The One Show 1982

The One Show

Judged To Be Advertising's Best
Print, Radio, TV

Volume 4

A Presentation of
The One Club for Art and Copy

Published by
American Showcase, Inc.
New York

The One Club
For Art and Copy

Len Sirowitz
PRESIDENT

Bill Weinstein
CHAIRMAN, PUBLICATION COMMITTEE

Beverley Daniels
DIRECTOR

American Showcase

Tennyson Schad
CHAIRMAN AND CO-PUBLISHER

Ira Shapiro
PRESIDENT AND CO-PUBLISHER

Christopher Curtis
DIRECTOR OF SPECIAL PROJECTS

Seymour Chwast and Michael Aron
Pushpin Lubalin Peckolick Inc., New York
DESIGNERS

Terry Berkowitz, New York
PRODUCTION AND MECHANICALS

Elise Sachs and Beverley Daniels
EDITORIAL COORDINATION

Sunlight Graphics, New York
TYPESETTING

Dai Nippon Printing Co., Ltd., Tokyo, Japan
COLOR SEPARATIONS, PRINTING AND BINDING

PUBLISHED BY
American Showcase, Inc.
724 Fifth Avenue, 10th Floor
New York, New York 10019
(212) 245-0981

IN ASSOCIATION WITH
The One Club for Art and Copy, Inc.
251 East 50th Street
New York, New York 10022
(212) 935-0121

U.S. AND CANADIAN BOOK
DISTRIBUTION:
Robert Silver Associates
95 Madison Avenue
New York, New York 10016
(212) 686-5630

OVERSEAS BOOK DISTRIBUTION:
American Showcase, Inc.
724 Fifth Avenue, 10th Floor
New York, New York 10019
(212) 245-0981

First Printing.
ISBN 0-960-2628-4-9
ISSN 0273-2033

Contents

The Board of Directors

PRESIDENT
Len Sirowitz
Rosenfeld, Sirowitz & Lawson

VICE PRESIDENT
David Saslaw
Leber Katz Partners

Anita Baron
Benton & Bowles

Ed Butler
Ed Butler, Inc.

Earl Cavanah
Scali, McCabe, Sloves

Harvey Gabor
SSC & B

Robert H. Lenz
Backer & Spielvogel

Jack Mariucci
Doyle Dane Bernbach

Thomas Nathan
TBWA Advertising

Norman Tanen
Backer & Spielvogel

Mike Tesch
Ally & Gargano

Judges Panel

Jack Aaker
Grey Advertising

Hy Abady
Calet, Hirsch, Kurnit & Spector

Judah Alper
Young & Rubicam

Dennis Altman
D'Arcy MacManus & Masius/De Garmo

David Altschiller
Altschiller, Reitzfeld, Solin/NCK

Ken Amaral
Doyle Dane Bernbach

Jack Anesh
Anesh Viseltear Gumbinner

Ellen Azorin
Kurtz & Tarlow

Katrine Barth
Frank Barth

Ron Becker
Geers Gross

Stanley Becker
Dancer Fitzgerald Sample

Norman Berry
Ogilvy & Mather

Bruce Bloch
AC&R Advertising

Jack Bloom
Trout & Ries

Mario Botti
Benton & Bowles

Nan Braman
Van Brunt & Company

Larry Cadman
Scali, McCabe, Sloves

Ed Caffrey
Benton & Bowles

Mavis Cain
SSC&B

Neil Calet
Calet, Hirsch, Kurnit & Spector

Sandy Carlson
Kurtz & Tarlow

John V. Chervokas
Warwick, Welsh & Miller

Jay Chiat
Chiat/Day

Agi S. Clark
N W Ayer

Robert Cole
Cunningham & Walsh

Rebecca Cooney
Benton & Bowles

Allan Corwin
Mingo-Jones Advertising

John Cross
Compton Advertising

George D'Amato
McCann-Erickson

Carlos Darquea
Sacks & Rosen

Francis DeVito
Young & Rubicam

Frank DiGiacomo
Della Femina, Travisano & Partners

John Doern
Compton Advertising

George Euringer
Ally & Gargano

Sanford Evans
Bozell & Jacobs

Gene Federico
Lord, Geller, Federico, Einstein

Marcella Free
Avrett, Free & Fischer

Botty Froodman
Grey Advertising

Jeff Frey
Wells, Rich, Greene

Hanno Fuchs
Sudler & Hennessey

Phil Geraci
Advertising to Women

Gary Geyer
The Marschalk Company

Frank Ginsberg
Avrett, Free & Fischer

Irwin Goldberg
Nadler & Larimer

Richard Goodman
Dancer Fitzgerald Sample

Peter Greeman
BBDO

Herb Green
McCann-Erickson

Barry Greenspon
Doyle Dane Bernbach

Jim Handloser
Mathieu, Gerfen & Bresner

Sharon Hartwick
Mathieu, Gerfen & Bresner

Robert Hildt
Geers Gross

Peter Hirsch
Calet, Hirsch, Kurnit & Spector

Paul Hodges
Laurence, Charles & Free

Jay Jasper
Ogilvy & Mather

Steve Kambanis
The Marschalk Company

Richard Karp
Grey Advertising

Richard Kiernan
Grey Advertising

Andy Langer
The Marschalk Company

Robert Larimer
Nadler & Larimer

John LaRock
Avrett, Free & Fischer

Robert Levenson
Doyle Dane Bernbach

Barry Z. Levine
Levy, Sussman & Levine

Joan Lipton
McCann-Erickson

Ted Littleford
Foote, Cone, & Belding

Peter Lubalin
Creamer

Ira B. Madris
McCann-Erickson

Ken Majka
Calet, Hirsch, Kurnit & Spector

Daniel S. Marshall
Martin, Sturtevant, Silverman & Marshall

Armand H. Mathieu
Mathieu, Gerfen & Bresner

Arthur Meranus
Cunningham & Walsh

Louis S. Miano
AC&R Advertising

W. Scott Miller
McCann-Erickson

Alex Mohtares
Leber Katz Partners

Hal Nankin
Benton & Bowles

Bruce Nelson
McCann-Erickson

John Noble
Doyle Dane Bernbach

Robert Oksner
Waring & LaRosa

Joe O'Neill
Ammirati & Puris

Curvin O'Rielly
BBDO

Larry Osborne
Rosenfeld, Sirowitz & Lawson

John Parkinson
Waring & LaRosa

Jim Perretti
Needham, Harper & Steers

Theodore Pettus
Lockhart & Pettus

Charles Piccirillo
Doyle Dane Bernbach

Jack Piccolo
Doyle Dane Bernbach

Frazier Purdy
Young & Rubicam

Richard Raboy
Epstein Raboy

Sam Reed
Mingo-Jones Advertising

Robert Reitzfeld
Altschiller, Reitzfeld, Solin/NCK

Les Richter
Ted Bates

Ronald Romano
Ted Bates

Ronald Rosenfeld
Rosenfeld, Sirowitz & Lawson

Leonard Sacks
Sacks & Rosen

Jay Schulberg
Ogilvy & Mather

Martin Shaw
Shaw & Koulermos

Brett Shevack
Laurence Charles & Free

Herman Siegel
Cunningham & Walsh

Jack Silverman
Leber Katz Partners

Paul Singer
Geers Gross

Murray Skurnick
Venet Advertising

Josephine Smith
Ogilvy & Mather

Mel Stein
The Marschalk Company

Joseph Stone
Berger, Stone & Ratner

Robert S. Sturtevant
Martin, Sturtevant, Silverman & Marshall

Len Sugarman
Foote, Cone & Belding

Abie J. Sussman
Levy, Sussman & Levine

Bob Tabor
Wells, Rich, Greene

Dick Tarlow
Kurtz & Tarlow

Richard Thomas
Lord, Geller, Federico, Einstein

Alex Tsao
Epstein Raboy

Ned Viseltear
Anesh Viseltear Gumbinner

John E. Warner
Warner, Bicking & Fenwick

Gerald Weinstein
Benton & Bowles

Kurt Willinger
Compton Advertising

Francine Wilvers
Doyle Dane Bernbach

Mike Withers
Calet, Hirsch, Kurnit & Spector

William Wurtzel
Hicks & Greist

President's Message

As an art director who has always believed in the power of the word, I am honored to have been elected President of The One Club for Art & Copy.

The One Club is truly the one club in our industry dedicated to the support of the total creative person. The art director who can think in words. The writer who can think in pictures. And both who can think strategically.

That coincides exactly with where our business is today. And how a creative person is being evaluated today.

That kind of forward thinking makes The One Club the most relevant and therefore, I believe, the most important club for creative people in our industry today.

About the Judging:

Unlike other shows, this One Show has been judged only by creative leaders in our business. Those men and women who have, over the years, walked away with our industry's fair share of awards themselves. That's why winning a One Show Award this year has more meaning than ever. And that's why this year The One Show is more important than ever.

Len Sirowitz

One Club Members

Donald Aaronson
Michael Abadi
Jeffrey Abbott
Ron Alberty
Richard Allen
Eileen Alleyne
David Altschiller
Jim D. Anderson
Jack Anesh
Leon Antman
Arnie Arlow
Deborah Armstrong
George Armstrong
Jeffrey L. Atlas
Neal Avener
Ellen Azorin
Carol Ann Baker
Cathy Bangel
Mel Barlin
Anita Baron
Cheryl Baron
Leo Baron
Yvonne Battle
Janeann Bean
Allan Beaver
Sandy Berger
Susan Berliner
William Bernbach
Raul Blade
Laurie Bleier
Richard K. Bloom
Francesca Blumenthal
Rob Boezewinkel
Muriel G. Bois
George R. Bonner, Jr.
Virginia Bonofiglio
James Bosha

Marina M. Brock
Ed Brodsky
Scott Bronfman
Devaughn Brown
Lonnie Brown
Gina Bruce
Casey Burke
Nelsena Burt
Ed Butler
Larry Cadman
Cathie Campbell
John Caples
Bob Carducci
David Carlin
Scott Carlton
Earl Carter
Earl Cavanah
R. Michael Chapell
David Chapman
Elaine Charney
Steven Chazanow
Lauren Cherry
Thomas Chiarello
Marcia Christ
Lisa L. Chu
Jo-ann E. Cirrincione
Joseph A. Civisca
Peter Clarke
Andrew Cohen
Dale Cohen
Ilene A. Cohn
Robert Cole
Adrienne Collier
Kay A. Colmar
Maria Compton
Shawne Cooper
Uriah Franklin Corkrum

Robert D. Corwin
Bob Costanza
Mindy Costanza
Constantin Cotzias
George Courides
Robert B. Cox
Robert Cramer
Marilyn Cull
Dale Cunningham
Sharon Curcio
James M. Dale
Boris Damast
Rebecca Dancour
Elizabeth L. Daniell
Wesley Davidson
Glenn Davis
Nancy Deckinger
Jerry Della Femina
Gregory Dellamonica
Bob Dion
Neil Drossman
Michael R. Duclos
Lorraine C. Duffy
Paula Dunn
Laurence Dunst
Arthur Einstein
Bernadette F. Elias
David C. Essertier
Sherie Fas
Oksana Fedorenko
Fritz Feik
Steve Feldman
Richard Ferrante
Jerry Fields
Peggy Fields
Lilly Filipow
Sal Finazzo
Carole Anne Fine
Len Fink
Peggy Flaum
Camille Focarino

Mel Freedman
Kent Freitag
Jeffrey Frey
Susan Friedman
Robert Funk
Jeff Furman
Harvey Gabor
Michael D. Gaffney
Karen Gallo
Lorraine Garnett
Rich Garramone
Judith Gee
Rose Geller
Gary Geyer
Frank Ginsberg
Sharon Glazer
Irwin Goldberg
Linda E. Goldman
Debbie Goldstein
Milt Gossett
Alison Gragnano
Betty Green
Steve Green
Barbara Greer
Dick Grider
John J. Griffin
Robert Haigh
Jim Hallowes
Alan Halpern
Jerome A. Handman
Carla Hardaway
Sharon Hartwick
Nancy Hauptman
Roy Herbert
Sharon Hewitt
Leonard D. Hickey II
Joan Orlian Hillman
Peter Hirsch
Seth Hochberg
Bruce Hopman
William Horvath

Douglas W. Houston
Graham Hubbel
Mike Hughes
Linda Huss
Patricia Hutt
Bennett Inkeles
Craig R. Jackson
Richard Jackson
Wendy Jackson
Fifi Jacobs
Corrin Jacobsen
Steven Janovici
Roberta Jaret
Bob Jefferson
Jo Ellen Johns
Caroline Jones
Jean R. Joslin
Alan B. Kahn
Barnaby Kalan
David J. Kaminsky
Charles H. Kane
Marshall Karp
Martin Kaufman
Louise Kittel
Jeffrey Klarik
M. Helen Klein
Murray Klein
Esther Kong
Gene Kong
Lois Korey
Haruo Koriyama
Tom Kostro
Judy Kozuch
Steven Krammer
George Kurten
Lucille Landini
Andrew Langer
Anthony E. LaPetri
Doris Latino
Mary Wells Lawrence
Karen M. Lee

David L. Leedy

David J. Leinwohl

Robert N. Lelle

Robert Leonard

Paul Lepelletier

Robert Levenson

Barry Z. Levine

Mark Levine

Carol Lewis

Evelyn Lief

Jeff Linder

Claire O. Lissance

Angela Locascio

Regina Lorenzo

David Lowenbein

Cecile T. Lozano

Peter Lubalin

Ted Luciani

Tony Macchia

Georgia Macris

Elisabeth Mansfield

Celeste Mari

Jack Mariucci

Elliot L. Markson

Arthur Cerf Mayer

Mary Means

Mario G. Messina

David C. N. Metcalf

Beryl Meyer

Lou Miano

S. Michael Minard

Jonathan L. Mindell

Ivy Mindlin

Robert Mizrahi

Jon S. Montgomery

Rafael Morales

Linda Morgenstern

Katrina Morosoff

Syl M. Morrone

David L. Morton

Yonatan Dov Mozeson

Norman Muchnick

Jill Murray

Ed McCabe

Ruth L. McCarthy

George McCathern

Michael McCray

Deanne McLean

Mary K. McMahon

Susan McTichecchia

Robert Nadler

Thomas Nathan

Sheldon Nechetsky

Charles Novick

Bill Oberlander

Dick O'Brien

Andrew O'Connor

Steve Ohman

Robert Oksner

Peter Oravetz

Curvin O'Rielly

Rowan O'Riley

Patricia O'Shaughnessy

Maxine Paetro

Gerard Pampalone

Thomas Pastore

Stanley Pearlman

Ellen Perless

Joseph C. Perz

Louise Petosa

Bob Phillips

Peter Phillips

Michael Pitts

Larry Plapler

Chris Pogreba

Mindy Pollack

Shirley Polykoff

Joseph Pompeo

Faith Popcorn

Louis Principato

Jeffrey Propper

Peggy Pulcini

Elissa Querze

Mary Quinn

Brandon Rabin

Richard Raboy

June Rachelson

Richard Radke

Bob Ralske

Jim Raniere

Neil Raphan

Ted Regan

Brigitte Regout

Jan Rehder

Michael T. Reid

Bob Reitzfeld

Robert Resnick

Anne Reilly

Ruthann M. Richert

L. Kenneth Ritter

Jean Robaire

Karen Robbins

Eric Robespierre

Phyllis Robinson

Karen L. Rogers

Leland Rosemond

Michael Rosen

Ron Rosenfeld

Susan Rossiello

John Russo

Antoinette Sacchetti

Thomas Sacco

Susan Sacks

Harry Sandler

David Saslaw

Nina Scerbo

Fran Schechter

Susan Schermer

Louis E. Schiavone III

Jennifer Schiffman

Barry Schoor

Jay Schulberg

Loretta M. Schurr

Mike Schwabenland

Aron J. Schwartz

Ron Seichrist

Ray Seide

Joan Seidman

Charles Sforza

Marylin Shakofsky

William Shea

Brett Shevack

Jamie Shevell

Paul Shields

Virgil Cox Shutze

John Siddall

Joanne Siegmann

Don Silberstein

Jonathan Sills

Marjorie Silver

Karen L. Simon

Leonard Sirowitz

Jo Smith

Raymond Smith

Stephen Smith

Martin Solow

Ron Spiegel

Helayne Spivak

Leon Sterling

Dawne Renee Steward

Lynn Stiles

Debora Stone

Scott Stooker

Richard Story

Ira Sturtevant

Len Sugarman

Abie Sussman

Milton Sutton

Daniel Swanson

Leslie Sweet

Norman Tanen

Donna Tedesco

Judith Teller

Douglas Thompson

Ian Tick

Brad Tillinghast

Jessie Tirsch

Cynthia Tocman

Peggy F. Tomarkin

Holly Tooker

Steve Toriello

Ron Travisano

David Tourin

Matthew Twomey

Ben Urman

Rudolph Valenti

Joan Van der Veen

Mary Vanderwoude

Angel Vasquez

Deyna Detroit Vesey

Larry Vine

Gloria Viseltear

Ned Viseltear

Larry Volpi

Nina Wachsman

Tom Wai-Shek

Judy Wald

Marvin Waldman

Stuart Waldman

Don Walley

Jessica Warren

Riva B. Weinstein

Jenny Wetmore

David S. Wheeler

Bob Whitworth

Peggy Wiggins-Rowan

Richard Wilde

C. Richard Williams

Kurt Willinger

Bruce Wilmoth

Lloyd Wolfe

Ed Wrenn

Elizabeth Wynn

Anthony Tsang Yee

Mark Yustein

1982
Gold & Silver
Awards

LAST YEAR, A CAR OUT-PERFORMED 318 STOCKS ON THE NEW YORK STOCK EXCHANGE.

If you'd bought a new BMW 320i in the beginning of 1980, and sold it at the end,
your investment would have retained 92.9% of its original value.*
If you'd done the same with any of 318 NYSE stocks, you'd have done less well.
And you'd have forfeited an important daily dividend:
The unfluctuating joy of driving one of the world's great performance sedans.

THE ULTIMATE DRIVING MACHINE.
BMW, MUNICH, GERMANY

*Based on average retail price according to January 1981 NADA Used-Car Guide. Your selling price may vary according to the condition of your car and whether you sell it privately or to a dealer © 1981 BMW of North America, Inc. The BMW trademark and logo are registered trademarks of Bayerische Motoren Werke, A.G.

1 GOLD

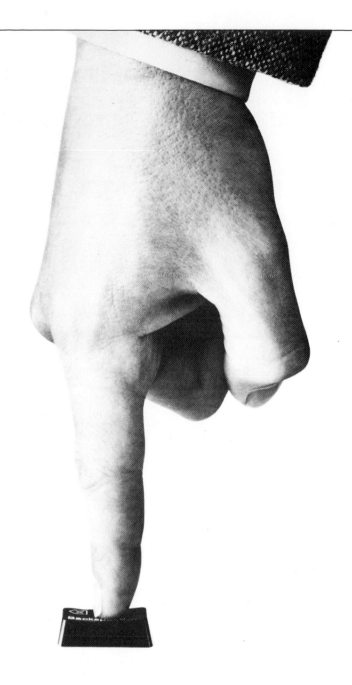

Untype 60 words per minute.

The IBM Electronic 75 Typewriter can erase faster than some people can type.

At the touch of a button, it can automatically lift a character, a word, or an entire line clean off a page.

But not only does the IBM Electronic 75 Typewriter offer you automatic erasing, it also offers you automatic indents, center-ing, underlining and column lay-out.

As well as a memory that can store up to 7,500 characters. (With optional memory: 15,500 characters.)

So if you're interested in sav-ing time, consider the IBM Elec-tronic 75 Typewriter.

You'll be sur-prised how fast your typing gets done.

And undone.

To order call *IBM Direct* at the toll-free numbers below. Or, for a free demonstration call your local IBM Office Products Division Representative.

Call *IBM Direct* 800-631-5582 Ext. 141. In New Jersey 800-352-4960 Ext. 141.
In Hawaii/Alaska 800-526-2484 Ext. 141.

2 SILVER

PERHAPS YOU CAN'T BUY HAPPINESS. BUT FOR $35,000 YOU CAN PURCHASE EXHILARATION.

If we have indeed entered the Era of Lowered Expectations, then nothing so captures the spirit of the times as the expensive luxury sedan.

Weighed down by their own ornamentation, and further compromised by the demands of fuel efficiency and anti-pollution devices, such cars are literally creating new standards of drivability—elevating sluggish, uninspired performance to the norm.

If driving ever becomes a totally joyless act, it will be accomplished without the complicity of the engineers at the Bavarian Motor Works in Munich, Germany.

There the credo has always been that no amount of refinement in an automobile can ever compensate for a lack of zeal—a belief that reaches its finest expression in the extraordinary BMW 733i.

DRIVING AS A VISCERAL EXPERIENCE.

The 733i "stands at the top of a select group of luxury sedans," wrote Car and Driver magazine, "that can take a limited amount of time and turn it into an experience to be savored for always."

What's behind such performance? The belief that only uncompromising engineering can prevent the creation of compromised cars.

While other automobile manufacturers were attempting to redeem their investments in anachronistic V-8's, BMW engineers were perfecting leaner, more efficient engines.

The 733i is powered by a 3.2-liter, electronically fuel-injected engine that's been called "the most refined in-line six in the world" (Road & Track).

While other manufacturers were placing ever more unconscionable demands on suspension systems to prop up ever more bargelike vehicles, BMW engineers introduced the "single most significant breakthrough in front suspension design in this decade" (Car and Driver). It's called a double-pivot front axle, and enables the 733i to negotiate even zigzagged stretches of roadway with an eerie nonchalance.

While other sedans were developing cushioned steering to buffer the driver from any contact with the road, BMW engineers devised one of the world's most tactile steering systems. It scans the road, reporting back all manner of topographical data while weeding out jolts and jars.

Even stopping a 733i is gratifying. Huge power-assisted disc brakes bring you from cruising speeds to a straight-line halt with none of the anxiety to which you may be accustomed.

In fact, driving a 733i is an experience for which no prior ownership of a luxury sedan has properly prepared you. The 733i may well get you to the country club faster; but its truly distinguishing characteristic is that it does so while providing the sort of pulse-quickening fun that's all but become another casualty of obsolescence in the conventional luxury sedan.

A PERFECTLY BALANCED ECOLOGY OF DRIVER AND ENVIRONMENT.

At BMW, the driver is presumed not to be human luggage but rather an integral part of the car—a belief that's evident everywhere inside the 733i.

It is almost anatomically impossible to be uncomfortable behind the wheel.

The adjustable bucket seats position you in postures that orthopedic specialists have determined to be correct for driving.

A telescopically adjustable steering wheel lets you correct for variations in arm length.

Controls and dials are large and easily visible without squinting—and displayed on a wraparound console so replete with instrumentation that Car and Driver called it a "space-age dash."

Nor have simple conveniences been ignored. A central electronic system lets you control the trunk lid lock, all four door locks, and even correctly position the outside rearview mirror from inside the car, even when the engine is off.

In fact, so perfectly balanced is this ecology of driver and environment that one journalist was moved to exclaim, "to drive (the 733i) is to know all the wonderful things machines can do for man."

If your present luxury sedan has moved no one to such paroxysms of praise, we suggest that you contact your local BMW dealer. He will be happy to arrange a thorough and quite revealing test drive.

THE ULTIMATE DRIVING MACHINE.

BMW MUNICH GERMANY

© 1981 BMW of North America, Inc. The BMW trademark and logo are registered trademarks of Bayerische Motoren Werke, A.G.

3 GOLD

LAST YEAR, A CAR OUT-PERFORMED 318 STOCKS ON THE NEW YORK STOCK EXCHANGE.

If you'd bought a new BMW 320i in the beginning of 1980, and sold it at the end, your investment would have retained 92.9% of its original value.

If you'd done the same with any of 318 NYSE stocks, you'd have done less well.

And you'd have forfeited an important daily dividend:

The unfluctuating joy of driving one of the world's great performance sedans.

THE ULTIMATE DRIVING MACHINE.

THE WORLD'S MOST ELEGANT PROTEST AGAINST MEDIOCRE ENGINEERING.

The protest we have in mind is against prestigious luxury cars that succeed as symbols, but disappoint as cars.

Cars whose underlying engineering seems to have lagged behind their considerable reputations.

Luxury car buyers dissatisfied with this state of affairs will find a perfect vehicle for dissent in the BMW 733i—the $35,000 luxury car engineered to lead where others have lagged.

INTRODUCING DIGITAL MOTOR ELECTRONICS.

The 733i is the first automobile in America to offer Digital Motor Electronics—a system that illustrates the difference between technology and gadgetry.

"DME" measures, reports on and, most importantly, governs engine efficiency.

It assures that the optimum mixture of fuel and air is ignited at the optimum time in the ignition cycle. It adjusts idling speed, cuts off fuel flow to cylinders when they're not needed, and even helps report back, through a fuel economy indicator, your actual mpg figures as you drive.

The figures will make interesting reading. The 733i with standard five-speed transmission now delivers a pleasantly surprising (19) EPA-estimated mpg, 29 mpg highway. Automatic is also available.

(Fuel efficiency figures are for comparison purposes only. Your actual mileage may vary, depending on speed, weather and trip length. Your actual highway mileage will most likely be lower.)

Inside, an onboard computer provides such useful functions as anti-theft protection and speed monitoring—and even helps control the weather. A special climate control adjusts temperatures to a preset level, going so far as to warn you of potential icing conditions.

All these technological advances accompany a car that's fairly steeped in amenities.

Its deep molded bucket seats are upholstered in wide, supple rolls of fine leather. Carpeting is thick and plush.

And the attentiveness to luxury and comfort throughout caused Car and Driver magazine to single out the 733i as "the height of refined elegance."

PERFECTION IS UNATTAINABLE. SUPERIORITY ISN'T.

Of course, the true measure of any machine is how well it performs —an axiom that confers an almost unfair advantage on the 733i.

Its 3.2-liter, electronically fuel-injected engine has been called "without a doubt, the most sophisticated production in-line six in the world" (Road & Track magazine), delivering the exhilarating performance that's conspicuously absent among cars in its class.

Its revolutionary double-pivot front suspension is so advanced it has earned an international patent.

And its amazingly agile steering reflects the precision inherited from over six decades of building high-performance vehicles.

The sum is a car whose "parts and pieces…work so well together they must have been melded in another world" (Car and Driver).

If your present luxury sedan suggests more mundane origins, you might contact your nearest BMW dealer, who will be happy to arrange a test drive at your convenience.

THE ULTIMATE DRIVING MACHINE.

TOO MANY WORK BOOTS LAY DOWN ON THE JOB.

| **SPLIT SOLE** | **CRACKED LEATHER** | **SPLIT SEAM** | **WATER DAMAGE** |
| Construction Worker–Chicago, Illinois | Gas Station Owner–Troy, New York | Truck Driver–Providence, R.I. | Mailman–Des Moines, Iowa |

If you spend a good part of your day working in a pair of boots, obviously, you depend a lot on them.

Unfortunately, though, most boots don't deliver.

Their problems run from shoddy and uncomfortable construction on the one foot to no waterproofing and no insulation on the other.

At Timberland, we make what we think are the best work boots around.

Here's why:

YOU HAVE TO WORK IN RAIN AND SNOW. SO DO OUR BOOTS.

If there's one time people who save a few dollars on a pair of boots really pay the price, it's when it rains or snows. Because most boots won't keep you dry.

But it's in weather like this that Timberland boots really shine.

Our boots are made of silicone or oil-impregnated waterproof leathers.

To resist rust, we use only solid brass eyelets.

And because any needle hole is a potential water hole, we seal every seam with not just one coat of latex but two.

How dry will Timberland boots keep you?

Well, on a machine called a Maser Flex that tests waterproof leathers, Timberland leathers must withstand a minimum of 15,000 flexes, equal to U.S. Military standards.

WE WON'T LEAVE YOU OUT IN THE COLD.

It's been estimated that on extremely cold days, you lose 80% of your body heat through the top of your head.

Yet, inevitably, your feet are always the first things to go.

To prevent the inevitable, your feet are surrounded with a layer of nitrogen filled closed cell insulation that'll keep your feet warm to temperatures well below zero.

Our boots aren't just better insulated than most boots, they're better insulated than most houses.

OUR BOOTS ARE TOUGH ON THE JOB. NOT ON YOUR FEET.

One of the biggest qualifications a work boot must have is an ability to take punishment.

Timberland's stand up to whatever you dish out.

Thanks to little things like four rows of nylon stitching instead of cotton in all key stress points. And big things like heavy duty molded soles permanently bonded to the uppers, so they can withstand a tremendous amount of abuse.

But there's a soft side to our boots as well.

It includes leather linings, geometrically

graded lasts, and a unique, 4-ply innersole construction. It results in boots so comfortable they eliminate the painful breaking-in period other boots force you to suffer through.

But don't just take our word for it. Step into any store that carries Timberland boots and try on a pair.

They come in a variety of styles, for men and women, starting at about $60.00. Which, in all honesty, might be a few dollars more than you now spend.

But we think you'll find it's worth spending a little more money to get a lot more boot.

Timberland

The Timberland Company, P.O. Box 370, Newmarket, New Hampshire 03857

WHY SAVING A FEW DOLLARS ON A PAIR OF WORK BOOTS NOW, COSTS YOU MORE IN THE LONG RUN.

These two work boots have been sitting in water for three hours. The boot on the left costs about $90. The boot on the right is a Timberland, which start at about $60 more. But come the middle of the winter, which boot would you rather have your feet in?

Just about anyone who has ever gone out to buy a pair of work boots has been guilty of making the same mistake.

You narrow your choice down to two pairs, with one costing a few dollars less than the other.

Then, you decide on the cheaper pair, figuring that for a better price, they look like a better buy.

But, with work boots, looks can be deceiving.

Because if you put that extra money into boots like Timberland's, you'd be out a few dollars now, but you'd be a lot better off when winter sets in, a couple of months from now.

MOST WORK BOOTS LAY DOWN ON THE JOB IN RAIN AND SNOW. TIMBERLAND'S DON'T.

If there's one time people who save a few dollars on a pair of boots really pay the price, it's when it rains or snows. Because most boots won't keep you dry.

But it's in weather like this that Timberland® boots really shine.

Our boots are made of silicone or oil-impregnated waterproof leathers.

To resist rust, we use only solid brass eyelets.

And because any needle hole is a potential water hole, we seal every seam with not just one coat of latex but two.

How dry will Timberland boots keep you?

Well, on a machine called a Maser Flex that tests waterproof leathers, Timberland leathers withstand a minimum of 15,000 flexes, equal to U.S. Military standards.

WE WON'T LEAVE YOU OUT IN THE COLD.

It's been estimated that on extremely cold days, you lose 80% of your body heat through the top of your head.

Yet, inevitably, your feet are always the first things to go.

To prevent the inevitable, your feet are surrounded with a layer of nitrogen-filled closed cell insulation that'll keep your feet warm to temperatures well below zero.

Our boots aren't just better insulated than most boots, they're better insulated than most houses.

OUR BOOTS ARE TOUGH ON THE JOB. NOT ON YOUR FEET.

One of the biggest qualifications a work boot must have is an ability to take punishment.

Timberland's stand up to whatever you dish out.

Thanks to little things like four rows of nylon stitching instead of cotton in all key stress points. And big things like heavy-duty molded soles permanently bonded to the uppers, so they can withstand a tremendous amount of abuse.

But there's a soft side to our boots as well.

It includes leather linings, geometrically graded lasts, and a unique, 4-ply innersole construction. It results in boots so comfortable they eliminate the painful breaking-in period other boots force you to suffer through.

But don't just take our word for it. Step into any store that carries Timberland boots and try on a pair.

They come in a variety of styles, for men and women, starting at about $60.00. Which, in all honesty, might be a few dollars more than you now spend.

But we think you'll find it's worth spending a little more money to get a lot more boot.

Timberland ®

See adjoining page for nearest Timberland dealer.

IF YOU PAY $45.00 OR MORE FOR NON-WATERPROOF WORK BOOTS, YOUR FEET AREN'T THE ONLY THINGS GETTING SOAKED.

Chances are, your wallet is taking a little bit of a soaking as well.

Because the fact is, if you're spending that kind of money for boots that aren't waterproof, you simply aren't getting your money's worth.

Especially when, for just a few dollars more, you could be getting work boots like Timberland's.

YOU HAVE TO WORK IN RAIN AND SNOW. SO DO OUR BOOTS.

If there's one time people who save a few dollars on a pair of boots really pay the price, it's when it rains or snows. Because most boots won't keep you dry.

But it's in weather like this that Timberland® boots really shine.

Our boots are made of silicone or oil-impregnated waterproof leathers.

We use waterproof leathers, nitrogen filled closed-cell insulation, and genuine leather linings. Steps most boot manufacturers don't take.

To resist rust, we use only solid brass eyelets.

And because any needle hole is a potential water hole, we seal every seam with not just one coat of latex but two.

How dry will Timberland boots keep you?

On a machine called a Maser Flex that tests waterproof leathers, Timberland leathers must withstand a minimum of 15,000 flexes, equal to U.S. Military standards.

WE WON'T LEAVE YOU OUT IN THE COLD.

It's been estimated that on extremely cold days, you lose 80% of your body heat through the top of your head.

Yet, inevitably, your feet are always the first things to go.

To prevent the inevitable, your feet are surrounded with a layer of nitrogen filled closed cell insulation that'll keep your feet warm to temperatures well below zero.

Our boots aren't just better insulated than most boots, they're better insulated than most houses.

An inside look at some of the things that separate Timberland® boots from other boots.

OUR BOOTS ARE TOUGH ON THE JOB. NOT ON YOUR FEET.

One of the biggest qualifications a work boot must have is an ability to take punishment.

Timberland's stand up to whatever you dish out.

Thanks to little things like four rows of nylon stitching instead of cotton in all key stress points. And big things like heavy-duty molded soles permanently bonded to the uppers, so they can withstand a tremendous amount of abuse.

But there's a soft side to our boots as well.

Four rows of nylon stitching plus two coats of latex add up to a strength not found in most work boots.

It includes leather linings, geometrically graded lasts, and a unique, 4-ply innersole construction. It results in boots so comfortable they eliminate the painful breaking-in period other boots force you to suffer through.

But don't just take our word for it. Try on a pair.

They come in a variety of styles, for men and women, starting at about $60.00. Which, in all honesty, might be a few dollars more than you now spend.

But we think you'll find it's worth spending a little more money to get a lot more boot.

Timberland ®

Gold & Silver Awards

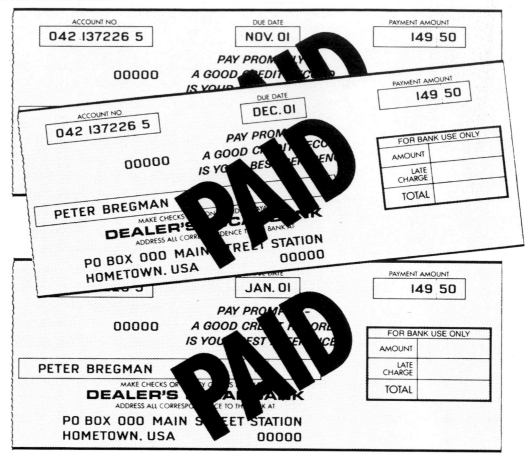

The first 3 payments on your next VW are on us.

No kidding! Come in and make your best deal on any 1981 Volkswagen. After you've made the down payment and 48-month or longer financing has been approved, we'll take care of the first three monthly payments for you.

For example, if you put down $1555** on an '81 Rabbit L sedan (at $6755*), 48 monthly payments comes to $149.50 each. But we'd pay for three months' worth or $448.50.

And, you still wouldn't owe a penny more until February, 1982. Offer ends November 15.

*Manufacturer's suggested retail price. Includes freight and dealer delivery charges. Taxes and title fees, extra.
**Down payment and finance charge will vary depending on model and options. Based on total cash price of $6755, which excludes taxes and title fees. 48 monthly payments with approved credit, A.P.R. 16.8% total deferred payment of $8731.

5 GOLD

We knew Len Sirowitz when

...when he rode the subway every day from the Bronx to study Advertising Design at Pratt.

Len Sirowitz went on from Pratt to become one of the foremost advertising art directors in the country, and was named "The Number One Art Director in America" twice in national polls. He is co-chairman of Rosenfeld, Sirowitz & Lawson, one of the fastest-growing advertising agencies in America with an impressive list of blue-chip clients.

Len Sirowitz has come a long way since Pratt. And on the way he brought a lot of Pratt with him.

Pratt Institute
LOOK HOW FAR YOU CAN GO FROM PRATT

Pratt Institute, 200 Willoughby Avenue, Brooklyn, New York 11205 (212) 636-3669
Graduate programs in Architecture, City and Regional Planning, Urban Design; Art Therapy; Fine Arts; Industrial, Interior, Package, Communications Design; Computer and Decision Science; Library and Information Science.

7 GOLD

LAST YEAR, A CAR OUT-PERFORMED 318 STOCKS ON THE NEW YORK STOCK EXCHANGE.

If you'd bought a new BMW 320i in the beginning of 1980, and sold it at the end, your investment would have retained 92.9% of its original value.*

If you'd done the same with any of 318 New York Stock Exchange stocks, you'd have done less well. And you'd have forfeited an important daily dividend: The unfluctuating joy of driving one of the world's great performance sedans.

THE ULTIMATE DRIVING MACHINE.
BMW, MUNICH, GERMANY.

LET YOUR GREATER SEATTLE/TACOMA BMW DEALERS ARRANGE A THOROUGH TEST DRIVE.

BELLEVUE	EDMONDS	MOUNT VERNON	SEATTLE	TACOMA
BELLEVUE BMW	**ALAN BMW, INC.**	**BLADE BMW, INC.**	**PHIL SMART, INC.**	**BMW NORTHWEST, INC.**
13817 Northrup Way (20th N.E.)	21420 Hwy. 99 South	1100 Freeway Drive	600 East Pike St.	7507 Bridgeport Way West
(206) 643-4544	(206) 771-7100	(206) 424-3231	(206) 324-5959	(206) 456-8115

*Based on average retail price according to January 1981 NADA Used-Car Guide. Your selling price may vary according to the condition of your car and whether you sell it privately or to a dealer.
© 1981 BMW of North America, Inc. The BMW trademark and logo are registered trademarks of Bayerische Motoren Werke, A.G.

8 SILVER

O e thi g our pri t wheels wo 't do.

They wo 't break, like this o e did.

Because the entire wheel is reinforced. With metal.

Which means characters won't snap off, and typewriters won't edit people without their consent.

That's guaranteed for a full year.

Now, this is what our print wheels will do. They'll print in 21 different typefaces. And in different type sizes.

They'll print signs and symbols, such as π and ¶.

Best of all, each wheel can be custom-made.

At Xerox, we offer a wide variety of supplies that help prevent communications breakdowns. Everything from magnetic cassettes to Telecopier supplies to data storage systems.

So before you send for any more Information Processing or Telecopier supplies, send in the coupon. Or call

1-800-527-1868.

After all, which would you rather supply your office with:

The thi gs it eeds?

Or the things it needs?

– – – – – – – – – – – – – – – – – –

I'd like more information on the complete line of Xerox Office Supplies.

Send to: Xerox Corporation, P.O. Box 470065, Dallas, Texas 75247.

Name _____

Title _____

Company _____

Address _____

City _____ State _____ Zip_____

Phone _____

85-I   NSPS-7-81

XEROX

*In Texas, Alaska and Hawaii, call collect 1-214-630-6145.

XEROX® and TELECOPIER® are trademarks of XEROX CORPORATION.

9 GOLD

THERE'S ALWAYS BEEN A PLACE FOR GOOD WRITING.

HENRY W. LONGFELLOW | OLIVER WENDELL HOLMES | HARRIET BEECHER STOWE | WALT WHITMAN | HENRY THOREAU | JAMES RUSSELL LOWELL | NATHANIEL HAWTHORNE | JOHN GREENLEAF WHITTIER | CHARLES DICKENS

BRET HARTE | MARK TWAIN | RUDYARD KIPLING | THEODORE ROOSEVELT | JOHN MUIR | JACK LONDON | BOOKER T. WASHINGTON | EDITH WHARTON | HENRY MENCKEN

JOHN MASEFIELD | JANE ADDAMS | ARCHIBALD MACLEISH | AMY LOWELL | D.H. LAWRENCE | VIRGINIA WOOLF | EMILY DICKINSON | JULIAN HUXLEY | JOHN MAYNARD KEYNES

HELEN KELLER | B.F. SKINNER | RACHEL CARSON | WILLIAM SAROYAN | THOMAS WOLFE | GERTRUDE STEIN | ERNEST HEMINGWAY | WILLIAM FAULKNER | VLADIMIR NABOKOV

ARTHUR SCHLESINGER, JR. | TRUMAN CAPOTE | SOMERSET MAUGHAM | DYLAN THOMAS | EDWIN O'CONNOR | HARRY TRUMAN | JAMES JONES | JOSEPH HELLER | JOHN KENNETH GALBRAITH

ROBERT FROST | JOHN F. KENNEDY | E.E. CUMMINGS | JOHN STEINBECK | BERTRAND RUSSELL | EVELYN WAUGH | KATHERINE ANNE PORTER | ARTHUR MILLER | ALBERT SCHWEITZER

ROBERT COLES | MARTIN LUTHER KING, JR. | JAMES DICKEY | SAUL BELLOW | LILLIAN HELLMAN | IRWIN SHAW | W.H. AUDEN | ROBERT PENN WARREN | PHILIP ROTH

Since 1857, *The Atlantic* has been the home of good writing. And, as you can see, good writers.

Fiction, poetry, humor, essays, reviews, comment, investigative reporting. Important, entertaining articles on politics, science, travel, medicine, business, economics, art, film, television, education.

And this 124-year tradition continues in the April issue of *The Atlantic*, on your newsstand now.

You'll find new fiction by Philip Roth. A disturbing

portrait of America's volunteer army by James Fallows. A humorous look at the economy through the eyes of Roy Blount, Jr. A report from Paris by Mavis Gallant. Poetry by Robert Penn Warren.

They're just a few examples of the good writing in *The Atlantic* this April.

And good writing is what good reading is all about.

THE Atlantic

Gold & Silver Awards

Hello?
How's the Great American Novel going?

So far it reads more like the turgid insights of a lonely Albanian date-plucker.
Did I hear the word "lonely"?

There's a fog rolling in.
You're in Pawegansett, dear. It holds the world record for fog.

The "t" in my typewriter is sticking. I have seventeen cans of lentil soup. And my Paco Rabanne cologne, which I use to lure shy maidens out of the woods, is gone, all gone.
You're going to have to do better than that.

All right, I'm lonely. I miss you. I miss your cute little broken nose. I miss the sight of you in bed in the morning, all pink and pearly and surly.
And you want me to catch the train up.

Hurry! This thing they call love is about to burst the bounds of decency. And, darling...
Yes?

Bring a bottle of Paco Rabanne, would you? The maidens are getting restless.
Swine!

Paco Rabanne
A cologne for men
What is remembered is up to you

Our greatest achievement.

After 75 years of making vacuum bottles, we've made ones that don't break. Because
they're solid steel inside and out. They've been dropped
off roofs. And from speeding motorcycles. The one seen here belongs to Leonard Weeks, Jr.
of Lacoochee, Florida. He accidentally ran over it with a 7-ton bulldozer.
Four years later, it's still keeping his coffee hot.
Thermos® brand unbreakable steel bottles. Backed by a 5-year limited warranty.
Every dent is a mark of quality. ® Thermos is a Registered Trademark of the King-Seeley Thermos Co.

The Original American
THERMOS®
Company

12 SILVER

O e thi g
our pri t wheels
wo 't do.

They wo 't break, like this o e did. Because the entire wheel is reinforced. With metal.

Which means characters won't snap off, and typewriters won't edit people without their consent.

That's guaranteed for a full year.

Now, this is what our print wheels will do. They'll print in 21 different typefaces. And in different type sizes.

They'll print signs and symbols, such as π and ¶.

Best of all, each wheel can be custom-made.

At Xerox, we offer a wide variety of supplies that help prevent communications breakdowns. Everything from magnetic cassettes to Telecopier supplies to data storage systems.

So before you send for any more Information Processing or Telecopier supplies, send in the coupon. Or call

1-800-527-1868.

After all, which would you rather supply your office with:

The thi gs it eeds?

Or the things it needs?

I'd like more information on the complete line of Xerox Office Supplies.

Send to: Xerox Corporation,
P.O. Box 470065,
Dallas, Texas 75247.

Name_____
Title_____
Company_____
Address_____
City_____State____Zip____
Phone_____

XEROX

Xerox proudly announces paper you can't copy on.

It isn't your average 8½" X 11".

Actually it's more like 33000" X 147⁄8". And while your copier won't know what to do with it, your computer or word processor will.

Now you can feed your computer printer or word processor high-quality Xerox Computer Forms.

Stock forms that are available in combined volume discounts, so you can conveniently order them together with copier paper, and save on both. And forms that are backed by our money-back quality guarantee.

For more information on how to order, make excellent use of this paper. And send in the coupon.

I'd like more information on how I can save on Xerox Computer Forms. Send to: Xerox Corporation, P.O. Box 24, Rochester, N.Y. 14601.

Name_____
Title_____
Company_____
Address_____
City_____
State_____
Zip_____
Tel._____

XEROX

Improve your memory.

If your word processor or mini-computer seems absentminded it may not be its fault. It could be the diskette that forgets to remember.

Xerox floppy diskettes, on the other hand, keep track of more of what you've typed, and have no trouble recollecting it.

They're compatible with almost any equipment. Because chances are that your machine's memory system is made by Shugart, a Xerox company.

Xerox Floppy Diskettes

And they come in both 5¼" and 8" sizes.

Here's something else you won't want to forget. High quality Xerox diskettes can save you up to 40%. And even better, we're giving you an introductory 10% discount on top of that. If you're dissatisfied for any reason during the first year, we'll replace the diskettes free of charge.

So, if your diskettes are suffering from amnesia, just send in the coupon below. Or call 1-800-648-5600, operator 665.*

You'll thank us for the memories.

I'd like more information on how to improve my memory.

Send to: Xerox Corporation, P.O. Box 24, Rochester, N.Y. 14601

Name_____
Title_____Company_____
Address_____
City_____State____Zip____Phone_____

*In Nevada, call 1-800-992-5710, operator 665.

XEROX® is a trademark of XEROX CORPORATION.

13 GOLD

You can now reach Xerox at the following numbers.

$1750 $3295 $3995

The Xerox 660, 2600 and 3100 copiers are now easier than ever to reach. Just refer to the numbers listed above.

All three machines give you sharp, clear copies on plain paper, mailing labels, even your own letterhead.

And all three give you the quality and reliability of Xerox. Backed by the largest service organization in the industry.

Other Xerox copiers are also available at easy to reach numbers. Machines that do everything from reduce to copy two-sided originals automatically.

Just send in the coupon. Or call us at 800-648-5600, operator 658.*

We'll keep our lines open. Although it won't be easy.

You see, we've been very busy ever since we lowered our numbers.

☐ I'd like a sales representative to contact me.
☐ I'd like a demonstration.
☐ I'd like more information about Xerox small copiers.

Send to: Xerox Corporation, P.O. Box 24, Rochester, N.Y. 14601.

Name_____

Title_____

Company_____

Address_____

City_____State_____Zip_____

Telephone_____
658

XEROX

*In Nevada call 800-962-5710, operator 658.
XEROX®, 660®, 2600 and 3100® are trademarks of XEROX CORPORATION.

Machines may be newly manufactured or remanufactured or reconditioned. Some models are available only as remanufactured or only as reconditioned.

17 GOLD

THE TRAVELLING COMPANION THAT COMES WITH ITS OWN SUITCASE.

This Bulova travel alarm packs away in a snap. In a genuine leather case of black, burgundy or white.

But best of all, it's made of solid brass. And it has a fine quartz movement that makes it the most accurate travel clock you can buy.

At Bulova, time only flies first class.

The Hideaway, pictured above, has a suggested retail price of $59.95.

Nobody ever has enough clocks. Except Bulova.

Gold & Silver Awards

**Consumer Magazine
Less than a Page
B/W or Color
Campaign**

19 GOLD
ART DIRECTOR
Charles Abrams
WRITER
George Rike
ARTISTS
James Stevenson
Robert Weber
Frank Modell
CLIENT
General Wine & Spirits
Company/Chivas Regal
AGENCY
Doyle Dane Bernbach

*"Just once I'd like to see some
Chivas in this thing."*

Chivas Regal • 12 Years Old Worldwide • Blended Scotch Whisky • 86 Proof. General Wine & Spirits Co., N.Y.

"It's eleven o'clock.
Do you know where your Chivas Regal is?"

"You never bought _me_ Chivas Regal."

Gold & Silver Awards

**Consumer Magazine
Less than a Page
B/W or Color
Campaign**

20 SILVER

ART DIRECTOR
Dolores Mollo

WRITER
Bob Potesky

DESIGNER
Dolores Mollo

PHOTOGRAPHER
Gerald Zanetti

CLIENT
Oroweat Foods

AGENCY
Foote, Cone & Belding

Fresh whole wheat flour, and 5 other natural grains for a unique flavor.

Walnuts and sunflower seeds for a crunchy texture.

Sweetened only with brown sugar and honey for a taste you could never call plain.

Brownberry Health Nut.
Even when you eat this bread plain, you're not eating plain bread.

**BROWNBERRY®
Honest Bread**

© 1981 Oroweat Foods Company

Arnold Brick Oven® White.
There are so many rich ingredients in this white bread, it isn't white.

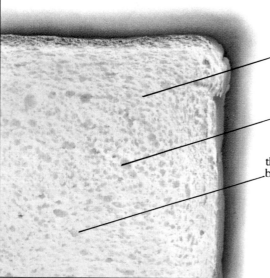

Just enough golden honey and creamery butter for a richer taste and color.

Slow baked with fresh yeast for a unique texture.

Unbleached wheat flour that's high in protein. Other white breads look pale by comparison.

**ARNOLD
Honest Bread**

© 1981 Oroweat Foods Company

20 SILVER

Brownberry Natural Wheat.
The natural goodness is preserved
by leaving out the preservatives.

Coarsely ground whole grain for a chewy
texture and nut-like flavor.

Unbleached spring wheat that's high
in protein.

Fresh natural yeast and naturally,
no preservatives.

BROWNBERRY.
Honest Bread

O e thi g our pri t wheels wo 't do.

They wo 't break, like this o e did.

Because the entire wheel is reinforced. With metal.

Which means characters won't snap off, and typewriters won't edit people without their consent.

That's guaranteed for a full year.

Now, this is what our print wheels will do. They'll print in 21 different typefaces. And in different type sizes.

They'll print signs and symbols, such as π and ¶.

Best of all, each wheel can be custom-made.

At Xerox, we offer a wide variety of supplies that help prevent communications breakdowns. Everything from magnetic cassettes to Telecopier supplies to data storage systems.

So before you send for any more Information Processing or Telecopier supplies, send in the coupon. Or call

1-800-527-1868.

After all, which would you rather supply your office with:

The thi gs it eeds?

Or the things it needs?

— — — — — — — — — — — — — — —

I'd like more information on the complete line of Xerox Office Supplies.

Send to: Xerox Corporation, P.O. Box 470065, Dallas, Texas 75247.

Name _____
Title _____
Company _____
Address _____
City _____ State _____ Zip _____
Phone _____

85-I   NSPS-7-81

XEROX

*In Texas, Alaska and Hawaii, call collect 1-214-630-6145.

XEROX® and TELECOPIER® are trademarks of XEROX CORPORATION.

21 GOLD

A CHICKEN DIVIDED MULTIPLIES PROFITS.

You don't have to be a mathematical genius to know you make more money selling chicken parts than you do selling whole chickens. And if the chicken parts you're selling are Perdue, you make even more. The fact is, people are willing to pay more for Perdue. Because Perdue Pedigreed Chicken Parts are the only ones tagged with a money-back quality guarantee.

So if you want the most profitable chicken parts you can sell, buy the ones that come from the most profitable chicken. Perdue.

One of the few things on the Space Shuttle that didn't have a backup system.

Backup systems are essential to any manned space flight.

But space inside the shuttle is precious. How did the crew of the NASA Space Shuttle Columbia get a 35mm camera they could depend on, without having to take along a lot of 35mm cameras?

They took off with a Nikon.*

With good reason.

No Nikon has ever failed on a NASA space mission. In every manned mission into space since 1971, no Nikon has had structural damage from blast off. Or jammed.

Or had a mechanical problem. Or any problem that affected its performance.

A Nikon, as you may have gathered, is incredibly reliable.

So reliable it's the choice of more professional photographers than all other 35mm cameras combined.

There are four Nikon models designed for your special professional needs. The F3, the finest Nikon ever built for the professional photographer. The FE, a compact full-featured automatic. The FM which offers full manual control. And the

Nikonos IV-A—the world's only fully automatic 35mm underwater camera.

Whatever your needs as a professional, one thing is certain. Whether up in space, down on earth, or underwater, there's a Nikon to help take pictures that are out of this world.

Nikon
We take the world's greatest pictures.

*Camera used was a modified Nikon F. Future flights will use a modified F3 that has been customized with special wiring, lubrication and finish for use in space. © Nikon Inc., 1981. Garden City, New York 11530

23 GOLD

THESE WOMEN ARE TWO GENERATIONS APART.

Never before has a point-of-purchase or packaging material (on the right) captured so brilliantly the qualities of an original (on the left).

It's new Converpak™ from Continental Group's Bleached Board Mill. And it's the most visually acute boxboard we've ever created.

Note the definition. Color. Texture. The little things that make point-of-purchase grab you. The little extra that makes packages pop from the shelf.

But reproduction isn't Converpak's only strength. Its unique formation makes it stronger, more uniform, so it runs through your filling system faster. It holds its integrity through distribution to protect your product without distortion to the printed image. And it's produced in a wide-caliper range to satisfy all of your packaging needs.

Converpak can make your carton designs look even better than you see here. So call John R. Curtin at (203) 964-6631 and see. Call now, because your competition could be reading this, too.

 CONTINENTALGROUP

Bleached Board Operations
21 Harbor Plaza, Stamford CT 06904

Packaging
Forest Products
Insurance
Energy

MOST AGENCIES LOOKING FOR A WRITER WANT TO SEE YOUR WORK.

WE THOUGHT YOU'D LIKE TO SEE OURS FIRST.

We're in the market for a good writer who'd like to build a great book.

Naturally, we'll want to take a look at your work. Just so we know what we're getting into.

But that works both ways.

So here's some of our work. We think it's pretty good stuff. And there's a lot more award-winning print, radio and television where that came from.

But, quite frankly, we're more interested in the awards you're going to win than the ones we've already won.

If you like what you see here, send some of your best work to me, Bill LaWarre, Sr. V.P./Creative Director.

If we like what we see, you'll be building a great book in no time. At a salary that'll make you never want to use it.

NORTHLICH, STOLLEY, INC.
200 West Fourth Street, Cincinnati, Ohio 45202

25 GOLD

Hollywood weather
without Hollywood overhead.

In Florida you can produce as good a film as you could in Hollywood or New York.

On a much better budget.

With the nation's third-largest pool of acting talent.

Experienced, professional technicians.

State-of-the-art equipment, facilities, and services.

Call us for all the help you need in planning your next location shoot.

You'll bring back New York or Hollywood film in the can. On a Florida budget.

Ben Harris, Motion Picture and Television Bureau; Suite HR4-4, Collins Building; Tallahassee, Florida 32301.

(904) 487-1100

WHY THE BEST BOOTS AND HANDSEWNS MONEY CAN BUY ARE THE BEST BOOTS AND HANDSEWNS YOU CAN SELL.

Over the past few years, we, at Timberland, have developed a reputation for making quality footwear.

It's a reputation that we feel is well deserved.

Because while some manufacturers may combine a few of the features we put into our boots and handsewns, no other manufacturer combines all of the features.

Obviously, this commitment to craftsmanship benefits people who buy Timberland products.

But it also benefits people who sell them.

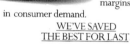

OUR BOOTS COME WITH RUGGED SOLES, LEATHER UPPERS, AND HIGHER-PROFIT MARGINS.

At Timberland, we've always put higher quality craftsmanship into our boots, so our dealers can get a better price for them.

And they do.

Today, Timberland boots are the fastest-selling premium quality boots in the United States. And they sell at a premium price.

Our boots also come with something else other boots don't come with: built-in consumer demand.

Which means that you can sell a pair of Timberlands in less time than it takes to sell a pair of ordinary boots. And make more money.

THE FIRST LINE OF HANDSEWNS WITH THE QUALITY OF TIMBERLAND.

For us, making a line of quality handsewns was a tough pair of shoes to fill.

Because, as the makers of the world's finest boots, we couldn't come out with anything less in a handsewn.

Timberland handsewns, including our boat shoes, are made from the same quality materials as our boots.

They are made with the same quality craftsmanship. And, most important, they come with the same high-profit margins and built-in consumer demand.

WE'VE SAVED THE BEST FOR LAST.

Unlike other manufacturers, we've never thought our job ends when shipping begins.

Every year, we invest more money in consumer boot advertising than any of our competitors.

And this year, we'll be putting more money than ever before behind our handsewns, as well as a new boat shoe.

We also have the most complete dealer support program, including p.o.p., in-store promotions, and dealer co-op.

The result of these investments?

Well, just in the last few years alone, Timberland's growth has been unmatched by any of our competitors. And our dealers' profits have grown just as quickly.

See, we told you we were saving the best for last.

Timberland

THE BOAT SHOE THAT'S ABOUT TO BLOW SPERRY TOP-SIDER OUT OF THE WATER.

At first glance, the statement above might be a little shocking. But not when you consider what's below it.

The new boat shoe from Timberland.

HOW TIMBERLAND IMPROVED THE BOAT SHOE.

Today, most people who wear boat shoes never set foot on a boat.

So while the sole on Sperry's most popular boat shoe is made of a soft rubber compound, Timberland's is a long-lasting rugged Vibram® sole.

Ours holds up just as well as theirs on boats. But it holds up a lot better than theirs on land.

As proof, something called an abrasion count measures a sole's resistance to wear and tear.

Sperry's abrasion count is about 70. Timberland's is twice that.

But the heart of a Timberland boat shoe isn't just the sole.

Timberland's uppers are made of only waterproof leathers, which are silicone-impregnated. They remain soft and supple even after repeated soakings. Sperry's leather has a painted-on pigment finish, causing it to eventually dry out and crack.

To prevent rusting and resist salt, we use only solid brass eyelets. Sperry uses painted metal ones. So when the paint goes, so does the protection.

Finally, Timberland boat shoes are completely hand-sewn. Which means they're so comfortable, the breaking-in period ends the day they're put on. And they're handcrafted in a small town in New England, by people whose families have been practicing this art for generations.

While Sperry's are often made by machine, a long boat ride away.

HOW WE'VE IMPROVED THINGS FOR PEOPLE WHO SELL BOAT SHOES.

Recently, Sperry ran a rather unusual trade ad. Unusual in that it was filled with apologies.

It seems Sperry felt the need to apologize for the way they've treated their dealers in the past. And they promised to make amends.

At Timberland, we have no apologies to make. We've always felt that if we're good to our dealers, our dealers will be good to us.

So when it comes to delivery on our boat shoes, we think you'll find we're better than any of our competitors.

If you want to run co-op, or need p.o.p., we give it to you.

And very shortly, we'll be launching our new boat shoe with a major advertising campaign. So dealers who buy our boat shoes will have no problem selling them.

What it all comes down to is this:

You can do business with a company that promises to improve the way they do things. Or a company that doesn't have to.

Timberland®

The Timberland Company, P.O. Box 370, Newmarket, New Hampshire 03857

WHY TIMBERLAND® HAS TAKEN AN APPROACH TO MAKING SHOES THAT'S YEARS BEHIND OTHER COMPANIES.

Over the years, the shoe industry has seen many changes. Materials that cost less money, machines that turn out more shoes—changes that have enabled manufacturers to make shoes faster and more economically.

But not necessarily better.

At Timberland, we've always believed the only way to make shoes is the way shoes were made years ago.

TIMBERLAND'S HANDSEWN MOCCASIN CONSTRUCTION.
THE ART OF HANDSEWING TAKEN TO ITS ULTIMATE.

Consider just the materials:

Where other companies may be satisfied using less expensive leathers, Timberland uses only premium full-grain leathers. In fact, on the average, we believe we invest more money in leathers and soles than any of our competitors.

They cost more in the short run but, because they hold up better, they're worth more in the long run.

We use only solid brass eyelets, so they won't rust. Nylon thread and chrome-tanned rawhide laces because they last longer. And long-wearing rugged Vibram® soles that are unbeatable for resistance to abrasion.

But what we do with these materials is even more impressive.

We all know how comfortable slippers are. Well, before the outer soles are attached, our handsewns are actually leather slippers to which we add full mid-soles. Ours provide excellent support on the bottoms of the shoes, while the tops form molds around the feet. (In other words, our shoes conform to the feet instead of vice versa.)

Here, Timberland hand-sewers take over.

Where others are often satisfied machine-sewing the vamp and kicker, our handsewers sew every stitch by hand. One at a time.

In addition, unlike machine-sewn shoes, Timberland handsewns are dampened and made on the last. Then, they're allowed to dry on the last, ensuring no wrinkles on the uppers.

But, more important, this total control by man instead of machine results in handsewns that, unequivocably, are the finest, most comfortable shoes in the world.

WE'RE COMBINING OLD WORLD CRAFTSMANSHIP WITH NEW WORLD SELLING.

A lot of companies would be satisfied merely making a product as good as our handsewns.

But Timberland isn't a lot of companies.

Soon, we'll be launching a major advertising campaign for our handsewns.

We'll also supply you with a complete package of p.o.p. material.

The reason for all this? Very simple.

Surely, we take great pride in how all Timberland handsewns are made.

But we take even greater pride in how well they sell.

Timberland®

The Timberland Company, P.O. Box 370, Newmarket, New Hampshire 03857

COULD YOUR SCHOOL PASS AN ENTRANCE EXAM?

A lot of schools pass in the education department, but fail in the security department.

That's why you need Medeco High Security Locks. We offer more than 23-million key combinations. And four levels of key control to give you exactly the degree of security your system needs.

By combining tumbler elevation and rotation in our patented double-locking mechanism, we make our locks virtually pick-proof. And with hardened steel inserts, they're practically impossible to pry, drill, or force open.

So upgrade your security system with Medeco. Choose from our complete UL-listed line of high security cam locks, switch locks, padlocks, and deadbolt locks. Or use our high security replacement cylinders to make your existing hardware intruder-resistant.

With Medeco, your institution of higher learning won't let just anyone pass.

Security Locks, Inc.
medeco®
P.O. Box 1075, Salem, Virginia 24153 (703) 387-0481

PROFIT SHARING IS BAD FOR BUSINESS.

If you don't like others getting an unfair share of your business — put a stop to splitting up the profits in your coin boxes.

With high security Medeco locks on your vending machines, you get the absolute protection you need. With a factory-restricted key control system that prevents unauthorized key problems.

Medeco's hardened steel inserts provide maximum vandal resistance. And our patented double-locking action combines tumbler rotation with tumbler elevation. So even a pro can't pick, pry, drill, or force our locks open.

There's an easy-to-install, UL-listed Medeco lock to keep all your equipment safe, including cam, rod, and pop-out inner cylinders. So specify Medeco in the future and order replacement locks for your equipment today.

With Medeco locks, you'll never have undeserving partners in your business.

Security Locks, Inc.
medeco®
P.O. Box 1075, Salem, Virginia 24153 (703) 387-0481

28 SILVER

**Collateral
Brochures Other
Than by Mail**

29 GOLD
ART DIRECTOR
Ann-Marie Light

WRITER
Mitch Epstein

DESIGNER
Ann-Marie Light

PHOTOGRAPHER
Anthony Edgeworth

CLIENT
Fieldcrest Mills

AGENCY
Epstein Raboy

30 SILVER
ART DIRECTOR
Sara Meyer

WRITER
Sandra Bucholtz

PHOTOGRAPHER
Kent Severson

CLIENT
Rhodes Frozen Bread Dough

AGENCY
Martin/Williams Advertising/Mpls.

Thoroughbred Tweed

Pictured at Borris House, Borris, County Carlow, "Thoroughbred Tweed" by Fieldcrest is the most contemporary design of the collection, blending heather, texture and tweed to achieve a woven plaid effect. From the Fieldcrest collection, "The Ireland I Love."

29 GOLD

How did Rhodes become the #1 frozen dough at retail?

Gold & Silver Awards

Collateral Sales Kits

31 SILVER

ART DIRECTOR
Jim Heck

WRITERS
Joel Jamison
Melanie Barker

ARTISTS
Margaret Buchanan
Norman Rainock

PHOTOGRAPHER
Sam West

CLIENT
Virginia Marine Products
Commission

AGENCY
Lawler Ballard Advertising/
Virginia

Collateral Direct Mail

32 GOLD

ART DIRECTOR
Lynda Transou

WRITER
Jack S. Allday

DESIGNER
Lynda Transou

CLIENT
Lincorp

AGENCY
Allday & Associates/Dallas

33 SILVER

ART DIRECTOR
Hal Tench

WRITER
Barbara Ford

DESIGNER
Hal Tench

PHOTOGRAPHER
John Whitehead

CLIENT
Collegiate Schools

AGENCY
The Martin Agency/Virginia

31 SILVER

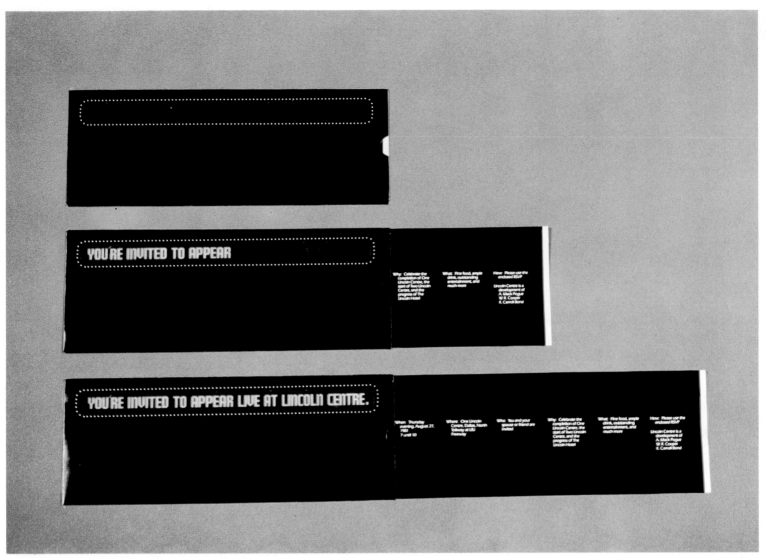

32 GOLD

33 SILVER

**Collateral
P.O.P.**

34 GOLD
ART DIRECTOR
George White

WRITER
Marc Deschenes

DESIGNER
George White

PHOTOGRAPHER
Jim Wood

CLIENT
Joseph M. Herman Shoes

AGENCY
Humphrey Browning
MacDougall/Boston

35 SILVER
ART DIRECTOR
Anthony Angotti

WRITER
Tom Thomas

DESIGNER
Barbara Bowman

PHOTOGRAPHER
Dick James

CLIENT
BMW of North America

AGENCY
Ammirati & Puris

34 GOLD

LAST YEAR, A CAR OUT-PERFORMED 318 STOCKS ON THE NEW YORK STOCK EXCHANGE.

If you'd bought a new BMW 320i in the beginning of 1980, and sold it at the end,
your investment would have retained 92.9% of its original value.
If you'd done the same with any of 318 NYSE stocks, you'd have done less well.
And you'd have forfeited an important daily dividend:
The unfluctuating joy of driving one of the world's great performance sedans.

THE ULTIMATE DRIVING MACHINE.
BMW, MUNICH, GERMANY

Gold & Silver
Awards

**Outdoor
Single**

36 GOLD
ART DIRECTOR
Dean Stefanides

WRITER
Earl Carter

DESIGNER
Dean Stefanides

PHOTOGRAPHER
Hashi

CLIENT
Nikon

AGENCY
Scali, McCabe, Sloves

37 SILVER
ART DIRECTOR
Lars Anderson

WRITER
Peter Levathes

DESIGNER
Lars Anderson

PHOTOGRAPHER
Steve Steigman

CLIENT
Maxell

AGENCY
Scali, McCabe, Sloves

36 GOLD

IF THERE'S A MAXELL CASSETTE IN THIS CAR AND IT DOESN'T WORK, WE'LL REPLACE IT.

37 SILVER

Gold & Silver Awards

Outdoor Campaign

38 GOLD
ART DIRECTOR
Bob Marberry

WRITER
Dick Thomas

PHOTOGRAPHER
Rick Dublin

CLIENT
Saigon Restaurant

AGENCY
Bobco/Mpls.

39 SILVER
ART DIRECTOR
John Knight

WRITER
Lyndon Mallett

DESIGNER
Geoff Halpin

PHOTOGRAPHER
Billy Wrencher

CLIENT
Wolverhampton & Dudley
Breweries

AGENCY
TBWA/London

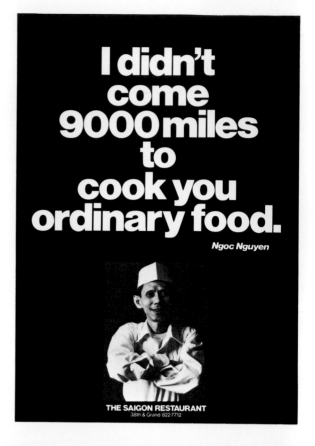

38 GOLD

It's New Year's Eve.

Don't get carried away.

There's no reason to beat around the bush when you're asking people not to kill themselves. If you're driving tonight, please drink responsibly.

If you've had too much to drink, don't get behind the wheel. Or you might find that you'll wind up in a more permanent resting place.

The way we see it, if one life is saved, this message is worth thousands of times the cost of publishing it. Have a happy and healthy New Year. **THE HOUSE OF SEAGRAM**

For reprints please write Advertising Dept. PE-1281.
The House of Seagram, 375 Park Ave., N.Y., N.Y. 10152

40 GOLD

The earthquake is over but the shock wave continues.

The quake in southern Italy happened back on November 23, 1980. Yet people are still homeless. Families still separated. Schools still shut. Hospitals still working overtime. Everywhere there are tens of thousands of people with only a past and very little future. They need your help. Please be generous and send a donation to the Red Cross.

That way the homeless will get shelter, the sick will get medicine, the hungry will get fed. Your donation could make a lot of people feel better. Including yourself.

The Italian Earthquake Relief Fund.

Yes, I would like to help the victims of the Italian earthquake. Here is my check for:

☐ $10 ☐ $20 ☐ Other _____

Name _____

Address _____

City _____

State _____ Zip _____

Make check to:
American Red Cross/Italian Earthquake Relief
Mail to: Jo Scott, 330 Madison Ave., 10th floor,
New York, N.Y. 10017

A public service announcement by the following U.S. advertising agencies:

N.W. Ayer ABH International • Ted Bates & Company, Inc. • BBDO International, Inc. • Benton & Bowles, Inc.
Compton Advertising Incorporated • Dancer Fitzgerald Sample, Inc. • Doyle Dane Bernbach Inc. • Foote, Cone & Belding
McCann-Erickson, Inc. • Ogilvy & Mather International Inc. • Young & Rubicam Inc.

Public Service Outdoor Single

42 GOLD
ART DIRECTORS
Richard Kurtz
Herb MacDonald

WRITER
Richard Kurtz

DESIGNERS
Richard Kurtz
Herb MacDonald

ARTIST
Herb MacDonald

CLIENT
Nova Scotia Department of
Mines and Energy/DREE

AGENCY
Corporate Communications/
Canada

43 SILVER
ART DIRECTOR
Ed Tajon

WRITER
Dave Newman

DESIGNER
Ed Tajon

ARTIST
Ken Orvidas

CLIENT
American Red Cross-
Portland Chapter

AGENCY
Borders, Perrin & Norrander/
Oregon

Corporate Newspaper or Magazine Single

44 GOLD
ART DIRECTOR
Derek Chapman

WRITER
David Hayward

DESIGNER
Derek Chapman

ARTIST
Derek Chapman

PHOTOGRAPHER
Nigel Dickson

CLIENT
Allstate Insurance Companies
of Canada

AGENCY
Leo Burnett/Canada

45 SILVER
ART DIRECTOR
Peter Hirsch

WRITER
Neil Calet

DESIGNER
Peter Hirsch

CLIENT
Calet, Hirsch, Kurnit
& Spector

AGENCY
Calet, Hirsch, Kurnit
& Spector

42 GOLD

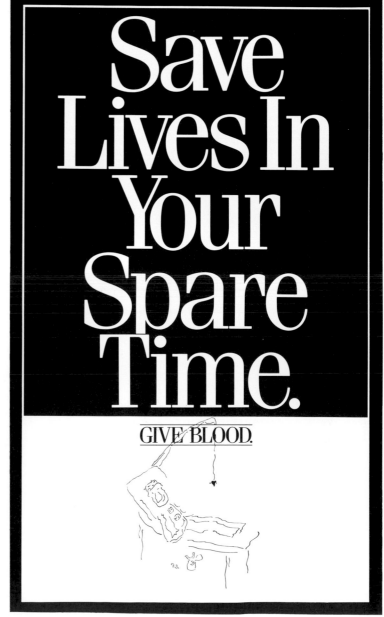

43 SILVER

Which bag would you prefer?

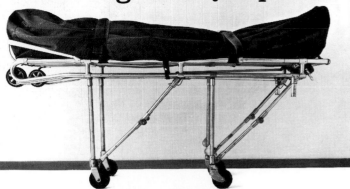

At this moment, President Reagan and his Cabinet are reviewing the future of U.S. Passive Restraint Legislation. (An act that would provide for factory installation of air bags in all cars.)

In Allstate's book, this is a perfectly reasonable and proper thing for the Executive Branch of the United States Government to be doing.

Except for one slightly disturbing note.

Whatever they decide will inevitably affect Canadians, because under the Canada-U.S. Auto Pact, most of our cars are designed in the U.S.

Why should Canadians worry about this?

After all, every car sold in Canada already has seat belts, and four provinces have even gone to the trouble of passing mandatory "buckle-up" laws.

And everybody knows that, even though nothing is perfect, seat belts provide reasonably good protection on the road.

In spite of these comforting thoughts, we think Canadians *should* worry.

Because seat belts by definition suffer from a potentially fatal flaw.

Human nature.

Unless the people in the car actually perform the voluntary act of doing up their seat belts, they end up with no protection at all.

And we all know about human nature when it comes to voluntary acts, even if they are life savers.

A typical example is drunk driving.

Why don't people perform the voluntary act of not driving when they're under the influence?

When you consider that impaired

driving is about as dangerous as Russian roulette, this particular voluntary act could be a real life saver.

It's the same with seat belts. By performing the voluntary act of buckling up, car occupants could help save their lives by the thousands.

(Not to mention the millions of dollars in hospital and highway emergency costs that are borne by us all.)

The sad truth is that even in provinces with strong "buckle up" laws, supported by advertising campaigns, seat belt use is *actually slipping*. (Example: in a recent B.C. survey, seat belt use was found to have slipped from 63% to 54% in just six months. Other provincial surveys could be worse.)

Without even counting in the people who are excluded from using seat belts such as Police, emergency vehicle drivers and individuals with certain medical

Allstate
A company with values

problems, this leaves a lot of Canadians dangerously unprotected. If only it weren't for human nature!

Do we have to stay on this merry-go-round?

No. Because there is an alternative.

Air bags.

Because they're in place, ready to operate 100% of the time, air bags don't depend on any voluntary act by the driver or passenger.

Because of this fundamental advantage over seat belts, and their protective capability proven by more than 750 million kilometres of actual highway driving experience, we estimate that if every car in Canada was equipped with air bags 900 lives and 6,500 injuries* could be saved in the next twelve months.

And because air bags could save some of the millions of dollars that insurance companies have to pay out now for death and injury claims, car insurance costs could better be brought under control.

Allstate understands the problems now being faced by the North American automobile industry.

We appreciate that losses of more than 4 billion dollars in 1980 can make car manufacturers somewhat reluctant to support air bag legislation that could add to the sticker price of their cars.

But Allstate also knows that because the technology exists, installing air bags on all cars at the factory would cost about the same as a vinyl roof or an AM/FM radio.

The choice is simple. A moderate investment in air bags to help save lives. Or another kind of bag.

Which would you prefer?

If you have an opinion on this issue, or if you'd just like more air bag information, we'd like to hear from you. Please write:
Consumer Information Group, Allstate Insurance Companies of Canada, 255 Consumers Road, Willowdale, Ontario. M2J 1R4

*An estimate for Canada based on U.S. Department of Transport Studies.

44 GOLD

DKG. A NAME TO FORGET.

It was a good name. And it stood for a lot of good things. Like award-winning creative. A blue-chip account list. And the kinds of marketing successes brand managers pray for. Which may be the reason DKG has received seven merger offers in the past twelve months.

After considering them carefully, we've decided. It's no dice.

We're not going to exchange our independence for someone else's stock. Or sacrifice our convictions to someone else's bottom line.

We're not going to merge.

Instead, we're going to emerge.

From now on, DKG will be known as Calet, Hirsch, Kurnit & Spector. After twenty years in the business, we're putting our names on the door. Our names. Not a combination of us and some merger-hungry monolith.

Because at Calet, Hirsch, Kurnit & Spector, the only ones we want to be responsible to are our clients.

AAMCO Transmissions
Alitalia Airlines
American Enka
Brown-Forman Distillers
Clairol Appliances
Corning Housewares
Corning Lenses
Dollar Savings Bank
Getty/Skelly
Martex/Lady Pepperell
Pocket Books
Ramada (Tropicana Hotel)
Remington Shavers
Ricoh Cameras
Simplicity Patterns
Talon Zippers
Thermos
Toshiba
True Temper
Uniroyal

Calet, Hirsch, Kurnit & Spector, Inc.
1271 AVENUE OF THE AMERICAS, NEW YORK, NY 10020/ (212) 489-7300

45 SILVER

Decriminalization of Marijuana. Let's understand all of the issues before it gets carved in tablets of stone.

Sometime in 1981, the House of Commons will debate a bill which will decriminalize the possession of marijuana.

If this legislation is subsequently passed into law, the act of possessing marijuana will be changed from a crime to a simple misdemeanor.

Which means something like a traffic ticket instead of a jail sentence if you're caught.

While the bill does not entirely legalize the act of smoking grass, the vast majority of people will interpret it as if it did.

After all, if you can practically carry it, you can smoke it.

And if you can smoke it, you can get stoned out of your mind on it.

Which brings us to the one discordant note in an otherwise humanitarian change in the law.

The Traffic Injury Research Foundation of Canada has irrefutable research findings obtained in a recent study of fatal highway accidents proving that one of every eight victims had been using cannabis.

In our book, this proves the popular belief that grass doesn't interfere with psychomotor response is wrong.

Dead wrong. Grass can kill on the highway just as lethally as alcohol can.

Allstate's position on this life and death matter is simple.

It's not our business to be either for or against decriminalization of marijuana.

That's up to Parliament.

But it _is_ our business to be against needless death and injury on the highways. From where we sit, we have a horrifyingly first-hand view of the increasing waste of life and money caused by road accidents and we know it has to be stopped.

So before Parliament passes a bill that may cause a road safety hazard as serious as that of alcohol, let's at least understand and discuss the issues.

Let's ask ourselves and our elected representatives if we have enough _facts_ to justify such a far reaching move at this time.

If, in our enthusiasm for freeing young people from the stigma of a criminal record, we aren't at the same time condemning them to a self-inflicted death.

And equally to the point, if laws as they apply to cannabis should not be changed to mirror existing statutes that provide stiff penalties for carrying open bottles of liquor or beer in a motor vehicle.

Allstate urges you to consider these issues.

Before they get carved in tablets of stone.

Like to know more about cannabis and its effect on driving? Write: Consumer Information Group, Allstate Insurance Companies of Canada, 255 Consumers Road, Willowdale, Ontario. M2J 1R4

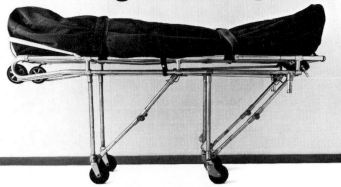

Gold & Silver Awards

**Corporate
Newspaper or Magazine
Campaign**

47 SILVER

ART DIRECTORS
Tom Shortlidge
Rich Kimmel

WRITERS
Mike Faems
Mark Fenske

PHOTOGRAPHERS
Mel Kaspar
NASA/Voyager 2

CLIENT
Motorola

AGENCY
Young & Rubicam/Chicago

WE USED TO BRING YOU THE SIX O'CLOCK NEWS. NOW WE ARE THE SIX O'CLOCK NEWS.

Back in the 1950s, when the 6 o'clock news first started finding its way into people's living rooms, Motorola was there.

Today, although we're no longer making television sets, we're still there when people all over the country sit down to the 6 o'clock news.

Except now, instead of making the sets they're watching, we're part of the history they're watching.

On November 12, 1980, a Motorola communications subsystem designed for the Jet Propulsion Laboratory and NASA sent photographs back to Earth from a billion miles away near the planet Saturn.

This equipment, the only link between Earth and the Voyager spacecraft, not only sent photos that thrilled a watching world, it also transmitted data that turned centuries of scientific thought upside down.

One month before, the world's largest auto maker was able to announce a giant step forward in improving gas mileage while at the same time decreasing emissions because of an engine management system that runs on a microprocessor Motorola designed.

And in the years ahead, technology we're pioneering may bring microelectronic devices into our lives that the world has only dreamed of before.

Like a portable telephone small enough to fit in your pocket.

Microprocessors that could allow industrial robots to function ten times faster than humans.

And microchips that make it possible to use computers to find oil miles beneath the earth's crust without drilling an inch.

All these advances and more are being pioneered by Motorola in our development centers around the world. And in many ways they're only the beginning of what we can do.

So the next time you see something on the 6 o'clock news that you never imagined possible, you'll know there's a chance someone at Motorola had a part in making it happen. And if that makes us sound like a company far different from the one that once made television sets for your living room, it's simply because we are.

Making electronics history. Ⓜ **MOTOROLA**

WHEN YOU'RE 966 MILLION MILES IN SPACE, YOU CAN'T DROP YOUR PICTURES OFF AT THE CORNER DRUGSTORE.

The planet Saturn is so far away, it has taken Voyager 2, travelling several times the speed of sound, four years to get there. Even a radio message takes almost an hour and a half to make the trip. Imagine the challenge of sending back pictures.

And yet, the pictures get back. And with amazing clarity.

A Motorola communications system designed for the Jet Propulsion Laboratory and NASA transmits all the pictures from Voyager 2.

This Motorola system also provides the link for all other communications between Earth and the spacecraft, and relays the scientific information Voyager 2 gathers on this remarkable journey, just as one of our systems did for Voyager 1.

In fact, Motorola electronic systems have been part of U.S. space programs since Explorer I in 1958. Our equipment has been used on every manned and most unmanned space shots without a single failure affecting mission success. Not one.

Bringing pictures back from 966 million miles away is just another example of Motorola's advanced technology and reliability meeting challenges around the world. And beyond.

Ⓜ **MOTOROLA** A World Leader In Electronics.

Quality and productivity through employee participation in management.

Motorola, Inc. is one of the world's leading manufacturers of electronic equipment, systems and components, including communications systems, semiconductors, equipment for military and aerospace use, industrial and automotive electronic equipment, and data communications products. ©1981 Motorola Inc. Motorola and Ⓜ are registered trademarks of Motorola Inc.

47 SILVER

WE USED TO BRING YOU THE SIX O'CLOCK NEWS. NOW WE ARE THE SIX O'CLOCK NEWS.

Motorola and (M) are registered trademarks of Motorola, Inc.

Back in the 1950s, when the 6 o'clock news first started finding its way into people's living rooms, Motorola was there.

Today, although we're no longer making television sets, we're still there when people all over the world sit down to the 6 o'clock news.

Except now, instead of making the sets they're watching, we're part of the history they're watching.

On November 12, 1980, a Motorola communications subsystem designed for the Jet Propulsion Laboratory and NASA sent photographs back to Earth from a billion miles away near the planet Saturn.

This equipment, the only link between Earth and the Voyager spacecraft, not only sent photos that thrilled a watching world, it also transmitted data that turned centuries of scientific thought upside down.

One month before, the world's largest auto maker was able to announce a giant step forward in improving gas mileage while at the same time decreasing emissions because of an engine management system that runs on a microprocessor Motorola designed.

And in the years ahead, technology we're pioneering may bring microelectronic devices into our lives that the world has only dreamed of before.

Like a portable telephone small enough to fit in your pocket.

Microprocessors that could allow industrial robots to function ten times faster than humans.

And microchips that make it possible to use computers to find oil miles beneath the earth's crust without drilling an inch.

All these advances and more are being pioneered by Motorola in our development centers around the world.

And in many ways they're only the beginning of what we can do.

So the next time you see something on the 6 o'clock news that you never imagined possible, you'll know there's a chance someone at Motorola had a part in making it happen.

And if that makes us sound like a company far different from the one that once made television sets for your living room, it's simply because we are.

Making electronics history. (M) **MOTOROLA**

Gold & Silver Awards

Student Competition

48 GOLD
ART DIRECTOR AND WRITER
Norm Johnson

PHOTOGRAPHER
John Kelly

SCHOOL
Art Center College of Design/
California

49 SILVER
ART DIRECTOR AND WRITER
Kirk Mosel

SCHOOL
School of Visual Arts

Consumer Radio Single

50 GOLD
WRITER
Helayne Spivak

CLIENT
MCI

AGENCY PRODUCER
Jerry Haynes

AGENCY
Ally & Gargano

51 SILVER
WRITERS
Dick & Bert

CLIENT
Granada TV Rental

AGENCY PRODUCER
Shelley Muller

AGENCY
TBWA

GOOD.

FOR NOTHING.

☐ Yes, I'd like to see a resume and samples of your work.

Agency _____
Address _____

Attn. _____
Mail to: Norm Johnson
2017 Berkshire Avenue
So. Pasadena, CA 91030
or call collect (213) 256-1270

48 GOLD

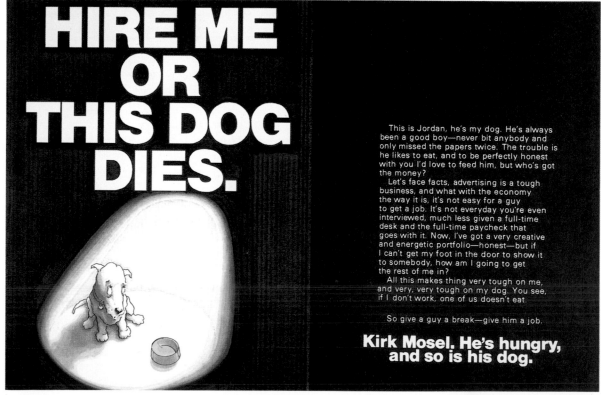

HIRE ME OR THIS DOG DIES.

This is Jordan, he's my dog. He's always been a good boy—never bit anybody and only missed the papers twice. The trouble is he likes to eat, and to be perfectly honest with you I'd love to feed him, but who's got the money?

Let's face facts, advertising is a tough business, and what with the economy the way it is, it's not easy for a guy to get a job. It's not everyday you're even interviewed, much less given a full-time desk and the full-time paycheck that goes with it. Now, I've got a very creative and energetic portfolio—honest—but if I can't get my foot in the door to show it to somebody, how am I going to get the rest of me in?

All this makes thing very tough on me, and very, very tough on my dog. You see, if I don't work, one of us doesn't eat.

So give a guy a break—give him a job.

Kirk Mosel. He's hungry, and so is his dog.

49 SILVER

50 GOLD

(A PHONE RINGS. THEN A VERY TIRED WOMAN'S VOICE.)

MOM: Hullo?

DAVE: Hi, Mom. Surprise. It's Dave.

MOM: Hullo?

DAVE: Mom. Wake up. It's your son, Dave. I'm calling long distance.

MOM: (STILL ASLEEP BUT KNOWS HIS NAME.) Dave?

DAVE: I'm sorry I'm calling so late, but the rates are cheapest weekdays after 11 pm.

MOM: (SOUND OF FEMALE SNORING.)

DAVE: Mom? Mom! Come on. Give the phone to Dad.

MOM: Here, Frank. It's for you.

DAD: (LOUD MASCULINE SNORING)

DAVE: Dad. It's me. Dave. Dad? Come on, Dad. Mom. Are you still there? (SOUND OF TWO PEOPLE SNORING.) Wake Dad! Wake Dad! Don't do this to me. Mom…Dad…

ANNCR: Reach out. Reach out and wake someone. That's one suggestion on how to get Bells' lowest rates on long distance calls. Want a better suggestion? Try MCI, the nation's long distance phone company, and save 30, 40, even 50% weekdays by calling after the very decent hour of 5:00 p.m. So call MCI. And find out how to save money when you want to. Not when Bell tells you to.

51 SILVER

BERT: You're sure this is the newest video cassette recorder? Huh?

DICK: The KX-2 records, plays back, freeze-frames, and has a laser-powered digital chronographical instrumentation panel.

BERT: Ooh, what's that?

DICK: A clock

BERT: Oh Boy. Here's my check!

DICK: And here's your KX-2.

GUY: Hey Mack, I got those video KX-3's here.

BERT: KX-3's?

DICK: Yeah, this one selects the best show on the air, edits out the commercials and chills beer.

BERT: What about my KX-2's?

DICK: It's now officially obsolete.

BERT: Obsolete?

ANNCR: Video cassette recorders are changing fast. So, why buy one for hundreds of dollars when you can rent a new brand name VCR from Granada TV Rental for as low as $29.95 a month? And, when you want a newer model, no problem. And no cost for delivery, installation or repairs. Granada believes that when it comes to TV's and VCR's, the only thing that's obsolete is the idea of "buying" one.

BERT: So the KX-3 is the state of the art, huh.

DICK: For at least a week.

BERT: A week!

DICK: Maybe 2 days

BERT: 2 days?

DICK: What time is it? Maybe an hour.

ANNCR: TV and VCR rental. A new concept in America from Granada. Fourteen locations in the New York metropolitan area. Look for us in the white pages. Granada TV rental. A whole new way of looking at TV.

Gold & Silver
Awards

**Consumer Radio
Campaign**

52 GOLD
WRITER
Helayne Spivak
CLIENT
MCI
AGENCY PRODUCER
Jerry Haynes
AGENCY
Ally & Gargano

53 SILVER
WRITERS
Dick & Bert
CLIENT
Granada TV Rental
AGENCY PRODUCER
Shelley Muller
AGENCY
TBWA

52 GOLD

(SOUND OF INTERCOM-LIKE BUZZ)

PICKING: Sara. Is the WATS line free?

SARA: No, Mr. Picking, it isn't.

PICKING: Call me when it is.

SARA: Sure will. (BUZZ) Yes?

LORD: Sara. I'd like the WATS line?

SARA: Sorry, Mr. Lord. Mr. Picking's next in line.

LORD: Forget Picking. Put me next.

SARA: Sure will. (BUZZ) Yes?

PICKING: Picking here. Is the WATS free yet?

SARA: Listen, Mr. Picking. Mr. Lord says his call should be next.

PICKING: We'll see about that. (BUZZ)

SARA: Yes?

KELLY: It's Mr. Kelly. Give me the WATS line.

SARA: Mr. Picking and Mr. Lord are waiting too, Mr. Kelly.

KELLY: Whose name is on your check every week, Sara?

SARA: Why, I believe the line is free now.

ANNCR: If you spend more in time than you save in money with Bell's WATS line, call MCI. The nation's long distance phone company. MCI offers your company many economical alternatives to Bell's services. Including one that will save you 30% more than their famous WATS line. So call MCI. Because your company hasn't been calling too much. You've just been paying too much.

52 GOLD

(A PHONE RINGS. THEN A VERY TIRED WOMAN'S VOICE.)

MOM: Hullo?

DAVE: Hi, Mom. Surprise. It's Dave.

MOM: Hullo?

DAVE: Mom. Wake up. It's your son, Dave. I'm calling long distance.

MOM: (STILL ASLEEP BUT KNOWS HIS NAME.) Dave?

DAVE: I'm sorry I'm calling so late, but the rates are cheapest weekdays after 11 pm.

MOM: (SOUND OF FEMALE SNORING.):

DAVE: Mom? Mom! Come on. Give the phone to Dad.

MOM: Here, Frank. It's for you.

DAD: (LOUD MASCULINE SNORING)

DAVE: Dad. It's me. Dave. Dad? Come on, Dad. Mom. Are you still there? (SOUND OF TWO PEOPLE SNORING.) Wake Dad! Wake Dad! Don't do this to me. Mom...Dad...

ANNCR: Reach out. Reach out and wake someone. That's one suggestion on how to get Bell's lowest rates on long distance calls. Want a better suggestion? Try MCI, the nation's long distance phone company, and save 30, 40, even 50% weekdays by calling after the very decent hour of 5:00 p.m. So call MCI. And find out how to save money when you want to. Not when Bell tells you to.

52 GOLD

(SOUND OF PHONE RINGING. FUMBLING WITH RECEIVER IS HEARD. A VERY SLEEPY VOICE SAYS...)

DENISE: Hullo?

HAROLD: Denise? It's me. Harold. Did I wake you?

DENISE: Not yet. But if you keep talking, you will.

HAROLD: Come on. This is a long distance call.

DENISE: What time is it?

HAROLD: 2 a.m. your time.

DENISE: Harold. I have to wake up all over again in four hours. Call me in the morning.

HAROLD: Denise. Wait. I can't. Look how much money I save by calling weekdays after 11 p.m.

DENISE: I can save you even more money, Harold.

HAROLD: How?

DENISE: (SOUND OF RECEIVER BEING HUNG UP.)

ANNCR: Bell suggests that to save the most money on your long distance calls, you should call after 11 p.m. We have a better suggestion: call MCI, the nation's long distance phone company, and save 30, 40 even 50% between the civilized weekday hours of 5 and 11 p.m. Not to mention the savings you can get all day long and weekends. So call MCI now. And stop talking in someone else's sleep.

BERT: (On phone filter) Hello?

MIR: Is this Bernie Blenstrum?

BERT: Yes...

MIR: The guy I met yesterday at the supermarket?

BERT: We grabbed the same rump roast.

MIR: And today, you sent me a brand new color television set?

BERT: Some guys send candy, or flowers, but *me*...

MIR: They're just delivering it, it's *gorgeous!*

BERT: Well, if anything happens to it, it'll be fixed for free!

MIR: What a man!

BERT: Yes I am!

MIR: Bernie, would you like to come over and...

BERT: Yes I would!

DICK: ...'scuse me, lady, could you sign this receipt from Granada TV Rental?

MIR: Rental? What rental?

BERT: Pay no attention to him, Gloria!

DICK: Granada TV Rental. It's the newest thing. You can rent new, brand name TVs for as little as $11.95 a month!

MIR: *$11.95???!*

DICK: So you save hundreds of dollars renting, cuz there's no big cash outlay, and no repair bills!

MIR: Bernie, you spent a measly $11.95?

BERT: With the money I saved on renting from Granada, I was going to get you some flow... can...a...car! Yeah, a car!!

MIR: A car?? Oh, Bernie, you hurry right over!!!

(SFX: HANG UP)

BERT: Where's that number, rent a car, rent a car

ANNCR: TV and VCR rental. A new concept in America from Granada. Fourteen locations in the New York metropolitan area. Look for us in the white pages.

Granada TV Rental. A whole new way of looking at TV.

BERT: You're sure this is the newest video cassette recorder? Huh?

DICK: The KX-2 records, plays back, freeze-frames, and has a laser-powered digital chronographical instrumentation panel.

BERT: Ooh, what's that?

DICK: A clock

BERT: Oh Boy. Here's my check!

DICK: And here's your KX-2.

GUY: Hey Mack, I got those video KX-3's here.

BERT: KX-3's?

DICK: Yeah, this one selects the best show on the air, edits out the commercials and chills beer.

BERT: What about my KX-2's?

DICK: It's now officially obsolete.

BERT: Obsolete?

ANNCR: Video cassette recorders are changing fast. So, why buy one for hundreds of dollars when you can rent a new brand name VCR from Granada TV Rental for as low as $29.95 a month? And, when you want a newer model, no problem. And no cost for delivery, installation or repairs, Granada believes that when it comes to TV's and VCR's, the only thing that's obsolete is the idea of "buying" one.

BERT: So the KX-3 is the state of the art, huh.

DICK: For at least a week.

BERT: A week!

DICK: Maybe 2 days.

BERT: 2 days?

DICK: What time is it? Maybe an hour.

ANNCR: TV and VCR rental. A new concept in America from Granada. Fourteen locations in the New York metropolitan area. Look for us in the white pages. Granada TV Rental. A whole new way of looking at TV.

DICK: Couple more questions Mr. Bim, and you'll be a...

BERT: A certified TV repairman!

DICK: Right!

BERT: Don't I have to take apart a TV set or something?

DICK: It's just a lot of wires and glowy things. This is more important!

BERT: Go ahead.

DICK: What's the first thing you say when you look at the set?

BERT: Oh—it's the picture tube.

DICK: Then what?

BERT: It'll take 2 weeks to a year.

DICK: And finally...

BERT: I catch 'em when they faint!

ANNCR: There is a way to beat the TV repair game! Rent your TV set from Granada TV Rental. You can rent a brand new, brand name, color TV for as low as $11.95 a month. And if anything should happen, Granada will promptly fix it free, or give you a free loaner. With Granada TV Rental, you'll never have to worry about TV repairs again!

DICK: So you toss the set into the back of the van, you drive away, you say and you shout back

BERT: Tough luck, sucker!

DICK: Very good!

ANNCR: TV and VCR rental. A new concept in America from Granada. Fourteen locations in the New York metropolitan area. Look for us in the white pages. Granada TV Rental. A whole new way of looking at TV.

Gold & Silver Awards

**Consumer Television
60 Seconds
Single**

54 GOLD
ART DIRECTOR
Michael Tesch

WRITER
Patrick Kelly

CLIENT
Federal Express

DIRECTOR
Joe Sedelmaier

PRODUCTION CO.
Sedelmaier Films/Chicago

AGENCY PRODUCER
Maureen Kearns

AGENCY
Ally & Gargano

55 SILVER
ART DIRECTOR
Ray Black

WRITER
Ray Black

CLIENT
Tip Top Bakery

DIRECTOR
Ray Lawrence

PRODUCTION CO.
Window Productions/Australia

AGENCY PRODUCER
Robert Bateson

AGENCY
Pope & Kiernan & Black/
Australia

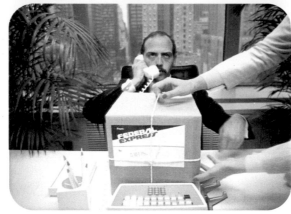

54 GOLD

MR. SPLEEN(OC): OkayEunice,travelplans.Ineedtobe
inNewYorkonWednesday,LAonThursday,NewYorkon
Friday.Gotit?

EUNICE (VO): Got it.

MR. SPLEEN (OC): Soyouwanttoworkhere,wellwhatmakes
youthinkyoudeserveajobhere?

GUY: Wellsir,Ithinkonmyfeet,I'mgoodwithfiguresandI
haveasharpmind.

SPLEEN: Excellent.CanyoustartMonday? Guy: Yessir.
Absolutelywithouthesitation.

SPLEEN: Congratulation,welcomeaboard.

(SFX) (OC): Wonderful,wonderful,wonderful.Andin
conclusionJim,Bill,Bob,Paul,Don,Frank,andTed,

businessisbusinessandasweallknow,inordertoget
somethingdoneyou'vegottodosomething.Inordertodo
somethingyou'vegottogettoworksolet'sallgettowork.

Thankyouforattendingthismeeting. (SFX)

(OC): Peteryoudidabang-upjobI'mputtingyouin
chargeofPittsburgh.

PETER: (oc) Pittsburgh,perfect.

SPLEEN: Iknowit'sperfectPeterthat'swhyIpicked
Pittsburgh. Pittsburgh'sperfectPeter.
MayIcallyouPete?

PETER: CallmePete. SPLEEN: Pete.

SECRETARY (OC): there'saMr.Snitlerheretoseeyou.

SPLEEN (OC): Tellhimtowait15seconds.

SECRETARY: Canyouwait15seconds.

MAN: I'll wait 15 seconds.

SPLEEN (OC): CongratulationsonyourdealinDenverDavid.
I'mputtingyoudowntodealinDallas.Donisitadeal?Do
wehaveadeal?It'sadeal.Ihaveacallcomingin...

ANNCR (VO): In this fast moving high pressure,
get-it-done-yesterday world

(VO): Aren't you glad that there's one company that can
keep up with it all?

SPLEEN (OC): Dickwhat'sthedealwiththedeal.Arewe
dealing?We'redealing.Daveit'sadealwithDon,Dork
andDick.Dorkit'sadealwithDon,DaveandDick.

Dickit'saDorkwithDonDealandDave.Dave,gotago,
disconnecting.Dorkgotago,disconnecting.Dick
gottago,disconnecting...

ANNCR (VO): Federal Express. (SFX) When it absolutely,
positively has to be there overnight.

55 SILVER

(SINGERS): *No other multigrain is quite like*
Bornhoffen...
There's flaxseed, malted grain, buckwheat and
bran...
so the aroma and taste of Bornhoffen is something
to look forward to...
Bornhoffen Wholefood bread.
Man does not live on bread alone...
However, with Bornhoffen he comes close.

**Consumer Television
30 Seconds
Single**

56 GOLD
ART DIRECTOR
Dean Hanson

WRITER
Tom McElligott

CLIENT
Donaldsons

DIRECTOR
Jim Lund

PRODUCTION CO.
EmCom

AGENCY PRODUCERS
Dean Hanson
Tom McElligott

AGENCY
Fallon McElligott Rice/Mpls.

57 SILVER
ART DIRECTOR
Michael Tesch

WRITER
Patrick Kelly

CLIENT
Federal Express

DIRECTOR
Joe Sedelmaier

PRODUCTION CO.
Sedelmaier Films/Chicago

AGENCY PRODUCER
Maureen Kearns

AGENCY
Ally & Gargano

**Consumer Television
10 Seconds
Single**

58 GOLD
ART DIRECTOR
Michael Tesch

WRITER
Patrick Kelly

CLIENT
Federal Express

DIRECTOR
Joe Sedelmaier

PRODUCTION CO.
Sedelmaier Films/Chicago

AGENCY PRODUCER
Maureen Kearns

AGENCY
Ally & Gargano

59 SILVER
ART DIRECTOR
Michael Tesch

WRITER
Patrick Kelly

CLIENT
Federal Express

DIRECTOR
Joe Sedelmaier

PRODUCTION CO.
Sedelmaier Films/Chicago

AGENCY PRODUCER
Maureen Kearns

AGENCY
Ally & Gargano

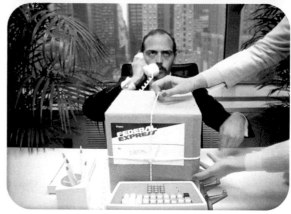

56 GOLD

ANNCR (VO): Christmas may be for *children*...but *after* Christmas is for *adults*.

MAN: I want a new color TV!

ANNCR (VO): Donaldsons presents the *After* Christmas Sale and Clearance.

WOMAN: And a coffee pot and a sweater and a toaster...

ANNCR (VO): ...with *20 to 50 percent savings* on housewares, clothing and more.

MAN: I want a new ski jacket and gloves...

ANNCR (VO): Donaldsons After Christmas Sale and Clearance...

WOMAN: And if I don't get it, I'm going to hold my breath!

57 SILVER

MR. SPLEEN (OC): OkayEunice,travelplans.Ineedtobe inNewYorkonMonday,LAonTuesday,NewYorkon Wednesday,LAonThursday,

andNewYorkonFriday. Gotit? Soyouwanttowork here,wellwhatmakesyouthinkyoudeserveajobhere?

GUY: Wellsir,Ithinkonmyfeet,I'mgoodwithfiguresandI haveasharpmind.

SPLEEN: Excellent.CanyoustartMonday?

(OC): AndinconclusionJim,Bill,Bob,andTed,

Businessisbusinesssolet'sgettowork. Thankyoufor takingthismeeting.

(OC): Peteryoudidabang-upjobI'mputtingyouinchargeof Pittsburgh.

PETER (OC): Pittsburgh'sperfect.

SPLEEN: Iknowit'sperfect,Peter,that'swhyIpicked Pittsburgh. Pittsburgh'sperfect,Peter,MayIcall youPete?

SPLEEN (OC): CongratulationsonyourdealinDenverDavid.

I'mputtingyoudowntodealinDallas.

ANNCR (VO): In this fast moving, high pressure, get-it-done-yesterday world, aren't you glad there's one company that can keep up with it all?

ANNCR (VO): Federal Express. (SFX) When it absolutely, positively has to be there overnight.

58 GOLD

ANNCR (VO): Federal Express is so easy to use, all you have to do is pick up the phone.

(SFX: RRRRRRRIIIIIIIIPPPPPPPPPPPPPPPPP!!)
(SFX: WATER)

59 SILVER

SPLEEN (OC): CongratulationsonyourdealinDenver,David. I'mputtingyoudowntodealwithDon.

DonisitadealꞏDowehaveadealꞏIhaveacallcoming through.

ANNCR (VO): In this fast paced world aren't you glad there's one company that can keep up with it all?

SPLEEN: Dick,what'sthedealwiththedealꞏArewedealing?

SUPER: Federal Express.

Gold & Silver Awards

Corporate Televison Single

60 GOLD
ART DIRECTORS
Phil Dusenberry
Ted Sann

WRITERS
Phil Dusenberry
Ted Sann

CLIENT
General Electric

DIRECTOR
Bob Giraldi

PRODUCTION CO.
Bob Giraldi Productions

AGENCY PRODUCER
Jeff Fischgrund

AGENCY
BBDO

61 SILVER
ART DIRECTORS
Ted Sann
Phil Dusenberry
Mike Moir

WRITERS
Ted Sann
Phil Dusenberry

CLIENT
General Electric

DIRECTOR
Bob Giraldi

PRODUCTION CO.
Bob Giraldi Productions

AGENCY PRODUCER
Jeff Fischgrund

AGENCY
BBDO

Public Service Television Single

62 SILVER
ART DIRECTOR
Arnold Wicht

WRITERS
Bill Martin
Ian Parker

CLIENT
Ontario Secretariat for
Social Development

DIRECTOR
Fred Stenger

PRODUCTION CO.
Rabko

AGENCY PRODUCER
Tim Heintzman

AGENCY
Camp Associates/Canada

60 GOLD

(MUSIC)

AVO: On a summer's evening in 1924, in Lynn, Massa-chusetts, perhaps the most significant game in the long history of baseball was played.

It wasn't the pitching that was so extraordinary, nor the hitting. And the fielding, well, it was less than exemplary.

No, what made this game truly historic was the time of day. (SFX) Nightfall.

For it was on this night that this small group of GE engineers ushered in the era of night baseball. Baseball under the lights.

And while the names of "Yugo" Fee and Tommy Perkins and Hank Innes will never be recorded in the Hall of Fame,

It was this earnest band of GE pioneers that made possible for us all the many brilliant nights to come. (SFX)

SINGERS: *GE. We bring good things to life.*

61 SILVER

(MUSIC)

(AVO): To all you students of innovation, to you, inspired to try what's never been tried before,

To all those consumed with an insatiable curiosity,

a penchant for ingenuity,

To you who seek and search

And blaze new trails,

Who try and fail and try again;

To all you children of imagination,

You sons and daughters and mothers of invention,

Dreamers and doers, thinkers and

Tinkerers all, we at General Electric salute you.

For, as advanced as our technology has become, we've never forgotten that from small beginnings big ideas grow.

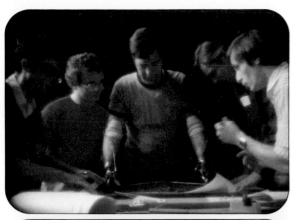

62 SILVER

ANNCR: It's often assumed that people with mental or physical disabilities cannot participate in today's complex society. We've produced this commercial to set the record straight. Of the 68 people involved in this production, 42 are mentally or physically disabled; among them the director, the cameraman, the set designer and the builders, the sound engineer, many of the musicians, and Beethoven who was deaf when he wrote this music.

Even me. I'm blind.

We put it all together to make this point: consider what we can do–LABEL US ABLE

Gold & Silver Awards

**Consumer Television
60 Seconds
Campaign**

63 GOLD
ART DIRECTORS
Jim Nawrocki
Lynn Crosswaite
Rich Seidelman

WRITERS
Josephine Cummings
Bob Scarpelli
Christie McMahon

CLIENT
McDonald's

DIRECTORS
Rob Lieberman
Dan Nichols
Denny Harris

PRODUCTION COS.
Harmony Pictures
Michael/Daniel Productions
Denny Harris

AGENCY PRODUCERS
Sheila Hayden
Helmut Dorger
Patricia Caruso

AGENCY
Needham, Harper & Steers/
Chicago

63 GOLD

DENISE (VO): Chrissie's my very best friend in the whole world. We're exactly alike. We both have trouble with math.

CHRISSIE (OC): What's the square root of 164?

DENISE (VO): We both love horses. And we both hate our hair.

GIRLS (OC): Yuck!!

DENISE (VO): We even liked the same guy. Then found out he likes Marcia Wilk.

GIRLS (OC): Marcia Wilk?!

SINGERS: *No two are closer than you*

She shares in all that you do

*A best friend's someone to care
Someone who'll always be there*

*Everything is more fun
When it's done with someone*

We've got a place to get away

*When you deserve a break today
At McDonald's.*

DENISE (VO): The best thing about Chrissie is . . . she's my best friend.

SINGERS: *Here's to the two of you.*

MALE SOLO: *Where did all the day go*

GIRL SOLO: *I'm so sleepy, goodnight*

MALE SOLO: *Miss her more than she knows
Sometimes you can't seem to find . . .*

GIRL SOLO: *Do you have to go Dad?*

MALE SOLO: *. . . A minute of time
There's so much to be said.*

GIRL SOLO: *I've got homework to do*

MALE SOLO: *How can it be so tough*

GIRL SOLO: *Have to go to my class.*

DAD SOLO: *A little time's all you need
You never see her enough*

GROUP: *Get together, get away*

GIRL: Yes, I'll have a cheeseburger, fries . . .

DAD: And a sundae?

GIRL: Yeah!

GROUP: *You deserve a break today*

GIRL SOLO: *At McDonald's.*

(MUSIC)

SINGERS: *Sometimes you can't slow down*
You're movin'
Can't stop that feeling inside
You're dancin'
It keeps you spinnin' around
Keep goin'
You gotta go for the ride
Yeah, just look at you go
You're rollin'
Look at you doin' the town
You're shinin'.
Big Mac
And a Coke on the go
McDonald's
You know we won't slow you down
You're movin' to your own song

SINGERS: *In your heart.*
We'll keep you goin' along
You know it
You don't have to slow down
No...no...no...
Because you know we're around
You've been going strong all day.
Yeah, you deserve a break today
At McDonald's we'll keep moving
Cause you're rollin'
We'll keep ya movin'.

**Consumer Television
60 Seconds
Campaign**

64 SILVER

ART DIRECTORS
Nicholas Gisonde
Eric Steinhauser
Doreen Fox
Mark Nussbaum

WRITERS
Barry Udoff
Charlie Breen
Charlie Ryant

CLIENT
Miller Brewing

DIRECTORS
Steve Horn
Bob Giraldi
Jeff Lovinger

PRODUCTION COS.
Steve Horn Productions
Bob Giraldi Productions
Lovinger, Tardio, Melsky

AGENCY PRODUCERS
Eric Steinhauser
Marc Mayhew

AGENCY
Backer & Spielvogel

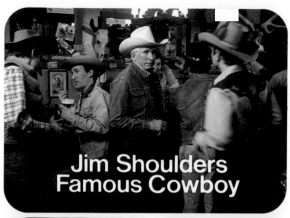

Jim Shoulders
Famous Cowboy

Baseball Greats
Numazawa and Boog Powell

64 SILVER

SHOULDERS: I can tell a real cowboy from the drugstore kind clean across Texas. The way he wears his hat'll tell you. And the beer that they drink is a sure-fire give-away too. A lot of us drink Lite beer from Miller. We love the taste, but we surely appreciate that it's got a third less calories than their regular kind. You see, you don't wanna be filled up when you're out there punching doggies...right, cowboy?

MARTIN: I didn't punch that doggie!

ANNCR (VO): Lite Beer from Miller. Everything you always wanted in a beer. And less.

POWELL: You know, baseball is the same in Japan as it is in America.

NUMA: (In Japanese) That's right.

POWELL: You play nine innings...

NUMA: (In Japanese) That's right.

POWELL: Three strikes and you're out...

NUMA: (In Japanese) One, two, three...

POWELL: And after the game, there's nothing like a beer. When Numa's in town, I treat him to Lite Beer from Miller, because it tastes great.

NUMA: (In Japanese) No, we drink it because it's less filling.

POWELL: Yeah, I know it's less filling, but we drink it because it tastes great.

NUMA: (In Japanese) No, because it's less filling.

POWELL: Listen Numa, it tastes great!

NUMA: (In Japanese) I say less filling!!!

POWELL: (Sheepishly) all right, it's less filling.

ANNCR (VO): Lite Beer from Miller. Everything you always wanted in a beer. And...

NUMA (VO): (In Japanese) Less!!!

DEFORD: I've had to write some tough things about some tough guys, but there's one guy I can't write anything bad about. His unique brand of baseball has made him a living legend. So have his commercials. They got me to try his favorite beer, Lite Beer from Miller. Lite's less filling and it really tastes great. So I'd like to give this Lite to that renowned yet humble man...Marv Throneberry.

THRONEBERRY: Cheer up Billy. Someday you'll be famous just like me.

ANNCR (VO): Lite Beer from Miller. Everything you always wanted in a beer. And less.

Gold & Silver Awards

**Consumer Television
30 Seconds
Campaign**

65 GOLD

ART DIRECTOR
Michael Tesch

WRITER
Patrick Kelly

CLIENT
Federal Express

DIRECTOR
Joe Sedelmaier

PRODUCTION CO.
Sedelmaier Films/Chicago

AGENCY PRODUCER
Maureen Kearns

AGENCY
Ally & Gargano

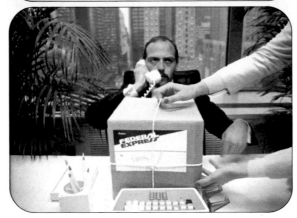

65 GOLD

MR. SPLEEN (OC): OkayEunice,travelplans.Ineedtobe
inNewYorkonMonday,LAonTuesday,NewYorkon
Wednesday,LAonThursday,

andNewYorkonFriday. Gotit? Soyouwanttowork
here,wellwhatmakesyouthinkyoudeserveajobhere?

GUY: Wellsir,Ithinkonmyfeet,I'mgoodwithfiguresandI
haveasharpmind.

SPLEEN: Excellent.CanyoustartMonday?

(OC): AndinconclusionJim,Bill,Bob,andTed,

Businessisbusinesssolet'sgettowork. Thankyoufor
takingthismeeting.

(OC): Peteryoudidabang-upjobI'mputtingyouinchargeof
Pittsburgh.

PETER (OC): Pittsburgh'sperfect.

SPLEEN: Iknowit'sperfect,Peter,that'swhyIpicked
Pittsburgh. Pittsburgh'sperfect,Peter,MayIcall
youPete?

SPLEEN (OC): CongratulationsonyourdealinDenverDavid.

I'mputtingyoudowntodealinDallas.

ANNCR (VO): In this fast moving, high pressure, get-it-
done-yesterday world, aren't you glad there's one
company that can keep up with it all?

ANNCR (VO): Federal Express. (SFX) When it absolutely,
positively has to be there overnight.

(MUSIC UNDER THROUGHOUT) (SFX: WHISTLE UNDER)

BOSS (OC): Kraddock, Kraddock, Kraddock, Kraddock...
Keener, have you seen Kraddock?

KEENER (OC): Not me, maybe Krenshaw.

BOSS (OC): Krenshaw, have you seen Kraddock?

KRENSHAW (OC): Not me, maybe Keener.

BOSS (OC): Are you sure you haven't seen Kraddock?

KEENER (OC): I'm sure, maybe Krenshaw isn't sure!

BOSS (OC): Ok. Look, if either of you guys see
Kraddock, tell him the parts I told him to send to
Kalamazoo yesterday did not get there. And I tell
you, when we get our hands on Kraddock...

Are you sure you haven't seen Kraddock?

ANNCR (VO): Next time send it Federal Express.

BOSS (OC): Where's Kraddock?

ANNCR (VO): When it absolutely, positively has to be
there overnight.

(MUSIC THROUGHOUT) (SFX: BIRDS CHIRPING)

(SFX: RATTLE OF ALARM CLOCK)

(SFX: ENGINE)

(SFX: FLAT TIRE)

(SFX: DOG BARKING)

ANNCR (VO): You cant' count on anything these days...

(SFX: FOOTSTEPS)

(SFX: TYPING)

MAN (OC): Did you type the letter I told you to type?

SECRETARY (OC): No.

ANNCR (VO): With possibly one exception: Federal
Express.

When it absolutely, positively has to be there
overnight.

**Consumer Television
30 Seconds
Campaign**

66 SILVER
ART DIRECTORS
Rich Silverstein
Jeff Goodby

WRITERS
John Crawford
Jeff Goodby

CLIENT
The Oakland A's

DIRECTOR
Bob Eggers

PRODUCTION CO.
Eggers Films

AGENCY PRODUCER
Deborah Wagner

AGENCY
Ogilvy & Mather/
San Francisco

66 SILVER

TIMID SOUL: Reserved seat, pl—...oh...

MARTIN: Right. And I s'ppose you came out here just to sit on your hands.

TS: uh...no...

MARTIN: Okay, Armas is up. Three and one. Let's hear it.

TS: (HESITANTLY) Uh...hey·go, Tony.

MARTIN: C'mon, talk it up!

TS: (STILL EMBARRASSED) Atta way, Tony.

MARTIN: Let's hear some chatter!

TS: (BUILDING) Atta way to watch him, Tony.

MARTIN: C'mon! C'mon!

TS: This guy's got nothin, Tony! Make him pitch to you. That's not an arm, that's a noodle.

MARTIN: (CUTTING HIM OFF) Okay. We'll give you a tryout.

ANNCR: Billyball. It's a different brand of baseball.

ANNCR (VO): A's manager Billy Martin grew up right here in West Berkeley. Mr. and Mrs. Ed Sims remember:

OLD WOMAN: Billy was a good boy.

A quiet boy.

He stayed out of trouble.

He was a *shy* child who was polite to everybody.

I remember...

OLD MAN: Mother doesn't remember too good anymore.

ANNCR (VO): Billyball.

It's a different brand of baseball.

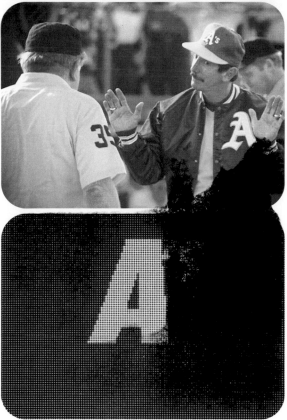

UMPIRE: He's *out*, Billy!

MARTIN: (MILDLY) Gosh, Ron, from the dugout it sure looked like he held up on that pitch.

UMPIRE: He swung, Billy!

MARTIN: Of course, you have a much better vantage point than I.

UMPIRE: (BELLIGERENTLY) You wanna appeal, go ahead!

MARTIN: That won't be necessary, Ron. Your word is good enough for me. If you say he went around, I'm sure he went around. (WALKING OFF) My mistake... my mistake.

UMPIRE: (REACTS)

ANNCR: It's a different brand of baseball: It's Billyball.

Gold & Silver Awards

**Consumer Television
10 Seconds Campaign**

67 GOLD

ART DIRECTOR
Michael Tesch

WRITER
Patrick Kelly

CLIENT
Federal Express

DIRECTOR
Joe Sedelmaier

PRODUCTION CO.
Sedelmaier Films/Chicago

AGENCY PRODUCER
Maureen Kearns

AGENCY
Ally & Gargano

67 GOLD

ANNCR (VO): Federal Express is so easy to use, all you have to do is pick up the phone.

(SFX: RRRRRRRIIIIIIIIPPPPPPPPPPPPPPPPPP!!)
(SFX: WATER)

ANNCR (VO): The nice thing about Federal Express is

(SFX: HORN) we'll come to your office and pick up the package.

You don't have to take it anywhere. (SFX: HORN)

SPLEEN (OC): Congratulationsonyourdealin Denver, David. I'mputtingyoudowntodealwithDon.

Donisitadeal? Dowehaveadeal? Ihaveacallcoming through.

ANNCR (VO): In this fast paced world aren't you glad there's one company that can keep up with it all?

Dick, what'sthedealwiththedeal? Arewedealing?

ANNCR (VO): Federal Express. When it absolutely, positively has to be there overnight.

**Consumer Television
10 Seconds Campaign**

68 SILVER
ART DIRECTOR
Lindy Junor

WRITER
Keith Davidson

CLIENT
Australian Apple &
Pear Corporation

DIRECTORS
John Street
Pablo Albers

PRODUCTION CO.
Zoetrope Film Productions

AGENCY PRODUCERS
Keith Dunn
Heather Moors

AGENCY
Ogilvy & Mather/Australia

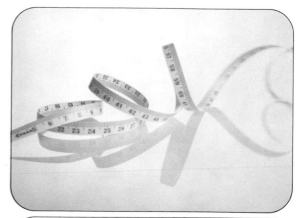

68 SILVER

(VO): Thirsty? There's artificial flavour, artificial fizz, or natural juicy apples.

For a thirst, grab an apple.

(SFX: CRUNCH)

(VO): Most snacks are cruel to diets.

(SFX: WHIPLASH)

But not apples. For a diet snack, grab an apple.

(SFX: CRUNCH)

(vo): When it comes to mouth fresheners, apples really clean up. For a mouth freshener, grab an apple.

(SFX:CRUNCH)

**Corporate Television
Campaign**

69 GOLD

ART DIRECTORS
Phil Dusenberry
Ted Sann

WRITERS
Phil Dusenberry
Ted Sann

CLIENT
General Electric

DIRECTOR
Bob Giraldi

PRODUCTION CO.
Bob Giraldi Productions

AGENCY PRODUCER
Jeff Fischgrund

AGENCY
BBDO

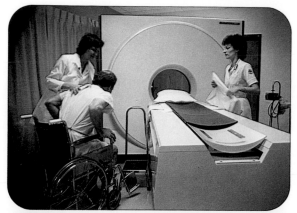

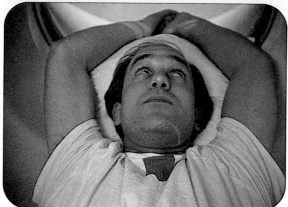

69 GOLD

(MUSIC)

ANNCR (VO): You're about to see surgery performed without anesthesia, without sutures, even without a scalpel. This is the CT Scanner by GE.

It's a remarkable machine that lets doctors see and explore the human body without a single incision.

It actually takes tens of thousands of images and assembles them into a clear precise picture. This allows doctors to see clearly the most intricate details of the human anatomy, which until now could only be seen through conventional surgery.

The CT Scanner by GE.

NURSE: That's it.

PATIENT: That's it?

DOCTOR: That's it.

ANNCR (VO): Bringing new vision to exploratory medicine.

PATIENT: I'm okay.

WIFE: Oh, great!

PATIENT: Let's go home.

ANNCR (VO): GE. We bring good things to life.

(MUSIC)

ANNCR (VO): On a summer's evening in 1924, in Lynn, Massachusetts, perhaps the most significant game in the long history of baseball was played.

It wasn't the pitching that was so extraordinary, nor the hitting. And the fielding, well, it was less than exemplary.

No, what made this game truly historic was the time of day.

(SFX) Nightfall

For it was on this night that this small group of GE engineers ushered in the era of night baseball. Baseball under the lights.

And while the names of "Yugo" Fee and Tommy Perkins and Hank Innes will never be recorded in the Hall of Fame,

It was this earnest band of GE pioneers that made possible for us all the many brilliant nights to come.
(SFX)

SINGERS: *GE. We bring good things to life.*

(MUSIC)

ANNCR (VO): To all you students of innovation, to you, inspired to try what's never been tried before,

To all those consumed with an insatiable curiosity,

a penchant for ingenuity,

To you who seek and search

And blaze new trails,

Who try and fail and try again;

To all you children of imagination,

You sons and daughters and mothers of invention,

Dreamers and doers, thinkers and

Tinkerers all, we at General Electric salute you.

For, as advanced as our technology has become, we've never forgotten that from small beginnings big ideas grow.

 The Gold Award
Winners on
The Gold Award
Winners

**Consumer Newspaper
Over 600 Lines, Single**

AGENCY: Ammirati & Puris
CLIENT: BMW of North America

It seems that cars these days regularly ask
five-figure sums and promise in return nothing more
substantive than instant popularity, regained youth, etc.

BMW has always offered more tangible justifications,
and its resale value is one of them.

We began with a fact—that the BMW 320i retained
some 92.9% of its original value in the used car
market. That fact isn't new to BMW advertising. What
is new is the way it's used here—as an underpinning
to a claim of investment superiority. We simply related
it to other investments which people in our target
audience might make. When we found that the BMW
320i retained more of its value than several hundred
NYSE stocks, we had an ad.

But there's another explanation as to how this ad got
done...and that is that the client not only approved
it, but encouraged it to the point of demanding it.

It's often said that clients ultimately get the
advertising they deserve. We like to think this is one of
those instances where it's true.

Anthony Angotti
Tom Thomas

LAST YEAR, A CAR OUT-PERFORMED 318 STOCKS ON THE NEW YORK STOCK EXCHANGE.

If you'd bought a new BMW 320i in the beginning of 1980, and sold it at the end,
your investment would have retained 92.9% of its original value.
If you'd done the same with any of 318 NYSE stocks, you'd have done less well.
And you'd have forfeited an important daily dividend:
The unfluctuating joy of driving one of the world's great performance sedans.

THE ULTIMATE DRIVING MACHINE.

1 GOLD

**Consumer Newspaper
Over 600 Lines, Campaign**

AGENCY: Ammirati & Puris, Inc.
CLIENT: BMW of North America

The One Show book is usually full of wry and entertaining stories of art director and writer wrestling with frustration, procrastination, deadlines and each other toward the completion of an ad or campaign.

This isn't one of those stories. This was a peacefully-conceived campaign based more on logic than on mysterious inspiration and dark urges.

The point of it all was to demonstrate why BMW is a superior value. It is a superior value because it performs better. And it performs better because it's engineered better, which is also why it holds its resale value better.

The ads in this campaign demonstrate all that in ways that, it seems to us, are self-evident. The best explanation of these ads is the ads themselves—including the body copy, which at least one of us involved in their creation recommends highly.

*Anthony Angotti
Jerry Whitley
Tom Thomas*

3 GOLD

**Consumer Newspaper
600 Lines or Less, Single**

AGENCY: Doyle Dane Bernbach
CLIENT: Volkswagen

The proposition was this: instead of giving a rebate, VW dealers were willing to make the first three payments on your next car for you.

Now guess which one of us really related to that.

*Peter Bregman
Joe Del Vecchio*

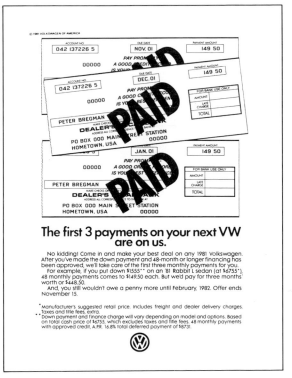

5 GOLD

**Consumer Newspaper
600 Lines or Less
Campaign**

AGENCY: Rosenfeld, Sirowitz & Lawson
CLIENT: Pratt Institute

Ron: We're doing this campaign for Pratt.
Debbie: I went to Pratt.
Jessie: So did I.
Len: I did, too. Remember when...
Debbie: ...when?
Len: You're too young—
Ron: —or you'd have known him then.
Jessie: When?

*Debra Goldstein
Jessie Tirsch*

We knew Len Sirowitz when

...when he rode the subway every day from the Bronx to study
Advertising Design at Pratt.
  Len Sirowitz went on from Pratt to become one of the foremost
advertising art directors in the country, and was named "The Number
One Art Director in America" twice in national polls. He is co-chairman of
Rosenfeld, Sirowitz & Lawson, one of the fastest-growing advertising
agencies in America with an impressive list of blue-chip clients.
  Len Sirowitz has come a long way since Pratt. And on the way he
brought a lot of Pratt with him.

Pratt Institute
LOOK HOW FAR YOU CAN GO FROM PRATT

Pratt Institute, 200 Willoughby Avenue, Brooklyn, New York 11205 (212) 636-3669
Graduate programs in Architecture, City and Regional Planning, Urban Design; Art Therapy; Fine Arts; Industrial,
Interior, Package, Communications Design; Computer and Decision Science; Library and Information Science.

7 GOLD

**Consumer Magazine
Color One Page or Spread
Including Magazine Supplements**

AGENCY: Ogilvy & Mather
CLIENT: Par Perfums

  We started from the notion that most advertising
for men's fragrances was a crashing bore: Man meets
himself, falls in love, splashes on some Olde English
Saddle or Hunk, waits for line of compliant women
to form.
  What if we dispensed with the usual sophomoric
winks and nudges and heavy-breathing promises?
  What if, for a change, readers were given a
chance to exercise their imaginations?
  What if there were a little playfulness, a little
romance, a little tenderness?
  Simple, isn't it?

*Roger Proulx
Alan Sprules
Jay Jasper*

11 GOLD

**Consumer Magazine
Color Campaign
Including Magazine Supplements**

AGENCY: Ammirati & Puris
CLIENT: BMW of North America

This campaign is the result not so much of inventiveness as of simple observation.

It's difficult to drive anywhere these days without noticing all the cars that look suspiciously like the BMW 320i. (After the campaign broke, one automotive writer came right out and called them "cookie-cutter copies.") At the time we were doing the campaign, BMW was appearing over and over as the standard of comparison in ads paid for by other car makers. In fact, it got to the point where BMW was being mentioned more often in other car ads than our own.

The point was to add our voice to all those others, and agree with what they were acknowledging, albeit unwittingly: that BMW was the superior choice for performance-minded drivers.

The objective, in the follow-the-leader world of cars and car advertising, was to make clear exactly who was doing the leading, and who the following.

*Anthony Angotti
Tom Thomas*

15 GOLD

**Consumer Magazine
Less than One Page
B/W or Color, Single**

AGENCY: Needham, Harper & Steers
CLIENT: Xerox

We'd like to dedicate this space to every art director and writer who ever grumbled about being thrown a piddly price-off or small space ad while the agency heavies hogged all the juicy corporate and 4-color stuff.

You don't have to be working on a big assignment to come up with a big idea.

Nevertheless, we hope we get something decent to work on this year. We're getting tired of all these piddly price-off and small space ads.

*Kevin McKeon
Mike Ciranni*

17 GOLD

The Gold Award Winners on The Gold Award Winners

**Consumer Magazine
Less than One Page
B/W or Color, Campaign**

AGENCY: Doyle Dane Bernbach
CLIENT: General Wine & Spirits/Chivas Regal

Over the years, we've all done ads that are just plain downright work. Doing Chivas Regal cartoons is work that is also fun. Rita Selden and Bert Steinhauser started them back in 1962 (they also created the Chivas four-color campaign at DDB). Since then, Chivas sales have risen from 135,000 cases a year to well over a million. As Bernbach once said, "Beware of arithmetic —you can't always make music with it." But in this business, that's the kind of arithmetic that does make music.

*Charles Abrams
George Rike*

*"Just once I'd like to see some
Chivas in this thing."*

Chivas Regal · 12 Years Old Worldwide · Blended Scotch Whisky · 86 Proof. General Wine & Spirits Co., N.Y.

19 GOLD

**Trade
Color, One Page or Spread
Outdoor Single**

AGENCY: Scali, McCabe, Sloves, Inc.
CLIENT: Nikon

It was a typical work day at Scali—10 p.m., Sunday. We were tired, hungry, looked like hell, and having imaginary conversations with Ed McCabe. He had hated our first effort on Thursday, and the plan was to show him a new ad on Monday. Understandably, the Space Shuttle wasn't going to wait for us.

Both of us were losing consciousness when the 'One of the few things...' headline "popped out." When it happened, we both smiled—shook hands— and hoped Ed would like it as much as we did.

When we presented it to him, he said, "You don't have to show me anything else!" Which sounded like an okay to us.

After that, even though there were zillions of reasons why the Space Shuttle might not go up on time...or why a Nikon might not be used on the first flight...or why the flight might not be a total success, we never gave those possibilities a second thought. After all, Ed McCabe had approved the ad.

*Earl Carter
Dean Stefanides*

23 GOLD AND 36 GOLD

AGENCY: Northlich, Stolley, Incorporated/Ohio
CLIENT: Northlich, Stolley, Incorporated

This ad was an act of open hostility against all those agency ads that ask you to send your best work to a box number in New York or Chicago.

Maybe you read one once and were interested enough to stuff your life's work into a manila envelope, send it Federal Express, and wait for who knows how long to hear from who knows who in who knows where.

We doubt it.

So Lloyd (Wolfe) and I decided on a different approach.

Instead of setting up an interview with the writer, we created an ad in which the writer interviewed us. We "sent" 3 samples of our best work. We chatted about winning awards, making money, and putting together a better book.

We gave the ad a look, something most recruitment advertising in our business sorely lacks. We wrote copy that demonstrated some sort of understanding with our prospect. We did what we always try to do.

A nice ad.

Lloyd and I liked it so much, in fact, we responded to it. We're still waiting for a reply.

(Incidentally, now that this ad is reaching more good art directors and copywriters than we ever anticipated, the offer still stands. Call 513-421-8840 and ask for me.)

Craig Jackson

AGENCY: Ally & Gargano
CLIENT: Timberland

We got Timberland account in the fall of 1980. And, as luck would have it, the first assignment we got was this trade campaign.

I say, as luck would have it, because it immediately ruled out doing what everyone usually does: take the consumer ads that have already been done, change a few words in the copy, and run them in the trade.

So one day, Dennis D'Amico and I called our clients, Stanley Kravetz and Jens Bang. We said, "why don't we do a trade campaign that talks to dealers in a language they understand?"

"What language is that?" Stanley asked.

"You know, profit margins, deliveries, dealer support, that language."

"For this we came to a New York agency," he said. We pushed on.

"Do your dealers work on higher margins?" we said.

"Only the smart ones."

"Do you invest more money in advertising than your competitors?"

"We never checked."

"How are your deliveries?"

"We're afraid to ask."

"What about dealer co-op?"

"What about it?"

"Thanks for everything," we said, "we'll get back to you next week." "Sounds great," they said, "can't wait to see the stuff."

Out of this came the trade campaign that won the Gold Award.

Which only goes to prove that when you have solid information to work with, doing good ads is easy.

*Ron Berger
Dennis D'Amico*

MOST AGENCIES LOOKING FOR A WRITER WANT TO SEE YOUR WORK.

WE THOUGHT YOU'D LIKE TO SEE OURS FIRST.

We're in the market for a good writer who'd like to build a great book.

Naturally, we'll want to take a look at your work. Just so we know what we're getting into.

But that works both ways.

So here's some of our work. We think it's pretty good stuff. And there's a lot more award-winning print, radio and television where that came from.

But, quite frankly, we're more interested in the awards you're going to win than the ones we've already won.

If you like what you see here, send some of your best work to me, Bill LaWarre, Sr. V.P./Creative Director.

If we like what we see, you'll be building a great book in no time. At a salary that'll make you never want to use it.

NORTHLICH, STOLLEY, INC.
200 West Fourth Street, Cincinnati, Ohio 45202

WHY THE BEST BOOTS AND HANDSEWNS MONEY CAN BUY ARE THE BEST BOOTS AND HANDSEWNS YOU CAN SELL.

**Collateral
Brochure Other than By Mail**

AGENCY: Epstein Raboy
CLIENT: Fieldcrest Mills

Expectation: two weeks in Ireland to travel the country, Dublin to Aran, writing and shooting as we went. And the account executive, my bride-to-be.

Reality: I'd broken my ankle on St. Patrick's night, 72 hours before we went; so, on crutches in a nation without an elevator. The rain never stopped. Nobody could drive on the left side of the road. Our budget was cut by transAtlantic cable. Up at 5 a.m. Warm beer (but nice people).

In the fun-and-glamour ad game, there's always the part they don't tell you about.

*Ann-Marie Light
Mitch Epstein*

29 GOLD

**Collateral
Direct Mail**

AGENCY: Allday & Associates, Inc/Dallas
CLIENT: Lincorp

This job started with a good budget, ample time, and a cooperative client who encouraged good work.
The rest was easy.

Lynda Transou

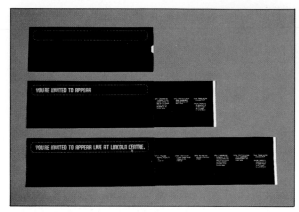

32 GOLD

Collateral P.O.P.

AGENCY: Humphrey Browning MacDougall/Boston
CLIENT: Joseph M. Herman Shoes

"Marc, we have to do a Herman poster."
"When's it due?"
"Last Thursday."
"Oh,_____"
"Why don't we do what we did for the ad? It got us a silver in the One Show last year."
"Okay."

Marc Deschenes
George White

34 GOLD

Outdoor Campaign

AGENCY: Bobco/Mpls
CLIENT: Saigon Restaurant

Some of us who work on restaurant advertising can't always draw on our personal experience or knowledge relating to food.

There are those of us, for example, who happen to like bologna sandwiches on white bread with Miracle Whip.

And some of us know as much about oriental food as we know about Wittgenstein's *Tractatus Logico-Philosophicus*, which is zilch.

Still, we have to live. And one way to approach an advertising problem is not with a net for snaring facts, but with a fielder's glove for catching the odd hops that ideas take when they bounce off the imagination.

We spend a lot of time running after foul balls. (Their trajectories are no less graceful because they fall on the wrong side of the line.)

In the case of the Saigon Restaurant, when one of us tasted the Nguyen's sweet and sour chicken, we liked it as well as bologna sandwiches, which is as well as we like any food.

At the time, Mr. Nguyen was attempting to impact the psyches of the restless bands of culinary pilgrims who roam our streets, using a small-space ad adorned with pretty bamboo leaves.

Whatever this man needed, it was not a leaf motif.

But what did he need? Advertising based on facts like menu selection, atmosphere, service? That line of exploration led to a series of dry holes. The mind kept wandering instead to the Vietnam war, to French colonialism, and to the immense distances traveled by the Nguyen family as they fled the certain horrors of South Vietnam to arrive at the uncertain prospects awaiting them in South Minneapolis.

Once we settled on what appeared to be some promising ideas, Bob Marberry fiddled, finessed, fussed, tinkered, trued, fine-tuned, adjusted, reworked, readjusted, took out, put back in, rearranged, lined up, realigned, stepped back, moved close, squinted, smiled, and, finally, pronounced the posters done.

Since the posters were delivered, the Nguyen family have opened a second restaurant.

Post hoc ergo propter hoc.

Dick Thomas

38 GOLD

**Public Service
Outdoor, Single**

AGENCY: Corporate Communications/Canada
CLIENT: NS Dept. of Mines and Energy/DREE

Cecil B. DeMille leaned across the desk and spoke in an intense, hushed voice, "Budget be damned, you can do anything."

"Anything?"

"Anything."

We didn't hesitate, "Ten-color, three dimensional, forty foot long visuals, hundreds of them swarming all over the city in perfect choreography."

"What else?" said Mr. DeMille, slightly bored at the mundanity of our suggestion.

"A label on the back for identification, black and white."

A look of puzzlement crossed DeMille's face, "Why, you think they'll get lost?"

"No, sir," we said confidently, "We think they'll win."

*Richard Kurtz
Herb MacDonald*

THE BIG SECRET TO SAVING GAS
IS RIGHT IN FRONT OF YOU

42 GOLD

**Corporate
Newspaper or Magazine, Single
Corporate
Newspaper or Magazine, Campaign**

AGENCY: Leo Burnett/Canada
CLIENT: Allstate Insurance Companies of Canada

As a major automobile insurer in Canada, Allstate believes they have a special obligation to help create a safer driving environment—one which will serve to reduce automobile accidents, save lives and prevent injuries, and hold down the cost of car insurance. The corporate advertising campaign grew out of this commitment to road safety and is part of an overall corporate program. The campaign was launched in February 1981.

The first two issues Allstate chose to speak out on were air bags and the decriminalization of marijuana. All too often, Allstate sees people killed or injured needlessly because they did not use their seat belts or were the innocent victims of accidents caused by drivers whose abilities were impaired by alcohol or drugs.

The marijuana ads were in response to the government's intention to amend the present laws with respect to marijuana and its use. Allstate felt that liberalization of the law could have a serious impact on highway safety and that more appropriate and responsive legislation would result if there were greater public understanding of the issues involved.

The air bag ad was designed to increase understanding of and support for air bags. These proven safety devices can prevent hundreds of deaths and injuries because they solve the problem of seat belts— human nature. They require no voluntary act by the driver or passenger.

Allstate feels that the campaign was successful because as a result of the ads, Allstate received hundreds of letters from all across Canada and the issues received broad coverage on television, radio and in newspapers. They succeeded in increasing awareness of the issues and opening up a public dialogue.

*Derek Chapman
David Hayward*

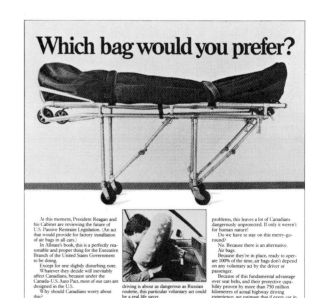

Which bag would you prefer?

44 GOLD AND 46 GOLD

Student Competition

SCHOOL: Art Center College of Design/California

The assignment was to develop a self-promotion ad taking into account current economic conditions.

A coupon ad seemed a natural, self-promotional vehicle for kicking off a career as an advertising art director. Once I determined the offer I was prepared to make to the *right agency,* the design took on a straightforward look. I do remember struggling over how to treat the copy portion— whether to use bullets and call-outs or a few short paragraphs. I opted for the latter. I felt it gave a cleaner, less spotty overall appearance. In the end I felt the ad had *stopping power.* Obviously, some other people felt the same.

Norm Johnson

48 GOLD

Consumer Radio Single
Consumer Radio Campaign

AGENCY: Ally & Gargano
CLIENT: MCI

Right after the One Show dinner, someone came up to congratulate me on the Gold Awards in question. What he said, right before he ran off, was "And the best thing about radio is that you do it all alone. The credit's all yours."

So I'd like to mention actors Lester Rawlins, Lynn Lipton, Harry Goz, Andy Duncan, Bill Fiore, Jerry Sroka, and Claudette Sutherland.

And Bob Verno, President of Judrac, one of the best engineers I've ever had the pleasure of working with.

And our agency producers, Jerry Haynes and Maureen Kearns.

And, finally, MCI, a very open-minded client.

All of whom helped me do it "all alone."

Helayne Spivak
SEE GOLD AWARD WINNERS 50 AND 52.

The Gold Award
Winners on
The Gold Award
Winners

**Consumer Television
60 Seconds, Single
10 Seconds, Single
30 Seconds, Campaign
10 Seconds, Campaign**

AGENCY: Ally & Gargano
CLIENT: Federal Express
4 Golds, 3 Silvers.

Does good advertising come easy?

Here's what you need:

Extra strength Tylenol
Pepto-Bismol
A good chiropractor
Lots of No-Doze
One psychiatrist
Plenty of aspirin
Magic markers
A good product
Alka-Seltzer
A good client
Endless cups of coffee
Loads of Bufferin
Joe Sedelmaier
Patrick Kelly

Mike Tesch

**Consumer Television
30 Seconds, Single**

AGENCY: Fallon McElligott Rice/Mpls
CLIENT: Donaldsons

When Fallon McElligott opened its doors less than a year ago, we announced the event with a newspaper ad in which the agency expressed a simple and direct philosophy: don't out-spend the competition, out-smart them.

We think the Donaldsons spot accomplishes just that goal.

The purpose of the commercial was to advertise a post-holiday department store clearance sale.

The production budget was $7,000. When talent costs were deducted, it was clear that we wouldn't have the opportunity to outspend the competition.

The creative process was relatively painless in spite of a very tight deadline. We met briefly on a Saturday, tossed a number of ideas around, and quickly agreed that this was the one. It was clear that the lip-synching would make for an unusual spot, but a couple of questions persisted: First, would the end result be humorous or just strange.? Second, to what degree would humor make our audience more receptive to the selling proposition?

It was not until the day of production that we knew just how well it would click. We were happily surprised at the way things fell into place.

We think this ad works because it relates to a human experience shared by all of us as children—unbounded greed—and makes us laugh at it.

*Dean Hanson
Tom McElligott*

54 GOLD

58 GOLD AND 67 GOLD

65 GOLD

56 GOLD

**Consumer Television
60 Seconds Campaign**

AGENCY: Needham, Harper & Steers/Chicago
CLIENT: McDonald's

Just when we thought all the emotional situations had
been done...and redone and redone...along came
"Daddy's Girl" to solve the very real problem of finding
a spare minute and a great place— McDonald's—for a
father and daughter to be together.
And just when we thought there wasn't one more story
to tell about good friends, along came the best pals in
the world to show us that there's nobody better or
more important than our "Best Friends."
And just when we thought every great music track had
been recorded and every vignette in the world had
been shot, along came "Can't Stop" to show us that
there still are magic moments to be captured and great
songs to be sung.
And just when we thought that maybe awards didn't
mean much anymore, we won.

Josephine Cummings
Bob Scarpelli
Christie McMahon
Jim Nawrocki
Lynn Crosswaite
Rich Seidelman

63 GOLD

**Corporate Television
Single**

**Corporate Television
Campaign**

AGENCY: BBDO
CLIENT: General Electric

A client as diverse and innovative as G.E.
A theme as flexible as "We bring good things to life."
And three weeks to deliver.
What more could we ask for.

    Great client. Great theme.
    What else could we ask for?

Ted Sann
Phil Dusenberry

60 GOLD AND 69 GOLD

1982 Print Finalists

Fly To The Big Apple For Small Potatoes.

$23 To Newark. $43 To LaGuardia.*

If you'd like to fare better on your next trip to the Big Apple, fly Piedmont. Nobody gives you as many nonstops to the New York area. And nobody gives you lower fares.

As low as $23 to Newark, as low as $43 to LaGuardia. Every seat on every Piedmont flight saves you money.

And even though our fares are strictly small potatoes, you'll get service that treats you like a big cheese. We'll even serve you a complimentary drink along the way.

So call Piedmont, or your travel agent. And we'll help you take a big bite out of air fares to the Big Apple.

Piedmont. Most Nonstops To New York.

*To Newark: $23 weekends and daily at 7:40a. $35 all other times. Depart 7:40a, 11:10a, 2:35p, 4:00p, 6:40p. To LaGuardia: $43 weekends. $55 weekdays. Depart 8:10a, 2:05p, 5:10p, 8:50p.

70

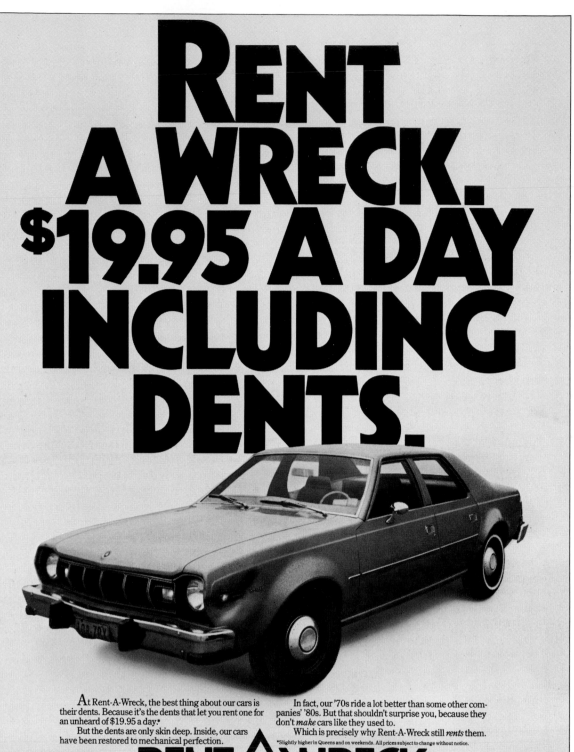

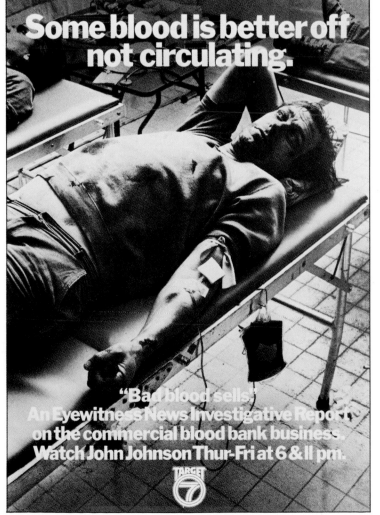

You're right, it does look like a check. That's because it is a check. But if you have BB&T's Constant Credit, it's something else as well.

It's a way to get a loan. A loan you can grant yourself anytime, anywhere, for any amount up to your credit limit in the length of time it takes you to write a personal check.

Because with Constant Credit, that's all you have to do.

Say an emergency arises. Or you need to pay some bills. Or you spot a great bargain but haven't enough in your checking account to take advantage of it. You simply write a check for more than your balance, and we automatically advance the amount required to cover it in units of $100.

Until you need Constant Credit there's no charge at all. And when you use it, you pay interest for only the number of days you owe the money.

Visit your nearest BB&T office soon and apply for Constant Credit. Then the next time you need a loan, all you'll have to do is put it in writing.

Nobody works harder for your money.

79

COME TO A PLACE WHERE YOU CAN STILL FIND BURIED TREASURE.

Two centuries ago, the pirate Blackbeard roamed the North Carolina coast.

It was here he won his legendary treasures.

And it was here that, in the end, he lost his life.

The pirates and their gold have come and gone.

But the real treasures are still here for the taking.

The ocean, gold in the sunset, diamond-sparkled in the cool Atlantic dawn.

Gleaming shells in jewel colors, half-buried in pearl-white sand.

Bright rivers that wind like silver threads through the soft, rich tapestries of growing fields.

Tall sapphire peaks, set into emerald valleys.

The perfume of pines and azalea blossoms and fresh-turned earth.

In North Carolina, the treasures are everywhere. From the mountains, to the midlands, to the secluded cove where Blackbeard fought his last battle.

Some, like the shells, are the kind you can carry away in your hands.

But most of them are the kind you'll probably carry away in your mind.

SHOULD YOU BE FORCED TO BEAR YOUR RAPIST'S CHILD?

As if being raped isn't horrifying enough, you may soon be denied the freedom to choose an abortion if you become pregnant.

Because right now, United States Senate hearings are being held on a Constitutional Amendment which would allow any state to outlaw abortion. Overnight.

Even if the pregnancy is the result of rape. Or incest.

Even if your sanity depends on it.

And that's not the worst of it. It is even possible that if you have an abortion, you could be prosecuted for murder.

So even a miscarriage could be investigated as manslaughter.

Backing this amendment are radical right-wing political forces including New York's very own Senator Alfonse D'Amato. This small but noisy group of people want to impose their religious beliefs on you. Your friends. Your family.

Don't stand by silently and let this injustice become law. Fill out the Planned Parenthood coupon. Give generously of your time and money. With your contribution we can work to preserve safe and legal abortion.

Act now.

Before the minority rules.

JOIN PLANNED PARENTHOOD
Planned Parenthood of New York City, Inc.
380 Second Avenue, New York, N.Y. 10010
212/777-2002

☐ I believe that abortion is something personal, not political. Please keep me informed and add me to your mailing list.

☐ I want to keep abortion legal and wish to make a tax-deductible contribution. Here is my check in the amount of
$ _____

NAME _____

ADDRESS _____

CITY·STATE·ZIP _____

TELEPHONE (DAY) _____ (EVE) _____

This advertisement has been paid for with private contributions

A copy of our financial report can be obtained from us or from the New York Department of State, Office of Charities Registration, Albany, New York 12231

© 1981 Planned Parenthood of New York City, Inc.   NYT 10·25

ABORTION IS SOMETHING PERSONAL. NOT POLITICAL.

IN CHICAGO, BEATING A TRAFFIC TICKET IS ALMOST AS EASY AS GETTING ONE.

Every week, thousands of tickets are served in Chicago. And every week, thousands of those tickets are dismissed in court. In fact, for many people, the most severe punishment ever imposed is a movie on how to drive safely.

This week, in a special four-part series, Target 7 reporter Peter Karl investigates the causes and effects of Chicago's overcrowded, ineffective traffic court.

Join him, each night at 10, as he explains why the system is coming apart, and how we can put it together again.

"TRAFFIC COURT: JUSTICE OR A JOKE." A TARGET 7 REPORT BY PETER KARL. TONIGHT AT 10 PM. EYEWITNESS NEWS.

©1981 American Broadcasting Companies, Inc.

Spirits aren't the only things that get lifted at Christmas.

So do wallets and purses.
Pickpockets and purse snatchers do terrific business this time of year.
So be careful and don't carry cash.

Carry American Express Travelers Cheques.
If lost or stolen they can usually be replaced the same day.
And no other travelers

cheque is as widely known and accepted.
American Express Travelers Cheques.
Don't spend the holidays without them.

88

89

YOUR TAX PROBLEMS DON'T GO AWAY AFTER APRIL 15TH. WHY SHOULD THE PERSON WHO PREPARES YOUR TAXES?

It's easy to find people to prepare your taxes for you *before* April 15th. The problem may be finding them *after* April 15th.

When you bring your taxes to TAX-AID, however, you can be sure we'll be there all year round. Because each intensively trained TAX-AID preparer is available through your AID agent, who has a full-time office right in your community.

And if the IRS decides to audit your account at *any* time, not only will TAX-AID accompany you but we'll also pay *any penalties and interest* that are a result of mistakes made by us.

So this year, bring your taxes to the people who are there *before* April 15th, and *after* April 15th. TAX-AID.

TAX AID
INSURANCE SERVICES

90

Every month, another 30,000 people find themselves unable to resist the indisputable logic of this chart.

LONG DISTANCE CALLS	MINUTES	BELL	MCI
Ann Arbor to Chicago	12	$ 3.15	$1.88
Ann Arbor to New York City	1	.39	.17
Ann Arbor to Washington, D.C.	27	7.47	4.54
Ann Arbor to Milwaukee	36	9.23	5.63
Ann Arbor to Miami	19	5.56	3.36
Ann Arbor to Los Angeles	54	16.27	9.97
Ann Arbor to Providence	40	11.04	6.75
Ann Arbor to Denver	7	2.13	1.24
Ann Arbor to Boston	28	7.76	4.72
Ann Arbor to Albuquerque	2	.70	.35
Ann Arbor to Cleveland	32	7.39	4.75
Ann Arbor to Kansas City	17	4.76	2.87
Ann Arbor to Salt Lake City	22	6.42	3.89
Ann Arbor to Minneapolis	3	.94	.51
Ann Arbor to Atlanta	56	15.41	9.45
Ann Arbor to Richmond	41	11.31	6.92
Ann Arbor to Phoenix	8	2.41	1.41
Ann Arbor to Houston	33	9.56	5.83
Ann Arbor to Philadelphia	4	1.21	.67
Ann Arbor to Indianapolis	16	4.16	2.50
Ann Arbor to Portland	27	8.20	4.98
Ann Arbor to Omaha	55	15.13	9.28
Ann Arbor to Cincinnati	1	.36	.16
Ann Arbor to Memphis	39	10.77	6.58
Ann Arbor to Little Rock	46	12.68	7.76
Ann Arbor to New Orleans	5	1.48	.84
Ann Arbor to Charlotte	23	6.40	3.88
Ann Arbor to St. Louis	51	14.02	8.57
Ann Arbor to San Francisco	9	2.82	1.66
Ann Arbor to Oklahoma City	17	4.76	2.87
Ann Arbor to Louisville	22	6.11	3.70
Ann Arbor to Toledo	10	2.06	1.22

Rates show comparative pricing between Bell's evening rate and MCI's evening rate. Final rate authorities on all tariffed services are MCI Tariff FCC 1 and AT&T Tariff FCC 263.

Given the choice, wouldn't you rather be charged 30%, 40%, even 50% less on MCI for the same long distance phone call you now place with Bell?

There's nothing elaborate to install. All you need is the same push-button phone you use now. You simply punch in a few extra numbers and, just like that, you're talking to the same person in the same place you were before — only for a lot less money.

The fact is, if your long distance phone bills run more than $25 a month, you could cut those bills substantially by using MCI, the nation's long distance phone company.

Which is precisely what hundreds of thousands of personal callers and over 85,000 businesses, including half the *Fortune* 500, have done.

Who knows, you might even get carried away like a woman from San Diego did and write us a letter saying, "I've never been so happy to pay a phone bill."

For a free brochure that tells you everything you need to know about MCI, just send in the coupon below. Or call us at (313) 352-7600 or 1-800-482-1730.

If, however, you have any lingering doubts, there's really only one logical thing to do.

Take another look at the chart.

MCI
The nation's long distance phone company.

Please send me more information on how to cut the cost of my long distance calls.
For Home ☐   For Business ☐
Name_____
Address_____
City_____
State_____ Zip Code_____
Telephone Number_____
Please call me after 5:00 p.m. ☐

MCI Telecommunications Corp.
24901 Northwestern Highway, Suite #214C
Southfield, MI 48075

91

IF YOU THINK AVIS GIVES YOU A GOOD DEAL WITH THIS CARD, BRING IT TO HERTZ.

Lately, Avis has been mailing "Private Offer Card" coupons to American Express Card members. These coupons entitle card members to a 30% discount on Avis time and mileage rates at participating locations, through April 30th, 1981. But there's a catch.

You can't take advantage of this discount unless you use the American Express Card. Avis doesn't even give this 30% discount offer if you use their own credit card.

Hertz will accept any major credit card.

Now Hertz will match Avis' discount on time and mileage rates in the U.S. when you present us with their "Private Offer Card." Only we'll accept any major credit card you want to use. Even Avis' or National's.

Get a 33% discount with a Hertz credit card.

And if you use a Hertz credit card when you rent one of our cars, we'll give you a bigger, 33% discount.

All in addition to the great services that make Hertz the #1 car rental company.

• #1 Express.® The world's fastest way to rent a car. Be sure to ask for #1 Express when you reserve your car.

• More cars, locations and people to serve you than any other rent-a-car company.

To obtain this special discount, just show Avis' "Private Offer Card" at any participating Hertz location along with one of the following credit cards: Hertz, Avis, National, American Express, Carte Blanche, Diners Club, Master Card or Visa when you're renting one of our cars.

This offer expires April 30th, 1981, and may not be combined with any other discount. Gas, insurance and taxes not included.

All standard Hertz rental requirements apply.

WHERE WINNERS RENT. For details, call Hertz at 800-654-3131.

HERTZ FEATURES THE EXCITING NEW FORD ESCORT.

GETTING A LONG TERM CAR LOAN? DON'T GET A SHORT TERM CAR.

Some of the figures you hear rattled off in banks these days can be downright frightening.

Interest rates on car loans have been as high as 16%. And car loans can now run as long as four years.

Paying one back is starting to look like settling the national debt.

If you're going to sign up for that kind of commitment, make sure you select a car that justifies it. One that will outlast the payment book.

Consider a Volvo. Volvos have always had a reputation for lasting a long time in Sweden.

And recent findings show they do well in this country, too. In fact, the life expectancy of a Volvo is 1/3 longer than the average life expectancy of all other cars on the road.*

What's even more important, Volvo's long list of comfort and performance features make it the kind of car you'll want to keep for a long time.

So this year, finance a Volvo. You may not laugh all the way to the bank. But you won't cry, either.

VOLVO

A car you can believe in.

93

IF WE CAN LOWER YOUR PHONE BILL BY 35% WHY CAN'T THE TELEPHONE COMPANY?

If everyone in your office could make their business calls at home, your company could probably save a lot of money.

To begin with, Wisconsin Bell charges substantially higher rates for "business service" than for personal phones at home.

Secondly, your company has to pay those high monthly rental fees for all your extensions.

And finally, Bell Telephone charges two or three times as much for long distance calls during business hours.

That's why if you want to lower your company telephone bill, you should make all your business calls at home. After 5PM and on weekends. Or make one call to National Telecom, instead.

At National Telecom, we specialize in providing telephones and PBX Systems to companies with 50 phones or more. At prices that will cost you substantially less.

How much less? Well, since we installed National Telecom equipment at Western Publishing, they estimate they're saving about 39% a month. Mortgage Guarantee Insurance Company figures their savings at about 38%. And National Survey, Funjet, and Guarantee Savings & Loan all estimate their savings at 35% a month. Or more.

What's more, our equipment is actually more dependable and superior to most Bell Telephone equipment most companies have.

For example, our digital PBX will not only deliver a louder, cleaner sound, but will automatically search through your WATS, Sprint or MCI lines for the cheapest route. You just have to dial the area code and number, and our PBX does the rest.

And our PBX equipment costs less than the less sophisticated PBX from the telephone company.

If you'd like to know what a National Telecom System could do for you, why not call our president, Mr. L.A. McLernon at 414-276-6244.

Of course, you'll have to pay Bell Telephone's rates for the call. But it's one call that's worth the money.

NATIONAL TELECOM. WE WANT TO PUT WISCONSIN BELL OUT OF THE PHONE BUSINESS.

94

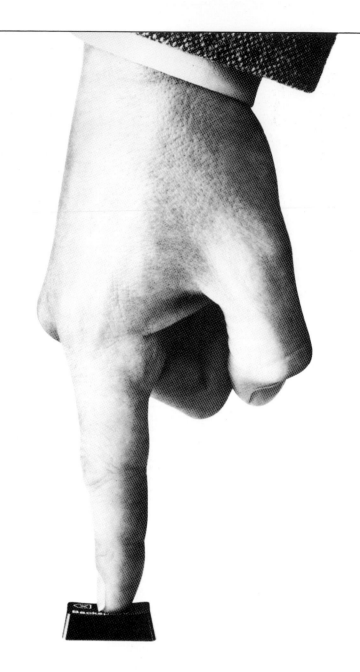

Untype 60 words per minute.

The IBM Electronic 75 Typewriter can erase faster than some people can type.

At the touch of a button, it can automatically lift a character, a word, or an entire line clean off a page.

But not only does the IBM Electronic 75 Typewriter offer you automatic erasing, it also offers you automatic indents, center-ing, underlining and column lay-out.

As well as a memory that can store up to 7,500 characters. (With optional memory: 15,500 characters.)

So if you're interested in sav-ing time, consider the IBM Elec-tronic 75 Typewriter.

You'll be sur-prised how fast your typing gets done. And undone.

To order call *IBM Direct* at the toll-free numbers below. Or, for a free demonstration call your local IBM Office Products Division Representative.

Free demonstration
For a free demonstration of the IBM Electronic 75 Typewriter, write today to: IBM Office Products Division, 400 Parson's Pond Drive/Dept. 804 L, Franklin Lakes, N.J. 07417.

NAME _____ TITLE _____
COMPANY _____
STREET ADDRESS _____
CITY _____ STATE _____ ZIP _____
BUSINESS PHONE _____

IBM.
Office Products Division

Call *IBM Direct* 800-631-5582 Ext. 141. In New Jersey 800-352-4960 Ext. 141.
In Hawaii/Alaska 800-526-2484 Ext. 141.

95 SILVER

Fleas are bad enough during the day. The intense itching, the constant scratching can drive your dog round the bend.

He can become tired, nervous and lose condition. But because fleas live not only on your dog, but also in his bedding, going to sleep can be a nightmare.

It can also be a serious threat to his health.

Should your dog become allergic to fleas, he could get eczema or summer itch.

In extreme cases, this may result in hair loss on the back and nasty sores on the body.

Fleas can also carry diseases such as dermatitis and a species of tapeworm.

To guard your best friend against these parasites, Exelpet has a prevention programme that's totally effective.

The Exeldog 3-Month Flea Collar will control fleas for a full three months.

Also available is the Exeldog Longer-Life Flea Collar which will control fleas for five months.

(It will also control most ticks for four months and the lethal Paralysis tick, found on the East Coast, for one month.)

And because your pet's bedding is a breeding ground for parasites, Exeldog collars should be used in conjunction with the Exelpet range of shampoos, dusting powders and bedding sprays. These will free your pet and his environment of harmful fleas and ticks. You'll find these products on the Exelpet rack at your supermarket.

Look for them.

He deserves a good night's sleep as much as you do.

FLEAS WON'T LET A SLEEPING DOG LIE.

98

Removes those unwanted lines in seconds.

When you use an IBM Electronic 75 Typewriter, you'll never be embarrassed by unsightly typing errors again.

At the touch of a button, you can automatically rid yourself of a character, a word, even an entire line—with no tell-tale signs.

But that's not all.

The IBM Electronic 75 also offers you automatic indents, centering, underlining, and column layout.

You also get a memory that can store up to 7,500 characters. (With optional memory: 15,500 characters.)

So when you have something to retype, the typewriter automatically types it.

What do all these features mean to you?

They mean that your work can look perfect in a matter of seconds.

And when your work looks perfect, you can never look bad.

For more information call your local IBM Office Products Division Representative. Or call *IBM Direct* at the toll-free numbers below.

IBM

Call *IBM Direct* 800-631-5582 Ext. 141. In New Jersey 800-352-4960 Ext. 141.
In Hawaii/Alaska 800-526-2484 Ext. 141.

99

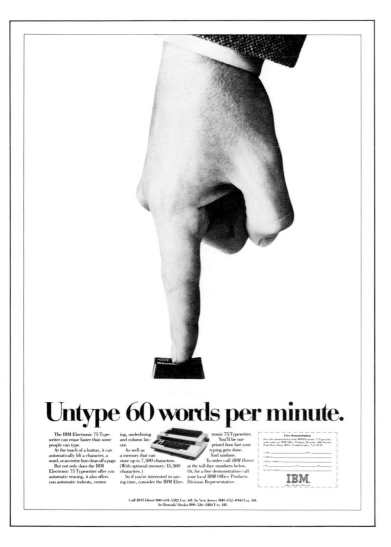

100

ART DIRECTOR
Stan Kovics

WRITER
Lesley Teitelbaum

DESIGNER
Stan Kovics

PHOTOGRAPHERS
Cityana Gallery
Magnum Photo House

CLIENT
Recycling Carroll Gardens

AGENCY
Great Scott Advertising

101

ART DIRECTOR
Tana Klugherz

WRITER
Debbie Kasher

PHOTOGRAPHER
Manny Gonzalez

CLIENT
Planned Parenthood of New
York City

AGENCY
Levine, Huntley, Schmidt,
Plapler & Beaver

2 BDRMS RIV VU $66,000.

CARROLL GARDENS
The Cooperative

505 Court Street • 855-8720 • Prices: $43,000 to $130,000 • Estimated monthly maintenance: $277 to $836 • Below market financing

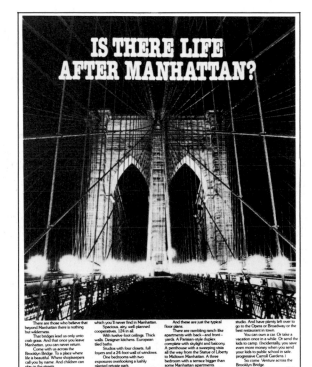

IS THERE LIFE AFTER MANHATTAN?

CARROLL GARDENS
The Cooperative
A GARDENS GROWS IN BROOKLYN

505 Court Street • 855-8720 • Prices: $43,000 to $130,000 • Estimated monthly maintenance: $277 to $836 • Below market financing

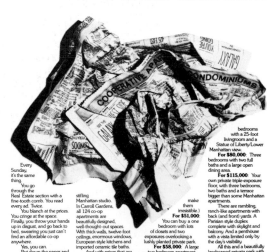

SAVE $100,000. LIVE IN BROOKLYN.

CARROLL GARDENS
The Cooperative

505 Court Street • 855-8720 • Prices: $51,000 to $130,000 • Estimated monthly maintenance: $328 to $836 • Below market financing

IN 1982, IF YOU HAVE A MISCARRIAGE YOU COULD BE PROSECUTED FOR MURDER.

Last week, right-wing U.S Senators took the first step toward making this nightmare a reality.

They held hearings on a Human Life Statute that would make a fertilized egg a person. If this law is passed, all abortions will be outlawed overnight. Even if the pregnancy is a result of rape. Or incest.

Even a miscarriage could be investigated as a criminal offense. Amazing as it sounds, you could be prosecuted for manslaughter.

Backing this bill are radical right-wing political forces, the right-to-lifers, the Moral Majority, and the electronic churchmen. This handful of people want to impose their religious views on everyone. They will stop at nothing to strip you of your most basic personal rights.

Only you can stop them. But you must begin to fight back now. Before outrage becomes law.

Fill out this Planned Parenthood coupon immediately. We'll advise you as to how you can stop this small group from imposing their beliefs on you. Your friends. Your family. Everyone.

Act now. Before the minority rules.

JOIN PLANNED PARENTHOOD
Planned Parenthood of New York City, Inc.
380 Second Avenue, New York, N.Y. 10010
212/777-2002

☐ I believe that abortion is something personal, not political. Please keep me informed and add me to your mailing list.
☐ I want to keep abortion legal and wish to make a tax-deductible contribution. Here is my check in the amount of $

NAME
ADDRESS
CITY/STATE/ZIP
TELEPHONE (W)

ABORTION IS SOMETHING PERSONAL. NOT POLITICAL.

MAKING ABORTION ILLEGAL WON'T MAKE IT UNAVAILABLE. JUST UNSAFE.

Before abortion was legalized in this country, more than 600,000 women each year took their lives into their own hands by having illegal, back-alley abortions.

How many were seriously injured?

How many died?

Right now, there are a handful of U.S. Senators who are determined to bring back those days of dangerous, clandestine abortions.

They are holding the second round of hearings on a proposed statute that would make a fertilized egg a person. If this bill becomes law, any state could outlaw abortion. Overnight.

And this time, it will be even worse than it ever was. Because if you have an abortion it will be considered premeditated murder.

Even a miscarriage could be investigated as manslaughter.

Backing this bill are radical right-wing political and religious forces including New York's very own Senator Alfonse D'Amato. This small but noisy group of people want to impose their beliefs on you. Your friends. Your family.

Don't stand by silently and let outrage become law. Fill out this Planned Parenthood coupon. Give generously of your time and money. With your contributions we can continue our work. to preserve safe and legal abortion.

Give now. Before the minority rules.

JOIN PLANNED PARENTHOOD
Planned Parenthood of New York City, Inc.
380 Second Avenue, New York, N.Y. 10010
212/777-2002

☐ I believe that abortion is something personal, not political. Please keep me informed and add me to your mailing list.
☐ I want to keep abortion legal and wish to make a tax-deductible contribution. Here is my check in the amount of $

ABORTION IS SOMETHING PERSONAL. NOT POLITICAL.

BECAUSE SHE'S OLD ENOUGH TO HAVE A BABY, DOESN'T MEAN SHE'S OLD ENOUGH TO BE A MOTHER.

40% of all girls who turn 14 this year will become pregnant while they are still teenagers.

Needless to say, many of these girls are not ready to become mothers.

Yet right now, U.S. Senate hearings are being held on a Constitutional Amendment which could force a woman to bear a child. Even if she's only a child herself.

If this amendment becomes law, any state could outlaw abortion. Overnight. Even if the pregnancy is the result of rape. Or incest.

It is even possible that if you have an abortion, you could be prosecuted for murder.

Backing this amendment are radical right-wing political forces including New York's very own Senator Alfonse D'Amato. This small but noisy group of people want to impose their religious beliefs on you. Your friends. Your family.

Don't stand by silently and let this injustice become law. Fill out the Planned Parenthood coupon. Give generously of your time and money. With your contributions we can work to preserve safe and legal abortion.

Act now. Before the minority rules.

JOIN PLANNED PARENTHOOD
Planned Parenthood of New York City, Inc.
380 Second Avenue, New York, N.Y. 10010
212/777-2002

☐ I believe that abortion is something personal, not political. Please keep me informed and add me to your mailing list.
☐ I want to keep abortion legal and wish to make a tax-deductible contribution. Here is my check in the amount of $

NAME
ADDRESS
CITY STATE ZIP
TELEPHONE (W)

ABORTION IS SOMETHING PERSONAL. NOT POLITICAL.

102

ART DIRECTORS
Steve Graff
Roy Grace
Marion Sackett

WRITERS
Patty Volk
Tom Yobbagy
Hal Kaufman

ARTIST
Roy Grace

PHOTOGRAPHER
Harold Krieger

CLIENT
IBM

AGENCY
Doyle Dane Bernbach

103

ART DIRECTOR
James Caporimo

WRITER
Enid Schindle

PHOTOGRAPHER
Steve Steigman

CLIENT
The Itkins

AGENCY
Smith/Greenland

102

103

The three most important letters in typing.

IBM

Call *IBM Direct* 800-631-5582 Ext. 141. In New Jersey 800-332-4960 Ext. 141. In Hawaii/Alaska 800-526-2484 Ext. 141.

It hath Math.

And it can check your Spelling in 6 different languages.

The New IBM Displaywriter System.

Announcing A Big Plus: Math
Now you can add, subtract, multiply and divide on the Displaywriter. And it verifies your figures by checking them against the figures you're typing from. So you don't have to worry about mistakes.

It Checks Your Spelling In 6 Languages
The Displaywriter has an electronic dictionary. It can check the spelling of about 50,000 words in English. And over 150,000 words in 5 other *languages*. At 1,000 words a minute. Muy bueno, n'est-ce pas?

The Urge To Merge
Now you can merge all different kinds of information into documents. Say you have a series of forms. You type the information only once, and the Displaywriter puts whatever data is needed where it's needed. And with our new diskette and diskette unit you can store almost 4 times as much information as before.

It's Easy To Remember Because There's Nothing To Forget
The Displaywriter uses prompts. We call them our Task Selection Menus and they appear on our screen to guide you step by step. You don't have to remember a series of confusing codes. That means that almost as soon as you get a Displaywriter System, you use a Displaywriter System.

How Much Is That In Dollars?
Surprise. The basic IBM Displaywriter System costs $7,895. With program license fees starting at $15 a month. Amazing, when you realize how much time and money a word processor saves you in the first place.

Extraordinary, when you compare its features to other word processors. Which is precisely why this ad hath been written.

IBM
Office Products Division—Dept. 804J, 400 Parsons Pond Drive, Franklin Lakes, N.J. 07417

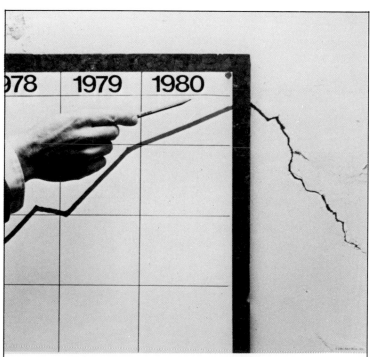

What to do when your business looks great on an annual basis, but your quarters are on the decline.

Quite often, while your business is going uphill, you can lose sight of the fact that your office is going downhill.

Before your reputation is on the line, call The Itkins.

As office furnishings professionals, The Itkins can start from scratch, or crack, as the case may be, and put together a great new office.

Your first step is to come into our showroom. Or, if you think we should see what we're up against, we'll send a consultant to you. Whether you're furnishing one new office or one office building, this staff member will personally handle your entire order. And you'll have no problem handling the price either. Our sheer volume allows us to give you great values.

Then, step by step, we go to work with our extensive resources. For instance, we have huge stock in our tremendous New York warehouse. So if your furniture is there, which is likely, you'll have it within 48 hours. And we're fast with special orders too. Because when they reach us, our own fleet of trucks is standing by for immediate delivery.

To expedite things even further, we are fully computerized. Which means anytime you call us, your order will always be in order. Our computer can tell you what's happening or confirm your order at the touch of a button.

Call The Itkins. While you make your quarters look good on your books, we'll make your quarters look good in person.

The Itkins

Office Furniture • Systems • Carpets • Draperies • 290 Madison Ave. at 41st, N.Y. 10017 Tel. 646-5978. Open weekdays 8:30 A.M. to 5:30 P.M. Saturdays 9:00 A.M. to 5:00 P.M. In New Jersey call our Morristown sales office at (201) 285-1171.

Has your executive suite gone sour?

Are you so busy looking toward the future, you don't see what's going on around you? Or behind you?

Before your office looks like a total shambles and your clients start looking elsewhere, call The Itkins.

We're professionals at office furnishings. Whether you want to furnish one new office or one new office building, our years of experience will make your experience a satisfying one.

You'll work with a staff member who'll personally oversee your entire order. Starting in our showroom where you can experience the furniture live, and in color. And in comfort. Plus, you'll be comfortable with the price too. Our sheer volume allows us to give you great values.

Then we go to work with our extensive resources. For instance, we have huge stock in our tremendous New York warehouse. So if your furniture is there, which is likely, you'll have it within 48 hours. And we're fast with special orders too. Because when they reach us, our own fleet of delivery trucks is standing by for immediate delivery.

To expedite things even further, we are fully computerized. Which means anytime you call us, your order will always be in order. Our computer can tell you what's happening or confirm your order at the touch of a button.

Before your executive suite turns your business sour, call The Itkins. We'll give you and your office a fresh start.

The Itkins

Office Furniture • Systems • Carpets • Draperies • 290 Madison Ave. at 41st, N.Y. 10017 Tel. (212) 646-5978. Open weekdays 8:30 A.M. to 5:30 P.M. Saturdays 9:00 A.M. to 5:00 P.M. In New Jersey call our Morristown sales office at (201) 285-1171.

**Consumer Newspaper
Over 600 Lines Campaign**

104
ART DIRECTOR
Bob Needleman

WRITER
Jamie Seltzer

DESIGNER
Bob Needleman

PHOTOGRAPHER
Steven Meisel

CLIENT
Ski Barn

AGENCY
Altschiller, Reitzfeld,
Solin/NCK

105
ART DIRECTORS
Jim Perretti
Tony Angotti
Priscilla Croft
Neil Leinwohl

WRITERS
Tom Thomas
Neil Leinwohl
Debby Mattison

PHOTOGRAPHERS
Howard Menken
Joe Toto

CLIENT
Xerox

AGENCY
Needham, Harper & Steers

The most popular styles this winter
aren't on 5th Avenue. They're off Route 17

The style you're missing in New York
can be found in New Jersey.

This winter the best dressed people
come from New Jersey.

EVERY DAY THE AVERAGE BUSINESSMAN COMMUTES TO THE NINETEENTH CENTURY.

MOZART HAS IMPROVED PRODUCTIVITY IN HEN HOUSES. NOW, WHAT CAN BE DONE FOR OFFICES?

ARE YOU TOO BUSY DOING YOUR JOB TO GET ANY WORK DONE?

**HOW MADISON AVE.
IS SUPPORTING JOCKS.**

The Hogwash Hills Diet.

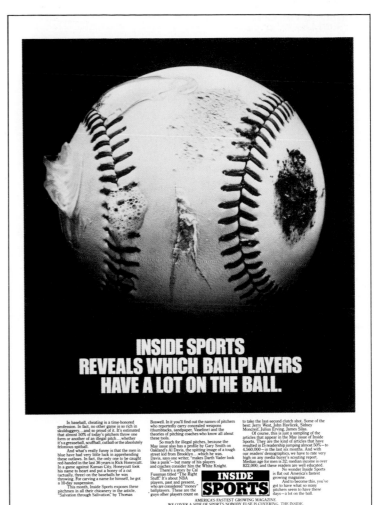
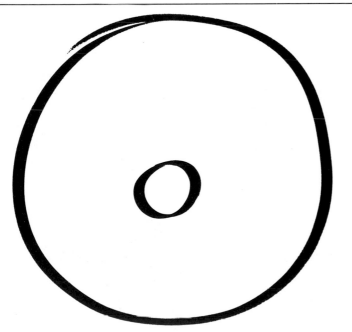

**Consumer Newspaper
Over 600 Lines Campaign**

108 GOLD
ART DIRECTORS
Anthony Angotti
Jerry Whitley
WRITER
Tom Thomas
DESIGNERS
Barbara Sharman
Barbara Bowman
Denise Monaco
Dominique Singer
PHOTOGRAPHER
Dick James
CLIENT
BMW of North America
AGENCY
Ammirati & Puris

109
ART DIRECTOR
Mike Eakin
WRITER
Ray Thiem
ARTIST
Harlan Scheffler
CLIENT
Terminix
AGENCY
Young & Rubicam/Chicago

PERHAPS YOU CAN'T BUY HAPPINESS. BUT FOR $35,000 YOU CAN PURCHASE EXHILARATION.

THE WORLD'S MOST ELEGANT PROTEST AGAINST MEDIOCRE ENGINEERING.

LAST YEAR, A CAR OUT-PERFORMED 318 STOCKS ON THE NEW YORK STOCK EXCHANGE.

If you'd bought a new BMW 320i in the beginning of 1980, and sold it at the end,
your investment would have retained 92.9% of its original value.*
If you'd done the same with any of 318 NYSE stocks, you'd have done less well.
And you'd have forfeited an important daily dividend:
The unfluctuating joy of driving one of the world's great performance sedans.

THE ULTIMATE DRIVING MACHINE.

Ah spring, when termites take wing looking for a new home to eat.

For eleven months out of the year you never see a termite.

They're busy tunneling back and forth from below ground to your house, chewing away at your subfloors, floors, structural timbers and other choice edibles.

But then along comes spring and warmer weather. And suddenly the termites leave their nest in swarms, sprout wings, and go fluttering into the air looking for new worlds to conquer.

Soon they drop down, mate, burrow back into the ground and start up new colonies of ravenous little termites.

It's a fascinating ritual. But for homeowners it spells nothing but trouble.

Which is why it pays to call Terminix.

What we do is make a complete scientific inspection of your building's foundation, carefully charting all areas of infestation or possible access.

Then we place a chemical barrier between your home and the ground that kills termites on contact.

Terminix is so sure we can stop termites that we'll guarantee your house and its contents for up to $100,000 against future termite damage.

So give us a call. We'll keep those termites out of your house. And that's a promise.

Stop termites scientifically. Call Terminix.

Each year these little critters damage more homes than fires, tornadoes or hurricanes.

The common termite. An insect no bigger than a grain of rice.

Yet every year they tunnel up from their nests below ground and damage more homes than tornadoes, hurricanes or even fires.

The worst of it is you never even know it's happening until it's too late.

Until one day you've got serious structural damage to your home and suddenly you're faced with thousands of dollars in repair bills to fix it up again.

Which, of course, is why it pays to call Terminix. Terminix scientists have developed the surest way to stop termites.

What we do is put a chemical barrier between your home and the ground that kills termites on contact.

In fact, Terminix is so sure we can stop termites that we'll guarantee your house and its contents for up to $100,000 against future termite damage.

Give us a call. We'll keep those termites out of your house. And that's a promise.

Stop termites scientifically. Call Terminix.

These creatures will literally eat you out of house and home.

You can't see them or hear them but they could be all around you.

Right now, while you're reading this ad, they could be chewing their way through your roof, rafters, ceiling, walls, floor boards, even the chair you're sitting in.

They're drywood termites, one of nature's most destructive villains. Every year they cause millions of dollars in damage to homes in your area.

But how can you tell if they've moved into *your* home? You can't. And that's why it pays to call Terminix.

Terminix scientists pioneered termite control.

What we do is make a thorough top to bottom inspection of your home and structure, carefully charting any infested areas or areas vulnerable to attack.

Then, if termites are detected, we fumigate. Because fumigation is the most effective way to penetrate hard-to-treat walls, studs and structural timber.

If you're worried about termites, give us a call. We'll get them out of your house. And that's a promise.

Stop termites scientifically. Call Terminix.

YOU CAN STILL GET MANHATTAN FOR $24.

Central Park to Battery Park.
Lincoln Center to Rockefeller Center.
Fifth Avenue to Broadway.
   You can still enjoy it all because Amtrak has extended its incredibly low, Get Up and Go fare, through May 31st, just $24 each way, when you buy your roundtrip ticket for any regular train.
   There are no reservations. No advance purchases. No gas bills. No tolls. No airport cab fares.
   And Amtrak has convenient schedules all week long,

including Saturdays and Sundays.
   What's more, if you're traveling with your family, you can save an additional 50 to 75%.
   If you're interested, and it's pretty hard not to be, call your professional travel planner or Amtrak.
   But don't wait too long. Because at this price a lot of other people will be interested too.

Amtrak **AMERICA'S GETTING INTO TRAINING**

UNTIL MAY 31. $24 EACH WAY. 24 HOURS A DAY.

OUR NEW NEW YORK TIMES.
AMTRAK'S HUDSON HIGHLANDER

DEPARTS 6:40 AM   ARRIVES 8:56 AM

As you can see, Amtrak's got a brand new way to help you get a head start on the business day. With a brand new early morning train from Hudson that gets you into New York's Grand Central Station before 9AM. That makes seven trains daily to choose from.
   So climb aboard. And make good use of your travel time instead of wasting it on the highway.
   You'll get plush reclining seats. Lots of room to

stretch. A snack bar right nearby for some "wake up" coffee. And friendly Amtrak service.
   But most of all, we'll give you the uninterrupted time you need to get some work done. Or to just plain relax.
   So call your professional travel planner or Amtrak. And on your next business trip, ride the train. We'll get you to New York refreshed and ready to get down to business.

Amtrak **AMERICA'S GETTING INTO TRAINING**
Amtrak Station, 69 S. Front St., Hudson, call toll free 800-523-5700

THIS AD WILL PULL YOU IN BOTH DIRECTIONS.

Whether you pick beautiful Washington or charming Boston, you're going to get a whole lot of enjoyment for very little money. That's because Amtrak has extended its incredibly low Get Up and Go fare, through May 31: just $24 each way, when you buy a roundtrip ticket for any regular train.
   There are no reservations. No advance purchases. No gas bills. No tolls. No airport cab fares.
   And Amtrak has convenient schedules, all week long, including Saturdays and Sundays.
   What's more, if you're traveling with your family, you

can save an additional 50 to 75%.
   And as if that isn't enough, in Washington, we can even arrange two nights' accommodations for the price of one on a weekend at any one of 33 of the best hotels.
   So what will it be? The White House, the Capitol and the Smithsonian Institution? Or the Boston Pops, Bunker Hill and Old Ironsides? Call your professional travel planner or Amtrak. But hurry. At this price a lot of other people will be calling, too.

Amtrak **AMERICA'S GETTING INTO TRAINING**

**WASHINGTON. BOSTON.
UNTIL MAY 31. $24 EACH WAY. 24 HOURS A DAY.**

Consumer Newspaper
Over 600 Lines Campaign

112 SILVER
ART DIRECTOR
Dennis D'Amico
WRITER
Ron Berger
PHOTOGRAPHER
Hunter Freeman
CLIENT
Timberland
AGENCY
Ally & Gargano

113
ART DIRECTOR
Pete Coutroulis
WRITER
Jim Weller
DESIGNER
Pete Coutroulis
PHOTOGRAPHER
IBID
CLIENT
National Telecom
AGENCY
Della Femina, Travisano &
Partners

WHY 100 OF WISCONSIN'S MOST SUCCESSFUL CORPORATIONS HAVE DISCONNECTED THEIR PHONES.

If you'd like to make your company more cost efficient, we have an easy solution.

Simply take the Bell off your phones.

Because you can probably save a lot of money by removing your Wisconsin Bell equipment. And replacing it with a system from National Telecom, instead.

At National Telecom, we specialize in providing telephones and PBX Systems to companies with 50 phones or more. At prices that will cost you substantially less.

How much less?

Well, since we installed National Telecom equipment at Western Publishing, they estimate

they're saving about 39% a month.

Mortgage Guarantee Insurance Company figures their savings at about 38%. And National Survey, Funjet, and Guarantee Savings & Loan all estimate their savings at 35% a month. Or more.

What's more, since all our equipment was developed utilizing the more modern technology of today, it's actually more dependable and superior to the Bell Telephone equipment most companies have.

For example, our digital PBX will not only deliver a louder, cleaner sound, but will automatically search through your WATS, Sprint or MCI

lines for the cheapest route. Every time someone in your company makes a long distance call. You just have to dial the area code and number, and our PBX does the rest.

And our PBX equipment costs less than the less sophisticated PBX from the telephone company.

If you'd like to know what a National Telecom System could do for you, why not call our President, Mr. L.A. McLernon at 414-276-6244.

Cost saving equipment from National Telecom.

So now if you want to leave Ma Bell, we can help you cut the cord.

NATIONAL TELECOM. WE WANT TO PUT WISCONSIN BELL OUT OF THE PHONE BUSINESS.

IF WE CAN LOWER YOUR PHONE BILL BY 35% WHY CAN'T THE TELEPHONE COMPANY?

If everyone in your office could make their business calls at home, your company could probably save a lot of money.

To begin with, Wisconsin Bell charges substantially higher rates for "business service" than for personal phones at home.

Secondly, your company has to pay those high monthly rental fees for all your extensions.

And finally, Bell Telephone charges two or three times as much for long distance calls during business hours.

That's why if you want to lower your company telephone bill, you should make all your business calls at home. After 5PM and on weekends. Or make one call to National Telecom, instead.

At National Telecom, we specialize in providing telephones and PBX Systems to companies with 50 phones or more. At prices that will cost you substantially less.

How much less? Well, since we installed National Telecom equipment at Western Publishing, they estimate they're saving about 39% a month.

Mortgage Guarantee Insurance Company figures their savings at about 38%. And National Survey, Funjet, and Guarantee Savings & Loan all estimate their savings at 35% a month. Or more.

What's more, our equipment is actually more dependable and superior to the Bell Telephone equipment most companies have.

For example, our digital PBX will not only deliver a louder, cleaner sound, but will automat-

ically search through your WATS, Sprint or MCI lines for the cheapest route. You just have to dial the area code and number, and our PBX does the rest.

And our PBX equipment costs less than the less sophisticated PBX from the telephone company.

If you'd like to know what a National Telecom System could do for you, why not call our president, Mr. L.A. McLernon at 414-276-6244.

Of course, you'll have to pay Bell Telephone's rates for the call. But it's one call that's worth the money.

NATIONAL TELECOM. WE WANT TO PUT WISCONSIN BELL OUT OF THE PHONE BUSINESS.

WISCONSIN BELL'S EARS MUST BE BURNING.

For years, a lot of businessmen have been saying a lot of unpleasant things about the telephone company in Wisconsin.

"That their rates are too high."

"That their service is too slow."

"That their equipment isn't as good as it could be."

Even worse, we think a lot of the nasty things they've been saying are true.

At National Telecom, we specialize in providing telephones and PBX Systems to companies with 50 phones or more. At prices that will cost you substantially less.

How much less?

Well, since we installed National Telecom equipment at Western Publishing, they estimate they're saving about 39% a month.

Mortgage Guarantee Insurance Company figures their savings at about 38%. And National Survey, Funjet, and Guarantee Savings & Loan all estimate their savings at 35% a month. Or more.

What's more, since all our equipment was developed utilizing the more modern technology of today, it's actually more dependable and superior to the Bell Telephone equipment most companies have.

For example, our digital PBX will not only deliver a louder, cleaner sound, but will automat-

ically search through your WATS, Sprint or MCI lines for the cheapest route. Every time someone in your company makes a long distance call.

And our PBX equipment costs less than the less sophisticated PBX from the telephone company.

If you'd like to know what a National Telecom System could do for you, why not call our president, Mr. L.A. McLernon at 414-276-6244.

After all, the most obscene thing about a phone call shouldn't be the price.

NATIONAL TELECOM. WE WANT TO PUT WISCONSIN BELL OUT OF THE PHONE BUSINESS.

Success story.

Failure can be a great teacher.

Not to slight the instruction of success. Business Week knows and covers well the valuable lessons learned from the winners. But it is a Business Week philosophy that sometimes people learn more when things go wrong, than when things go booming along.

In a regular, continuing review of corporate strategies, Business Week discusses why a company decides to do what it does. What its motivations are. The people making the moves.

And the likelihood of success or failure.

Business Week lays out how a business got into trouble. What they're doing about it. And what the ripples may be.

Not to embarrass or poke fun at someone else's mistakes, but to help others avoid repeating them.

Business Week has the careful, looking-ahead reporting and analyses that over six million readers depend on. The kind of business analyses readers know they cannot get consistently from daily journals and other publications. The kind that keeps their pockets filled.

BusinessWeek 🏢

I bet you my job.

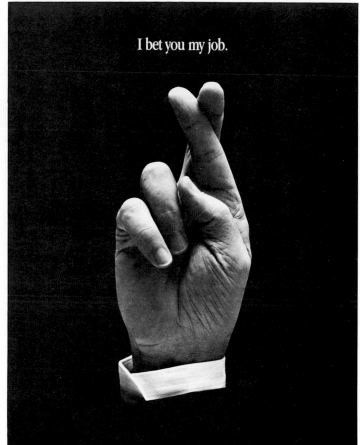

A dangerous game.

But like it or not, you put your future on the line every time you make an important business decision. You cannot eliminate risk altogether, of course. But you can improve your chances of success. Not by trusting to luck. But by making it your business to keep informed, so you can base your judgments on reliable information, objective interpretation and analysis.

That's why over six million business decision makers follow the on-going coverage provided by the 156 full-time worldwide business journalists who bring their expertise to Business Week.

Every week, Business Week editorial departments such as Corporate Strategies, Money and Banking, Information Processing, Marketing, and Technology offer you solid information to help you make responsible decisions.

Business Week offers you an award-winning combination of superior reporting and wide-ranging editorial focus not found anywhere else. Not in Forbes. Not in Fortune. Not in The Wall Street Journal.

Business Week. It leaves you both hands free to do your job.

BusinessWeek 🏢

SEE DICK RUN. SEE JANE JUMP.

See Harold hurl a hammer.

They'll be running, jumping, and hurling right here in Sacramento. At what's been called the most important track and field event in the U.S. all year.

It's a meet of Olympian proportions. Which is why the competition includes half a dozen Olympians. Not to mention dozens of hopeful hopefuls.

The winners here will become the 1981 U.S. National Team. They'll go on to carry the flag at the U.S.A./U.S.S.R. Meet in Moscow. And after that, at the World Cup Games in Rome.

And speaking of sports around the world, ABC's *Wide World of Sports* will be here watching. So the rest of the world can watch you in the stands.

If you want tickets, we suggest you buy them now. On your mark. Get set. Go.

And we further suggest you buy them with the American Express® Card.

Because from June 1 to August 31, for every local purchase you make on the Card, American Express will make a contribution to the Sacramento International Track & Field Association (they're the people who brought this event to Sacramento).

Each contribution will be a modest fifteen cents. But when you multiply that by thousands of purchases (over 107,000 purchases were made on the Card in the same three months last year), SITFA will have a sum no one has to feel modest about.

So run to the telephone, or jog over to the Community Center box office. You'll see the meet and support SITFA, besides.

Which means you'll see Dick run. You'll see Jane jump. But sorry. You won't see Spot.

 NATIONAL OUTDOOR TRACK & FIELD CHAMPIONSHIPS, JUNE 19, 20, & 21, HUGHES STADIUM. FOR TICKETS CALL 442-7827. THE AMERICAN EXPRESS CARD IS WELCOMED.

115

Got a good job? Quit.

Let's face it. You could be making a lot more money than you are right now. And as an investment executive at Paine Webber, we give you every opportunity to.

We'll provide you with professional help, advice, and good solid tools. In fact, we know of no better support system in the business.

You'll have direct access to our product managers and marketing people. And probably more direct contact with our research department than brokers at any other brokerage firm.

Then there's our Portfolio Dynamics program. An amazing computerized program that lets you provide free risk analysis for your clients, overnight. It's an incredible prospecting tool. And our brokers say that it's their most valuable investment.

The point is, the facilities are all there. The rest is entirely up to you.

So if a good job just isn't good enough for you, get a better one. Write to Mr. Joseph A. Cerbone, Director of Career Development. Paine Webber Inc., 140 Broadway, New York, NY 10005. Or call (212) 437-2732. And you, too, can say "Thank You, Paine Webber."

Thank you PaineWebber

An equal opportunity employer M/F/H   Member SIPC

116

117

118

119

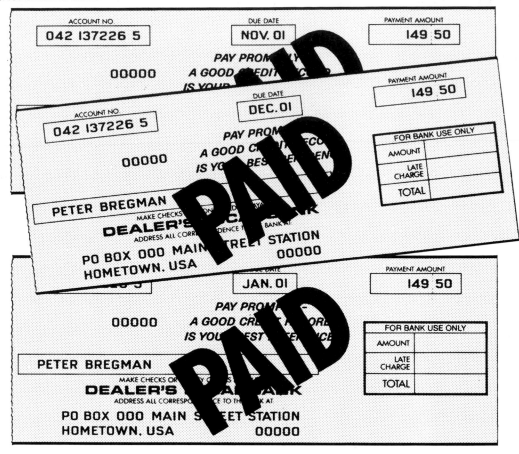

© 1981 VOLKSWAGEN OF AMERICA

The first 3 payments on your next VW are on us.

No kidding! Come in and make your best deal on any 1981 Volkswagen. After you've made the down payment and 48-month or longer financing has been approved, we'll take care of the first three monthly payments for you.

For example, if you put down $1555** on an '81 Rabbit L sedan (at $6755*), 48 monthly payments comes to $149.50 each. But we'd pay for three months' worth or $448.50.

And, you still wouldn't owe a penny more until February, 1982. Offer ends November 15.

*Manufacturer's suggested retail price. Includes freight and dealer delivery charges. Taxes and title fees, extra.
**Down payment and finance charge will vary depending on model and options. Based on total cash price of $6755, which excludes taxes and title fees. 48 monthly payments with approved credit, A.P.R. 16.8% total deferred payment of $8731.

COME SEE SOME OF AMERICA'S FINEST ATHLETES RUN AND JUMP AND THROW THINGS.

They'll run races and jump hurdles. They'll throw hammers and javelins.

At what's been called the most important track and field event in the U.S. all year.

It's a meet of Olympian proportions. Which is why the competition includes half a dozen Olympians. Not to mention dozens of hopeful hopefuls.

The winners here will become the 1981 U.S. National Team. They'll go on to carry the flag at the U.S.A./U.S.S.R. Meet in Moscow. And after that, at the World Cup Games in Rome.

And speaking of sports around the world, ABC's *Wide World of Sports* will be here watching. So the rest of the world can watch you in the stands.

If you want tickets, we suggest you buy them now. On your mark. Get set. Go.

And we further suggest you buy them with the American Express® Card.

Because from June 1 to August 31, for every local purchase you make on the Card, American Express will make a contribution to the Sacramento International Track & Field Association (they're the people who brought this event to Sacramento).

Each contribution will be a modest fifteen cents. But when you multiply that by thousands of purchases (over 107,000 purchases were made on the Card in the same three months last year), SITFA will have a sum no one has to feel modest about.

So run to the telephone, or jog over to the Community Center box office. You'll see the meet and support SITFA, besides.

And if you're lucky, you'll watch the drama as the athletes think of other things to throw.

The losers, their hands up in despair. Or the winners. A party.

 NATIONAL OUTDOOR TRACK & FIELD CHAMPIONSHIPS, JUNE 19, 20, & 21, HUGHES STADIUM. FOR TICKETS CALL 442-7827. THE AMERICAN EXPRESS CARD IS WELCOMED.

121

WEST SIDE STORY

If you have business on the West side of Manhattan, downtown or in New Jersey, Newark's your most convenient airport.

And Continental will take you there in style. With nonstops at 11:10am and 3:30pm.

So fly Continental to Newark. Because it's a lot closer to where you're going. And you'll never be part of the traffic jam at JFK.

For information and reservations, call your travel agent, company travel department or Continental Airlines today in Denver at 398-3000; in Grand Junction at 243-7105; in Colorado Springs at 473-7580.

NEWARK

EAST SIDE STORY

If your business takes you to the East side of town, Westchester, Connecticut, the north shore of Long Island or the Bronx, LaGuardia's most convenient for you.

LA GUARDIA

And only Continental can take you to LaGuardia nonstop. At 4:30pm every afternoon, starting October 25.

So fly Continental nonstop to LaGuardia. And the only sight you'll miss is the traffic jam that's called Kennedy Airport.

NEW YORK ON CONTINENTAL AIRLINES

122

IF YOU MADE AS MUCH MONEY AS MERRILL LYNCH, YOU'D BE BULLISH ON AMERICA, TOO.

You'd be more than bullish. You'd be downright ecstatic.

Because you'd be making profits on services you offer your customers. Services they may not use.

Kingsley Boye doesn't just give you the chance to be bullish. It also gives you the chance to be brainy. We offer our customers the opportunity to pay commissions that are up to 75% less than the major brokerage houses charge.*

Every Kingsley Boye client has his or her own personal broker. And they are among the best available with all the background and experience you could want. In fact, many of them began their careers at one of the brokerage houses you're probably using now.

Kingsley Boye has four seats on The New York Stock Exchange and has been active on Wall Street for the past 20 years.

If you'd like to know more about the advantages of dealing with Kingsley Boye, send for our free, informative brochure. We think it offers you an opportunity to be a lot more than bullish.

*Based on 1975 full commission rates. Minimum transaction $40.
©Kingsley, Boye & Southwood Inc.

Please send me information about Kingsley Boye, including your commission schedule.
LAT-05-17-1

Name _____
Address _____
City _____
State _____ Zip _____
Phone _____

**KINGSLEY BOYE
(213) 553-2900**

1900 Avenue of the Stars, Suite 1526
Los Angeles, CA 90067
In California, call 800-252-2068
Member N.Y.S.E.   Est. 1961

IN SAN DIEGO	IN NEWPORT BEACH	OUT OF STATE
600 B Street, Suite 1148	660 Newport Center Drive, Suite 235	CALL
(714) 233-9555	**(714) 644-2983**	**(800) 421-4617**

123

SMITH BARNEY MAKES MONEY THE OLD-FASHIONED WAY. FROM YOU.

The only thing more old-fashioned than profits is more profits. And that's exactly what Smith Barney and all the other major brokerage houses make. Because every time you trade with them you're paying a much higher commission than you have to. You're paying for all the services they offer. Services you're probably not using.

Kingsley Boye also offers you something old-fashioned. Common sense. At Kingsley Boye you pay a commission, too. But it's up to 75%* less than the big houses charge.

With Kingsley Boye you get a lot more than reduced commissions. You get your own experienced, licensed broker. A broker who very often got his experience with one of the brokerage firms you're probably dealing with now.

And with all that expertise, it's only natural that a Kingsley Boye broker is able to offer you additional, specialized services, like Money Market Funds, Bonds, and Options.

Kingsley Boye has four seats on The New York Stock Exchange and offers you all the expertise that over 20 years on Wall Street brings with it.

If you'd like to know some more about the advantages of dealing with Kingsley Boye, send for our free informative brochure.

You'll find out about something just as old-fashioned as making money.

It's called saving money.

*Based on 1975 full commission rates.   Minimum transaction $40.
⌐Kingsley, Boye & Southwood Inc.

Please send me information about Kingsley Boye, including your commission schedule.
LAT-06-14-1

Name_____

Address_____

City_____

State_____ Zip_____

Phone_____

SIPC
SECURITIES IN
YOUR ACCOUNT
PROTECTED UP TO
$500,000

**KINGSLEY BOYE
(213) 553-2900**

1900 Avenue of the Stars, Suite 1526
Los Angeles, CA 90067
In California, call **800-252-2068**
Member N.Y.S.E.   Est. 1961

IN SAN DIEGO
600 B Street, Suite 1148
(714) 233-9555

IN NEWPORT BEACH
660 Newport Center Drive, Suite 235
(714) 644-2983

OUT OF STATE
CALL
(800) 421-4617

IF YOU MISS THE JUNE TRACK & FIELD MEET HERE IN SACRAMENTO, DON'T WORRY. THERE'S ANOTHER ONE IN JULY. IN MOSCOW.

Frankly, we recommend the one right here. After all, Hughes Stadium is just a hop, a skip, and a high jump away.

And people are calling this the most important track and field event in the U.S. all year.

It's a meet of Olympian proportions. Which is why the competition includes half a dozen Olympians. Not to mention dozens of hopeful hopefuls.

The winners here will become the 1981 U.S. National Team. They'll go on to carry the flag at the U.S.A./U.S.S.R. Meet in Moscow. And after that, at the World Cup Games in Rome.

And speaking of sports around the world, ABC's *Wide World of Sports* will be here watching. So the rest of the world can watch you in the stands.

If you want tickets, we suggest you buy them now. On your mark. Get set. Go.

And we further suggest you buy them with the American Express® Card.

Because from June 1 to August 31, for every local purchase you make on the Card, American Express will make a contribution to the Sacramento International Track & Field Association (they're the people who brought this event to Sacramento).

Each contribution will be a modest fifteen cents. But when you multiply that by thousands of purchases (over 170,000 purchases were made on the Card in the same three months last year), SITFA will have a sum no one has to feel modest about.

So run to the telephone, or jog over to the stadium box office. You'll see the meet and support SITFA, all at the same time.

And if you want tickets to Moscow or Rome, call the American Express Travel Service.

We'll have them for you in less time than it takes to do a 100-meter dash.

NATIONAL OUTDOOR TRACK & FIELD CHAMPIONSHIPS, JUNE 19, 20, & 21, HUGHES STADIUM. FOR TICKETS CALL 442-7827. THE AMERICAN EXPRESS CARD IS WELCOMED.

© American Express Company. 1981

© 1981. Hebrew National Kosher Foods, Inc.

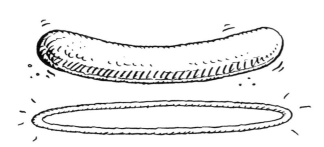

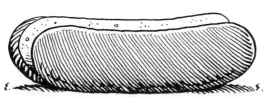

OUR STANDARDS ARE EVEN HIGHER THAN KOSHER.

At Hebrew National, our standards for making hot dogs are not only higher than U.S. Government standards and higher than our competition's standards, they're even higher than Kosher standards.

We don't use the non-meat fillers, the artificial color, the artificial flavor that Kosher hot dogs are allowed to use.

Why does Hebrew National go this far for a hot dog? Because to us, anything less would simply be a sin.

HEBREW NATIONAL®

We make them like we used to.

PAINE WEBBER SHOULD BE THANKING YOU.

Thanks to you, and many investors just like you, the big brokerage firms are getting bigger every day.

Because each time you trade with them you may pay commissions substantially higher than what you have to pay. You're paying for services they offer that in many cases you don't use.

At Kingsley Boye you'll find a lot to be thankful for. First and foremost is our greatly reduced commissions. Up to 75%* less than the major houses charge.

Paying less, by the way, doesn't mean you're getting less service.

With Kingsley Boye you get a lot more than reduced commissions. You get your own experienced, licensed broker. A broker who very often got his experience with one of the brokerage firms you're probably dealing with now.

And with all that expertise, it's only natural that a Kingsley Boye broker is able to offer you additional, specialized services, like Money Market Funds, Bonds, and Options.

Kingsley Boye has four seats on The New York Stock Exchange and offers you all the expertise that over 20 years on Wall Street brings with it.

If you'd like to know more about what those things are, and what they can mean to you, send for your free, informative brochure.

Once you've read it we think you'll be saying "thank you" Kingsley Boye.

And "good-bye" Paine Webber.

*Based on 1975 full commission rates. Minimum transaction $40.
©Kingsley, boye & Southwood Inc.

Please send me information about Kingsley Boye, including your commission schedule.
LAT-05-31-1

Name
Address
City
State_____ Zip_____
Phone

**KINGSLEY BOYE
(213) 553-2900**
1900 Avenue of the Stars, Suite 1526
Los Angeles, CA 90067
In California, call 800-252-2068
Member N.Y.S.E.   Est. 1961

IN SAN DIEGO
600 B Street, Suite 1148
(714) 233-9555

IN NEWPORT BEACH
660 Newport Center Drive, Suite 235
(714) 644-2983

OUT OF STATE
CALL
(800) 421-4617

SMITH BARNEY MAKES MONEY THE OLD-FASHIONED WAY. FROM YOU.

The only thing more old-fashioned than profits is more profits. And that's exactly what Smith Barney and all the other major brokerage houses make. Because every time you trade with them you're paying a much higher commission than you have to. You're paying for all the services they offer. Services you're probably not using.

Kingsley Boye also offers you something old-fashioned. Common sense. At Kingsley Boye you pay a commission, too. But it's up to 75%* less than the big houses charge.

With Kingsley Boye you get a lot more than reduced commissions. You get your own experienced, licensed broker. A broker who very often got his experience with one of the brokerage firms you're probably dealing with now.

And with all that expertise, it's only natural that a Kingsley Boye broker is able to offer you additional, specialized services, like Money Market Funds, Bonds, and Options.

Kingsley Boye has four seats on The New York Stock Exchange and offers you all the expertise that over 20 years on Wall Street brings with it.

If you'd like to know some more about the advantages of dealing with Kingsley Boye, send for our free informative brochure.

You'll find out about something just as old-fashioned as making money. It's called saving money.

*Based on 1975 full commission rates. Minimum transaction $40.
©Kingsley, Boye & Southwood Inc.

Please send me information about Kingsley Boye, including your commission schedule.
LAT-06-14-1

Name
Address
City
State_____ Zip_____
Phone

**KINGSLEY BOYE
(213) 553-2900**
1900 Avenue of the Stars, Suite 1526
Los Angeles, CA 90067
In California, call 800-252-2068
Member N.Y.S.E.   Est. 1961

IN SAN DIEGO
600 B Street, Suite 1148
(714) 233-9555

IN NEWPORT BEACH
660 Newport Center Drive, Suite 235
(714) 644-2983

OUT OF STATE
CALL
(800) 421-4617

IF YOU MADE AS MUCH MONEY AS MERRILL LYNCH, YOU'D BE BULLISH ON AMERICA, TOO.

You'd be more than bullish. You'd be downright ecstatic.

Because you'd be making profits on services you offer your customers. Services they may not use.

Kingsley Boye doesn't just give you the chance to be bullish. It also gives you the chance to be brainy. We offer our customers the opportunity to pay commissions that are up to 75% less than the major brokerage houses charge.*

Every Kingsley Boye client has his or her own personal broker. And they are among the best available with all the background and experience you could want. In fact, many of them began their careers at one of the brokerage houses you're probably using now.

Kingsley Boye has four seats on The New York Stock Exchange and has been active on Wall Street for the past 20 years.

If you'd like to know more about the advantages of dealing with Kingsley Boye, send for our free, informative brochure. We think it offers you an opportunity to be a lot more than bullish.

*Based on 1975 full commission rates. Minimum transaction $40.
©Kingsley, Boye & Southwood Inc.

Please send me information about Kingsley Boye, including your commission schedule.
LAT-05-17-1

Name
Address
City
State_____ Zip_____
Phone

**KINGSLEY BOYE
(213) 553-2900**
1900 Avenue of the Stars, Suite 1526
Los Angeles, CA 90067
In California, call 800-252-2068
Member N.Y.S.E.   Est. 1961

IN SAN DIEGO
600 B Street, Suite 1148
(714) 233-9555

IN NEWPORT BEACH
660 Newport Center Drive, Suite 235
(714) 644-2983

OUT OF STATE
CALL
(800) 421-4617

128

ROWLETT'S SALE ON NIKES, ADIDAS AND BROOKS IS RUNNING NOW THROUGH SATURDAY.

Brooks Villanova
Sugg. Retail $22.95
Sale Price $16.95

Adidas SL72
Sugg. Retail $39.98
Sale Price $30.98

Nike LDV
Sugg. Retail $39.98
Sale Price $28.98

All this week, you can get 25%
to 30% off top name running shoes
at Rowlett's.
But you'd better make tracks.
At these prices, everything will be
moving fast.
Rowlett's, at the corner of
Staples Mill and Broad.
We're open till 9 on Fridays
and Saturdays till 5.

NOW AT ROWLETT'S, EVEN THE PRICE OF DOWN IS DOWN.

Woolrich® Down Vests
Sugg. Retail $49.98 Sale Price $29.98

Woolrich® Down Parkas
Sugg. Retail $106.95 Sale Price $69.98

Ski Mittens
Sugg. Retail $19.98 Sale Price $13.50

Duxbak® Hunting Trousers
Sugg. Retail $50.00 Sale Price $31.98

Chamois Shirts
Sugg. Retail $22.00 Sale Price $16.50

Kaufman Sorrel® Boots
Sugg. Retail $44.98 Sale Price $36.98

Now through Saturday, Rowlett's
is cutting 20-40% off the price of
selected items of warm, well-known
outdoor wear.
Come by Rowlett's at Staples
Mill and Broad. We're open till 9 on
Fridays and till 5 on Saturdays.

ROWLETT'S HAS ENOUGH CANOES TO SINK A SHIP.

Aluminum Canoes by Grumman.
Now $50-150 off.

ABS Canoes by Old Town, Mohawk,
and Mad River.
Prices start at $450.

Fiberglass Canoes by Mohawk,
Grummon, Mad River, and Old Town.
Prices start at $295.

It's true. In fact, Rowlett's has
more canoes than anybody else in
Central Virginia.
Canoes by Grummon, Old Town,
Mohawk, Mad River, and Coleman.
Plus paddles, cushions, car racks,
and many other accessories.
Now when you're anxious to
get afloat, you know the best place
to get a canoe.
Rowlett's, at the corner of
Staples Mill and Broad. We're open
daily till 6, Fridays till 9, and
Saturdays till 5.

THE CLOSEST A CAR COMPANY CAN COME TO A MONEY-BACK OFFER.

No one buys a house or stock with the expectation of watching its value plummet; why buy a car in which that's not just an expectation, but a virtual certainty?

Particularly when you can avoid all inferior performance, investment or otherwise, by buying a BMW 320i.

According to the October 1981 NADA Used-Car Guide, if you'd bought a new BMW 320i in 1979 and sold it this year, you'd get an astonishing 101% of your money back.*

That's more than Audi 4000, Dat-sun 280ZX, or any other car in its price class. Even more than many other cars in substantially higher price classes, such as Cadillac Seville and Mercedes-Benz 280E.

All of which makes the BMW 320i one of the world's most exhilarating cars to leave a dealership in:

A car that leaves you enriched by the experience. Instead of impoverished by it.

THE ULTIMATE DRIVING MACHINE.
BMW, MUNICH, GERMANY.

*Based on average retail price. Your selling price may vary according to the condition of your car and whether you sell it privately or to a dealer. © 1981 BMW of North America, Inc. The BMW trademark and logo are registered trademarks of Bayerische Motoren Werke, A.G.

LET YOUR BAY AREA BMW DEALERS ARRANGE A THOROUGH TEST DRIVE.

CONCORD
IMPORT MOTORS, INC.
1945 Market Street
(415) 682-3577

EMERYVILLE
WEATHERFORD MOTORS, INC.
1710 59th Street
(415) 654-8280

MILL VALLEY
MILL VALLEY IMPORTS
383 Miller Avenue
(415) 388-2750

NAPA
AL LYON MOTORS, INC.
570 Soscol Ave.
(707) 224-8351

PALO ALTO
H & E GERMAN CAR SALES & SERVICE
275 Alma Street
(415) 324-4488

SAN FRANCISCO
GERMAN MOTORS CORPORATION
1201 Van Ness Ave.
(415) 775-9070

SAN LEANDRO
WEBER MOTORS, INC.
2000 Washington Ave.
(415) 351-2003

SAN MATEO
PETER PAN MOTORS, INC.
2695 South El Camino Real
(415) 349-9077

SAN RAFAEL
BMW AUTOZENTRUM
1826 Fourth Street
(415) 457-1441

SANTA CLARA
DON LUCAS BMW
3737 Stevens Creek Rd.
(408) 249-9070

SANTA ROSA
VEALE BMW
2800 Corby Avenue
(707) 545-6602

SUNNYVALE
ALLISON BAVARIAN MOTORS
750 East El Camino Real
(408) 733-2400

HOW TO AVOID THE DEVALUATION OF THE CAR.

These days, owning a car has largely become a process of presiding over its rapid depreciation.

BMW owners, on the other hand, have found a way to reverse that process.

Consider, for example, those who purchased a new BMW 320i in 1979. Today, according to the October 1981 NADA Used-Car Guide, their car is worth 101% of its original purchase price—literally more than they paid for it.*

During that same period, some cars in its class have lost over 25% of their value.

And at a time when the performance of most cars is declining as steadily as their resale value, the 320i has reversed that decline as well.

Its engine still delivers exhilarating response, even by prepollution control standards. And its suspension still offers "a balance of handling that's leagues ahead of most other sports sedans" (Road & Track).

To experience a car that's leading the advance rather than the retreat of the automobile, contact your nearest BMW dealer to arrange a thorough test drive at your convenience.

THE ULTIMATE DRIVING MACHINE.

*Based on average retail price. Your selling price may vary according to the condition of your car and whether you sell it privately or to a dealer. © 1981 BMW of North America, Inc. The BMW trademark and logo are registered trademarks of Bayerische Motoren Werke, A.G.

LET YOUR SOUTHERN FLORIDA BMW DEALER ASSOCIATION ARRANGE A THOROUGH TEST DRIVE.

Fort Lauderdale
FRANK HILSON BMW
1812 South Andrews Ave.
(305) 525-0336

Miami
BMW SOUTH
16165 South Dixie Highway
(305) 238-0900

Miami
BRAMAN MOTORS, INC.
2020 Biscayne Boulevard
(305) 576-6900

Pompano Beach
VISTA BMW
700 North Federal Highway
(305) 942-7400

LAST YEAR, A CAR OUT-PERFORMED 318 STOCKS ON THE NEW YORK STOCK EXCHANGE.

If you'd bought a new BMW 320i in the beginning of 1980, and sold it at the end, your investment would have retained 92.9% of its original value.*

If you'd done the same with any of 318 New York Stock Exchange stocks, you'd have done less well. And you'd have forfeited an important daily dividend: The unfluctuating joy of driving one of the world's great performance sedans.

THE ULTIMATE DRIVING MACHINE.
BMW, MUNICH, GERMANY.

LET YOUR BAY AREA BMW DEALERS ARRANGE A THOROUGH TEST DRIVE.

CONCORD
IMPORT MOTORS, INC.
1945 Market Street
(415) 682-3577

EMERYVILLE
WEATHERFORD MOTORS, INC.
1710 59th Street
(415) 654-8280

MILL VALLEY
MILL VALLEY IMPORTS
383 Miller Avenue
(415) 388-2750

NAPA
AL LYON MOTORS, INC.
570 Soscol Ave.
(707) 224-8351

PALO ALTO
H & E GERMAN CARS SALES & SERVICE
275 Alma Street
(415) 324-4488

SAN FRANCISCO
GERMAN MOTORS CORPORATION
1201 Van Ness Real
(415) 775-9070

SAN LEANDRO
WEBER MOTORS, INC.
2000 Washington Ave.
(415) 351-2003

SAN MATEO
PETER PAN MOTORS, INC.
2695 South El Camino Real
(415) 349-9077

SAN RAFAEL
BMW AUTOZENTRUM
1826 Fourth Street
(415) 457-1441

SANTA CLARA
DON LUCAS BMW
3737 Stevens Creek Rd.
(408) 249-9070

SANTA ROSA
VEALE BMW
2800 Corby Avenue
(707) 545-6602

SUNNYVALE
ALLISON BAVARIAN MOTORS
750 East El Camino Real
(408) 733-2400

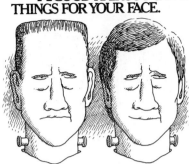

Buy IBM
for 10 cents a share.*

TEN CENTS

TEN 10¢

NAME

ADDRESS

CITY, STATE, ZIP

PHONE

☐ Please send me your brochure

SEAPORT SECURITIES CORPORATION
50 Broadway, New York N.Y. 10004

* Or sell it for 10¢ a share. With Seaport you can buy or sell any stock at any price for only 10 cents a share. That's all the commission you pay for market orders–$50 minimum. Our Unirate is among the simplest, lowest, across the board brokerage rates you can find. Just multiply the number of the shares by .10¢ and you've got your total transaction cost. Compare Seaport's Unirate with the commissions you are now paying and you will see how Seaport can save you up to 83% or even more when buying or selling listed and OTC stocks.

Seaport also offers you substantial saving for bonds and options.

Seaport Securities is a subsidiary of a member of the New York Stock Exchange. Your orders are executed efficiently, professionally, and so quickly, that some can be confirmed before you even hang up the phone.

Call Seaport Securities today and start saving commission dollars in 1981. You'll be pleased with how much service 10 cents will buy you.

**Call Toll Free 1-(800)-221-9894
In New York 212-482-8689**

SEAPORT SECURITIES
CORPORATION

NASD

SIPC

133

Xerox won't stop at nothing.

These days, even nothing costs something to send. That is, if you're using ordinary facsimile equipment.
Because ordinary facsimile equipment takes the time to read every line of type, and all the "nothing" in between.

The new Xerox Telecopier 455

Xerox, on the other hand, has three machines -- two of them brand new --that know the difference between a line of something and a line of nothing: The Telecopier 485 terminal. The new automatic Telecopier 495 digital terminal, that can send and receive unattended. And the new -- and very economical -- desktop Telecopier 455 terminal. When they come to a space like this:

they'll skip it -- the way your eyes just did -- and go on to the next line of type.
As a result, you can send a crisp, clear copy of the original document in as little as a minute. For up to 40% less than you'd normally spend on telephone charges.
Besides being fast, these machines are also very friendly. They're all on speaking terms with the other members of our Telecopier family. Even relatives working in remote parts of the world. In fact, they can talk to many competitive facsimile machines, as well.

The Xerox Telecopier 485

Only Xerox offers so many ways to get your message across. Or so many ways to save time and money doing it.
And the Telecopier 485, 495, and 455 terminals are just the beginning.
You see, Xerox will stop at nothing to bring you new machines that won't.

The new Xerox Telecopier 495

For more information on the Xerox family of Telecopiers, call your local Xerox facsimile sales rep. or call 1-800-527-1868. In Texas, call 1-800-442-5030. Or send this coupon to Xerox Corporation, P.O. Box 470065, Dallas, Texas 75247.

Name _____ Title _____

Company _____ Address _____

City _____ State _____ Zip _____ Tel. _____

XEROX®, TELECOPIER®, 485, 495, and 455 are trademarks of XEROX CORPORATION.

XEROX

134

Sony invent the world's smallest personal hi-fi.

Sorry, the cassette was in the way.

The latest Sony Walkman is the smallest stereo cassette player there's ever been.

Any smaller and a cassette couldn't fit in.

But put its lightweight headphones on, and it sounds like a hi-fi a hundred times its size.

And the beauty is, only you can hear it. Even when belting out Bach in a crowded park.

The Walkman's front-mounted controls operate at a touch.

And it plays all types of tape. Even metal.

Your Sony dealer can let you hear how amazing it sounds.

If he hasn't mislaid it behind a cassette. **SONY.**

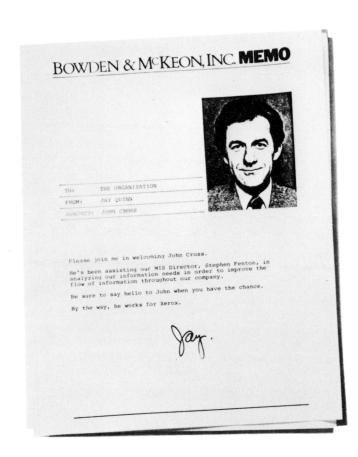

How to add to your staff without adding to your payroll.

Xerox helps business manage information.

But we don't just provide equipment your company can live with. In many cases we also provide a person who virtually lives with your company.

These people are called National Account Managers.

Their job is to get to know your company's information requirements. So they can analyze your needs and recommend solutions that are just right for you.

At the same time they can also help you get the most out of your existing equipment. And advise you on future needs with everything from plain paper copiers to information processors to machines that print out computer data much faster than ordinary computer printers.

Xerox equipment, you see, helps you make the best possible use of information. While Xerox people like National Account Managers, as well as Technical and Marketing Representatives and Systems Consultants, help you make the best possible use of equipment.

That way you not only get people who help you manage time and money.

They'll also show you the best way to manage information.

XEROX

XEROX® is a trademark of XEROX CORPORATION

If this is your only retirement plan, don't plan on retiring.

Pretend you're retired.
And you're living on a monthly Social Security check.
You pay your bills.
You buy some food.
And you wait for your next check.

It's probably not the comfortable retirement you had in mind.

That's because there's not much security left in the Social Security system.

Oh sure, your monthly dividends might go up. But then, so will everything else.

So what do you do?
At Southwest Savings, we think you can still look forward to a comfortable retirement later, by investing in one of our retirement accounts now.

And because the money you put into your retirement account, along with the interest it earns, is tax-deferred, you'll benefit today, as well as tomorrow.

Stop into any Southwest Savings office. Or call 241-4400 and ask about our tax-sheltered retirement accounts.

It's the surest way to put the security you want back into your retirement plan.

SOUTHWEST SAVINGS

Southwest Savings tax-sheltered retirement accounts.

137

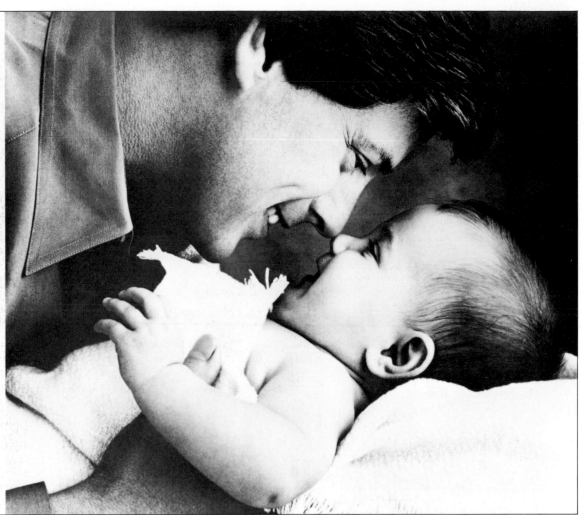

140

141

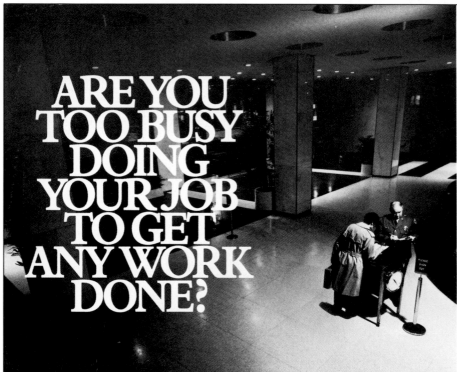

142

The prize for spotting the difference is 25% off your international phone bill.

It doesn't cost much to keep in touch. British TELECOM International

A SYSTEM TO MANAGE TRAVEL AND ENTERTAINMENT SPENDING.
NO MATTER HOW SMALL YOU ARE OR BIG YOU GET.

Your company can't avoid spending money on travel and entertainment. It's just one of the costs of doing business.

What you *can* avoid is spending too much.

With the American Express Corporate Card System, each employee you select gets the American Express® Card.

So they're ready for up to 95% of all business travel and entertainment. (As you know, the Card is welcomed at airlines, hotels, restaurants, and car rentals around the world.)

And they don't have to carry a walletful of credit cards, or a lot of cash. Because if the American Express Card is lost or stolen, they can get it replaced, fast. Usually by the end of the next business day. And with no liability for your company.

How does that help you with spending?

Well, with the Corporate Card System, you get one organized bill for *all* your company's travel and entertainment. With copies of almost every transaction.

So you know exactly where your money is going. What you spent. When. And where.

But if you think that's useful now, just wait.

It'll be even more useful when you join the ranks of the FORTUNE 500.

William R. Sullivan, V.P.
Commercial Marketing
American Express Company
P.O. Box 3603, New York, N.Y. 10008
I'd like to find out how the Corporate Card System can benefit my company.

Name

Company

Title

Address

City

State   Zip

Phone

No. of Travelers

THE AMERICAN EXPRESS CORPORATE CARD SYSTEM

IF SOMETHING ISN'T DONE ABOUT IT, NEARLY HALF THE CLASS WILL DIE OF CARDIOVASCULAR DISEASE.

That, believe it or not, is the proportion of deaths now caused by diseased hearts and blood vessels. And it's a proportion that could be tremendously reduced if people would only take better care of their bodies.

Knowing this, Blue Cross and Blue Shield Plans are doing something about it. Because we're committed to raising health standards and containing rising medical costs at the same time.

We're sponsoring a comprehensive physical fitness package, in cooperation with the President's Council on Physical Fitness and Sports, that's now available from the State Department of Education for use in all junior and middle schools in Virginia.

This program, entitled "Fit To Be You", features films produced by Walt Disney Educational Media Company as well as teachers' guides. Its aim is to encourage good fitness habits early in life to last a healthful lifetime.

So if you hear that your kids are watching Walt Disney movies in school, don't worry. They're learning something that will be vitally important all their lives.

They're learning that if they aren't using their bodies properly, they simply aren't using their heads.

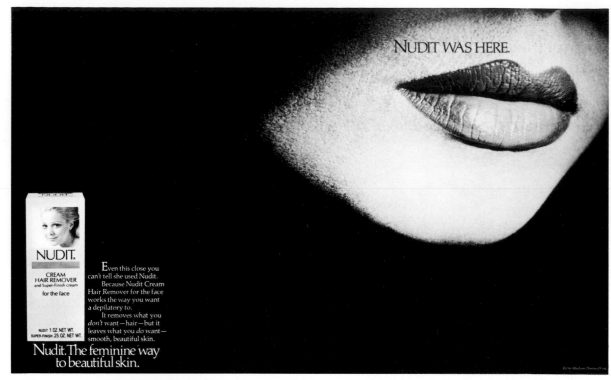

148

149

HOW THE IRS VIEWS TRAVEL AND ENTERTAINMENT SPENDING.

Closely.

Of course they understand it's one of the essential costs of doing business. That's why a lot of travel spending is deductible.

But when they get your company's tax return, they scrutinize this area...carefully. Which doesn't mean, *worry*. It just means, *be prepared*.

What the IRS really wants is information. Exactly what you spent. Where. With whom. And why.

The kind of information that's more easily provided when you have the American Express Corporate Card System.

With the Corporate Card System, each employee you select gets the American Express Card. So they're ready for up to 95% of all business travel and entertainment. (As you know, the Card is welcomed at airlines, hotels, restaurants, and car rentals around the world.)

And they don't have to carry a walletful of credit cards, or a lot of cash. Because if the American Express Card is lost or stolen, they can get it replaced, fast. Usually by the end of the next business day. And with no liability for your company.

Which brings us back to information.

With the Corporate Card System, you get one organized bill for all your company's travel and entertainment. With copies of almost every transaction.

You'll have a record of everything. Which is just what you need.

Because it's just what the IRS wants.

THE AMERICAN EXPRESS CORPORATE CARD SYSTEM

DISCOVERING THE HIDDEN FLOAT IN YOUR TRAVEL AND ENTERTAINMENT BUDGET.

Your company probably spends a lot of money on travel and entertainment.

You could be making money on that money.

It's simple. Don't pay for anything until you have to. And then, use the float you get to invest.

With the American Express Corporate Card System, your company doesn't pay travel and entertainment bills for as long as a month. The system helps control costs. Improves your cash flow. Simplifies expense reporting.

And it also gives you information on expenditures, while making travel easier for your employees.

To find out how the system could work for your company, send us the coupon. And discover how easy controlling your travel budget can be.

THE AMERICAN EXPRESS CORPORATE CARD SYSTEM

WITH SO MANY PEOPLE WORKING SO LATE, WHY ISN'T MORE WORK GETTING DONE?

**GRAND CENTRAL STATION
10:18 P.M.**

The trouble with commuter railroad stations is that they tend to be misleading economic indicators.

Crowded late-night trains are supposed to mean busy executives, soaring output and higher productivity.

Today there are plenty of busy executives, but productivity is anything but higher. In fact, it's fallen during six of the past seven quarters.

All of which illustrates something we've believed for some time: Productivity has less to do with how late people work than how well.

At Xerox, helping people work better is our business. And has been since the first Xerox copier revolutionized the way businesses reproduce information.

Today we make advanced machines that not only copy, but also automatically collate, reduce and even staple sets together.

Machines that let you create, store and re-

trieve documents much faster than humanly possible.

Machines that print out computer information much faster than ordinary computer printers.

And a special cable—called the Ethernet cable—that lets office machines work together so that they can literally save businesses millions of dollars in wasted time and effort. We even supply productivity experts to help your people make the best possible use of it all.

The purpose is obvious. To relieve people of various time-consuming chores so they'll have the time to do their jobs.

Not by working longer hours or shorter hours—but better hours.

XEROX

XEROX® and Ethernet are trademarks of XEROX CORPORATION.

At what age does your skin start to get dry?

Dry skin is a fact of life for most women.

Not only is it uncomfortable, it can also make you look older than you really are.

From the beginning.

Unfortunately, your skin started to get dry the moment you were born.

Immediately, it was under attack. Cold winter wind. Dry indoor heat. Air conditioning. Even soap. All these things can make your skin dry. Right from the start.

But as a baby, you had an advantage. You had a built-in protection system.

The older, the drier.

As you get older, this built-in protection system for your skin starts to fail.

Somewhere in your twenties or thirties, you begin to feel it. Your skin starts feeling drier.

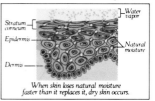

When skin loses natural moisture faster than it replaces it, dry skin occurs.

For many women, this is a time of trying any and all kinds of creams and lotions that promise relief. Searching for one that really works.

Keri lotion really does.

Why Keri works.

Keri does what a baby's skin does naturally.

It helps retain your skin's own natural moisture.

And Keri gives you long-lasting protection against dryness. You can even feel its effect long after you put it on.

Keri also has a high concentration of emollients to smooth and soften dry skin.

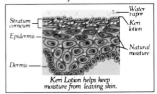

Keri Lotion helps keep moisture from leaving skin.

And it contains oils that help keep skin from losing water. All these things work together

to help keep your skin smooth and healthy looking.

Dermatologists know.

While Keri lotion may be new to you, the people who know all about skin have been using it for years.

Ever since Keri lotion was introduced years ago, dermatologists have been using it in hospitals, recommending it to patients and even using it themselves. Because they know it works.

Which all means, the sooner you start using Keri, the better.

No matter what your age.

Keri® lotion.

c 1982 Westwood Pharmaceuticals Inc.

TOO MANY LAY DOWN ON

WORK BOOTS THE JOB.

SPLIT SOLE
Construction Worker - Chicago, Illinois

CRACKED LEATHER
Gas Station Owner - Troy, New York

WATER DAMAGE
Mailman - Des Moines, Iowa

If you spend a good part of your day working in a pair of boots, obviously, you depend a lot on them.

Unfortunately, though, most boots don't deliver.

Their problems run from shoddy and uncomfortable construction on the one foot, to no waterproofing and no insulation on the other.

At Timberland,® we make what we think are the best work boots around.

Here's why:

YOU HAVE TO WORK IN RAIN AND SNOW. SO DO OUR BOOTS.

If there's one time people who save a few dollars on a pair of boots really pay the price, it's when it rains or snows. Because most boots won't keep you dry.

But it's in weather like this that Timberland boots really shine.

Our boots are made of silicone or oil-impregnated waterproof leathers.

To resist rust, we use only solid brass eyelets.

And because any needle hole is a potential water hole, we seal every seam with not just one coat of latex but two.

How dry will Timberland boots keep you?

Well, on a machine called a Maser Flex that tests waterproof leathers, Timberland leathers must withstand a minimum of 15,000 flexes, twice U.S. Military standards.

WE WON'T LEAVE YOU OUT IN THE COLD.

It's been estimated that on extremely cold days, you lose 80% of your body heat through the top of your head.

Yet, inevitably, your feet are always the first things to go.

To prevent the inevitable, your feet are surrounded with a layer of nitrogen filled closed cell insulation that'll keep your feet warm to temperatures well below zero.

Our boots aren't just better insulated than most boots, they're better insulated than most houses.

OUR BOOTS ARE TOUGH ON THE JOB. NOT ON YOUR FEET.

One of the biggest qualifications a work boot must have is an ability to take punishment. Timberland's stand up to whatever you dish out.

Thanks to little things like four rows of nylon stitching instead of cotton in all key stress points. And big things, like heavy-duty molded soles permanently bonded to the uppers so they can withstand a tremendous amount of abuse.

But there's a soft side to our boots as well.

It includes leather linings, geometrically graded lasts, and a unique, 4-ply innersole construction. It results in boots so comfortable they eliminate the painful breaking-in period other boots force you to suffer through.

But don't just take our word for it. Step into any store that carries Timberland boots, and try on a pair.

They come in a variety of styles, for men and women,

starting at about $60.00. Which, in all honesty, might be a few dollars more than you now spend.

But we think you'll find it's worth spending a little more money to get a lot more boot.

Timberland ®

The Timberland Company, P.O. Box 170, Newmarket, New Hampshire 03857

O e thi g our pri t wheels wo 't do.

They wo 't break, like this o e did.

Because the entire wheel is reinforced. With metal.

Which means characters won't snap off, and typewriters won't edit people without their consent.

That's guaranteed for a full year.

Now, this is what our print wheels will do. They'll print in 21 different typefaces. And in different type sizes.

They'll print signs and symbols, such as π and ¶.

Best of all, each wheel can be custom-made.

At Xerox, we offer a wide variety of supplies that help prevent communications breakdowns. Everything from magnetic cassettes to Telecopier supplies to data storage systems.

So before you send for any more Information Processing or Telecopier supplies, send in the coupon. Or call

1-800-527-1868.*

After all, which would you rather supply your office with:

The thi gs it eeds?

Or the things it needs?

‒ ‒ ‒ ‒ ‒ ‒ ‒ ‒ ‒ ‒ ‒ ‒ ‒ ‒

I'd like more information on the complete line of Xerox Office Supplies.

Send to: Xerox Corporation, P.O. Box 470065, Dallas, Texas 75247.

Name
Title
Company
Address
City_____State____Zip____
Phone

NSPS-7-81

XEROX

*In Texas, Alaska and Hawaii, call collect 1-214-630-6145.

XEROX® and TELECOPIER® are trademarks of XEROX CORPORATION.

One of the few things on the Space Shuttle that didn't have a backup system.

Backup systems are essential to any manned space flight.

But space inside the shuttle is precious.

How did the crew of the NASA Space Shuttle Columbia get a 35mm camera they could depend on, without having to take along a lot of 35mm cameras?

They took off with a Nikon.®

With good reason.

No Nikon has ever failed on a NASA space mission. In every manned mission into space since 1971, no Nikon has had structural damage from blast off. Or jammed. Or

had a mechanical problem. Or any problem that affected its performance.

A Nikon, as you may have gathered, is incredibly reliable. So reliable it's the choice of more professional photographers than all other 35mm cameras combined.

Your nearest Nikon dealer can give you all the down-to-earth reasons for owning a Nikon. There are five models to choose from. The F3 for professionals and serious amateurs. The FE automatic with manual override. The FM which offers full manual control. The Nikonos IVA—the

world's only fully automatic 35mm underwater camera. And the Nikon for people buying their first 35mm camera—the EM.

Whatever your choice, one thing is certain. Whether you're up in space, down on earth, or underwater, a Nikon can help you take pictures that are out of this world.

Nikon
We take the world's greatest pictures.

© NIKON INC. 1981

PORTABLE TAPE DECKS REQUIRE A MORE DURABLE TAPE.

You can take a portable cassette deck practically anywhere. But, take the average cassette tape out of its natural habitat, the living room, and you're asking for trouble.

Ordinary cassettes just aren't designed to stand up to life in the outside world. Even weather that's a little too hot or too cold can cause them to jam.

At Maxell, our cassettes are built to standards that are up to 60% higher than the industry calls for. They can withstand temperatures from subfreezing to subtropic. And they're tough enough to survive mishaps that would be fatal to a less durable cassette.

In fact, Maxell cassettes are so well made they'll even outlast your portable cassette deck. And that's not an idle promise. We guarantee it.

IT'S WORTH IT.

160

How do you explain something that's never existed before?

He had a similar problem.

It's not just a new machine. It's a totally new concept.

Xerox introduces Star.

The Xerox 8010 Star Information System is the first office tool (with the possible exception of the pad and pencil) designed specifically for professionals.

You see, people like engineers, analysts, researchers, etc., don't deal just with words or numbers or graphics. They deal with ideas.

The Star System lets them create, revise, and visualize their ideas on a screen, before anything is committed to paper.

And makes it possible for projects that might otherwise take days to be completed in just a few hours. For a fraction of the cost.

Here's how it works.

Say, for example, you're putting together a report or proposal.

With a basic keyboard and four simple commands, Star lets you call up stored information, even from computers. Add to it. Rearrange paragraphs. Choose the style and size of the typeface. Illustrate complex equations. Process records. Create a virtually limitless variety of forms, charts and graphs. And otherwise design a document precisely the way you want it.

Once you're satisfied with what you've created, it can be printed exactly the way it appears on the screen.

Your Stars can form a galaxy.

You can also plug your Star into the Xerox Information Outlet. Then, through a Xerox Ethernet cable, you can share information with other Stars throughout your company, including other offices in other cities. So several professionals can work together on one page, or on a whole report, without leaving their desks.

In other words, professionals can spend less time running from office to office,

doing tedious jobs, or waiting for outside help. And more time doing the productive work there never seems to be enough time to do.

"But I can't type."

Because Star was designed for professionals, it requires no previous experience with keyboards or display screens. What they work with on the screen are symbols of what they work with every day (such as a file drawer or an in/out box). So most people can become familiar with it in just a few minutes.

For more information, write Xerox Corporation, P.O. Box 470184, Dallas, Texas 75247. Or better yet, ask for a demonstration.

You'll see why Star—just like the wheel—is a lot easier to use than explain.

XEROX

161

"BEFORE THERE WAS KODAK THERE WAS KONICA".

Eastman Kodak was founded back in 1880. That's a long time ago.

But Konishiroku —the makers of Konica*—was founded in 1873. That's an even longer time ago. And it gives us a 7 year head start on The Legend.

But that's just the start of the untold story of Konica.

Konica made Japan's first camera. Japan's first SLR. Japan's first automatic SLR. And the first auto-focus camera. And... and...and...

If these firsts are news to you, that's because Konica is piloted by pioneers, not public relations experts.

Why are we telling you this? Because only a company with a heritage this rich could have developed a camera like the Konica FS-1. And today's cameras are what count.

The Konica FS-1. If we didn't invent it, who would have?

Probably nobody.

Because in a world of cosmetic improvements, the Konica FS-1 is built upon wall-to-wall innovation.

To begin with, the Konica FS-1

Just drop film in...

...close the back, and you're loaded!

is the first 35mm SLR to solve the problem of film loading. Simply put in the film, close the back and the camera loads itself—then automatically advances the film to the first frame.

What does that? A built-in winder. The first ever in an SLR. No clunky option, this autowinder is factory installed inside the camera. And it's all controlled by state-of-the-art electronics.

And the fully automatic Konica FS-1 can be operated manually, if you prefer. Its shutter is metal—our competition uses

cloth. And its shutter priority system eliminates the perfectly exposed blur.

Of course, the Konica system of lenses and accessories means the FS-1 grows right along with you.

We're not looking back.

We're proud of the fact that we are 108 years old.

But we're more proud that today, scientific equipment manufactured by us is used by the official Japanese inspection agency to test the performance of lenses made by every other manufacturer—including Canon, Nikon, and Pentax. You see, being the oldest is something our great-great-grandfathers were responsible for.

But being the boldest—that's something we live up to every day.

For more information write: Konica Corporation, Woodside, N.Y. 11377. In Canada: General Photographic Products Ltd., Ontario.

Konica®
THE OLDEST AND THE BOLDEST

MOST BOOTS COPING WITH THE HAVE A HARD TIME REALITIES OF LIFE.

If life was filled with nothing but clear skies, 60° temperatures, and leisurely strolls through the park, most boots would be adequate.

But since that's not the case, we've built a pair of boots with a more realistic view of things.

TIMBERLAND® THE BOOTS THAT REALIZE EVERY DAY ISN'T GOING TO BE A SUNNY DAY.

Last year, the average snow and rainfall, by state, was 32.02 inches.

It's in weather like this that Timberland® boots really shine.

Our boots are made of silicone or oil-impregnated waterproof leathers.

To resist rust, we use only solid brass eyelets.

And because any needle hole is a potential water hole, we seal every seam with not just one coat of latex but two.

How dry will Timberland boots keep you?

Well, on a machine called a Maser Flex that tests waterproof leathers, Timberland leathers must withstand a minimum of 15,000 flexes, twice U.S. Military standards.

WE WON'T LEAVE YOU OUT IN THE COLD.
It's been estimated that on extremely cold days, you lose 80% of your body heat through the top of your head.

Yet, inevitably, your feet are always the first things to go.

To prevent the inevitable, Timberland boots are filled on both sides and the innersole with layers of Nitrogen filled closed cell insulation that'll keep your feet warm to temperatures well below zero.

Our boots aren't just better insulated than most boots, they're better insulated than most houses.

WE'RE NOT JUST FOUL-WEATHER FRIENDS.
Because on beautiful days, the advantages of Timberland boots are equally clear.

Their durability, for example. Thanks to little things like four rows of nylon stitching instead of cotton in all key stress points. And big things like a heavy-duty Vibram® sole permanently bonded to the uppers so it can withstand a tremendous amount of abuse without separating.

But there's a soft side to our boots as well.
It includes foam-padded leather collars, leather linings, and a unique 4-ply innersole construction. And results in boots so comfortable, they eliminate the painful breaking-in period other boots force you to suffer through.

But don't just take our word for it. Step into any store that carries Timberland boots and try on a pair.

They come in a variety of styles for both men and women. They start at about $60. And they'll put an end to your search for the perfect pair of boots.

Timberland ®
The Timberland Company, P.O. Box 370, Newmarket, New Hampshire 03857

163

HE CAN READ EVERY BOOK IN THIS ROOM.

Jeff Vogel is completely blind.

But that can't stop him from reading virtually any book printed in English. Not since the development of the Kurzweil Reading Machine.

It scans books, page by page, converting each word into spoken English.

So through a simple pair of headphones, the blind are reading things they never could before.

The Kurzweil Reading Machine is being used in libraries and reading rooms throughout the country. Helping blind people finish graduate school, further their careers in law and teaching, or simply enjoy the latest best seller.

Similar technology is also being used to help computers. By translating the printed word into their language, other Kurzweil machines help make computers more productive.

Of course, a person doesn't have to be blind to learn from the Kurzweil Reading Machine.

We learn from it every day.

It helps us see just how much the blind have to offer.

XEROX

164

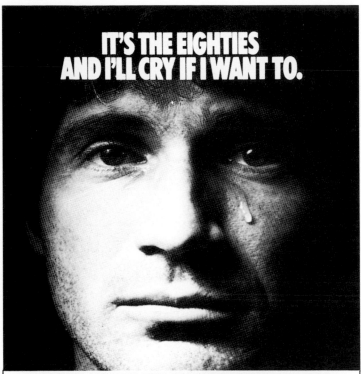

PERRYMAN, MARYLAND, 5:25 PM,
AS SEEN FROM AMTRAK'S TRAIN,
THE CRESCENT.
WHY NOT SEE AMERICA AT SEE LEVEL?

Amtrak ▸ AMERICA'S GETTING INTO TRAINING

169

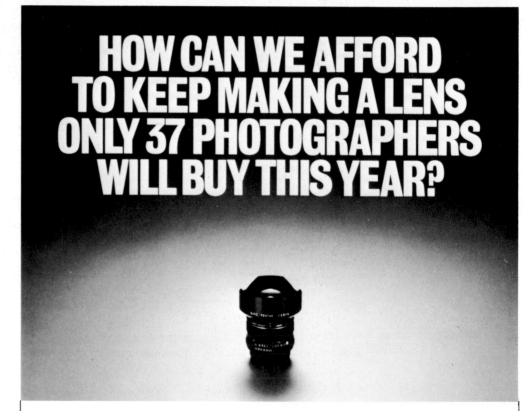

HOW CAN WE AFFORD TO KEEP MAKING A LENS ONLY 37 PHOTOGRAPHERS WILL BUY THIS YEAR?

The obvious answer is that we can't afford to stop making it if we want to keep calling ourselves a serious photographic company.

In an era where mass-produced, mass-market products are the rule, Pentax is a notable exception.

Not only do we continue to produce products that require lots of personal attention, but we're introducing new ones. Like the LX professional system camera.

When we make our lenses, for example, we coat every element seven times. It's called Pentax Super-Multi-Coating, and it's on our least expensive as well as our most expensive lenses. It's even on lens surfaces that are going to be cemented together. Because every surface is a potential source of flare.

We still make lens helicals out of brass and aluminum, because these two metals move freely against each other. So less lubrication is needed. (A lot of lubrication is not a sign of a well-made lens.)

In fact, there are a lot of shortcuts a company can take in lensmaking that can keep profits high and not degrade quality all that much. They can drop lenses that have a limited market. Or cut corners on materials. Or make lenses that don't meet acceptable quality standards, by trying to make them do too much.

Most photographers wouldn't notice if Pentax dropped its 15mm f/3.5 linear super-wide angle from the line tomorrow.

But Pentax is in business for the ones who would.

PENTAX®
© 1981 Pentax Corporation.

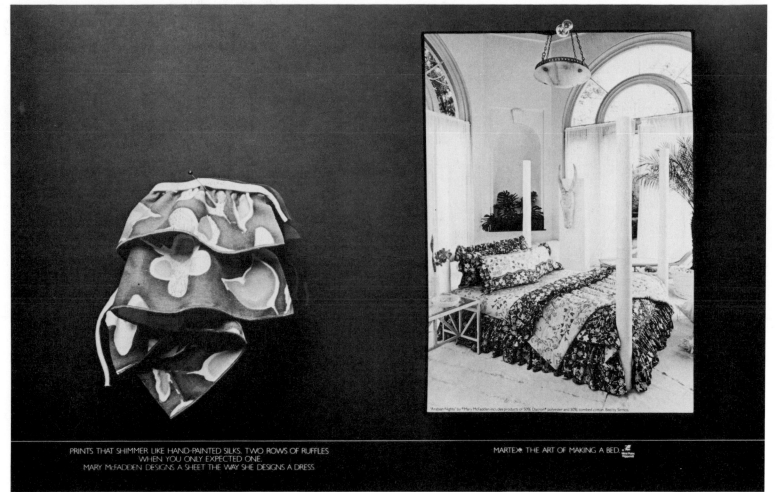
171

172

POINT ARGUELLO, CALIFORNIA, 4:35 PM
AS SEEN FROM AMTRAK'S TRAIN,
THE COAST STARLIGHT.

This time why not see America at see level?
AMERICA'S GETTING INTO TRAINING

173

DESIGNS YOU THOUGHT YOU COULD ONLY FIND IN SHEETS.
SOLIDS THAT ARE EVERYTHING BUT PLAIN.
AT MARTEX, WE MAKE AN ART OUT OF GETTING YOU DRY.

174

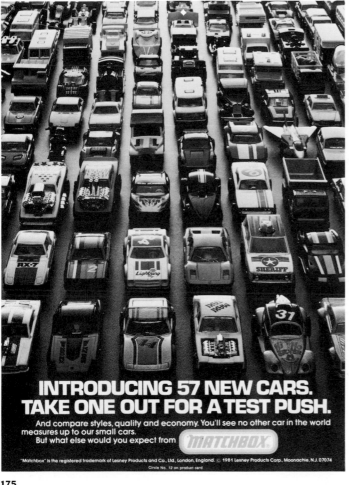

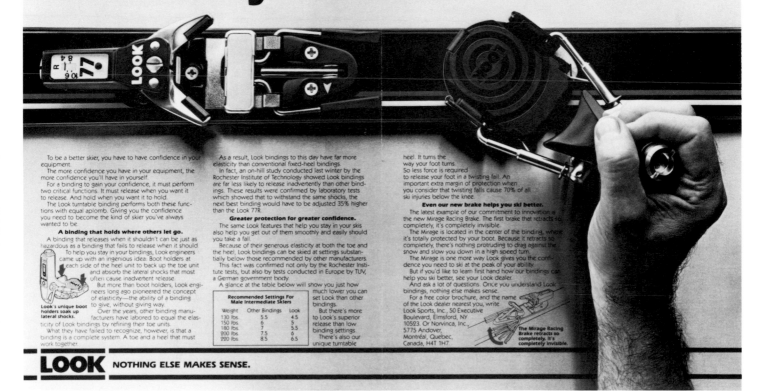

178
ART DIRECTORS
Richard Radke
Martin Lipsitt
WRITER
Ellen Azorin
DESIGNERS
Richard Radke
Martin Lipsitt
PHOTOGRAPHERS
Hunter Freeman
Joseph Standart
CLIENT
West Point Pepperell
AGENCY
Calet, Hirsch, Kurnit
& Spector

179 SILVER
ART DIRECTOR
Peter Hirsch
WRITER
Ken Majka
DESIGNER
Peter Hirsch
PHOTOGRAPHER
Phil Marco
CLIENT
King-Seeley Thermos
AGENCY
Calet, Hirsch, Kurnit
& Spector

180
ART DIRECTOR
Gary Shapiro
WRITER
Bernie Rosner
PHOTOGRAPHER
Terence Donovan
CLIENT
British Tourist Authority
AGENCY
Ogilvy & Mather

181
ART DIRECTORS
Richard Radke
Martin Lipsitt
WRITER
Ellen Azorin
DESIGNERS
Richard Radke
Martin Lipsitt
PHOTOGRAPHERS
Hunter Freeman
Joseph Standart
CLIENT
West Point Pepperell
AGENCY
Calet, Hirsch, Kurnit
& Spector

YES, OUR COLORS ARE UNUSUAL. BUT IT'S THE WAY WE PUT THEM
TOGETHER THAT REALLY SETS THEM APART.

MARTEX: THE ART OF MAKING A BED.

178

Our greatest achievement.

179 SILVER

"See the school where Shakespeare learned to write."

Ian Wollington, student, King Edward VI School

TWA Getaway® Vacations. Pound for pound, some of the best ways to see Britain.

These boys attend classes in the same Guildhall schoolroom where young William was educated some 400 years ago. In those days, Stratford was an important market town, and its grammar school was one of the best in England.

Stratford.
Today's Stratford is notable for its many 15th- and 16th-century buildings, romantic half-timbered houses, their dark oak beams framing whitewashed walls. In an easy walking tour of Stratford you can see Shakespeare's birthplace, Anne Hathaway's cottage, and Holy Trinity Church, where Shakespeare is buried. The bard lives on, in a Stratford little changed.

TWA Getaway Vacations.
But Stratford is only one stop on TWA's "Great Britain" Getaway Vacation, a fifteen-day escorted tour through England, Scotland, and Wales. Start in London with sightseeing that includes Buckingham Palace, Trafalgar and Parliament Squares, and Westminster Abbey. There's a reserved ticket to an evening of London theatre awaiting you as well.

Then north by luxury motor-coach to Cambridge and its hallowed university, and medieval York, its Roman fortress walls still standing. Travel up through Scotland's velvet green lowlands to Edinburgh, and over its misty Highlands to Inverness.

Then, down into the Lake District and on into rugged, mystical Wales. See Stratford, and the thatched-roof Cotswold cottages. Browse through ancient Bath, and wonder at inexplicable Stonehenge. Winchester Cathedral is the last stop before your London return. A grand adventure in history, for $1098 to $1168 per person, double occupancy, plus airfare.

Or a week of London theatre.
London's West End is the world's center of theatre. TWA's Getaway "London Theatre Week" lets you enjoy theatre by night, and sight-seeing by day. Choice tickets to three shows are included. Shopping discounts, dining discounts, and club memberships add to the value of this 9-day tour including tourist-class hotel with private bath and Continental breakfasts for only $279-$389 per person, double occupancy, plus airfare.

There are eleven vacations detailed in "TWA Getaway Britain"— yours free, along with a "Great Britain, Great Welcome" brochure. Send for both with the coupon below, then see your travel agent to learn about an affordable vacation through Britain's glorious past.

That's what makes Britain great.

British Tourist Authority
Box 3039, Grand Central Station
New York, N.Y. 10017

Send me your free brochures:
"TWA Getaway Britain," and
"Great Britain, Great Welcome."

Name _____
Address _____
City _____
State _____ Zip _____

180

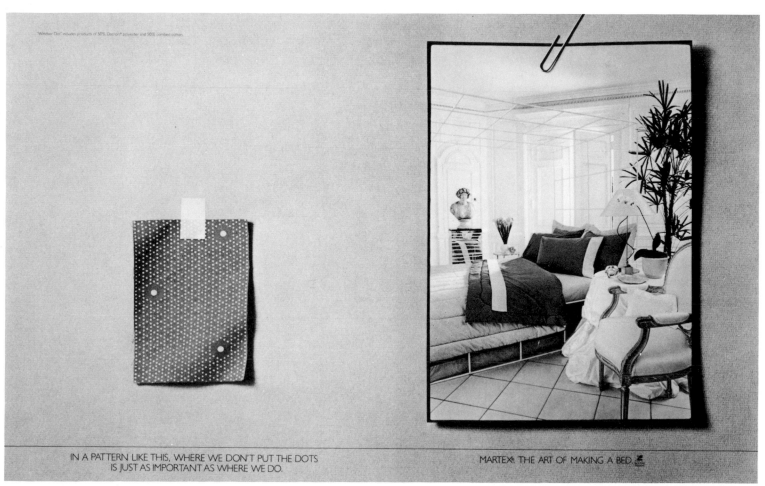

IN A PATTERN LIKE THIS, WHERE WE DON'T PUT THE DOTS IS JUST AS IMPORTANT AS WHERE WE DO.

MARTEX: THE ART OF MAKING A BED.

181

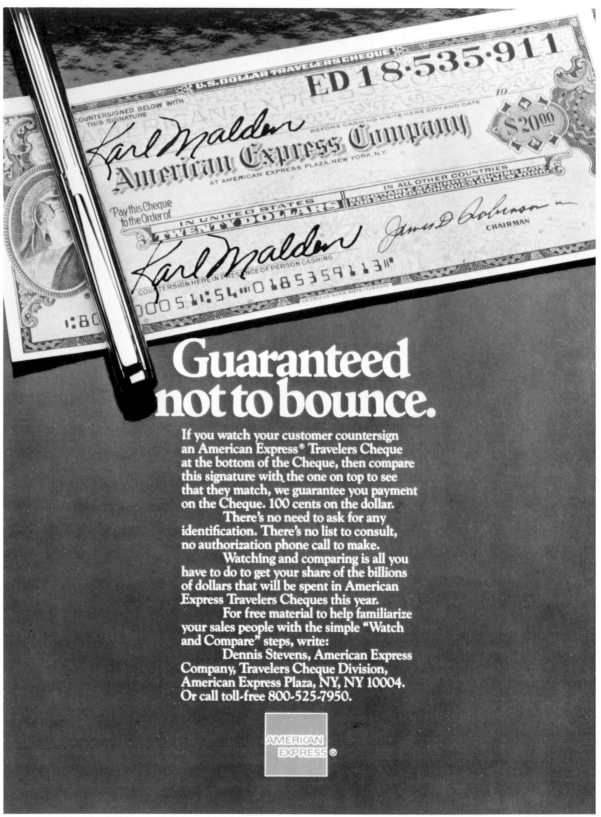

182

Sainsbury's are now selling their English grown Chinese Leaf. (Japanese variety, of course.)

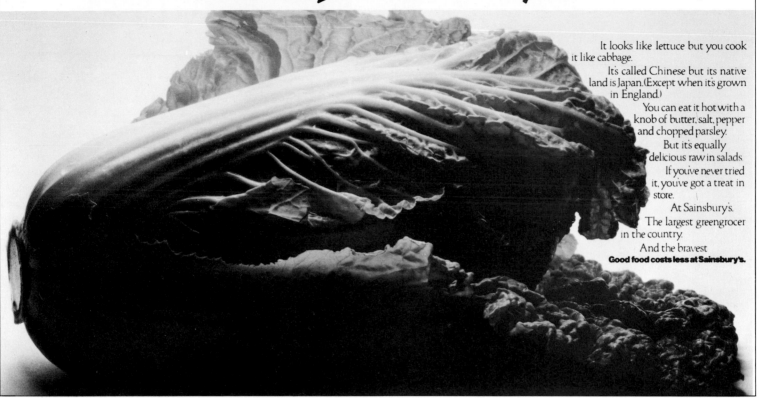

It looks like lettuce but you cook it like cabbage.

It's called Chinese but its native land is Japan. (Except when it's grown in England.)

You can eat it hot with a knob of butter, salt, pepper and chopped parsley.

But it's equally delicious raw in salads.

If you've never tried it, you've got a treat in store.

At Sainsbury's.

The largest greengrocer in the country.

And the bravest.

Good food costs less at Sainsbury's.

When something's brand new, it's best to wash it as gently as possible.

Johnson's® baby bath is gentle enough to bath even the newest babies.

Johnson & Johnson

WHEN YOU PLAY RACQUETBALL WITH 184 LITTLE SUCKERS, HOW CAN YOU LOSE?

We set out to build the top racquetball shoes on the market, so we started at the bottom: an innovative "suction cup" tread of durable rubber, designed for sure stops and quick starts. Then we used a Eurostripe pattern and stitching to give maximum support at the arch stress points for sure lateral movement. We topped the "Attack" with a speed lacing system for added stability, and gave the "Combat" a suede leather, full toe piece. Then covered them all in suede leather and mesh uppers for strength, comfort, and coolness on the court. "Attack" and "Combat," the premier racquetball shoes from PRO-Keds® Judge them by virtue of their design and performance, and you can't lose.

Combat Hi

Combat Lo

Men's Attack

Women's Attack

PRO-Keds®

185

Hello?
How's the Great American Novel going?

So far it reads more like the turgid insights of a lonely Albanian date-plucker.
Did I hear the word "lonely"?

There's a fog rolling in.
You're in Pawgansett, dear. It holds the world record for fog.

The "t" in my typewriter is sticking. I have seventeen cans of lentil soup. And my Paco Rabanne cologne, which I use to lure shy maidens out of the woods, is gone, all gone.
You're going to have to do better than that.

All right, I'm lonely. I miss you. I miss your cute little broken nose. I miss the sight of you in bed in the morning, all pink and pearly and surly.
And you want me to catch the train up.

Hurry! This thing they call love is about to burst the bounds of decency. And, darling...
Yes?

Bring a bottle of Paco Rabanne, would you? The maidens are getting restless.
Swine!

Paco Rabanne
A cologne for men
What is remembered is up to you

186 GOLD

At Sainsbury's if we don't sell our mince in a day, we don't sell it.

The best mince is fresh mince.

So all our ground beef and mince beef has a sell-by date of just one day.

What we don't sell in a day comes out of the cabinet as a fresh supply goes in.

Does this mean we waste a lot of mince?

On the contrary.

It seems when people know you sell good lean mince at good keen prices, they can't wait to buy it.

Not even for a day. **Good food costs less at Sainsbury's.**

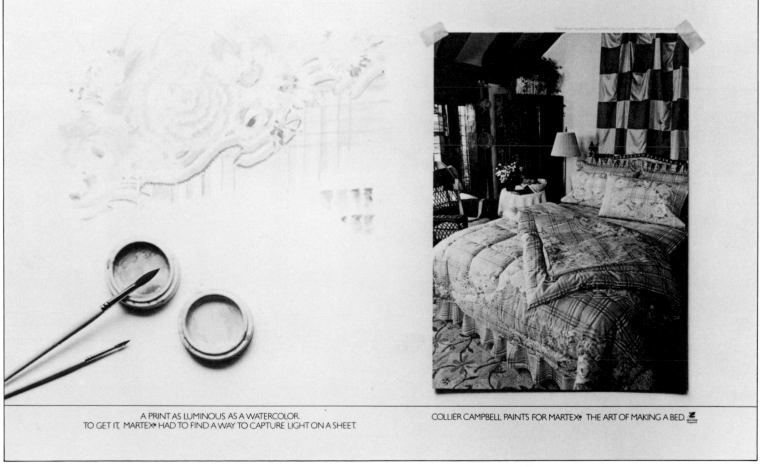

A PRINT AS LUMINOUS AS A WATERCOLOR.
TO GET IT, MARTEX® HAD TO FIND A WAY TO CAPTURE LIGHT ON A SHEET.

COLLIER CAMPBELL PAINTS FOR MARTEX® THE ART OF MAKING A BED.

189
ART DIRECTOR
Stuart Newman
WRITER
Lisa Dubose
DESIGNER
Stuart Newman
PHOTOGRAPHER
Jack Bankhead
CLIENT
Hartley's
AGENCY
Leo Burnett/London

190
ART DIRECTOR
Ron Brown
WRITER
David Abbott
DESIGNER
Ron Brown
PHOTOGRAPHER
Martin Thompson
CLIENT
J. Sainsbury
AGENCY
Abbott Mead Vickers/
SMS-London

191
ART DIRECTOR
Reggie Troncone
WRITER
Richard Gaetano Ferrelli
PHOTOGRAPHER
Hiro
CLIENT
U.S. Virgin Islands Div. of
Tourism
AGENCY
Greengage Associates

192
ART DIRECTOR
Ron Brown
WRITER
David Abbott
DESIGNER
Ron Brown
PHOTOGRAPHER
Martin Thompson
CLIENT
J. Sainsbury
AGENCY
Abbott Mead Vickers/
SMS-London

189

Can you tell which potato is badly bruised? Neither can Sainsbury's.

The potato on the top was the villain but you'd never have known just by looking.

It was harvested in frosty conditions and bruised beneath the skin where you can't see.

And what you can't see we can't see either.

So at Sainsbury's we've had to find another way round the problem.

It's called prevention.

We buy our potatoes direct from a select group of growers and we lay down very strict conditions.

No Sainsbury's potato should be handled in temperatures below 8° Centigrade.

And we don't simply take the growers' word for it.

We have four roving inspectors who make a habit of getting up early on cold mornings.

(If anyone's caught bending the rules he gets more than a frosty look.)

As the country's largest greengrocer we sell hundreds of tons of potatoes every day.

And whether you buy King Edwards, Maris Piper or Desiree (to name but three) you can be sure of one thing.

Their beauty will be more than skin deep.

Good food costs less at Sainsbury's.

190

The summer of 82°

82°F. That's the average mean temperature of summer in the United States Virgin Islands. With trade winds blowing almost without exception in an easterly direction. (Now that doesn't sound mean at all!)

In addition to beautiful weather, there's swimming, diving, sailing. Fishing, golfing, playing tennis. Sporting the day away. Then taking on the town at night. (You'll even have a chance to see our Mocko Jumbi—the "elevated spirit"–symbol of having a good time.)

This summer, with the prices in Europe just out of this world, but spending your vacation at home just out of the question–make it the American paradise. (The price at this time of year is just about as nice as you can get it!) See your travel agent.

United States Virgin Islands
St. Croix · St. John · St. Thomas

© 1981 United States Virgin Islands Division of Tourism, 1270 Avenue of the Americas, N.Y. N.Y. 10020.

191

A fickle fungus makes these wines remarkable. A fickle public keeps them reasonable.

In certain parts of Bordeaux the humid autumn weather encourages a particular kind of fungus to attack the grapes.

What might appear to be a catastrophe is in fact a blessing.

The fungus is called by the locals 'la pourriture noble' (the noble rot) and they watch its progress through the vineyard like anxious parents.

Anxious lest it should stop.

For the bizarre fact is the fungus causes a wonderful concentration of the grapes' juices that gives the wines of Sauternes and Barsac a unique rich texture and aroma.

Unfortunately, the fungus is fickle and doesn't attack all the grapes in the vineyard at the same time.

Some grapes may be ready for picking in September, others may not be graced with the noble rot until October or even November.

In a long fine autumn it can take as many as seven pickings to complete the harvest. In a severe autumn, the grapes can be ruined before the fungus does its work.

Small wonder that the production of these sweet Bordeaux wines is a hazardous and costly business.

Why then can you find Appellation Contrôlée wines from these regions sitting on Sainsbury's shelves for around £2 or £3 a bottle?

We'd like to claim it's because of our excellent buying powers – and that's largely true – but it's also due to the fickleness of public taste.

Many people still think it unsophisticated to enjoy a sweet wine.

Others don't quite know when to drink a Sauternes and consequently ignore it.

In the face of such prejudice the wines haven't yet been able to command the prices they deserve, but the picture is changing.

More and more wine experts are writing about these neglected wines.

Some recommend you drink your Sauternes with fruit – perhaps a fresh peach, strawberries or nectarine.

Others favour it accompanied by a biscuit or a bowl of nuts.

Many believe you should enjoy it on its own. All believe you should drink it chilled.

As for Sainsbury's we merely suggest you buy in a bottle or two while prices are still something of a bargain.

After all, with publicity such as this, the public could be fickle once more and cause quite a demand.

Good wine costs less at Sainsbury's.

192

Even with proper insulation, all walls are not created equal.

Fact is, brick has an equivalent "R" value of 41. Hence, a brick wall—insulated to the same "U" or "R" values as a wood frame wall—is a far better energy bargain.

That's because brick's mass doesn't react as quickly to winter's chill as insulated wood or aluminum siding. And that slow reaction softens the im-pact of cold temperatures on the interior. Which means greater comfort and lower heating bills.

Not only that, brick can store the sun's heat and radiate it inwardly at night.

No wonder brick is the preferred home exterior according to national surveys.

So if you're buying, building, or re-modeling, prescribe brick. It's been the leading cold remedy for ages.

9210 South 5200 West   West Jordan 561-1471 • 860 Wall Avenue   Ogden 394-7701 • 3037 South 300 West   Salt Lake City 487-9901 • 1155 East 350 North   St. George 673-9501

193

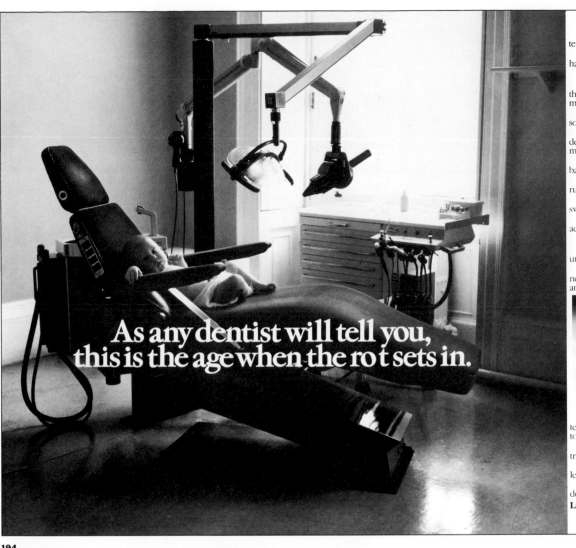

As any dentist will tell you, this is the age when the rot sets in.

The teeth of most of our children are in a terrible state.

By the time they enter school, half of them have had tooth decay. And who's to blame?

Sorry mothers, it's mothers.

The problem is, they simply don't realise that the damage can be done weeks, or even months, before a baby begins to cut teeth.

It happens when a baby starts on semi-solid food.

If it's unnecessarily sweet, the baby can develop a sweet tooth. And a sweet tooth now may mean bad teeth later.

So obviously the first food you give your baby is of vital importance.

If you've decided to start with a mashed-up rusk, then Liga is the one to choose.

The simple fact is, Liga rusks are far less sweet than most.

Indeed, the country's biggest-selling rusks actually contain 39% more sugar than Liga.

Sugar apart, Liga rusks lack very little.

They're made with natural ingredients to a unique formulation.

Many of the nutrients your growing baby needs are there. (Including extra calcium, iron and vitamins A and D.)

And when your baby does begin to cut teeth, you'll find they're the perfect teething rusk too: easy to hold and hard enough to gnaw on.

So when you buy your first packet of rusks, try to make sure they're Liga.

Your baby won't notice that they contain less sugar.

But in a few years' time, your dentist might. **Cow & Gate**

Liga. The rusk that won't encourage a sweet tooth.

Pick up a peaches and cream complexion where you pick up your peaches and cream.

J' Cleanser.

J' Moisturiser.

J' Foundation.

J' Eye Shadow

J' Nail Varnish.

J' Lipstick.

Sainsbury's announce their own exclusive beauty collection.

Its called 'J' Cosmetics and sparing the blushes of our beauty experts we think its a remarkable range.

First we look after your skin.

We started on the basis that a healthy skin is the basis of good looks.

So our beauty system begins with a collection of seven cleansers, toners and moisturisers.

As you'd expect, the formulae are of the highest quality.

Our 'J' Enriched Moisture Cream, for example, is rich in emollients, vitamin E and valuable wheat germ oil.

It helps give the skin a youthful freshness, smoothness and glow.

A process that's helped further by our creamy smooth foundations, powders and soft-toned blushers. (We're particularly

pleased with our 'J' All-In-One Foundation.

All three shades give a soft matt finish and the special oil-free formulation and sun-screen really protect the skin.)

Then we take care of your looks.

We haven't neglected your eyes, either.

Our mascaras are smudge proof, our eye pencils double ended (a kohl at one end, a fine liner at the other) and there's a glistening range of eye shadows.

For lips and nails we offer a selection of ten fashionable shades – some to match, some to tone in.

As for the colours themselves you really have to visit our stores to appreciate them.

But you can probably guess at one or two shades.

Having sold you peaches and cream were not likely to forget plum and apricot.

New 'J' Cosmetics. Exclusive to Sainsbury's.

**Consumer Magazine
Black and White
Campaign Including
Magazine Supplements**

196
ART DIRECTOR
Mark Nussbaum

WRITER
Charlie Breen

DESIGNER
Mark Nussbaum

PHOTOGRAPHERS
Beth Galton
Bettmann Archive

CLIENT
Miller Brewing

AGENCY
Backer & Spielvogel

197 SILVER
ART DIRECTORS
Jim Perretti
Anthony Angotti
Priscilla Croft
Neil Leinwohl

WRITERS
Tom Thomas
Neil Leinwohl
Debby Mattison

PHOTOGRAPHERS
Howard Menken
Joe Toto

CLIENT
Xerox

AGENCY
Needham, Harper & Steers

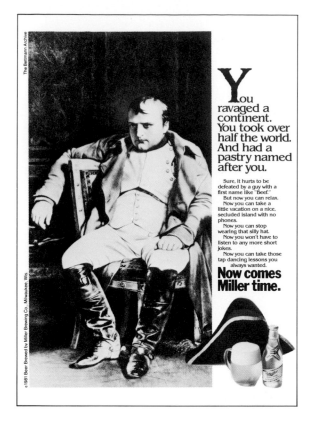

EVERY DAY THE AVERAGE BUSINESSMAN COMMUTES TO THE NINETEENTH CENTURY.

It wouldn't take very long for the average twentieth century businessman to feel right at home in the average nineteenth century office.

Because for the most part, the way office workers and executives work
and the tools they use are merely refinements of procedures
and products invented in the 1800s or before.

The typewriter was patented in 1827. The pencil with
an eraser attached was patented in 1858. The telephone was
invented in 1876 and the ball-point pen dates from 1888.

No wonder productivity in the office isn't keeping pace with the times.

At Xerox, helping people work more productively is our business.

Today we produce advanced machines that not only make copies of
incredible quality, but automatically reduce, collate and staple sets together.

Machines that create, store and retrieve documents faster than humanly
possible. Machines that print out computer information faster than ordinary
computer printers.

And machines that help business professionals, who earn
80% of the salaries paid by American business, create reports with
charts, tables and graphics, in hours instead of days.

There's even a special cable—called the Xerox Ethernet
cable—that can connect these machines into an information network. So that
the people in your office and in offices around the country can have
the information they need to get their jobs done.

In fact, Xerox people, machines and services can not only help
you stay on top of your job, but even get ahead of it.

Which can put you a century ahead of where you were
yesterday.

In this issue of The Best of Business, we'll be showing you some of the
specific ways Xerox can help businesses enhance productivity in the twentieth
century. We hope you'll find it both useful and interesting.

XEROX

ARE YOU TOO BUSY DOING YOUR JOB TO GET ANY WORK DONE?

Most jobs can be divided into two parts:
Meaningful work. And the time-
consuming chores that keep you from
getting to it.

This is one of those perennial problems
that business people have traditionally
chosen just to grin and bear.

But it's getting harder and harder to
grin—particularly when you consider all
the money wasted because people are increasingly busy and decreasingly productive.

At Xerox, we can help correct the
problem.

For example, we make
machines that can
help give you
finished reports
during the time you might otherwise spend
waiting. The machines are Xerox copiers,
and we've spent years making ones that not
only copy, but also collate, reduce and even
staple sets together automatically.

There are also Xerox machines that
create, edit, store and retrieve
information electronically.
Saving people hours of needless effort.

And Xerox machines
that take information right from computers,
then print it out using the typeface and
format you choose. All at two pages a second.

There's even a special cable—called the
Ethernet cable—that can link office
machines into a single network.
Organizing your information so
that it's always accessible, instead
of occasionally missing.

In other words, Xerox
machines help make you more productive
by doing the time-consuming chores you
shouldn't be doing.

Unlike you, our machines don't have
anything better to do.

XEROX

XEROX® and Ethernet are trademarks of XEROX CORPORATION.

MOZART HAS IMPROVED PRODUCTIVITY IN HEN HOUSES. NOW, WHAT CAN BE DONE FOR OFFICES?

It's been said that if you assemble an audience of chickens, sit them on nests
and have them listen to string quartets, productivity will increase.

This suggests many possibilities for poultry farms, but not
too many for offices.

Which is exactly our point. It's ironic that
so much effort has been expended helping
chickens become more productive, while
productivity for office workers and executives continues to decline.

At Xerox, helping people become more productive is our business. And
has been since the first Xerox copier revolutionized the way businesses
reproduce information.

Today we make machines that not only copy, but also
automatically collate, reduce, and even staple sets together.

Machines that let you create, store and retrieve documents
much faster than humanly possible.

Machines that print out computer information much
faster than ordinary computer printers.

And a special cable—called the Ethernet cable—that links office machines
into a single network. So that people throughout your office can have instant
access to the same information.

We even supply productivity experts to help your people make
the best possible use of it all.

In fact, Xerox people, machines and services can literally save
businesses millions of dollars in wasted time and effort.

That may not be Mozart. But in its own way, it can be just as
enriching.

XEROX

**Consumer Magazine
Black and White
Campaign Including
Magazine Supplements**

198
ART DIRECTOR
Lars Anderson
WRITER
Peter Levathes
DESIGNER
Lars Anderson
PHOTOGRAPHER
Steve Steigman
CLIENT
Maxell
AGENCY
Scali, McCabe, Sloves

WITH SOME TAPE YOU CAN'T TELL YOUR BRASS FROM YOUR OBOE.

When the oxide particles on recording tape aren't of a uniform size and shape, you can end up listening to distortion as well as music. The sounds of different instruments get blurred together, and your music loses its clarity.

At Maxell, every inch of our tape is checked and rechecked to make sure the oxide particles are perfectly uniform. Which means when you listen to music on Maxell tape, every instrument will sound perfectly clear.

So if you can't tell your brass from your oboe, try using our tape.

IT'S WORTH IT.

Maxell Corporation of America 60 Oxford Drive Moonachie N.J 07074

IF YOU'VE GOT THE WATTS, WE'VE GOT THE TAPE.

To get the most out of today's high performance stereos, you need a high performance tape.

Maybe that's why so many manufacturers of top-rated tape decks recommend Maxell. Our tape is designed to help good equipment live up to its specifications.

Unlike ordinary tape, Maxell can handle sudden bursts of power without any distortion. And it can deliver the extreme highs and lows that sometimes get left behind.

So if you'd like to get the most out of your sound system, try Maxell. But a word of caution. Always keep your seat belt securely fastened.

IT'S WORTH IT.

PORTABLE TAPE DECKS REQUIRE A MORE DURABLE TAPE.

You can take a portable cassette deck practically anywhere. But, take the average cassette tape out of its natural habitat, the living room, and you're asking for trouble.

Ordinary cassettes just aren't designed to stand up to life in the outside world. Even weather that's a little too hot or too cold can cause them to jam.

At Maxell, our cassettes are built to standards that are up to 60% higher than the industry calls for. They can withstand temperatures from subfreezing to subtropic. And they're tough enough to survive mishaps that would be fatal to a less durable cassette.

In fact, Maxell cassettes are so well made they'll even outlast your portable cassette deck. And that's not an idle promise.

We guarantee it.

maxell

IT'S WORTH IT.

A 4-piece suite for half the price of a 3-piece suite.

For the same money, you can buy a 1/2-piece lounge suite, or a beautiful, colourful 4-piece bathroom suite. £350.

Admittedly, a bathroom suite has to be plumbed in rather than just wheeled in.

But usually, the job can be done in 2 days for around £100.

Which still makes the bathroom far and away the cheapest room in the house to modernise.

And what a difference it would make.

The latest baths are curved and contoured to make them more comfortable to relax in.

And, would you believe, cheaper to run.

(They take less water to fill to a given depth.)

More innovations have been made in wash basins and loos too.

And let's not forget the 4th part of the suite.

The bidet.

In a few years time, you'll wonder how you ever managed without one.

You don't have to stop at 4 pieces, either. If you have a few extra square feet to play with, a separate shower should certainly fit into your plans.

There are all sorts of matching bathroom accessories too, from towel rails to toothbrush holders.

For brochures from all the leading manufacturers, and a list of local builders merchants and bathroom specialists, send the coupon.

And when you go to choose your new bathroom, look out for those products that bear the British Bathroom Council Seal of Approval.

It tells you they've been made to the highest standards of quality and workmanship.

If you don't believe us, try sawing a bath in half.

bbc
The British Bathroom Council

To: The British Bathroom
Council, P.O. Box 28,
Southwater, Near Horsham,
West Sussex.
Name
Address

DOES YOUR BATHROOM
MAKE YOU FEEL LIKE SINGING?

Could you live with a kitchen as old as your bathroom?

These days, you seldom see an old-fashioned kitchen.

Those antiquated cookers, fridges and sinks have long since been sent to the scrapheap.

(Which is where we found the one in the picture.)

But take a look at most people's bathrooms.

Some of them are so old, they'd look more at home in Steptoe's yard.

It's not as if a new bathroom is an extravagant luxury.

You can have a beautiful, colourful 3-piece suite for as little as £350, fully installed.

And usually, the job can be done in 2 days.

A new bathroom wouldn't just look better, it'd work better.

Modern baths are actually cheaper to run than old ones, because they're designed to take less water to fill to a given depth.

Loos have gone syphonic, to give you flush with hush.

And bidets, commonplace on the continent, are fast becoming standard equipment in British bathrooms.

It goes without saying that there are dozens of beautiful designs to choose from,

without affecting the flow.

Basins can be built into vanity units, making space for all those things that clutter up the bathroom.

The latest showers have independent controls, so that you can adjust the temperature and a range of colours that would have made Joseph's coat look positively drab.

For brochures from all the leading manufacturers and a list of local builders merchants and bathroom specialists, send the coupon.

And when you go to choose your new bathroom, look out for products that bear the British Bathroom Council Seal of Approval.

It tells you that they've been tested and approved for quality and workmanship.

To us, good old-fashioned reliability is one thing that'll never be out of date.

bbc
The British Bathroom Council

To: The British Bathroom
Council, P.O. Box 28,
Southwater, Near Horsham,
West Sussex.
Name
Address

DOES YOUR BATHROOM
MAKE YOU FEEL LIKE SINGING?

Are you afraid to go to the loo at night?

We're not talking about things that go bump in the night.

We're talking about cisterns that go KER-FLUSSSHHH!!! which means they need

In the wee small hours, it can sound like Niagara Falls.

It's about time you woke up to what's happening in bathrooms these days.

The latest loos are syphonic. They're so quiet, you've probably never heard of them.

Some even have concealed cisterns. So they're as easy on the eye as they are on the ear.

Many other innovations have been made in the bath and basin department too.

Modern baths are actually cheaper to run than old ones.

They're curved and contoured, which means they need less water to fill to a given depth.

Washbasins are cleverly designed to minimise splashing.

And they can be built into vanity units, to maximise space.

The question is, is your bank balance big enough?

The answer is probably yes.

You can have a beautiful, colourful 3-piece suite for as little as £350, fully installed.

And usually, the job can be done inside two days.

For those with slightly more accommodating bathrooms (and Bank Managers) we'd recommend a bidet, or a separate shower.

Not to mention some of the beautiful matching accessories available today.

To see all these things in their true colours, send the coupon.

In return, we'll send you the leading bathroom manufacturers' brochures, together with a list of local builders merchants and bathroom specialists.

And when you go to choose your new bathroom, look out for the British Bathroom Council Seal of Approval.

You'll find it attached only to those products tested and approved for quality and workmanship.

It's the kind of reassurance that helps you sleep at night.

bbc
The British Bathroom Council

To: The British Bathroom
Council, P.O. Box 28,
Southwater, Near. Horsham,
West Sussex.
Name
Address

DOES YOUR BATHROOM
MAKE YOU FEEL LIKE SINGING?

200 GOLD

**Consumer Magazine
Color Campaign
Including Magazine
Supplements**

201
ART DIRECTOR
Peter Harold
WRITER
Barry Smith
PHOTOGRAPHER
Geoff Senior
CLIENT
V.A.G. (U.K.) Ltd.
AGENCY
Doyle Dane Bernbach/London

202
ART DIRECTOR
Michael Winslow
WRITER
Harriet Frye
PHOTOGRAPHERS
Tim Olive
Phil Marco
Jay Maisel
CLIENT
North Carolina Dept. of
Commerce
AGENCY
McKinney Silver & Rockett/
North Carolina

WELCOME TO THE LAND OF MILK AND HONEY.

The long rows of jars on a roadside stand shine like soft, sweet gold in the morning sunlight.

Green pastures climb slowly through the mist to join the rising mountains.

The air is so fresh, you'd think somebody had washed it. The sound of a lone bird mingles with the sound of a stream.

Away to the East, the mountains flatten into hills, then into farmlands stretching out endlessly toward the island beaches of the Atlantic.

And everywhere the fields are rich with crops, the waters are rich with fish, and the air is rich with the smell of flowers.

And the land is rich in history. It is the land of colonists, of pioneers, of the Cherokee Nation.

North Carolina. It is a land of promises kept.

A land of plenty. A land civilization has touched, but never destroyed.

It is an abundant land, filled with good things.

And it is a land that reaches out and invites you to come and share.

NORTH CAROLINA

For more information, and the free North Carolina Travel Package, write North Carolina Travel Department 430, Raleigh, NC 27699.

COME TO A PLACE WHERE YOU CAN STILL FIND BURIED TREASURE.

Two centuries ago, the pirate Blackbeard roamed the North Carolina coast.

It was here he won his legendary treasures.

And it was here that, in the end, he lost his life.

The pirates and their gold have come and gone.

But the real treasures are still here for the taking.

The ocean, gold in the sunset, diamond-sparkled in the cool Atlantic dawn.

Gleaming shells in jewel colors, half-buried in pearl-white sand.

Bright rivers that wind like silver threads through the soft, rich tapestries of growing fields.

Tall sapphire peaks, set into emerald valleys.

The perfume of pines and azalea blossoms and fresh-turned earth.

In North Carolina, the treasures are everywhere. From the mountains, to the midlands, to the secluded cove where Blackbeard fought his last battle.

Some, like the shells, are the kind you can carry away in your hands.

But most of them are the kind you'll probably carry away in your mind.

For help in planning your vacation, just send us this coupon for the free North Carolina Travel Package.

Name

Address

City   State   Zip

NORTH CAROLINA

North Carolina Travel Department 430, Raleigh, NC 27699.
Plan to visit North Carolina during the 1982 World's Fair.

COME WATCH NORTH CAROLINA MAKE A SPECTACLE OF ITSELF.

When autumn comes to North Carolina, it puts on a show like P.T. Barnum never dreamed of.

Tall ridges roll away, as far as you can see.

The reds, greens and golds of a hundred kinds of trees fade into the soft blue of the distant haze.

But not all the color of autumn is in the leaves.

You find it at county fairs, where rows of purple beets and peach preserves compete for blue ribbons, and red ones, and yellow.

You see it in bright school banners over green playing fields. In age-old harvest celebrations and brand-new theme parks.

On beaches where even the shells are russet and purple and gold.

In the yellow slickers of fishermen casting for bluefish in the green surf.

In hang-gliders that stripe the autumn sky like shifting rainbows.

You can take it home in a handmade quilt. Or a jar of golden honey. Or just in photographs.

So come visit North Carolina, this year, when autumn does.

If you don't, you just may be missing out on the greatest show on earth.

NORTH CAROLINA

For more information, and the free North Carolina Travel Package, write North Carolina Travel Department 932, Raleigh, NC 27699.

**Consumer Magazine
Color Campaign
Including Magazine
Supplements**

203
ART DIRECTORS
Jerry Whitley
Clement McCarthy

WRITERS
Joe O'Neill
Martin Puris

DESIGNERS
Barbara Sharman
Barbara Bowman
Denise Monaco

PHOTOGRAPHER
Dick James

CLIENT
BMW of North America

AGENCY
Ammirati & Puris

204
ART DIRECTOR
Garry Horner

WRITER
Indra Sinha

DESIGNER
Garry Horner

ARTIST
Garden Studios

CLIENT
Metal Box

AGENCY
Ogilvy & Mather/London

NEVER HAS BEING FISCALLY RESPONSIBLE BEEN SO MUCH FUN.

THE PEOPLE WITH MONEY ARE STILL SPENDING IT. BUT WITH INFINITELY MORE WISDOM.

A LUXURY SEDAN THAT SATISFIES BOTH THE PEOPLE WHO KNOW MONEY AND THE PEOPLE WHO KNOW CARS.

There are more kinds of fruit in cans than most people think there are in orchards.

And they're canned on harvest day, fresh and juicy, saving their goodness for your family.

Uncan them, and hundreds of exciting fruit pies, flans, gateaux and other desserts are yours for the making.

Our free colour recipe book 'The Uncanny Knack' tells you how. Send for your copy from the address below. **Uncan a feast**

Order 'The Uncanny Knack' from The Canned Food Advisory Service, Tempo House, 15-27 Falcon Road, London SW11 2PL Or telephone 01-223 4768.

There are more kinds of fish and shellfish in cans than most people think there are in the sea.

And they're fresh and delicious, packed with nutritious protein and vitamins.

Uncan them, and hundreds of exciting soups, salads, mousses, risottos and other dishes are yours for the making.

Our free colour recipe book 'The Uncanny Knack' tells you how. Send for your copy from the address below. **Uncan a feast**

Order 'The Uncanny Knack' from The Canned Food Advisory Service, Tempo House, 15-27 Falcon Road, London SW11 2PL Or telephone 01-223 4768.

There are more kinds of vegetables in cans than most people think there are in the market.

And they're canned within hours of harvest, fresh and wholesome, saving their goodness for you.

Uncan them, and hundreds of delicious salads, stews, casseroles and side-dishes are yours for the making.

Our free colour recipe book 'The Uncanny Knack' tells you how. Send for your copy from the address below. **Uncan a feast**

Order 'The Uncanny Knack' from The Canned Food Advisory Service, Tempo House, 15-27 Falcon Road, London SW11 2PL Or telephone 01-223 4768.

RABBIT FLUNKS THE ISUZU TEST.

It takes a lot for a car to please the American buyer today. It takes even more to please an Isuzu inspector.

Isuzu inspectors reject any car that can't get an EPA estimated 27* miles per gallon of gas in the city, or more. Reject any car that isn't quick enough to go zero to sixty in 13 seconds, or less. And reject any car that can't measure up to more than 1680 stringent Isuzu quality standards.

It is this unwavering dedication to innovation, craftsmanship and performance that has led Isuzu to build a nearly perfect car. A car that can outperform the amazing Volkswagen Rabbit.

The five speed Isuzu gets better city gas mileage* than the five speed Volkswagen

Rabbit. The Isuzu has more horsepower than the Volkswagen Rabbit. And the Isuzu is constructed so well our anti-corrosion warranty is three times longer than that of the Volkswagen Rabbit.

Yet, remarkable though it may seem, an Isuzu I-MARK 4-door sedan is priced several hundred dollars less than a comparable Volkswagen Rabbit. What's more, an Isuzu is such a dependable car, we back it with a guarantee no Volkswagen dealer would make.

We guarantee you'll never have to pay for a tow on warranty repairs. Guarantee your dealer will be shipped almost any conceivable part in 48 hours or less (in the unlikely event your Isuzu ever breaks down). Even give you our hot line phone number in case you ever have a complaint or a problem.

The remarkable new Isuzu I-MARK. It beats the Rabbit by more than a hare.

ⅢISUZU
WE DIDN'T BRING IT TO AMERICA UNTIL IT WAS RIGHT.

T'was a man from Honolulu,
Who got a new Isuzu.
On a gallon of gas he could carry his lass,
Farther than his VW Beetle used to.

THE JAPANESE BEETLE.

Thirty-two years ago a homely, funny shaped car found a home in America.

A little car, that promised maximum efficiency, dependability and economy, at a truly economical price.

But over the years even Volkswagens change. To the point that the German Beetle has gone the way of the American Passenger Pigeon. Leaving American passengers to pay a lot more for a Volkswagen than they used to.

At Isuzu, we've been working for over 65 years with a single philosophy in mind. To build the toughest, most economical and dependable car any carmaker can build.

A practical car. That can deliver over 40* estimated MPG, over 50 MPG on the highway.

Yet go for under $6,800 in the showroom.**

Of course, driving a practical car like an Isuzu Diesel requires giving certain things up.

Like the necessity of paying for expensive tune-ups. Or the luxury of paying for what some car companies regard as options. (We think there's nothing optional about having front disc brakes or a diesel fuel/water separator.)

A car that's quick enough to be one of the fastest in its class, yet durable enough to last for years.

The Japanese Gas and Diesel Beetle from Isuzu.

Some people may consider its exterior a trifle plain. But then, an Isuzu has always had thick skin.

ⅢISUZU

Sainsbury's are now selling their English grown Chinese Leaf. (Japanese variety, of course.)

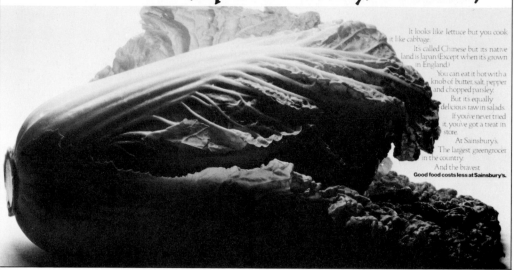

It looks like lettuce but you cook it like cabbage.

It's called Chinese but its native land is Japan. (Except when it's grown in England.)

You can eat it hot with a knob of butter, salt, pepper and chopped parsley.

But it's equally delicious raw in salads.

If you've never tried it, you've got a treat in store.

At Sainsbury's.

The largest greengrocer in the country.

And the bravest.

Good food costs less at Sainsbury's.

Eat the same pasta they eat on the Via Veneto. (Via Sainsbury's.)

No-one knows as much about pasta as the Italians.

There's evidence that it was a revered dish as early as 5000 BC and its popularity is certainly not on the wane.

Today, the average Italian eats 60lbs of pasta a year.

(In England, we manage only 2½ lbs each.)

Not unnaturally therefore, when we decided to start selling our own range of pasta we knew exactly where to go:

Italy.

We went, in fact, to Parma where the local pasta is as celebrated as the local ham.

And as you might expect, we demanded nothing but the best.

Sainsbury's pasta is made from durum wheat and no other.

(Softer wheats are cheaper but the pasta becomes floury and flavourless when cooked.)

We specified fresh eggs, never dried.

And in our tagliatelle verdi it's real spinach that gives the pasta its colour and flavour.

You'll find Sainsbury's new range of pasta in our larger stores right now.

And happily you'll also find the perfect wine to drink with it.

Sainsbury's chianti comes from the vineyards of Antinori near Florence.

Full bodied and in a traditional flask it has a pedigree as authentic as our pasta.

But that's a story for another advertisement...

Good food costs less at Sainsbury's.

Egg Tagliatelle.

Egg and Spinach Tagliatelle.

Tagliatelle Verdi.

Egg Vermicelli.

At Sainsbury's if we don't sell our mince in a day, we don't sell it.

The best mince is fresh mince.

So all our ground beef and mince beef has a sell-by date of just one day.

What we don't sell in a day comes out of the cabinet as a fresh supply goes in.

Does this mean we waste a lot of mince?

On the contrary.

It seems when people know you sell good lean mince at good keen prices, they can't wait to buy it.

Not even for a day. **Good food costs less at Sainsbury's.**

Consumer Magazine
Color Campaign
Including Magazine
Supplements

209
ART DIRECTOR
Jack Mariucci
WRITER
Patty Volk
PHOTOGRAPHER
Arthur Beck
CLIENT
Weight Watchers
AGENCY
Doyle Dane Bernbach

210 SILVER
ART DIRECTOR
Lars Anderson
WRITER
Rodney Underwood
DESIGNER
Lars Anderson
PHOTOGRAPHER
Jerry Friedman
CLIENT
U.S. Pioneer Electronics
AGENCY
Scali, McCabe, Sloves

ANNOUNCING THE TASTE YOU USED TO CHEAT FOR.

Bald, rubbery, hard-boiled eggs. Endless vistas of cottage cheese. The relentless boredom of carrots and celery.

Conventional diet food is enough to drive you *off* a diet. Happily, Weight Watchers 19 New Frozen Meals are good enough to drive

you on.

Like this Chicken Oriental in a snappy soy-spiked ginger sauce with crunchy Chinese vegetables.

Lean, juicy beefsteak smothered in a thick, brown gravy.

Lasagna dripping with spicy tomato sauce.

Yes, even *Sausage Pizza.* Now you can have them. Even if you're on a diet. So if you're really serious about dropping those extra pounds, our exciting new taste can help.

After all, how can you go off your diet, if the taste you want is on it?

WEIGHT WATCHERS® 19 NEW FROZEN MEALS. TRY IT. YOU'LL DIET.

AT LAST. DIET FOOD THAT'S GOOD ENOUGH TO EAT.

Parched, parsley-freckled fish. Endless vistas of cottage cheese. The relentless boredom of carrots and celery.

Conventional diet food is enough to drive you *off* a diet. Happily, Weight Watchers 19 New Frozen Meals are good enough to drive you on.

Like this turkey drenched in rich, velvety gravy seeping into a steamy mound of fragrant stuffing.

Lasagna dripping with spicy tomato sauce.

Lean, juicy beefsteak smothered in a thick brown gravy.

Authentic Chinese Food.

Yes, even *Sausage Pizza.* Now you can have them. Even if you're on a diet. So if you're really serious about dropping those extra pounds, our exciting new taste can help.

After all, how can you go off your diet, if the taste you want is on it?

WEIGHT WATCHERS® 19 NEW FROZEN MEALS. TRY IT. YOU'LL DIET.

THE NEW TASTE THAT DRIVES YOU ON A DIET.

Endless vistas of cottage cheese. Still life with radish.

The relentless boredom of carrots and celery.

Conventional diet food is enough to drive you *off* a diet. Happily, Weight Watchers 19 *New* Frozen Meals are good enough to drive you *on.*

Like this Lasagna dripping with spicy tomato sauce.

Rich, velvety gravy seeping into a mound of fragrant steamy turkey and stuffing.

Lean, juicy beefsteak smothered in a thick brown gravy.

Authentic Chinese food.

Yes, *even Sausage Pizza.* Now you can have them. Even if you're on a diet. So if you're really serious about dropping those extra pounds, our exciting new taste can help.

After all, how can you go off your diet, if the taste you want is on it?

WEIGHT WATCHERS® 19 NEW FROZEN MEALS. TRY IT. YOU'LL DIET.

WEIGHT WATCHERS IS THE REGISTERED TRADEMARK OF WEIGHT WATCHERS INTERNATIONAL, INC. © WEIGHT WATCHERS INTERNATIONAL, INC. 1981

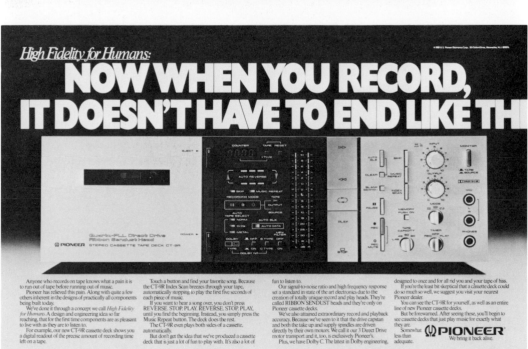

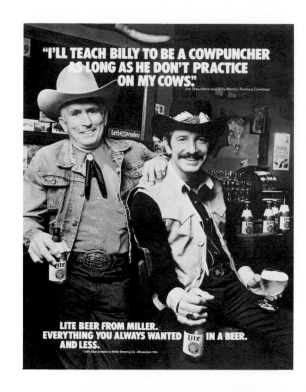

211

**Consumer Magazine
Color Campaign
Including Magazine
Supplements**

213
ART DIRECTOR
Reggie Troncone
WRITER
Richard Gaetano Ferrelli
PHOTOGRAPHER
Hiro
CLIENT
U.S. Virgin Islands Div. of
Tourism
AGENCY
Greengage Associates

214
ART DIRECTOR
Eric Hanson
WRITER
Bob Finley
DESIGNER
Eric Hanson
PHOTOGRAPHER
Alan Dolgins
CLIENT
Entex Industries
AGENCY
Sachs, Finley/Los Angeles

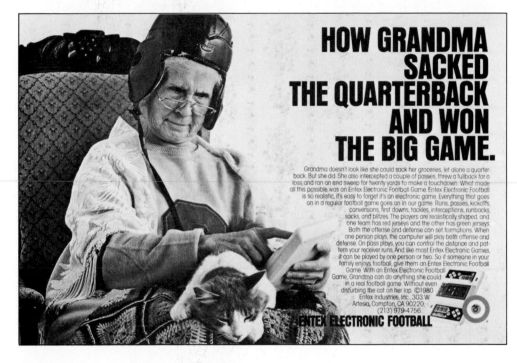

"*You never bought me Chivas Regal.*"

Chivas Regal • 12 Years Old Worldwide • Blended Scotch Whisky • 86 Proof. General Wine & Spirits Co., N.Y.

Running this red light can really get you in trouble.

When your oil light flashes on while you're driving, you don't have enough oil pressure. And running an engine this way can destroy it in minutes! For the life of your car, read this information now, then keep this page in your glove compartment.

1 What to do immediately.

Get safely and quickly off the road. Turn your engine off and put on your flashers. Now you're ready to find out if your oil supply is low or if you have bigger trouble.

2 How to check your oil.

Wait 3 to 4 minutes to let your engine cool. Locate the dipstick (consult your owner's manual), pull it out and wipe it clean. Then reinsert it as far as it will go and pull it back out. Your dipstick will be marked "add" and "full." Add oil if it is below the "add" mark and don't fill it above the "full" mark.

3 How to add oil.

Locate the oil fill tube on top of the engine. Remove the cap and wipe the area clean. Pour in the oil and allow several minutes for it to drain all the way down. Then check the oil level again.

4 Now should you drive your car?

If the oil level is normal, and the oil light goes off when you restart your car, drive to a service station and have the mechanic check for leaks. If the oil light remains on, don't drive. You may have a serious mechanical problem. Get your car checked by a licensed mechanic before it's driven.

5 How Gulf can help.

Our years of experience can help make driving better and safer for you. One example of our quality products is our line of fine Gulfpride motor oils. Should you have any questions about car care or driving safety, please write: Gulf Consumer Services Division, Post Office Box 1563, Houston, Texas 77001.

Gulf

Drive with experience.

© Gulf Oil Corporation 1981

TEAR THIS OUT AND KEEP IT IN YOUR GLOVE COMPARTMENT.

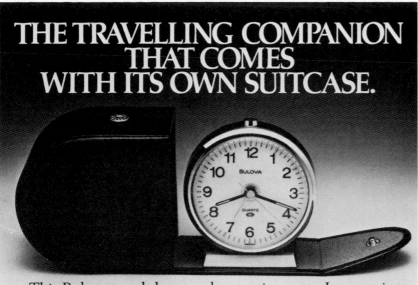

*"It's eleven o'clock.
Do you know where your Chivas Regal is?"*

Chivas Regal • 12 Years Old Worldwide • Blended Scotch Whisky • 86 Proof. General Wine & Spirits Co., N.Y.

How to have a flat tire and get away with it.

What to do if you have a blowout.
If a blowout happens while you're driving, let up on the accelerator, keeping a firm grip on the steering wheel. Brake only after your car has slowed down and is under control. Then put your flashers on and find a level place with at least six feet of clearance between you and the road. Stop.

Basic steps to changing a tire.

1 Put your car in "park" or in gear and put your emergency brake on. It's a good idea to "block" the wheels to keep the car from rolling.

2 With a screwdriver or the tapered end of a lug wrench, pry off the wheel cover.

3 With the lug wrench, loosen each lug nut one turn.

4 Now take your spare tire out. With the jack on solid ground, jack up the car so that the tire is at least two or three inches off the ground. Then remove the lug nuts and pull off the flat tire.

5 Put the spare tire on, tighten each lug nut, then jack the car down until the tire just touches the ground.

6 Go back and tighten each nut as tightly as possible, crosswise rather than clockwise, as shown.

7 Finish lowering your car and pack up your gear. And be sure to get your flat fixed as soon as you can. Remember, today's flat tire is tomorrow's spare tire.

How Gulf can help.
One way to avoid a potential mishap is to have the best-quality tires to begin with. Our 45,000-mile steel-belted Cruisemaster radial tire is one example of the high-quality automotive products you can be sure of from Gulf. If you have any questions about car care or driving safety, write: Gulf Consumer Services Division, Post Office Box 1563, Houston, Texas 77001.

Gulf

Drive with experience.

© Gulf Oil Corporation 1981

TEAR THIS OUT AND KEEP IT IN YOUR GLOVE COMPARTMENT.

222

Tell'em what a wonderful day you had at the beach. Call home.

Go ahead, rub it in. After all, how could you possibly forget the real reason you're vacationing in Florida this time of year in the first place?

General Telephone **GTE**

223

*"Just once I'd like to see some
Chivas in this thing."*

Chivas Regal • 12 Years Old Worldwide • Blended Scotch Whisky • 86 Proof. General Wine & Spirits Co., N.Y.

*"It's eleven o'clock.
Do you know where your Chivas Regal is?"*

Chivas Regal • 12 Years Old Worldwide • Blended Scotch Whisky • 86 Proof. General Wine & Spirits Co., N.Y.

"You never bought me Chivas Regal."

Chivas Regal • 12 Years Old Worldwide • Blended Scotch Whisky • 86 Proof. General Wine & Spirits Co., N.Y.

A million miles away on ½ tank of gas.

Forget passports and plane reservations.
Another world is just two hours away.

Palm Springs

Convention and Visitors Bureau, Palm Springs, California 92262

2 hours to splashdown.

To recreation, relaxation. To a world apart
that will put you back together.

Palm Springs

Convention and Visitors Bureau, Palm Springs, California 92262

THE ONE-TANK VACATION.

To Palm Springs.   **And back.**

Forget faraway places. One of the world's great
resorts is just over the horizon.

Palm Springs

Convention and Visitors Bureau, Palm Springs, California 92262

228

229

PEOPLE WHO BUY MAXELL TAPE BUY TWICE AS MANY RECORDS AS PEOPLE WHO DON'T.

According to research, not only do people who buy Maxell audio tape buy over 40% more cassettes in a year than the average cassette buyer, but they also purchase almost twice as many records as the average record buyer.

After all, people who are willing to pay more for an exceptional tape like Maxell must love good music. And can afford to buy the albums they really want.

So if you're wondering how you can boost record sales, maybe you should stock up on the tape that sells in record-breaking numbers. Maxell.

IT'S WORTH IT.

FEW THINGS REPRODUCE AS FAST.

The speed of the Toshiba BD-7501 is hard to duplicate.

The first copy appears clean, crisp and dry within 5 seconds of pressing the print button. It continues to create copies at the incredible rate of one every 2.4 seconds. Or, 25 in a minute flat.

Which means your customers can get a lot more done in a lot less time.

But haste doesn't mean waste. The BD-7501 is microprocessor controlled. So most important functions are carried out automatically.

Toner supply is maintained and adjusted to assure copy quality.

A toner-recycling system helps lower per-copy costs. Dual cassettes supply a 600-sheet paper capacity. Indicator lights tell when to replenish paper or toner. It even has a stationary exposure platen. And the deluxe BD-7511 model has all these features plus reduction capability.

Yet, with all it has going for it, the BD-7501 comes with a price tag most small offices can afford.

The Toshiba BD-7501 plain-paper copier. It's as quick as a rabbit. And that can mean a lot of lettuce for you.

Please rush me more information about the speedy Toshiba BD-7500 series copiers.

Name_____
Title_____
Company Name_____
Address_____ Zip____
Area Code/Phone_____

If you want your information even faster, call your Toshiba regional manager. East — Dirk Dowling (201) 628-8000. Midwest — Bill Tschannen (312) 964-5190. West — Dale Maier (415) 692-1360.

TOSHIBA

Toshiba America, Inc. 82 Totowa Rd., Wayne, NJ 07470

How to make fast dough.

In 1973, Mr. Coffee introduced a unique, patented process for making a better cup of coffee.

As soon as word reached the public, Mr. Coffee sales began a meteoric ascent and shot off the charts.

And those retailers who had spotted the Mr. Coffee trend and had stocked plenty of Mr. Coffee inventory enjoyed profits that shot off the charts as well.

Now from the same people who invented and made Mr. Coffee a landmark marketing success comes another unique, money-making new product: Mr. Pasta.

Mr. Pasta is an electric pasta machine that makes 1½ pounds of fresh, delicious pasta in just 6½ minutes. Simply. Quickly. And without mess.

Mr. Pasta lets you capitalize on the emerging trend toward Italian food, and toward fresh pasta in particular.

And because it comes from people who know your business, it's backed by all the support necessary to provide you with profitable growth.

Quality. Service. Packaging. And promotional support that includes a substantial commitment to network and spot television.

So if you want to make fast dough, get the machine that more and more of your customers will be using to make fast dough.

Mr. Pasta
Fresh, delicious pasta. Incredibly fast.

NORTH AMERICAN SYSTEMS INC. 24700 Miles Road, Bedford Heights, Ohio 44146. (216) 464-4000

233

234

O e thi g
our pri t wheels
wo 't do.

They wo 't break, like this o e did. Because the entire wheel is reinforced. With metal.

Which means characters won't snap off, and typewriters won't edit people without their consent.

That's guaranteed for a full year.

Now, this is what our print wheels will do. They'll print in 21 different typefaces. And in different type sizes.

They'll print signs and symbols, such as π and ¶.

Best of all, each wheel can be custom-made.

At Xerox, we offer a wide variety of supplies that help prevent communications breakdowns. Everything from magnetic cassettes to Telecopier supplies to data storage systems.

So before you send for any more Information Processing or Telecopier supplies, send in the coupon. Or call

1-800-527-1868*

After all, which would you rather supply your office with:
The thi gs it eeds?
Or the things it needs?

I'd like more information on the complete line of Xerox Office Supplies.

Send to: Xerox Corporation, P.O. Box 470065, Dallas, Texas 75247.

Name _____
Title _____
Company_____
Address_____
City_____State_____Zip_____
Phone_____

XEROX

*In Texas, Alaska and Hawaii, call collect 1-214-630-6145.

XEROX® and TELECOPIER® are trademarks of XEROX CORPORATION.

235 GOLD

TAKE YOUR BUSINESS ELSEWHERE.

Like Amsterdam, Athens, Barcelona, Beirut, Brussels, Copenhagen, Düsseldorf, Geneva, London, Madrid, Milan, Paris and Tokyo.

HBM can help you get there. That's because we're now a partner agency of Interpartners Communications S.A., a major international advertising corporation. Which gives HBM worldwide marketing capabilities. And gives you access to millions of consumers overseas.

Now you can coordinate an advertising campaign anywhere in the world. From one source. From One Beacon Street.

For example, we can get your message across in Greece. In Greek.

And our Greek affiliate, Lamda Alpha, will see that it doesn't lose anything in the translation.

In plain English, that means that HBM clients can now expect more than the hard-working, award-winning advertising which has made us Boston's top agency.

Our clients can expect the world of us.

Humphrey Browning MacDougall

236

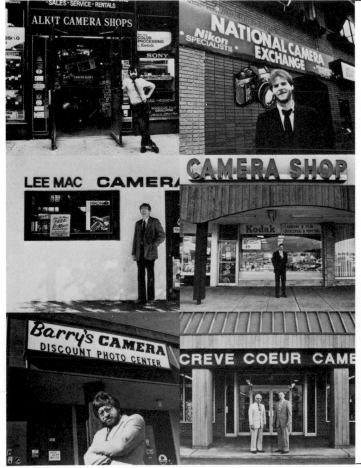

Some of photography's greatest names don't take pictures. But they do something just as important: they sell the cameras that take them. Their names can be seen at shopping centers, downtown malls, along highways—you name it.

A lot of these names have one name in common. Nikon. It's a big responsibility, but we welcome it. We also realize that when you carry a Nikon product it isn't just our reputation on the line, but yours as well. So we stand behind you.

We stand behind you with flexible purchase plans designed to help you plan your inventory months ahead without losing big discounts.

We stand behind you with a co-op program that cuts reimbursement time to the minimum.

We stand behind you with Nikon Dealer Focus Groups that give dealers like yourself a chance to express your needs and problems.

We stand behind you with immediate responsiveness to marketplace problems to protect your inventory.

And we stand behind you with a commitment to make the best product possible for each important segment of your market.

Because when a customer asks to see a Nikon product, we know you stand behind us.

Nikon
We take the world's greatest pictures.™

Nikon isn't
the only name
we stand
behind.

237

238

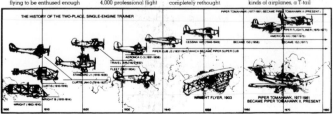

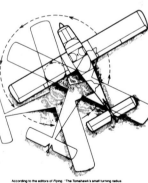

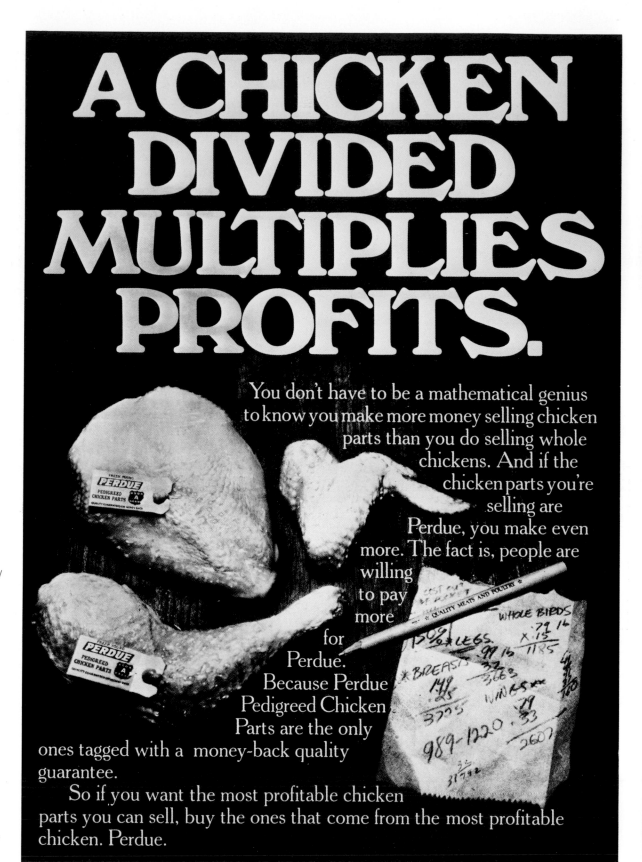

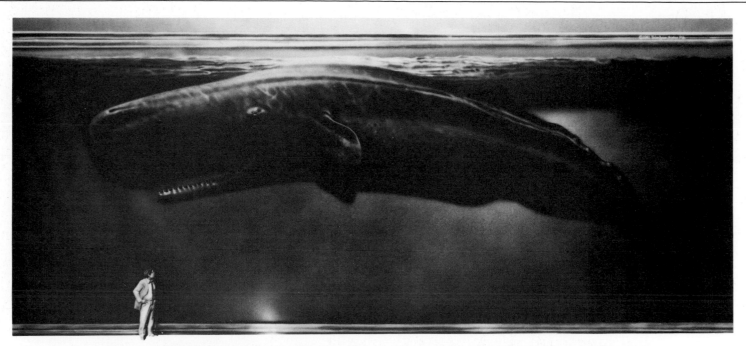

By installing The Shower Massage in your hotel you can save enough water each year to fill a large fish bowl.

374,000 gallons is a lot of water. Even to a whale.

That's how much water you can save each year with The Shower Massage by Water Pik.

Not to mention money.

Just imagine how much energy it would take to heat all that water.

Since The Shower Massage only uses about half as much water as

an ordinary showerhead, a typical hotel of 70 rooms* can save 1,025 gallons of water daily.

Within several months, in most cases, The Shower Massages will have paid for themselves. Best of all, you don't have to spend a lot in the beginning to save

a lot in the end. The Shower Massage is surprisingly low-priced.

Your guests will overflow with praise.

Your guests will actually enjoy greater luxury now that they're saving water than they did when

they were wasting it. There's just no substitute for the soothing yet invigorating massage that made The Shower Massage famous.

It's so popular you'll be glad we made it theft-resistant.

Some people like The Shower Massage so much they'll be tempted to take it with them when

they leave.

Which is why we built in unique theft-resistant features. Your maintenance people will like it too; it's durable and easy to clean.

If you want to save

water and energy and money, why not install The Shower Massage in your hotel?

If your guests aren't taking showers with The Shower Massage, you're taking a bath.

THE SHOWER MASSAGE
by Water Pik

Call today (800) 525-5302 for fast service or write: Teledyne Water Pik, 1730 E. Prospect St., Ft. Collins, CO 80525.

*Average 71% occupancy rate, projecting 1.5 showers per occupied room per day

244

Hollywood weather without Hollywood overhead.

You know it's going to happen again this year.

You're going to have to produce a storyboard that says you have to shoot in California. On a budget that says you can't.

Fortunately, there is a way to do it.

It's called Florida.

Florida gives you even more and longer days of good shooting light than California.

You pay less to get to Florida's weather. And considerably less to shoot in it.

Less to directors and produc-

tion houses that have won their share of Clios, Art Directors Club and One Show Awards, and Andys.

You don't pay a premium for the nation's third-largest pool of acting talent (which includes many New York actors who hate shooting in New York weather as much as you do). Or for professional crews. Or for all kinds of locations, from jungles to seashores to plains to deserts to cities to New England village greens—just about everything except snow-capped mountains.

And you don't waste time and

money coping with hassles and red tape, because those are about the only things we don't have here.

Call us for all the help you need, as fast as you need it, in planning your next shoot.

You'll bring back Hollywood footage and a Hollywood tan. On a Florida budget.

Ben Harris, Motion Picture and Television Bureau, Suite AW4-5, Collins Building, Tallahassee, Florida 32301.

(904) 487-1100

245

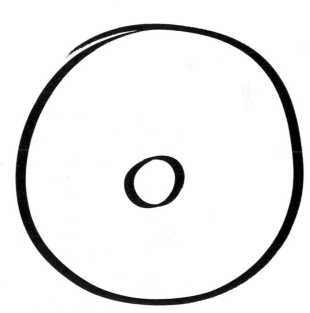

Inside the breast. Without x-rays.

Because breast cancer strikes one woman in eleven, anything that can help in its early detection is important news.

That's why the March issue of Discover, on your newsstand now, has the story of diaphanography.

This controversial technique, developed in Sweden, uses ordinary light instead of x-rays to look for abnormalities inside the breast.

Some doctors say it gives an even clearer view into the denser tissue of young women than x-rays. And of course, repeated use poses no danger from radiation. However, medicine is still debating the reliability of the technique.

© 1981 Time Inc.

Diaphanography. It's one more instance of how the news of science affects every aspect of our lives. People have come to realize that understanding science is a basic need.

It was to meet this need that Time Incorporated launched Discover last fall. Now, six issues later, Discover is firmly established as the newsmagazine of science. The only one.

Reader and advertiser acceptance of Discover has been so enthusiastic that we've been able to increase our circulation rate base 50%, from 400,000 to 600,000.

And since we began publication, we've sold more advertising pages and generated

more revenue than any of the new science magazines.

Discover is the leader in science news, news told in language non-scientists can understand and enjoy. For advertisers, it's a rare opportunity to catch the crest of a new wave of interest that is sweeping America.

Surround your advertising message with science, the great adventure.

DISCOVER
The newsmagazine of science from Time Inc.

246

247
ART DIRECTOR
Cathie Campbell
WRITER
Anders Rich
PHOTOGRAPHER
Dennis Chalkin
CLIENT
Maxell
AGENCY
Scali, McCabe, Sloves

248
ART DIRECTOR
Sal DeVito
WRITER
Norman Muchnick
DESIGNER
Sal DeVito
PHOTOGRAPHER
Martin Toranally
CLIENT
Savin
AGENCY
Wells, Rich, Greene

249
ART DIRECTOR
Bill Snitzer
WRITER
Bob Finley
DESIGNER
Bill Snitzer
PHOTOGRAPHER
Lamb & Hall
CLIENT
Tomy Toys
AGENCY
Sachs, Finley/Los Angeles

250
ART DIRECTOR
Priscilla Croft
WRITER
Debby Mattison
PHOTOGRAPHER
Steve Steigman
CLIENT
Xerox
AGENCY
Needham, Harper & Steers

247

248

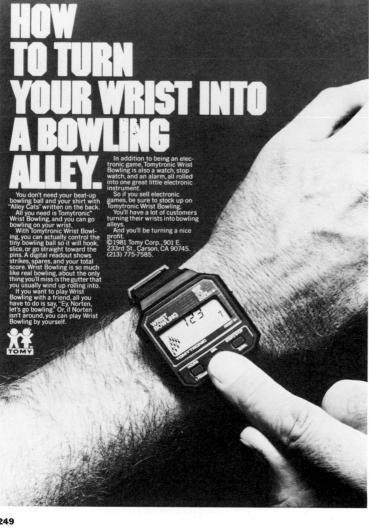

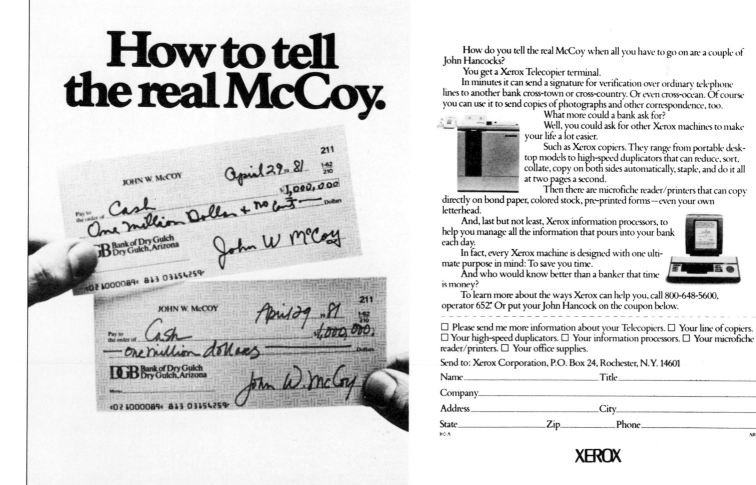

Introducing three new lamps from Sylvania.

Our new lamp is aptly called the SuperSaver™ III. You see, it's really three-lamps-in-one.

First, it's an energy-saving lamp that saves up to 15% more energy than standard 40-watt fluorescent lamps.

Second, it's an excellent color lamp that has a color-rendering index superior to both standard Cool White lamps and conventional Lite White energy-saving lamps.

And third, it's a high light level lamp that uses a unique Lite White Deluxe phosphor system that produces a light output unsurpassed by other energy-saving fluorescent lamps.

So your customers can use the same SuperSaver III to enhance retailing displays as well as cut energy costs in general lighting applications.

And SuperSaver III lamps can save up to $15.75 in energy over the life of the lamp (based on 5¢ per KWH). So if you multiply those savings by the number of lamps required, the bottom line will shine like never before.

For more information see your Sylvania Lamp Representative, or write or call GTE Products Corp., Sylvania Lighting Center, Danvers, MA 01923 (617) 777-1900 ext. 2650.

SYLVANIA Industrial/Commercial Lighting GTE

251

Why Abert, Newhoff & Burr turned to God.

When we started working with Brentwood Savings, we had one job: Make them look as big as the biggest.

We went right to the top.

After George hit TV, radio and newspaper, an independent research study reported name recognition up 400%.

New accounts opened: 10,000. 24% said George sent them.

Awareness is next to godliness.

Abert, Newhoff & Burr, Inc. In Century City, call Tom Burr, (213) 552-2217. In Newport Beach, call Bud Barnes, (714) 640-4894.

Abert, Newhoff & Burr

252

BLAME JACK KLUGMAN
BLAME LORETTA SWIT
BLAME JUDD HIRSCH
BLAME DICK TRACY
BLAME THAT GUY IN SOHO WITH 15 PEACH
BLAME FRANCE (if it'll help)

"Apparently the poor man's run out of Yoplait Yogurt."

We know there isn't enough Yoplait on your grocery store shelves. So tell your grocer you're "frustrated." He'll stock more. In fact, he's probably doing that right now. After all, who knew we'd sell out? 2,000,000 cups in the first month.

Who understands the mystery of why such phenomena occur? Was it seeing all those real Americans like Jack Klugman getting a little taste of French culture? Or just New Yorkers'

insatiable curiosity for anything new and incredible?

Anyway, you bought more Yoplait than our most optimistic minds estimated you would. Even though we knew that Yoplait is the yogurt of France. That it's creamy & smooth & different & all natural yogurt with active cultures from France & has real fruit throughout & so on & so on. Still, we did something no one should ever do. We underestimated N.Y.

✳ Yoplait. Yogurt
Get a little taste of French culture.

NOW MADE IN AMERICA. Yoplait, flower design, and container shape are trademarks of SODIMA, Paris, France. © Yoplait USA, Inc. 1981.

254

255

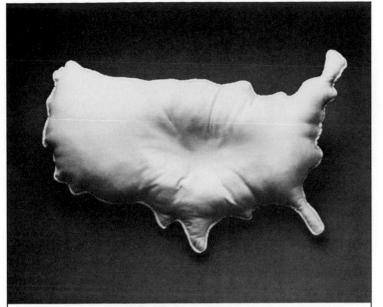

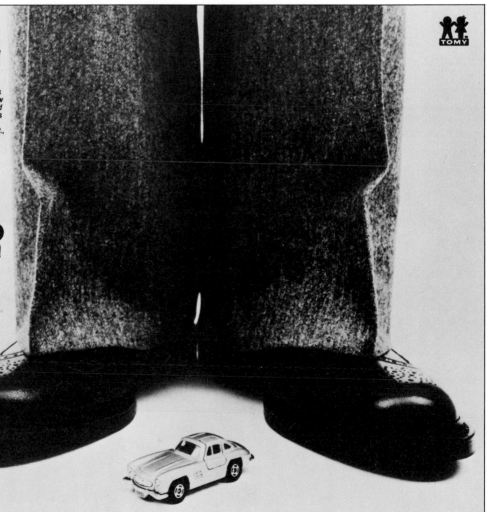

The egg came first.

We've just collected a couple of awards from the Institute of Sales Promotion.

They voted the commercial for our paint set offer the best promotional TV ad. Then they gave us another prize for our egg-recipe competition.

Picking up awards does wonders for the ego of course (our staff had a right old hen-party when they heard the news) but picking up sales is something else. Here again, with your help,

we won hands-down. During both promotions our production dept. were hard-pushed laying on all the extra stock needed.

We've warned them that an even greater effort will be required this year. To make sure we stay brand-leader we've upped our promotional budget to over £750,000.

A fact, no doubt, that will cause a few ruffled feathers among the competition.

Goldenlay
The taste of the country.

GOLDENLAY EGGS (U.K.) LIMITED, CARLTON HOUSE, SANDY WALK, WAKEFIELD. TEL. WAKEFIELD 78141.

259

"And that, son? That's the Big Zipper."

260

261

FREEZE FRAME ON ORDINARY VCR SYSTEMS*   FREEZE FRAME ON TOSHIBA'S FOUR-HEAD BETA SYSTEM*

Toshiba freezes without snow.

On an average VCR, you simply can't see a still or slow-motion picture without the usual avalanche of electronic noise.

But thanks to Toshiba's new portable V-9035 Betaformat VCR, the blizzard of interference has been lifted.

The V-9035 has four video heads instead of the usual two. These two extra heads have a single function: to trace the recorded tracks in still and slow motion.

No other VCR has two extra heads designed specifically for this purpose. So it's no surprise the V-9035 gives you totally clear still and slow-motion pictures no other portable can match.

Besides surpassing all others when slowing down or standing still, the V-9035 also lets you make visual searches at either double speed or, with Betascan, at 17 times normal speed. And features the unique programming capability of handling 8 different programs over 14 days.

And like any Toshiba VCR, it has precise electronic tuning and sensitive solenoid touch controls.

Toshiba also makes everything else that goes into the making of superior home video.

For starters, there's the incredible IK-1850 autofocus video camera. Its 2/3-inch Univicon/2 tube functions perfectly in low-light conditions and is housed in a strong, light magnesium body.

And for reviewing, there's the CA-045, America's smallest color television. It's small (the screen measures just 4 1/2 inches diagonally) light and has the input/output terminals for hooking it up as a playback monitor.

Toshiba's new portable Betaformat VCR, autofocus video camera and 4 1/2-inch color television. Put them together and you can't beat the system. And that's no snow job.

TOSHIBA
Again, the first.

*Actual TV Pictures.

Toshiba America, Inc. 82 Totowa Road, Wayne, NJ 07470

262

© 1981 Polaroid Corporation.
"Polaroid."

Hours.   Ours.

16 different black and white films. No waiting.

Type 52
Fine Grain

As a photographer, you're familiar with the use of Polaroid instant black and white professional films for test shots and determining exposure. But you may not know the many reasons they're so often used for finished work.

Wherever exceptional tonal rendition is required, our fine grain films give you superb prints with virtually no graininess, as evidenced by our Type 52, used for the portrait we've shown above.

If you're photographing on the fringes of light and time, any one of our high speed films will give you marvelous results in minute detail, in as little as 15 seconds.

For line art, charts, and artistic effects, our high contrast films hand over enhanced blacks and whites in 15-second prints, and 30-second transparencies.

And no film in the world simultaneously delivers a fully developed print and a

Type 55
Positive/Negative

high resolution negative as fast as our positive/negative films—which also allow you to make enlargements (up to 25 times, without objectionable graininess or loss of detail).

But the biggest benefit of all is that each of our films tells you instantly whether the picture you took is what you want.

To find out which film is best suited to the work you're doing, see a Polaroid professional film dealer, or write: Polaroid Corporation, Dept. 476, Cambridge, MA 02139. Or call Polaroid Technical Assistance, toll free in the continental U.S.: 800-225-1618. (In Massachusetts, call collect: 617-547-5177.)

We make sixteen different instant black and white professional films that are ready to give you the results you've been waiting for. Without the wait.

Type 51
High Contrast

Polaroid
Instant Professional Films

263

**Trade
Black and White
Page or Spread**

264
ART DIRECTOR
Ira Madris
WRITER
Bruce Nelson
CLIENT
The New York Times
AGENCY
McCann-Erickson

265
ART DIRECTOR
Nancy Rice
WRITER
Tom McElligott
DESIGNER
Nancy Rice
PHOTOGRAPHER
Tom Bach
CLIENT
Mr. Pasta
AGENCY
Fallon McElligott Rice/Mpls.

266
ART DIRECTOR
Mike Ciranni
WRITER
Kevin McKeon
PHOTOGRAPHER
Bill Stettner
CLIENT
Xerox
AGENCY
Needham, Harper & Steers

We have entered a new age.
The age of corporate clutter.
Page after page of every
business publication is devoted
to the paid corporate message.
Yet, because of the sheer number
of them, few retain their power
and importance.

Analysts may wade through
them. Decision makers may sift
through them. But for most of the
business and non-business publics,
the nearly one billion dollars
of corporate advertising is blending
into one amorphous logo.

Which is why the corporate
advertiser must look beyond the
traditional business publications
to a medium that allows his
message to stand out.

And which is why these times
demand The Times. Its environment of integrity surrounds your
message; framing it, elevating it,
separating it from the crowd.
With an immediacy that brings
with it additional power.

Here, the importance of
your ad cannot be denied. You
are in The New York Times.
You have entered a new arena,
but not as a spectator. As a player.

These times demand more of a corporate advertiser.
These times demand The Times.

The New York Times

The Chinese invented it.
The Italians improved it.
Mr. Pasta perfected it.

For centuries, pasta has been one of man's most loved foods.

And the fresher the pasta, the better man has loved it. But making fresh pasta has always been a difficult, time-consuming and messy job.

Until now.

Because now there's Mr. Pasta—a new way to make fresh, delicious pasta simply, quickly and without mess.

All you do with Mr. Pasta is pour one pound of all purpose flour into the top of a Mr. Pasta machine, add four eggs, and flip the switch. In only 1½ to 2 minutes, Mr. Pasta automatically mixes and kneads the flour and eggs into dough.

Then, with just a turn of the knob, Mr. Pasta

turns that fresh delicious dough into fresh delicious pasta.

Eight different kinds of pasta: Linguini, spaghetti, macaroni, egg noodles, fettucini, vermicelli, rigatoni and lasagne.

Mr. Pasta is safe, expertly engineered, maintenance-free, and designed to give your customer years and years of dependable pasta making.

And because it comes from people who know your business, it's also designed to give you years and years of profitable growth.

Mr. Pasta
Fresh, delicious pasta. Incredibly fast.

You can now reach Xerox at the following numbers.

$1750 $3295 $3995

The Xerox 660, 2600 and 3100 copiers are now easier than ever to reach. Just refer to the numbers listed above.

All three machines give you sharp, clear copies on plain paper, mailing labels, even your own letterhead.

And all three give you the quality and reliability of Xerox. Backed by the largest service organization in the industry.

Other Xerox copiers are also available at easy to reach numbers. Machines that do everything from reduce to copy two-sided originals automatically.

Just send in the coupon. Or call us at 800-648-5600, operator 658.*

We'll keep our lines open. Although it won't be easy.

You see, we've been very busy ever since we lowered our numbers.

☐ I'd like a sales representative to contact me.
☐ I'd like a demonstration.
☐ I'd like more information about Xerox small copiers.

Send to: Xerox Corporation, P.O. Box 24, Rochester, N.Y. 14601.

Name_____
Title_____
Company_____
Address_____
City_____ State____ Zip_____
Telephone_____

XEROX

I still haven't got over that night we let our hair down.

When Sean from Barnsley actually upstaged Diana Ross with his tuneful rendering of 'Reach out and touch...'

Nor have I forgotten the many useful conversations I had with you all during our week away.

I don't simply mean the formal discussions at our heating forum and sales meeting.

I'm referring to those long talks I had with many of you individually. Often long into the night.

Understanding our business better was, after all, at the heart of our trip.

And I, for one, felt I was well rewarded. (Which is more than can be said of my visits to the tables.)

Thank you all for your advice.

On just about everything you care to mention, except possibly how to play blackjack.

Have a good day!

Well, friends, none of us did walk alone. We'd probably have fallen over anyway.

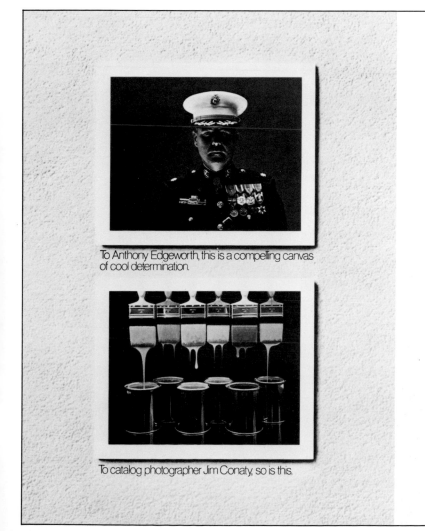

To Anthony Edgeworth, this is a compelling canvas of cool determination.

To catalog photographer Jim Conaty, so is this.

Both were taken with new Polacolor ER instant film.

When Jim Conaty wanted to turn a typical product shot into an alluring one, he selected the same medium esteemed photographer Anthony Edgeworth used to paint a stunning portrait of pride.

Polaroid's new Polacolor Extended Range instant film.

Little wonder. The same qualities that make new Polacolor ER film a great tool for artistic photography make it a great tool for commercial applications, too.

To begin with, this film features a medium-contrast emulsion—which results in excellent retention of detail in both highlight and shadow areas over a broad range of scene brightness conditions.

On top of that, Polacolor ER film's new magenta dye helps produce color quality that will do justice to the most worthy subject. Catalog or otherwise.

And its excellent skin tones and broad tonal range offer a useful neutral position from which you can easily change to versions with varying degrees of contrast.

Needless to say, Polacolor ER film provides pictures that are ready on the spot. So you can tell right away if you shot what you were shooting for.

All of which suggests, if you want to turn an ordinary catalog shot into an extraordinary one, use Polaroid's Polacolor ER film.

You'll find its look and feel, its versatility, sensitivity and responsiveness make it another good choice for finished art.

Polacolor ER film is balanced for daylight and electronic flash. And it is available in two formats: 8x10 (Type 809) and 4x5 (Type 59).

For further details see your Polaroid professional film dealer, or in the continental U.S. call 800-225-1618 (in Massachusetts, call collect 617-547-5177).

Polaroid
Instant Professional Films

THE TECHNOLOGY FOR OUTDOOR BOOTS HAS FINALLY COME OUT OF THE WOODS.

272

"Even the pigs know when Successful Farming comes. It's the only time of the month they get fed late."

273

We Discovered the World

National Geographic

274

"I told them to wash the suit, and hold the wax."

How the Haggar Washable Suit stood up to a torture test, thanks to an incredible Klopman Zephyr fabric.

The guys at the Campus Oaks Car Wash in Sacramento, California, had funny looks on their faces when they saw Dave Black come in.

They had washed a lot of things before — cars, trucks, trailers — but they'd never been asked to wash a suit.

What might have appeared as some wild publicity stunt was really a tough consumer test that the *Sacramento Union* was conducting. The newspaper wanted to see if the Haggar Washable Suit could live up to its claim that it could take the rigors of machine washing and drying and still "come out looking good — wash, after wash, after wash."

Reasoning that if the suit could survive the harsh detergents and powerful water jets in the car wash, it could stand up against any machine washing, they outfitted Mr. Black (a fashion model) in a new pinstripe suit and sent him out to face the watery proving ground.

In he went — first through the suds, then through the rinse, and finally the hot air dryer. He got the full treatment except for the wax and tire cleaner.

And how did the Haggar Washable Suit do? Well, everyone down at the car wash was pleasantly surprised. The linings, shoulder pads, and interfacings kept their shape. And the cool, comfortable Zephyr fabric from Klopman was still incredibly smooth and wrinkle-free.

What did Dave Black think? "You know," he smiled, "it looks like a guy can get a lot of mileage out of this suit."

If you thought the Haggar Washable Suit was incredible before, wait until you see it for Spring '82.

Haggar is taking another giant step forward for Spring '82 with Magic Stretch Lite™. This blended tropical-weight fabric from Klopman of DuPont Dacron® has the look and feel of natural fibers. Plus the washability and wrinkle-resistance today's consumer wants.

And, to appeal to an even wider segment of your sportswear market, you'll find Magic Stretch Lite now comes in a whole new collection of pinstripes for business; sporty checks and plaids; and bright, bold colorations in casual slacks.

The Haggar Washable Suit. It just keeps on making headlines.

HAGGAR
THE WASHABLE SUIT™

FINALLY. A TELEVISION SERIES THAT EXPLOITS SENSITIVITY AND GOOD TASTE.

They're called Young People's Specials. And they provide audiences with some of television's most graphic examples of hard-core decency.

Young People's Specials are true family entertainment. They communicate with gentleness and love. Never with violence. They provoke. Stimulate. Excite. Without ever resorting to cruelty or blatant acts of vengefulness.

About the only thing these beautiful programs do with a vengeance is attract viewers.

One recent special was beamed to over 5 million households. And not just to the

*Source: NTI Special Report 2 ('81)

young people in those homes. 60% of the total audience were 18 to 49 adults. 46% were women.

Which is one important reason why Multimedia's Young People's Specials have always proven highly saleable commodities.

We urge you to call Don Dahlman today, at (513) 352-5955. He can explain further why carrying this series is such a good decision for the family.

Your corporate family, as well as the ones at home.

YOUNG PEOPLE'S SPECIALS

 multimedia
Multimedia Program Productions, Inc.

A RARE OPPORTUNITY FOR PRINT ART DIRECTORS TO LOOK DOWN ON TV ART DIRECTORS.

Print art directors have always been left out in the cold when it comes to great Christmas parties.

While the TV production companies have stuffed their clients silly, we on the print side have starved ours of the attention they truly deserve.

At Spano/Roccanova we think it's about time the people who care about print art direction got their just desserts.

So, on Tuesday, December 22, we're going to elevate all of our clients to the top of the World Trade Center for lunch.

It will be as fine a party as befits New York's finest print art directors.

What! You say you do TV and you still care about print? And you use Spano/Roccanova? Well, you lucky @#$¢¥! It looks like lunch at the top of the World Trade Center and dinner at Roseland.

SPANO/ROCCANOVA'S FIRST ANNUAL CHRISTMAS LUNCH. DECEMBER 22, AT THE TOP OF THE WORLD TRADE CENTER.

SPANO/ROCCANOVA RETOUCHING, INC. • 16 WEST 46 ST. • N.Y. N.Y. 10036 • (212) 840-7450

277

All star.
All woman.
All yours.

This could be the beginning of a beautiful relationship.

The delicious, delightful, the lovely Miss Piggy and the rest of the Muppets are now representing Polaroid Time-Zero film and cameras—the OneStep, The Button and the SX-70 AutoFocus.

And you couldn't ask for better representation. To begin with, the Muppets mean fun. So does Polaroid. And when you put the two together they mean something else. Business.

Besides being fun, the Muppets are believable. Millions buy what the Muppets say. So it stands to reason they'll buy what the Muppets sell. And lots of it.

Miss Piggy is the kind of girl we're proud to bring home to mother, father and the whole family. And you'll be glad to know that we're bringing her and the rest of the Muppets home quite often.

We're spending millions of dollars through December to generate nearly two billion impressions on network television. The fact that consumers will be seeing a lot of the Muppets means you'll be seeing a lot of consumers.

We think you'll agree that the Muppets have what it takes to continue the tradition of advertising that helped make the OneStep America's best-selling camera. And SX-70 the best-selling instant film.

Speaking of tradition, in case you're wondering about the whereabouts of James Garner and Mariette Hartley, they're introducing the new Sun cameras in one of the biggest kickoff campaigns in Polaroid history.

So, to take advantage of the big fall buying season, call your Polaroid representative. We think you'll see that, when the Muppets go to market, the market goes to the Muppets.

Polaroid

278

THE BEST PLACE TO WORK ON YOUR OWN IDEAS IS NOT AT WORK.

Until now, the most sophisticated computers were found at work. Which meant anyone who needed a computer to develop his own ideas did so before anyone arrived in the morning. Or after everyone left at night.

Fortunately, that is no longer necessary. For some of the best parts of a big computer can now be had in a computer small enough (and inexpensive enough) to fit into anyone's budget (personal or corporate).

The MPT/100 computer you see here.

The MPT/100 runs a multi-tasking FORTRAN and a multi-tasking PASCAL that executes at assembly language speeds. An ANSI-compatible BASIC that lets you write quickly large programs that take up a small amount of space. A full range of user-friendly aids like a Command Line Interpreter, a Menu Editor, and a Debugger. And MP/OS, one of the most advanced operating systems in the business.

Such systems software is not only familiar and consequently easy to use. It also lets you get your software up and running faster. So you (and your ideas) can be on the road while everyone else is still on the drawing board.

You (and your ideas) can go anywhere in the world. Because we give the MPT/100 computer the same worldwide support we give every Data General computer. And when you've really taken off, you can grow with all your software, all your peripherals, everything you've learned. Because we've gone to great lengths to make our computers get along with each other.

What, you may ask, is inside the computer? A 16-bit microNOVA® computer. 64K-bytes of memory. 80-column by 24-line screen. Full keyboard with numeric pad. 716-KB of on-line storage on two 358 mini-diskettes.

Out back you'll find an I/O bus that accepts the standard microNOVA peripherals, including Data General Winchester-type disks. As well as your own interfaces. And two synchronous/asynchronous communications ports programmable to 19.2K baud.

And a host of operating features you'll have to see in action.

The point is that with an MPT/100 computer of your own, there is no reason why you can't do what a lot of other companies have done with other Data General computers.

Like Summagraphics Corporation of Fairfield, Connecticut, a company whose Computer Aided Drafting (CAD) systems have made their customer's draftsmen 3-10 times more productive. An achievement that has tripled Summagraphics systems business in 20 months.

If you would like more information about the MPT/100 computer, call your local Data General office, your Data General manufacturer's representative, or one of the distributors listed below. Or write us at MS C-228, 4400 Computer Drive, Westboro, MA 01580.

We would suggest, however, that you ask us to send this information to your home.

Unless, of course, you're planning to use the MPT/100 to work on your hot new project at work.

MPT/100 computers are available for delivery from SCHWEBER, HALL-MARK, KIERULFF, ALMAC, STROUM and R.A.E. in Canada.

◆ DataGeneral
We take care of our own.

microNOVA is a registered trademark of Data General Corporation. © 1980 Data General Corporation.

279

Johnson & Johnson announces a birth.

The most miraculous experience in life is giving life…giving birth to a tiny child who depends on you, the parent, for its loving. Its nurturing. And its care.

For over eighty-five years, we at Johnson & Johnson have been helping new parents care for their beautiful new babies.

Today, we're happy to announce a birth of our own.

It's the birth of three new magazines. Each designed to give new parents information specific to each stage of parenthood.

Pre-Parent Adviser is the first magazine, written for the months before you give birth.

Next is New Parent Adviser. The magazine for parents who have just given birth.

And finally, Parenting Adviser, filled with the knowledge a brand-new parent needs for the first year.

At Johnson & Johnson, we continue to put all our experience, all our knowledge, and all our resources behind our commitment to helping parents care for the most important people in the world. Babies.

© J&J 1981

You don't need us to tell you that it costs a lot to heat schools, hospitals and old people's homes. Or that the government has asked you to cut your costs.

But let us tell you how you can do both, with Glow-worm's Vangarde commercial boilers.

Spend less on fuel.

Vangarde boilers have lightweight fabricated heat-exchangers which are more efficient than cast iron, so they use less gas, particularly under partload conditions. In the summer, for example.

Their outputs range from 125,000 to 300,000 Btu/h.

They can be adjusted in 10,000 Btu/h stages to meet the exact heating requirements of the installation. Therefore they operate more efficiently, saving even more gas.

And they can be linked to give outputs of more than 1 million Btu/h.

So you can save even more gas in summer-

Here's an easy cut to make. Spend less on keeping them warm.

time by shutting down one or more boilers.

And, of course, gas is cheaper than other fuels. For the equivalent of a 200,000 Btu/h Vangarde boiler, solid fuel could cost 16% more to run and oil could cost 45% more.

Spend less on installation.

They weigh between 30% and 70% less than their cast-iron rivals. (Our 300,000 Btu/h boiler weighs 302 lbs. Its heaviest rival weighs more than 1000 lbs).

So they save man-hours because they're easier to get into awkward places. (Cellars, for example.) And they save building costs because you're unlikely to have to reinforce floors or build load-bearing roofs.

Spend less on servicing.

You can get at all the main parts by removing the front panel.

It takes less than an hour to replace a waterway, for example. With some other boilers, it can take days.

And if the boilers are linked in series, you can service one without closing down the whole system.

Spend less.

They never cost more to buy than cast-iron boilers. And usually they cost less.

So you needn't put money-eating boilers in your new buildings.

You can replace the money-eating boilers in your old buildings.

And everyone can keep warm during the freeze.

Glow "worm ⑦ *trust it*
THE LEADING AUTHORITY ON GAS CENTRAL HEATING AND FIRES
Glow-worm Limited, Nottingham Road, Belper, Derby DE5 1JT

282

35mm photography.
Why we cover it from every angle.

It started very simply with a roll of film. At Fuji, we believed that to make the very best roll of film we could, we had to know exactly what was happening inside the camera.

So we made cameras.

And discovered that we couldn't really know what was happening inside the camera unless we made our own lenses.

So we made lenses.

In fact, we didn't just make lenses, we even went so far as to manufacture our own optical glass for our lenses.

Now, in the entire world of 35 millimeter photography, how many companies do all that?

One. Fuji.

You see, we believe that to do the job right, we have to control the picture from the moment you see it in the viewfinder until the moment you have it in your hand. Obviously our competition doesn't share our philosophy. But then, there's something else they don't share: our technology. Technology has made Fuji the largest photographic manufacturer in Japan. And the second largest film maker in the world.

And it's the reason we can do so much and do it all well.

In fact, when it comes to 35 millimeter film, (prints or slides) Fuji's quality, color, and credentials are unsurpassed. After all, wasn't it Fuji that pioneered and introduced 100 and 400 ASA color negative print film?

Of course, there's more to 35mm photography than just making great film. That's why Fuji has created what may well be the most technologically advanced line of cameras in the world. The AX line. The AX-5 combines cybernation with a 7000 element micro computer to offer automatic compensation for over and under exposures as well as six different modes. And Fuji technology has created an oilless, self-lubricating shutter that is unparalleled for accuracy. But then, what else would you expect from the company that introduced the first compact SLR, manufactured the first SLR with a silicon cell light sensor, or pioneered L.E.D. technology for 35mm cameras?

Of course, when you make a great film and a great camera,

it's pretty hard to resist the temptation to make a great lens too. We didn't. We created a whole range of great lenses, everything from fisheye to telephoto. And each one is unique. Not only do we manufacture our own glass, we developed and patented the Electronic Beam Coating technique to reduce lens flare. (We won the Japan Society Invention Award for that one.)

In fact, if you saw the U.S. hockey team win the 1980 Olympics, you were seeing them through one of our Fujinon television camera lenses.

And every night Fuji makes the news. Our Fujinon lenses are used on 2 out of 3 of the network news programs.

We even helped the U.S. Navy. Fuji designed the optics for the new night landing system on U.S. aircraft carriers.

Surprised? You shouldn't be. You see when it comes to the technological side of photography a lot of people turn to Fuji. Maybe you should too.

Fuji. And you just thought we made great film.

Fuji. The company that gives you the whole picture.

Fuji Photo Film U.S.A., Inc., 350 Fifth Avenue, N.Y., 10118.

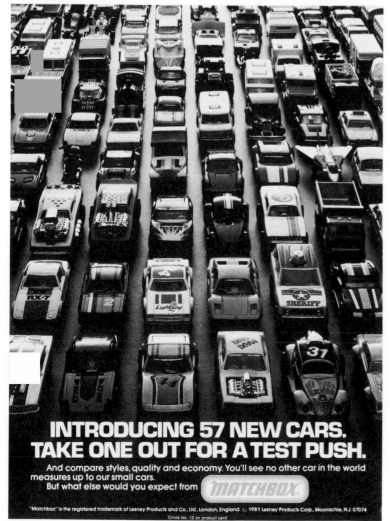

INTRODUCING 57 NEW CARS.
TAKE ONE OUT FOR A TEST PUSH.

And compare styles, quality and economy. You'll see no other car in the world measures up to our small cars.
But what else would you expect from **MATCHBOX**

Bulova points out that it has a long line of Caravelle quartz watches for under $100.

285

ANNOUNCING THE BIRTH OF THE 13 OZ. BLUES.™

We nursed it. Rehearsed it. And now we're spreading the news. J.P. Stevens has given birth to the 13 Oz. Blues.

They're the new Light Heavyweight Denims. In all cotton, a reverse blend and a new, unique mini-blend. All in a variety of weaves. And they're so cotton pickin' good, our crop of blues will help keep you in the black.

They're hi-test performance denims that act as a missing link between the 14 oz. standard of durability and the 12 oz. profit margin. And with their rich dark indigo color, they'll remain true blue till the end.

So come on, lighten up and slip into something more comfortable.

13 OZ. BLUES™ by J.P. STEVENS
THE NEW LIGHT HEAVYWEIGHTS

J.P. Stevens & Co., Inc., 1185 Avenue of the Americas, N.Y.C., 10036. (212) 930-2500.

One of the few things on the Space Shuttle that didn't have a backup system.

Backup systems are essential to any manned space flight.

But space inside the shuttle is precious. How did the crew of the NASA Space Shuttle Columbia get a 35mm camera they could depend on, without having to take along a lot of 35mm cameras?

They took off with a Nikon.* With good reason.

No Nikon has ever failed on a NASA space mission. In every manned mission into space since 1971, no Nikon has had structural damage from blast off. Or jammed.

Or had a mechanical problem. Or any problem that affected its performance.

A Nikon, as you may have gathered, is incredibly reliable.

So reliable it's the choice of more professional photographers than all other 35mm cameras combined.

There are four Nikon models designed for your special professional needs. The F3, the finest Nikon ever built for the professional photographer. The FE, a compact full-featured automatic. The FM which offers full manual control. And the

Nikonos IV-A—the world's only fully automatic 35mm underwater camera.

Whatever your needs as a professional, one thing is certain. Whether up in space, down on earth, or underwater, there's a Nikon to help take pictures that are out of this world.

Nikon
We take the world's greatest pictures.

*Camera used was a modified Nikon F. Future flights will use a modified F3 that has been customized with special wiring, lubrication and finish for use in space. © Nikon Inc., 1981. Garden City, New York 11530

THE ONE RETOUCHER'S SHOW AWARDS.

SPANO/ROCCANOVA. THE QUALITY OF OUR WORK IS RETOUCHING OTHER STUDIOS OUT OF THE PICTURE.
SPANO/ROCCANOVA RETOUCHING, INC.   16 WEST 46 STREET   NEW YORK, N.Y. 10036   212 840-7450

Trade
Color Page or Spread

289
ART DIRECTOR
Peter Begley
WRITER
Steven Landsberg
DESIGNER
Peter Begley
PHOTOGRAPHER
Larry Robins
CLIENT
Sherwin Williams
AGENCY
Doyle Dane Bernbach

290
ART DIRECTOR
David Demarest
WRITER
David Schneider
ARTIST
Carlo Basile
PHOTOGRAPHER
Paul Bowen
CLIENT
Piper Aircraft
AGENCY
Ally & Gargano

291
ART DIRECTOR
Nancy Rice
WRITER
Tom McElligott
DESIGNER
Nancy Rice
PHOTOGRAPHER
Vern Hammerlund
CLIENT
Meredith Corporation
AGENCY
Fallon McElligott Rice/Mpls.

292
ART DIRECTOR
Janet Ferguson
WRITER
Marty Lipkin
PHOTOGRAPHERS
Robert Stevens
Robert Latorre
CLIENT
Haggar
AGENCY
Tracy-Locke/Dallas

293
ART DIRECTOR
Anthony Angotti
WRITER
Elizabeth Cutler
DESIGNER
Barbara Bowman
CLIENT
Club Med
AGENCY
Ammirati & Puris

289

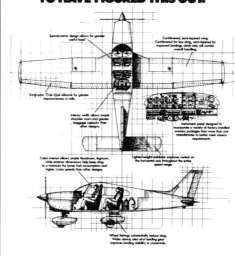

290

291

292

293

THESE WOMEN ARE TWO GENERATIONS APART.

Never before has a point-of-purchase or packaging material (on the right) captured so brilliantly the qualities of an original (on the left).

It's new Converpak™ from Continental Group's Bleached Board Mill. And it's the most visually acute boxboard we've ever created.

Note the definition. Color. Texture. The little things that make point-of-purchase grab you. The little extra that makes packages pop from the shelf.

But reproduction isn't Converpak's only strength. Its unique formation makes it stronger, more uniform, so it runs through your filling system faster. It holds its integrity through distribution to protect your product without distortion to the printed image. And it's produced in a wide-caliper range to satisfy all of your packaging needs.

Converpak can make your carton designs look even better than you see here. So call John R. Curtin at (203) 964-6631 and see. Call now, because your competition could be reading this, too.

Bleached Board Operations
21 Harbor Plaza, Stamford CT 06904

CONTINENTALGROUP

294 SILVER

How to get rich off inflation.

It's easy when you're selling Sevylor. America's favorite inflatables. Sevylor's been the flagship of inflatable boats for over 32 years.

This year we're offering a full line of kayaks, runabouts and fishing boats. There's one for every kind of life style. And every kind of budget!

Sevylor goes overboard with TV to help you sell.

We've just launched a national television and print ad campaign to tell millions of boat-lovers about the advantages of Sevylor inflatable boats. And to send them looking for Sevylor dealers.

Once they've found your store, our eye grabbing point-of-purchase displays and informative packaging will have your customers reaching for their wallets.

We pump-up your accessory sales too.

When you sell a Sevylor, you're not just selling a boat. You're selling everything that goes with it. Oars, pumps, anchors, motor mounts, sail kits, canopies. Not to mention your own line of motors, life jackets and other gear.

With our inflatables, there's a lot more profit in store than you thought.

Don't miss the boat.

Americans are buying more boats now than ever. They're buying boats that are easy to afford and easy to maintain. Like Sevylor inflatables.

Find out how our boats can land some big profits for you. Write or call: Sevylor, 6802 Watcher St., Los Angeles, CA 90040, (213) 927-3473. Outside California, call us on our dealer line: (800) 421-6731.

If you're not stocking-up on Sevylor, you're missing the boat.

SEVYLOR

295

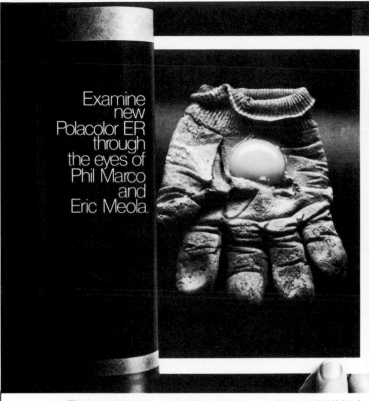

Examine
new
Polacolor ER
through
the eyes of
Phil Marco
and
Eric Meola.

Whatever your subject matter, Polacolor ER (Extended Range) instant film can make your subject truly matter. Sensitive, responsive and versatile, it offers professional photographers a new creative medium.

Its medium contrast emulsion, combined with an extended exposure latitude capable of handling scene brightness ranges up to 1:48, results in maximum detail in both highlight and shadow areas.

And its new magenta dye helps deliver a degree of color quality that is nothing short of striking.

Marco

This new Polacolor ER film's sensitivity and expressiveness are truly impressive. Its highlight and shadow detail, color fidelity and tonal gradation are remarkable.

Up until now, I used Polaroid instant film primarily as a tool to check and control both light and imagery. But the performance of Polacolor ER film so surpassed my expectations that I now look forward to using it as finished art.

Meola

Polacolor ER film provides a full tonal range and an extremely precise rendition of what appears to the eye. Simply put, what I see is what I get. No more, no less.

The tonal range and excellent skin tones of the new material create a neutral position from which I can readily shift to versions with more or less contrast, depending on what's called for. All in all, its singular look and feel offer a new avenue of expression.

Polacolor ER instant film is balanced for daylight and electronic flash and is rated at 125 ASA. It is available in two formats: 8x10 (Type 809) and 4x5 (Type 59).

For further details see your nearest Polaroid professional film dealer, or in the continental U.S. call: 800-255-1618 (in Massachusetts call collect: 617-547-5177).

Polaroid
Instant Professional Films

$119

$119

IF HERTZ STICKS IT TO YOU IN CALIFORNIA,

YOU CAN AUTOMATICALLY GO TO AVIS.

You probably know about the good deal Hertz has in California. $119 a week for a subcompact with unlimited mileage.

But did you know that deal is only good for one kind of car?

A stickshift.

For the same $119, Avis will give you an automatic (Chevy Chevette or similar). With the same unlimited mileage.

When you're in California, we don't think you want any unpleasant surprises. So we don't like to give you any.

That's why we suggest you reserve an Avis $119-a-week California Special. Then you'll be sure you'll get an automatic shift.

Which means you certainly won't get stuck with a stick. **AVIS**

Leave your worries behind.

$119

A WEEK
UNLIMITED MILEAGE.

CHEVY CHEVETTE

297

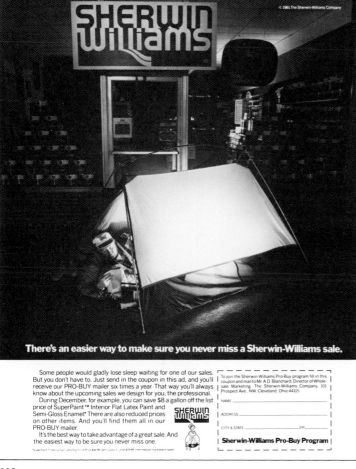

We think every computer cabinet should stand on its own five feet.

What makes one computer cabinet better than another?

Attention to details.

Like the extra stabilizer legs Digital recommends for all its cabinets. So when a top drawer is opened, the cabinet won't come crashing to the floor.

There are other details you'll like, too. All our metal cabinet parts are fully grounded, eliminating static shocks.

Mounts are designed for standard 19" EIA rack units, with a choice of 110 or 240 volt power controllers.

All air flow and electrical requirements have been integrated, so you need no separate air plenums or cable conduits.

Best of all, our new pricing structure makes Digital's cabinets more affordable than ever.

There's a lot of thought behind our cabinets.

And it shows.

For more information, call (603) 884-7054, from 9am-5pm, Eastern time. Or contact **Digital Equipment Corporation,** Accessories and Supplies Group, RQ/E72, 460 Amherst St., Nashua, NH 03063.

digital
We change the way the world thinks.

300

MOST AGENCIES LOOKING FOR A WRITER WANT TO SEE YOUR WORK.

WE THOUGHT YOU'D LIKE TO SEE OURS FIRST.

We're in the market for a good writer who'd like to build a great book.

Naturally, we'll want to take a look at your work. Just so we know what we're getting into.

But that works both ways.

So here's some of our work. We think it's pretty good stuff. And there's a lot more award-winning print, radio and television where that came from.

But, quite frankly, we're more interested in the awards you're going to win than the ones we've already won.

If you like what you see here, send some of your best work to me, Bill LaWarre, Sr. V.P./Creative Director.

If we like what we see, you'll be building a great book in no time. At a salary that'll make you never want to use it.

NORTHLICH, STOLLEY, INC.
200 West Fourth Street, Cincinnati, Ohio 45202

301 GOLD

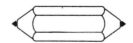

O e thi g
our pri t wheels
wo 't do.

They wo 't break, like this o e did.
Because the entire wheel is reinforced.
With metal.

Which means characters won't snap off,
and typewriters won't edit people without
their consent.

That's guaranteed for a full year.

Now, this is what our print wheels will
do. They'll print in 21 different typefaces.
And in different type sizes.

They'll print signs and symbols, such
as π and ¶.

Best of all, each wheel can be custom-
made.

At Xerox, we offer a wide variety of
supplies that help prevent communications
breakdowns. Everything from magnetic
cassettes to Telecopier supplies to data
storage systems.

So before you send for any more
Information Processing or Telecopier
supplies, send in the coupon. Or call

1-800-527-1868.

After all, which would you rather
supply your office with:
The thi gs it eeds?
Or the things it needs?

I'd like more information on the complete
line of Xerox Office Supplies.
Send to: Xerox Corporation,
P.O. Box 470065,
Dallas, Texas 75247.

Name_____
Title_____
Company_____
Address_____
City_____State_____Zip_____
Phone_____

XEROX

*In Texas, Alaska and Hawaii, call collect 1-214-630-6145.   XEROX® and TELECOPIER® are trademarks of XEROX CORPORATION.

306

WHY THE BEST BOOTS AND
HANDSEWNS MONEY CAN BUY
ARE THE BEST BOOTS AND
HANDSEWNS YOU CAN SELL.

Over the past few years, we, at
Timberland, have developed a reputation
for making quality footwear.

It's a reputation that we feel is well
deserved.

Because while some manufacturers
may combine a few of the features we put
into our boots and handsewns, no other
manufacturer combines all of the features.

Obviously, this commitment to
craftsmanship benefits people who buy
Timberland products.

But it also benefits people who
sell them.

OUR BOOTS COME WITH
RUGGED SOLES, LEATHER UPPERS,
AND HIGHER-PROFIT MARGINS.

At Timberland, we've always put
higher quality craftsmanship into our
boots, so our dealers can get a better price
for them.

And they do.

Today, Timberland boots are the
fastest-selling premium quality boots in the
United States. And they sell at a premium
price.

Our boots also come with something
else other boots don't come with: built-in
consumer demand.

Which means that you can sell a pair
of Timberlands in less time than it takes to

sell a pair of ordinary boots. And make
more money.

THE FIRST LINE OF
HANDSEWNS WITH THE QUALITY
OF TIMBERLAND.

For us, making a line of quality
handsewns was a tough pair of shoes to fill.
Because, as the makers of the world's
finest boots, we couldn't come out with
anything less in a handsewn.

Timberland handsewns, including
our boat shoes, are made from the same
quality materials as our boots.
They are made with the
same quality
craftsmanship.
And, most
important, they
come with the
same high-profit
margins and built-
in consumer demand.

WE'VE SAVED
THE BEST FOR LAST.

Unlike other manufacturers, we've
never thought our job ends when shipping
begins.

Every year, we invest more money
in consumer boot advertising than any of
our competitors.

And this year, we'll be
putting more money
than ever before
behind our
handsewns, as
well as a new
boat shoe.

We also have the most complete
dealer support program, including p.o.p.,
in-store promotions, and dealer co-op.

The result of these investments?

Well, just in the last few years alone,
Timberland's growth has been unmatched
by any of our competitors. And our dealers'
profits have grown just as quickly.

See, we told you we were saving the
best for last.

Timberland

307 GOLD

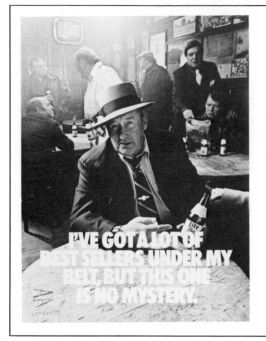

By Mickey Spillane,
Famous Mystery Writer

Being a celebrated mystery writer and a famous Lite Beer drinker, the guys at Miller asked me for a few words on their latest caper. It's a beaut. In fact, seven years ago, even they didn't know how good it would turn out to be.

I hear you thinking, "Okay, Spillane, eighty-six the small talk and get to the point."

Here it is: What beer has become *America's Number Three Best Seller?*

I'll give you a clue: Tastes great, less filling.

If you solved that little mystery, treat yourself to a Lite Beer. If you didn't solve it, have a Lite Beer anyway.

Nearly everyone else in America is drinking it. Which points to why Lite Beer sales are not only way ahead of any other low calorie beer, but why Lite is one of America's fastest growing beers.

And with Lite in the number *three* spot of *all* beers, you'd be smart to get a piece of the action.

All over the country, bar owners have proven that their business–and their take–is better since they started carrying Lite Beer. And it's no mystery why. Because a lot of guys will gladly go out of their way for a beer they know and love.

Especially when it's on tap (I never met a mug of Lite I couldn't spend time with). And since there's more money to be made in draft sales, you can imagine the kind of cash you'll rake in.

Cut yourself in on a piece of the action. Call your local Lite Beer distributor for the rundown on America's third largest selling beer: Lite Beer from Miller.

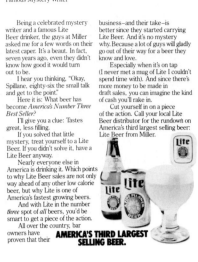

I'VE GOT A LOT OF BEST SELLERS UNDER MY BELT, BUT THIS ONE IS NO MYSTERY.

AMERICA'S THIRD LARGEST SELLING BEER.

By Grits Gresham,
Famous Fisherman

Let me tell you a true story about this bar owner named Merle.

He's got this watering hole down in Louisiana, see, and he did a decent business. But right across the street he's got this competition who was doing better than decent.

He was cleaning up. Hauling in all kinds of customers.

You know what he was luring them in with? Lite Beer from Miller.

Day in and day out, a whole slew of thirsty folks flocked there, including some of Merle's regulars (I got to admit, even I slipped in there once in a while) for some Lite Beer.

So I said, "Merle, why don't you sell Lite Beer from Miller? Not only is it America's number one low calorie beer, it's America's THIRD LARGEST SELLING BEER (Do you believe it?) It hasn't been around but seven years!) and moving up faster than a wet watermelon seed."

Merle, being nobody's fool, decided okay but went one better.

He sold Lite Beer on tap.

You know what happened? Not only did he reel in more customers, he sold nearly three times more low calorie beer than ever (He even increased his kitchen business). And since there is more profit in draft sales, you can well imagine the money he's making.

But the most surprising thing of all was the guy across the street. He drops into Merle's at least once a week!

Now if you are thinking this is some fish story, it's not. Because all over the country other smart bar owners are reporting the same kind of success stories: That their bar business–and profits–have never looked better since they started carrying Lite.

And I tell you, I'm not a bit surprised. I like Lite Beer. It really tastes great. It's also less filling (which is why *I* like it so much).

And most of America really likes it, too. Fact, they like it enough to make it the third largest seller around.

Which leads me to lend you a little piece of down-home advice. Give your local Lite Beer distributor a call. 'Cause to bring in the big ones you gotta use the right hook: Lite Beer from Miller.

DID YOU HEAR THE ONE ABOUT THE CUSTOMER WHO GOT AWAY?

AMERICA'S THIRD LARGEST SELLING BEER.

By Red Auerbach,
Famous General Manager

To stay way ahead of the game, you gotta make smart draft choices.

How do I know? Just ask Cousy, Heinsohn or Jones. They'll tell ya when it comes to draft picks, I know how to pick a winner.

That's Lite Beer from Miller.

Let me tell you why.

Lite was introduced only seven years ago. Seven years! You'd think it's been around forever, it's doing so well. It's America's *number one selling* low calorie beer!

Now, if you think that's something, let me bounce this off you– not only is Lite the top selling *low calorie beer,* it's America's NUMBER THREE selling beer. That's of *all* beers, period.

And in some cities, it's doing even better than that. (Fact is, Lite's one of the fastest growing beers in America.)

Which makes perfect sense to me. Because when you're a shrewd manager, you learn to look for smart combinations (kind of like putting Sam Jones and K. C. Jones together). And Miller put together one terrific combination with Lite: It tastes great and it's less filling.

A perfect team a lot of beer drinkers are looking for today.

So it's no wonder many bar managers tell me a big part of their profits come from serving Lite Beer.

But I also know a lot of managers who are not only putting this winning beer in their lineup, they're taking it all the way.

They're serving Lite on tap.

And since you know how much more profit there is in draft sales, you can imagine how well those guys are scoring.

If you know anybody who's serving Lite on tap, ask them how it's selling. Chances are, they're scoring big.

So why don't you sell it. You'll be a big step ahead of the game.

Call your local Lite Beer distributor and ask him for all the particulars on the fast breaking beer that should be your number one draft choice: Lite Beer from Miller.

YOU CAN ALWAYS TELL A SHREWD MANAGER BY HIS NUMBER ONE DRAFT CHOICE.

AMERICA'S THIRD LARGEST SELLING BEER.

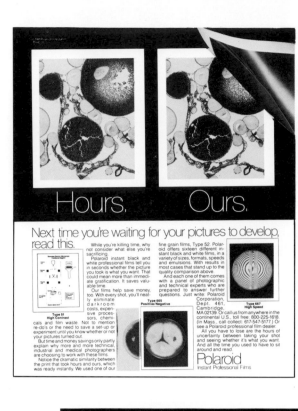

Hours. Ours.

Next time you're waiting for your pictures to develop, read this.

While you're killing time, why not consider what else you're sacrificing.

Polaroid instant black and white professional films tell you in seconds whether the picture you took is what you want. That could mean more than immediate gratification. It saves valuable time.

Our films help save money, too. You will neatly eliminate darkroom costs, expensive processors, chemicals, and film waste. Not to mention call-backs or the need to save a set until you know if your pictures turned out.

But time and money savings only partly explain why a lot more photographers are choosing to work with Polaroid instant black and white films for finished art.

Notice the dramatic similarity between the print that took hours and ours, which was ready instantly. We used one of our high contrast films, Type 51. Polaroid offers sixteen different instant black and white films, in a variety of sizes, formats, speeds, and emulsions. With results in most cases that stand up to the quality comparison above.

To find out which film is best suited to the work you're doing, see a local Polaroid professional film dealer, or write to: Polaroid Corp., Dept. 475, Cambridge, MA 02139. Or call us, toll free in the continental U.S.: 800-225-1618. (In Mass., call collect: 617-547-5177.)

All you have to lose are the hours of uncertainty between taking your shot and seeing whether it's what you want. And all the time you used to have to sit around and read.

Type 52
Fine Grain

Type 665
Positive/Negative

Type 667
High Speed

Polaroid
Instant Professional Films

310

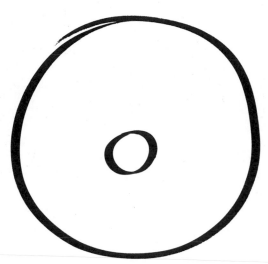

We intend to go as far
as the human mind can take us.

To what heights can the human
mind soar when we encourage
our thoughts to fly free?
If mankind's accomplish-
ments of the last 50 years are any
indication, the answer is evident.
For the barrier between what
is possible and what is not is
no match against the power of
human thought.
At Conoco Chemicals, we
have created an environment
where ingenuity truly flourishes.
From the limitless bounds of
the open mind came our answer
to pollution problems in America's
streams, and a chemical that
increases flow in the Trans Alaska
Pipeline.
But in spite of the gains we
have already made, our journey
has barely begun.
For we intend to go as far as
the human mind can take us. And
to share with you the benefits of
what we learn along the way.

Conoco Chemicals

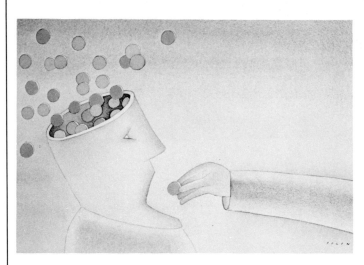

Without feeding a good idea, it will
bear no fruit.

An idea begins as a flash of
brightness in an amazing stream
of thought.
Incandescent, irresistible, it
blazes into our consciousness.
Invading our thoughts and
capturing our imagination, an
idea is born.
We value the power of a
good idea. But despite its price-
lessness, we are aware that
it cannot survive without financial support. We are aware, and
we are prepared.
Our position as part of
Conoco Inc., one of the world's
top 50 industrial companies,
allows us the financial ability to
transform our ideas into reality.
The many chemical inno-
vations for which we are responsible serve as ample proof.
For we are here to help
good ideas come to a fruition.
And to share with you their
brilliance and their benefits.

Conoco Chemicals

How the human mind
can expand the realm of possibility.

Technology began when some
forgotten genius took the wheel
and invented the nut.
Or the gear. Or the pulley.
These innovations are the
true foundation of our modern
technology.
But even more important,
they are proof of the universal
and insatiable need to know.
At Conoco Chemicals, we are
more than mindful of this need.
For it has compelled us to
develop a product that enables
the housing industry to use
more energy-efficient building
materials. And our large reactor
technology makes more of this
product at a lower cost.
We will continue to nurture
our need to know. For there are
no real boundaries to the realm
of possibility.
There are only opportunities.
Opportunities that we in-
tend to share with you.

Conoco Chemicals

Nikkor. The lenses that are made to take more than pictures.

Unlike most camera lenses which function well in a bright, sunny, perfect world, Nikkor lenses are made to function in the hottest, coldest, meanest conditions on earth.

Nikkor lenses have been strapped to rodeo horses, tied to the front fender of Indy race cars, and even bolted to a daredevil's cycle as he attempted to jump the Snake River Canyon. Nikkor lenses have been carried through forty below zero weather to shoot the top of K-2 in the Himalayas. And used to photograph the high-heat blast offs of NASA space missions. In every instance Nikkor lenses performed and got the picture.

Because some of the world's greatest pictures are taken under some of the world's worst conditions, Nikkor lenses have to be tough. Each lens barrel is made from a special aluminum alloy so that it can withstand years of demanding use. Each lens mount is made with brass then coated with hard chromium to inhibit corrosion. Even the screws holding the lens together are treated with special adhesives to prevent high-vibration (air travel for instance) from loosening them.

Nikkors are also designed to function simply under complicated conditions. For instance, every Nikkor lens has a wide non-slip rubber grip that makes it easy to focus in rain, snow, or severe cold (you can even wear your gloves). Click stops on the aperture ring are secure so your setting won't 'drift'. Lens markings are also color-coded for quick depth-of-field, focus distance, and lens-opening reference.

With a Nikkor lens there's also nothing to confuse you, or make you feel like you're all thumbs when you have to change a lens in a hurry. Every Nikkor lens has a special mounting ring so that it can be gripped and mounted easily. Every Nikkor lens also turns in the same direction to adjust exposure and to focus.

And because Nikkor offers you the widest selection of lenses in 35mm photography, no other system gives you more control over distance, depth, and perspective. Whether you're sitting inside the cockpit of a jet, or standing on top of a mountain, there's a Nikkor lens to help you achieve the effect you want. With Nikkor you get the most fisheyes. And the widest choice of wide angles. As well as the largest selection of telephoto lenses with both Internal Focusing for exceptionally quick focusing. And Extra-Low Dispersion Glass for spectacular color performance and sharpness. You also get a choice of zoom lenses that range from 28mm to 1200mm. And a selection of Micro-Nikkor lenses that give you incredible resolution whether you focus from infinity or inches from your subject. Optics, of course, are Nikon's passion. Unlike most camera manufacturers, and lens companies, Nikon makes its own optical glass and chooses only the best glass from each 'melt'—not just glass that meets minimum standards. And while others may coat their lenses to help improve color quality, every Nikkor lens is multi-coated to get the best color possible.

When you consider the dedication that goes into the making of every Nikkor lens, it's no wonder that more professionals use Nikkor for 35mm photography than any other brand of lens. Few things on earth, in fact, are as dependable as Nikkor lenses. Except the cameras they're designed for.

Nikon
We take the world's greatest pictures.

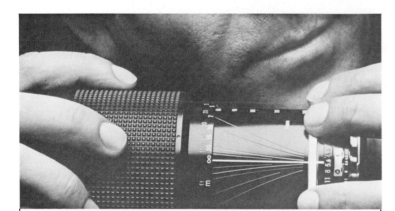

You can tell Nikkor zoom lenses are superior even with your eyes closed.

Most brand-new lenses look good on the store counter. Or when a salesman gives you a brief look through one.

But to really see how good a lens is you have to close your eyes. It's when you use your sense of touch and hearing that you begin to see the difference between a great lens and all the others.

Ask your Nikon dealer to hand you a Zoom Nikkor 80-200mm. And close your eyes. Feel the textured pattern of the rubber zoom/focusing ring and how easy it is to grip. Now move it forward and feel the incredible smoothness of the ring gliding across the barrel.

There are no "slow spots" to interfere with your zooming. No looseness to throw your concentration off.

Next, grasp the top of the lens barrel and try to move it from side to side. Notice the firmness. A lesser zoom would wobble indicating poor construction. Now turn the zoom/focusing ring. You'll notice that all it takes is a touch of your fingertips. Many lenses take much more effort.

Now put the lens on a Nikon camera body (Nikon makes changing lenses so easy, you can do that with your eyes closed). Feel the extraordinary balance of both Nikon camera and Nikkor lens locked snugly together. A non-Nikon lens on a Nikon body can feel uncomfortable in your hand.

Finally, in one movement, zoom in, zoom out, turn the zoom/focusing ring—and listen. You'll notice a quietness. A beautiful silence that attests to the quality control and precision fittings that go into every Nikkor zoom lens.

Of course the best part of owning a Nikkor lens—like the 80-200mm comes when you use it. And get edge-to-edge sharpness, vivid contrast, and spectacular color performance.

All of which adds up to pictures that will open your eyes.

Zoom Nikkor 80-200mm f4.5

Nikon
We take the world's greatest pictures.™

At Nikon we don't depend on someone else to make the most important part of a lens.

Unlike Nikon, most camera and lens companies depend on an outside source to make the heart of a lens—optical glass.

When a company doesn't make its own optical glass the performance of a lens can be compromised. For instance, the specifications of a lens design may have to be downgraded because the independent glass manufacturer cannot supply the proper glass. Or meet the close tolerances of the lens design.

Because Nikon makes its own optical glass, Nikon engineers can produce the exact type of glass needed for each element of each lens without compromise. In addition, having complete control over the glass-making process has enabled Nikon engineers to pioneer many optical-glass designs. For example, ED glass which gives you sharpness of color formerly not attainable with a telephoto lens at full aperture.

Every step in the Nikon lens-making process—grinding, polishing, assembling—is subject to the most demanding quality control standards in the world.

In fact Nikon's obsession with precision is so exacting, we have to make our own measuring instruments to test our lenses.

You can see the results of this dedication with our 24mm wide angle Nikkors (f2, f2.8). Both these lenses feature Nikon's Floating Element System for superior image quality even at the closest focusing distance. And both give you spectacular color, vivid contrast, and crisp detail even when your lens is wide open.

So the next time you're interested in a new lens—like a 24mm wide angle—and someone tells you that you can buy one that's just as good as a Nikkor for only half the price, remember one thing.

It's probably half the quality too.

Wide Angle Nikkor 24mm f2.8

Nikon
We take the world's greatest pictures.™

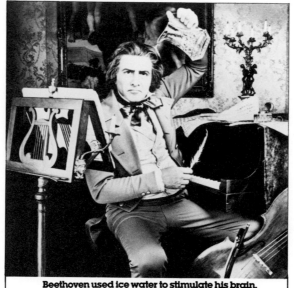

**Beethoven used ice water to stimulate his brain.
At GE, we have better ways.**

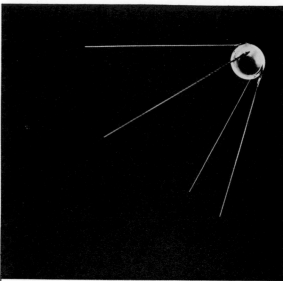

**24 years ago, this little object
launched an American revolution.**

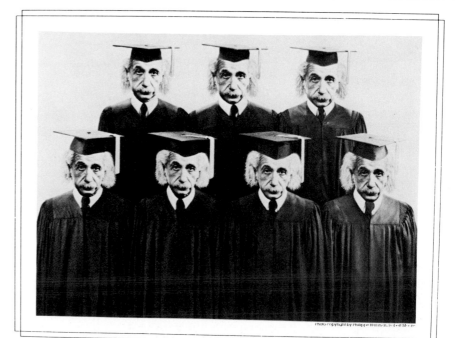

General Electric is looking for a few good men.

Why Cole Weston has switched to ILFOBROM GALERIE.

Why Jerry Uelsmann has switched to ILFOBROM GALERIE.

Why Arnold Newman has switched to ILFOBROM GALERIE.

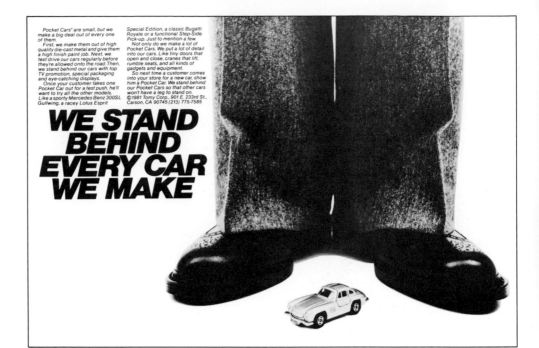

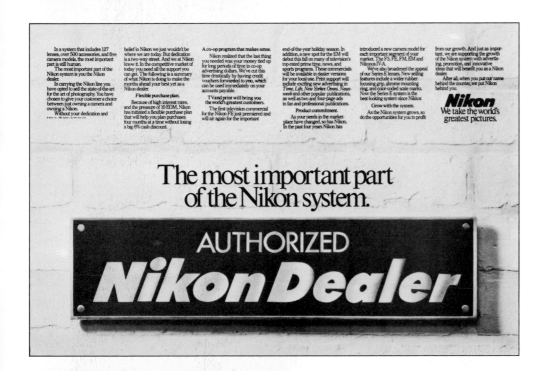

324
ART DIRECTOR
Jud Smith
WRITER
Ron Sackett
ARTISTS
Conrad Fialkowski
McNamara & Associates
PHOTOGRAPHER
Dennis Manarchy
CLIENT
Harley-Davidson
AGENCY
Carmichael-Lynch/Mpls.

325
ART DIRECTOR
Tom Schwartz
WRITER
Nancy Stevens
DESIGNER
Tom Schwartz
PHOTOGRAPHER
Bruno Zehnder
CLIENT
Nikon
AGENCY
Scali, McCabe, Sloves

326
ART DIRECTOR
Nick deSherbinin
WRITER
Chuck Matzell
DESIGNER
Nick deSherbinin
ARTIST
Roger Huyssen
PHOTOGRAPHER
Stein-Mason Studio
CLIENT
Acushnet Company
AGENCY
Humphrey Browning
MacDougall/Boston

327
ART DIRECTOR
Ron Spataro
WRITER
John Perry
DESIGNER
Ron Spataro
PHOTOGRAPHERS
Gary Blockley
Phil Terry
CLIENT
Cessna Aircraft
AGENCY
Bozell & Jacobs/Houston

324

325

326

327

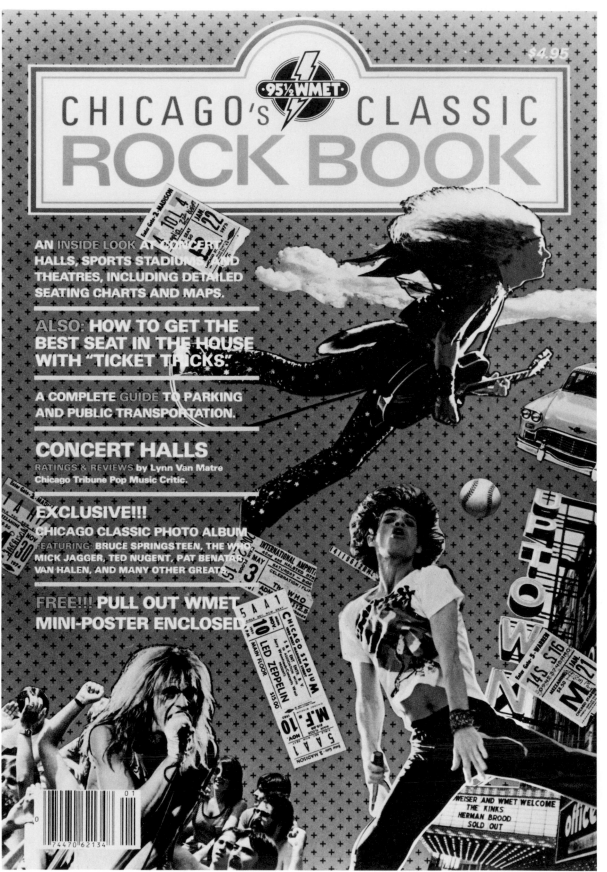

329

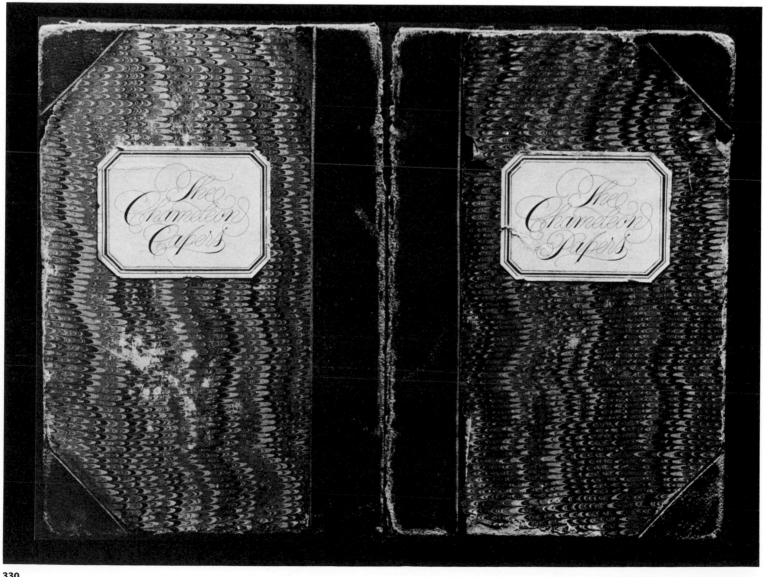

330

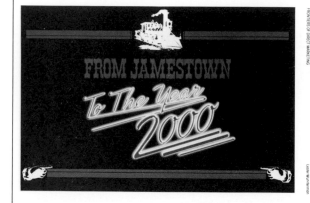

The Yankee Pedlars

For nearly 200 years the main form of American marketing was direct, door-to-door selling. The country was too large and its consumers too inaccessible to sell any other way. The customers needed to have the merchandise available, and the manufacturers or importers needed to find the customers. The main medium and marketplace was the Yankee pedlar. When the customers wouldn't, or couldn't, come to the goods–the goods had to go to them. Did this process end with the advent of roads, railroads and retailing? The answer is no.

The form has changed with time and the development of media. What goes door-to-door now is not necessarily the pedlar–but the personal service the pedlar provided.

However, these were ambitious, adventurous men living in a new land with new problems and new opportunities. They had vast distances to explore, settle and develop. The frontier was everywhere and in all dimensions. On every level it answered to a description Gertrude Stein expressed hundreds of years later when she wrote: "When you get there, there isn't any there there."

There wasn't any "there" yet in the technology required to convert handicrafts to manufacturing. There wasn't any "there" yet in the channels and techniques through which so varied and so great a volume of goods as would be needed could be distributed and sold. And there wasn't any "there" yet in the development of media to communicate with so many

10

3

331

332

333

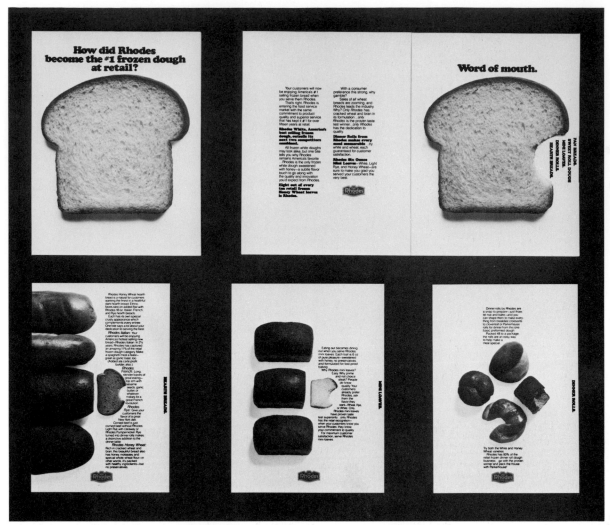

334 SILVER

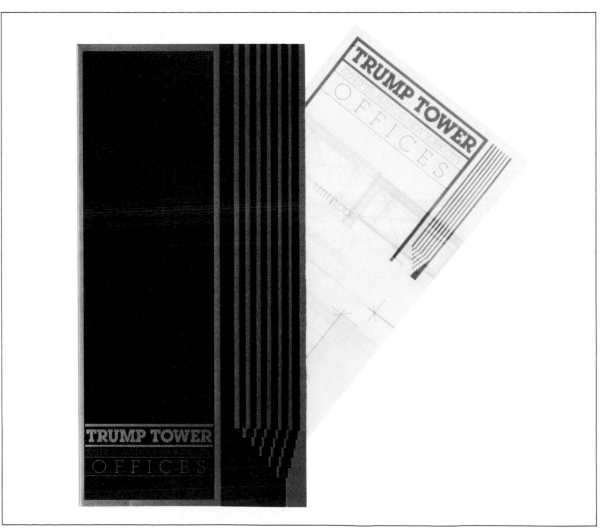

335

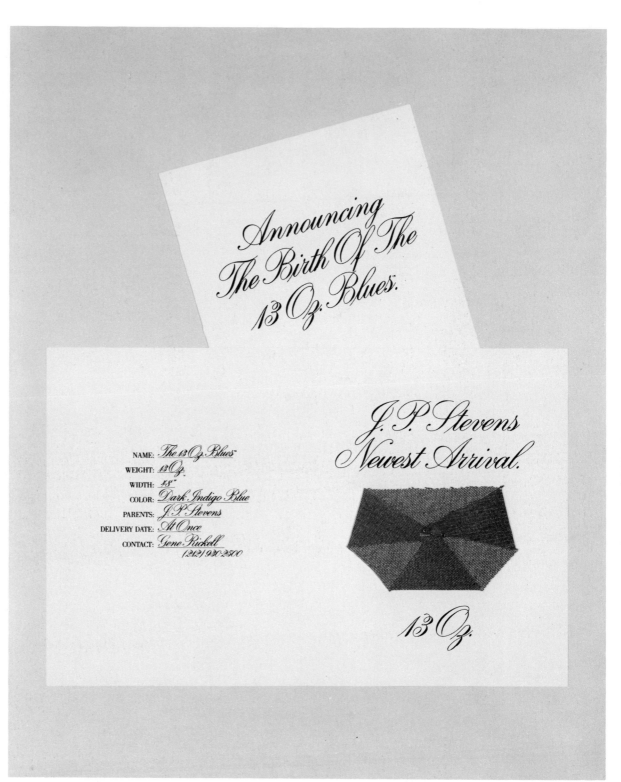

337

Thoroughbred Tweed

Pictured at Borris House, Borris, County Carlow, "Thoroughbred Tweed" by Fieldcrest is the most contemporary design of the collection, blending heather, texture and tweed to achieve a woven plaid effect. From the Fieldcrest collection, "The Ireland I Love."

340

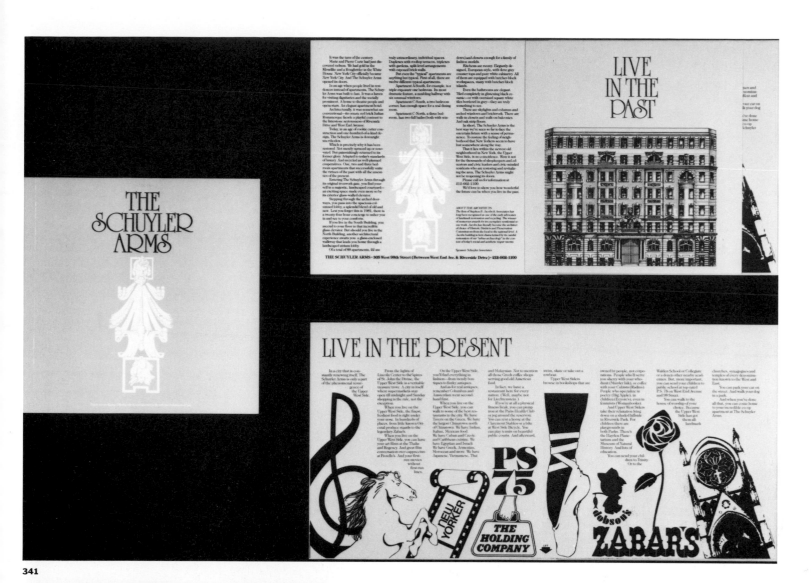

343
ART DIRECTOR
Gail Spruill-Hicks
WRITER
Steven Hicks
DESIGNER AND ARTIST
Gail Spruill-Hicks
PHOTOGRAPHERS
Arington Hendley
Steven Hicks
Mary Anne Smith
CLIENT
Natchez Convention Center
AGENCY
Lott/Spruill Advertising/
Mississippi

344
ART DIRECTOR
Alex Tsao
WRITER
Dick Raboy
DESIGNER
Alex Tsao
PHOTOGRAPHER
Mario Carrieri
CLIENT
Knoll International
AGENCY
Epstein Raboy

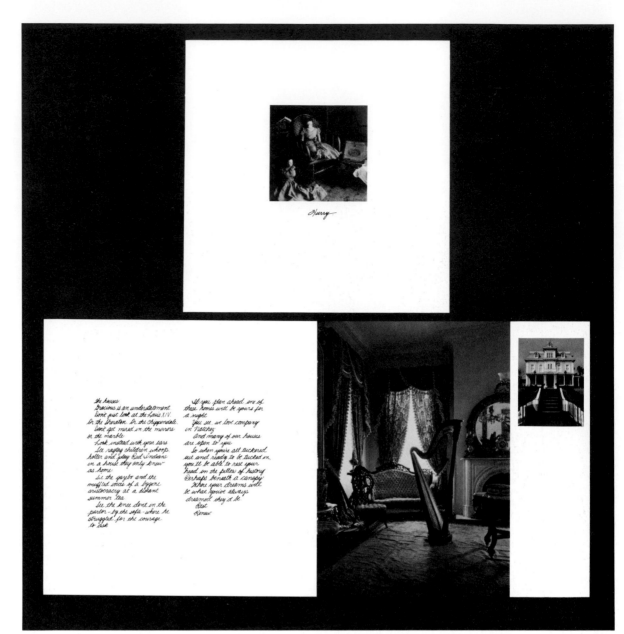

343

345

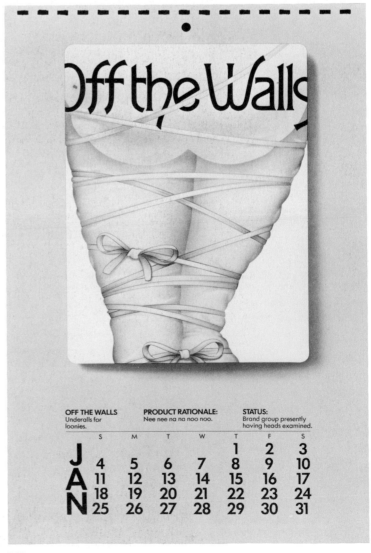

346

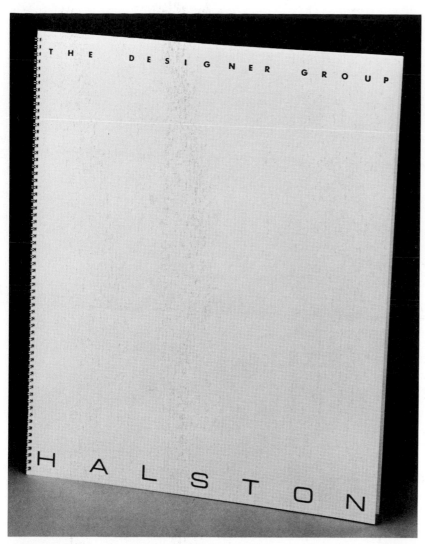

347

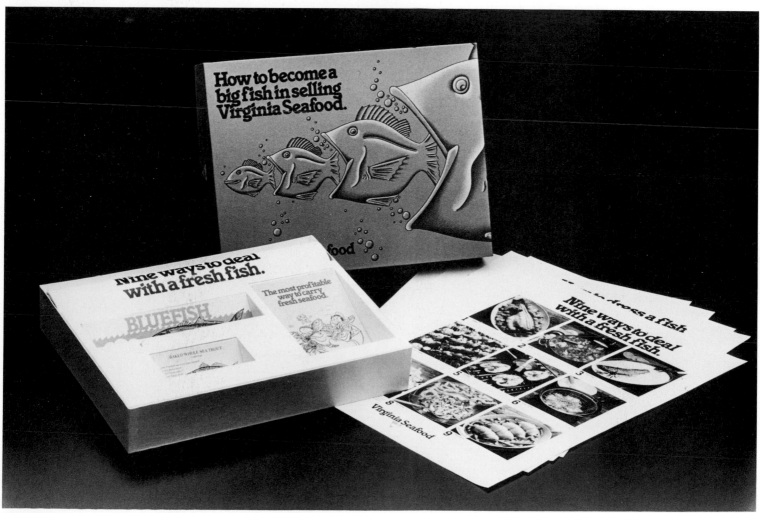

349
ART DIRECTOR
Ralph Burch

WRITER
Roger Myers

DESIGNER
Ralph Burch

PHOTOGRAPHER
Stuart Block

CLIENT
Kieffer-Nolde

AGENCY
Burch Myers Cuttie/Chicago

350
ART DIRECTOR
Jim Keane

WRITER
Richard Baron

DESIGNER
Jim Keane

PHOTOGRAPHER
Steve Niedorf

CLIENT
3M

AGENCY
BBDO/Mpls

351
ART DIRECTOR
Mark Greitzer

WRITER
Richard Dee

DESIGNERS
Marie Loeber
Mark Greitzer

ARTIST
Bill Wilkinson

CLIENT
Smithsonian Magazine

AGENCY
Millenium Design

349

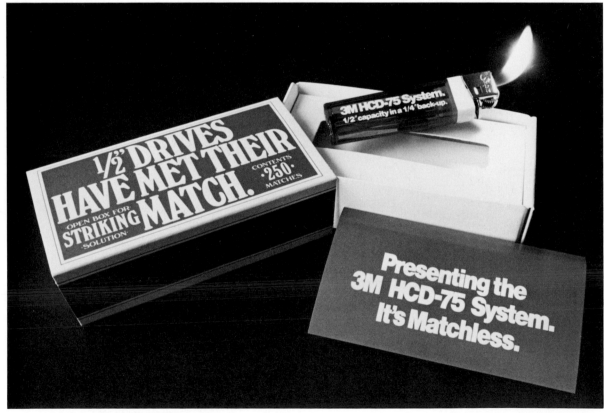

350

Smithsonian magazine

The selection and purchase of an automobile is a carefully considered one. In terms of performance, attractiveness and efficiency, purchasers want what they buy to be able to "go the distance."

In eleven short years, Smithsonian's circulation has accelerated from 175,000 to 1.8 million. That's performance!

Smithsonian is a beautifully designed creation reaching a total audience of more than 4.8 million readers.* That's attractiveness!

Among Smithsonian readers, there are more than 4.3 million cars, of which 72% were bought new. That's 40% better than the national buying rate. In terms of reaching the right market, that's efficiency!

Consider Smithsonian for your automotive sales messages. It's ideally designed to "go the distance."

*Source: 1980 SMRB

The classic Stutz Bearcat Speedster was more than merely a great car. It was a state of mind: synonymous with Scott Fitzgerald, raccoon coats and bathtub gin, it was the apogee of "cool" for the college freshmen of its day.

Powered by a dual-valve, T-head, mono-block Wisconsin engine, boasting 32 valves (2 intakes and 2 exhausts per cylinder), the Bearcat was capable of 155 mph, (although the factory only guaranteed 100), and carried a pricetag of $4,995—in 1931 dollars. The thing to do with your Bearcat on chilly mornings was to let it warm up in the driveway, murmuring throatily at 250 rpms, while you ate your breakfast.

Because of its dependability, power and performance, the Stutz Bearcat Speedster captured the imagination and respect of the public. For these reasons, it is our choice to represent to you the advantages of Smithsonian for automotive advertisers.

How to shift your Automotive Sales into high

Engine
The power source. Each month, the editors of Smithsonian fuel an editorial product that drives the magazine into the minds and interests of 4.8 million total readers.

Side-mounted Spares
For extra dependability. Readers know they can depend on Smithsonian to carry them convincingly and responsibly throughout the world around us. Smithsonian is a showcase for the whole world and the automotive world.

Headlights
Illumination. Automotive advertisers especially benefit from the intensity with which Smithsonian readers react. The interrelationship among the reader, the magazine and The Smithsonian Institution is unique because it is built of mutual respect and involvement. In Smithsonian, your automotive advertising is put in a special light.

The 1931 Stutz Bearcat Speedster

Running Boards
To help you in. If you haven't already experienced the Smithsonian ride, hop on! Ask one of our automotive account executives to take you for a spin through our pages. You'll enjoy the selling scenery. It's found only in Smithsonian.

Chrome Bumpers
For safety in the crunch. In today's volatile automotive market, Smithsonian affords advertisers the certainty of arriving at households where purchasing power and the desire to buy both live. One out of every five Smithsonian readers bought a new car last year.

Passenger Compartment
The 1931 Stutz Bearcat carried two people. These 4.8 million readers climb into Smithsonian each month for an entertaining and instructive trip through an unparalleled editorial scene.

Trunk
The place for extras. A valuable place to look into. Smithsonian has more subscriber households in the top-income 25 Zip Code markets than U.S. News and Newsweek; has a greater percentage of new car buyers than Time and Sports Illustrated; and has greater circulation concentration in the top 100 markets than the news weeklies. Little wonder that advertising investment by domestic and imported car manufacturers increased a whopping 31% in 1980.

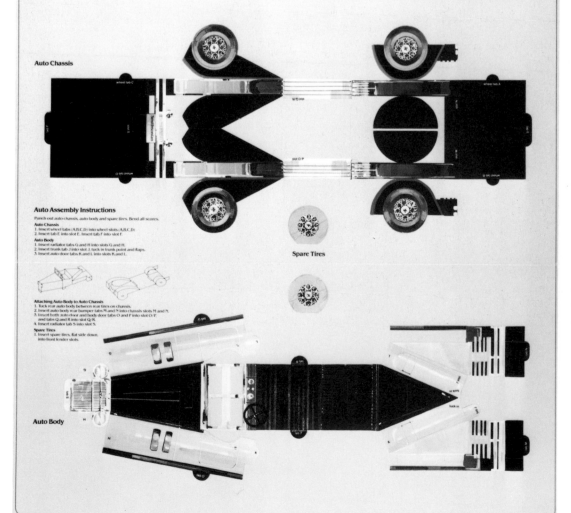

Auto Chassis

Spare Tires

Auto Assembly Instructions
Punch out auto chassis, auto body and spare tires. Bend all scores.

Auto Chassis
1. Insert wheel tabs (A,B,C,D) into wheel slots (A,B,C,D).
2. Insert tab E into slot E. Insert tab F into slot F.

Auto Body
1. Insert radiator tabs G and H into slots G and H.
2. Insert trunk tab J into slot J, tuck in trunk point and flaps.
3. Insert auto door tabs K and L into slots K and L.

Attaching Auto Body to Auto Chassis
1. Tuck rear auto body between rear tires on chassis.
2. Insert auto body rear bumper tabs M and N into chassis slots M and N.
3. Insert both auto door and body door tabs O and P into slot O-P, and tabs Q and R into slot Q-R.
4. Insert radiator tab S into slot S.

Spare Tires
1. Insert spare tires, flat side down, into front fender slots.

Auto Body

352 SILVER
ART DIRECTOR
Hal Tench
WRITER
Barbara Ford
DESIGNER
Hal Tench
PHOTOGRAPHER
John Whitehead
CLIENT
Collegiate Schools
AGENCY
The Martin Agency/Virginia

353
ART DIRECTORS
Dave Martin
Jack Mariucci
WRITERS
Mike Rogers
Stu Hyatt
DESIGNER
Dave Martin
PHOTOGRAPHERS
Stuart Peltz
Sean Eager
CLIENT
Eye Research Institute
AGENCY
Doyle Dane Bernbach

354
ART DIRECTORS
David Deutsch
Rocco Campanelli
WRITER
John Clarkson
CLIENT
Glamour Magazine
AGENCY
David Deutsch Associates

352 SILVER

**He's got his father's eyes.
Cataracts and all.**

For far too many children, the dark ages begin at an early age. With genetic disorders that cause cataracts and other serious eye problems.

The persistent work of the Eye Research Institute (the world's largest independent eye research center) gives physicians a greater ability to understand and treat these and many other blinding eye conditions.

In fact, the techniques and treatments we've developed help restore or preserve the vision of tens of thousands of people every year. With your support, we could help lots more.

Please send your tax deductible contribution to us at 20 Staniford Street, Dept. EB, Boston, MA 02114. Or write for further information.

If you see the light, chances are more visually impaired children will, too.

EYE RESEARCH INSTITUTE
Don't close your eyes to the problem of blindness.

BRING LIGHT INTO DARKNESS.
SUPPORT EYE RESEARCH.

353

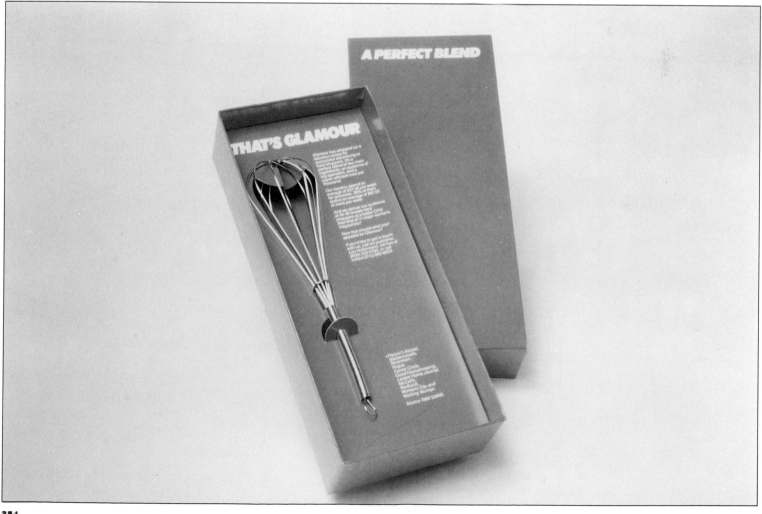

354

355
ART DIRECTOR
Ed Tajon
WRITER
Bill Borders
DESIGNER
Ed Tajon
ARTIST
Ken Orvidas
PHOTOGRAPHER
Pete Stone
CLIENT
Omark Industries/Oregon
Saw Chain Div.
AGENCY
Borders, Perrin & Norrander/
Oregon

356
ART DIRECTOR
Teddy Hwang
WRITER
Karen Loh
DESIGNER AND ARTIST
Teddy Hwang
CLIENT
Doyle Dane Bernbach/
Hong Kong
AGENCY
Doyle Dane Bernbach/
Hong Kong

357
ART DIRECTOR
Dianne Fiumara
WRITER
Ron Burkhardt
DESIGNER
Dianne Fiumara
PHOTOGRAPHER
Steve Bronstein
CLIENT
Minolta
AGENCY
Bozell & Jacobs

355

READ THIS OR GET LOST

From Nov. 9 Doyle Dane Bernbach 飛霸 Advertising is at : Hennessy Centre, 37th flr. Hong Kong. Tel: 5-765562
(You know . . . above Mitsukoshi Dept. Store.)

356

OLD COPIERS NEVER DIE.

THEY JUST

FADE AWAY

Your copier may be only _____ years old on the outside, but it's _____ years old inside.

Because copiers age 25 human years for each year of use.

So before you know it, yours can be out of service more often than in.

Your first warning will be funny little sounds coming from inside your machine. Metallic dings and pings. Strange groans and whines.

Or you'll see copies that once came out crisp and clear start to go grey around the edges. Or fuzzy in the middle.

These are all symptoms of old age. Telling you to trade in your old copier before it becomes an ooooold copier.

If you fear your copier's time has come, mail the enclosed coupon. We can tell you for sure in one ten-minute visit.

But be sure to send it today.

Your copier isn't getting any younger.

358

359

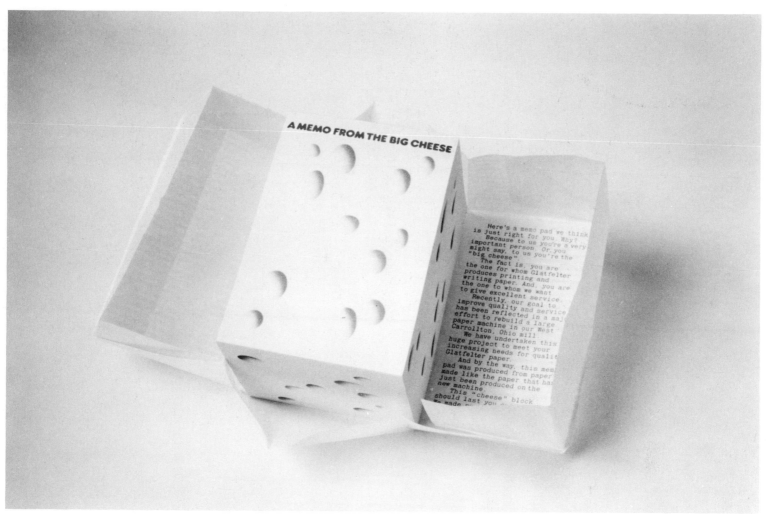

360

361

362

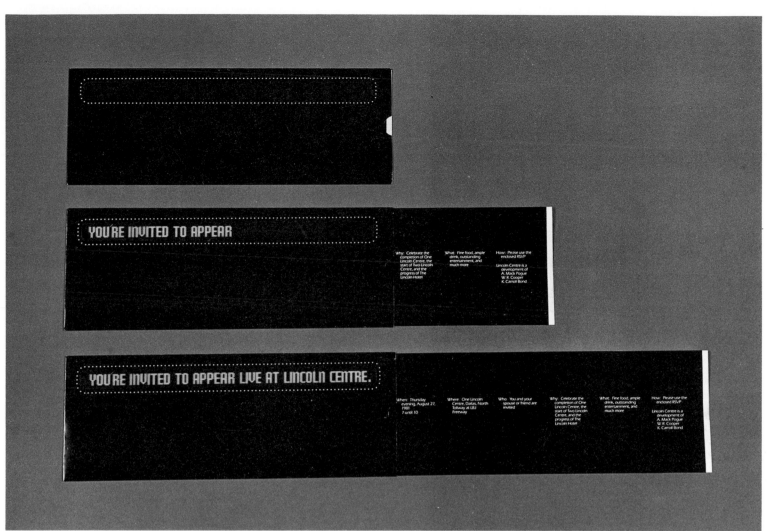

363 GOLD

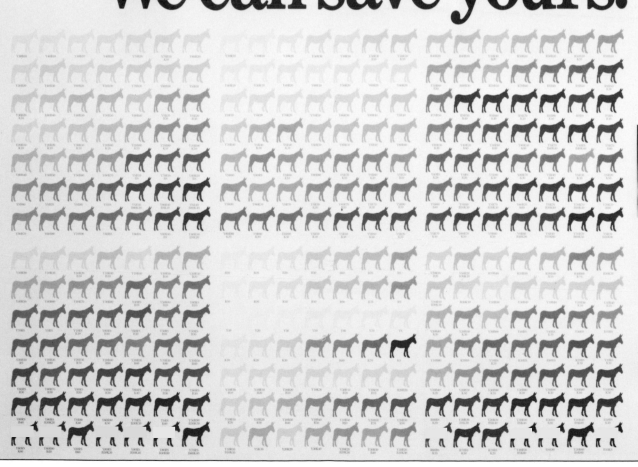

We can save yours.

Production problems, tight deadlines and sudden changes have a way of arising just when you thought things were under control.

That's why it's good to have Kieffer-Nolde full service quality working for you. We're as good at our job as you are at yours. We're experienced in offset, gravure and letterpress processes. We know how to keep projects from turning into problems. And we have a

track record for being able to handle whatever you trust to us. So, when you pick a color —any color—that's exactly what you'll get in return.

In a quarter-century serving the advertising community, we've seen some significant changes, but the way we work with production pros is still the same. Knowing where to save time and trouble is your job. And saving them for you is ours.

One less thing for you to worry about.

KIEFFER·NOLDE kn

*Kieffer-Nolde, Inc. Full Service Engravers
160 East Illinois, Chicago, Illinois 60611
(312) 337-5500 Toll Free 800-621-8114*

NOTE: This color chart was printed according to the following specifications: 100 lb. L.O.E. gloss paper; 4A Pert shade inks; B-R-Y-K inking sequence; 120-line screen; Miller 4-color press.

365
ART DIRECTOR
John LeeWong
WRITER
Dave Wollert
DESIGNER
John LeeWong
PHOTOGRAPHER
Tom Kelley Studio
CLIENT
Marantz
AGENCY
Chickering/Howell-Los
Angeles

366
ART DIRECTOR
Ed Tajon
WRITER
Dave Newman
DESIGNER
Ed Tajon
ARTIST
Ford Gilbreath
PHOTOGRAPHER
Pete Stone
CLIENT
Kah-Nee-Ta Resort
AGENCY
Borders, Perrin &
Norrander/Oregon

367
ART DIRECTORS
David Deutsch
Rocco Campanelli
WRITER
John Clarkson
CLIENT
Glamour Magazine
AGENCY
David Deutsch Associates

365

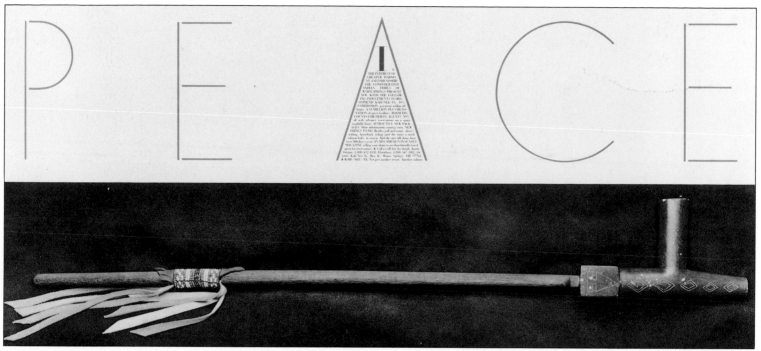

366

367

368
ART DIRECTOR
Anthony Angotti
WRITER
Tom Thomas
DESIGNER
Denise Monaco
PHOTOGRAPHER
Dick James
CLIENT
BMW of North America
AGENCY
Ammirati & Puris

369
ART DIRECTOR
Tom Kelly
WRITER
Bill Borders
DESIGNER
Tom Kelly
PHOTOGRAPHER
Aaron Jones
CLIENT
Blitz-Weinhard Brewing
AGENCY
Borders, Perrin &
Norrander/Oregon

370
ART DIRECTOR
John Constable
WRITERS
Steve Laughlin
Dennis Frankenberry
DESIGNERS
John Constable
Jay Filter
PHOTOGRAPHER
David Vander Veen
CLIENT
Oshkosh B'Gosh
AGENCY
Frankenberry, Laughlin
& Constable/Milwaukee

371
ART DIRECTORS
Kim Stuffelbeam
Mike Waterkotte
WRITERS
Tom Wolferman
Jim Corboy
DESIGNER
Mike Waterkotte
ARTIST
Steve Musgrave
CLIENT
WMET Radio
AGENCY
Eisaman, Johns
& Laws/Chicago

368

369

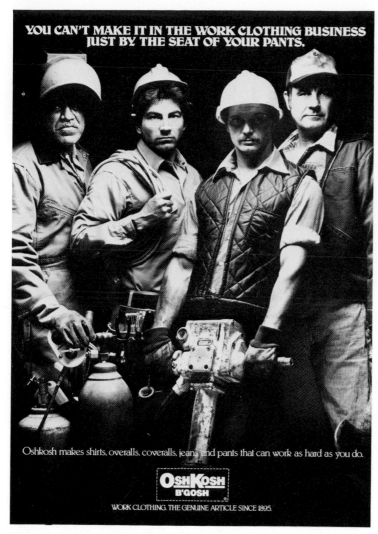

370

371

TRUE SAFETY IS THE ABILITY TO OUTMANEUVER DISASTERS, NOT MERELY SUSTAIN THEM.

It's often assumed that a safe car is one that's crash-worthy.

Actually, that's only half true. A safe car is also one that can avoid situations where it's called upon to prove its crash-worthiness.

Which is why BMWs are equipped with road-adhering fully independent suspensions, disc brakes, and sensitive steering systems pioneered by BMW race cars, quick enough to respond to the reflex corrections that emergencies require.

It is also why BMW passenger compartments are enclosed in steel pillars, roll bars, and rigid struts and cross-struts—and cushioned by computer-designed, energy-absorbing front and rear body sections.

It's obviously essential that a car make the maximum possible contribution to its own safe operation.

But it's no less vital that the driver be able to do the same.

THE ULTIMATE DRIVING MACHINE.

372

373

374 GOLD

EVERY BMW BEGINS LIFE AS A METICULOUSLY ENGINEERED BLUR.

BMWs are not created in a theoretical vacuum. They are the result of lessons learned on the great race-courses of the world.

So the blur shown above, the Kenwood-sponsored BMW M1/GTP, is considerably more than just a 200-mph race car.

It is very likely a forerunner of BMW passenger cars to come.

375

Give your right foot a hand.

Introducing new Bendix Cruise Control. It's the air-actuated electronically-controlled, road-tested, reliable relief driver that doesn't need a coffee break.

Minimizes fatigue, lets you concentrate on the road, not the speedometer.

Maximizes fuel efficiency by keeping speed steady.

Eliminates cable hand throttle for cold weather warm-ups.

Models for all popular engine and transmission combinations.

Designed especially for Class 7 & 8 linehaul tractors.

Available as an OE spec or in retrofit kits.

Dependable. Runs off air system with no drain on engine power.

You can't afford less.　**Bendix**

376

LAST YEAR, A CAR OUT-PERFORMED 318 STOCKS ON THE NEW YORK STOCK EXCHANGE.

If you'd bought a new BMW 320i in the beginning of 1980, and sold it at the end, your investment would have retained 92.9% of its original value.
If you'd done the same with any of 318 NYSE stocks, you'd have done less well.
And you'd have forfeited an important daily dividend:
The unfluctuating joy of driving one of the world's great performance sedans.

THE ULTIMATE DRIVING MACHINE.
BMW MUNICH, GERMANY

377 SILVER

WE RELUCTANTLY ANNOUNCE A CONVENIENT NEW PACKAGE

It has always been our belief that the only container which is appropriate to a true premium beer like Henry Weinhard's Private Reserve is a traditional glass bottle.

But bottles, unfortunately, are not appropriate to all the places where people like to drink Henry's. At the beach, for example. Or a soft-ball game. Or on a backpacking trip.

Recognizing this, and in response to numerous requests

from our customers and our friends in the retail trade, we have decided to make Henry's commercially available in the cans we originally intended only for service aboard airlines. While these cans lack the "bottling numbers" that distinguish the various limited brews of Henry Weinhard's Private Reserve, be assured that the product is identical in every respect to that offered in bottles and on draught.

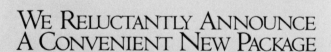

THE BLITZ-WEINHARD BREWING COMPANY OF PORTLAND, OREGON

378

379

380

IF THERE'S A MAXELL CASSETTE IN THIS CAR AND IT DOESN'T WORK, WE'LL REPLACE IT.

IT'S WORTH IT.

381 SILVER

One of the few things on the Space Shuttle that didn't have a backup system.

382 GOLD

383

386

ART DIRECTORS
Tim Hamill
Steve Nelson
Bob Jensen

WRITERS
Al Olson
Patrick DiNatale

CLIENT
Crown Center Redevelopment

AGENCY
Brewer Advertising/
Kansas City

387 GOLD

ART DIRECTOR
Bob Marberry

WRITER
Dick Thomas

PHOTOGRAPHER
Rick Dublin

CLIENT
Saigon Restaurant

AGENCY
Bobco/Mpls.

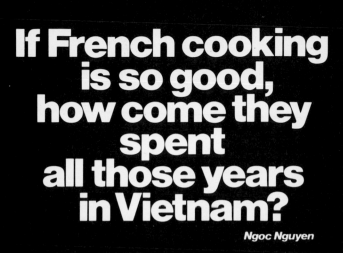

**If French cooking
is so good,
how come they
spent
all those years
in Vietnam?**

Ngoc Nguyen

THE SAIGON RESTAURANT
38th & Grand 822-7712

**I didn't
come
9000 miles
to
cook you
ordinary food.**

Ngoc Nguyen

THE SAIGON RESTAURANT
38th & Grand 822-7712

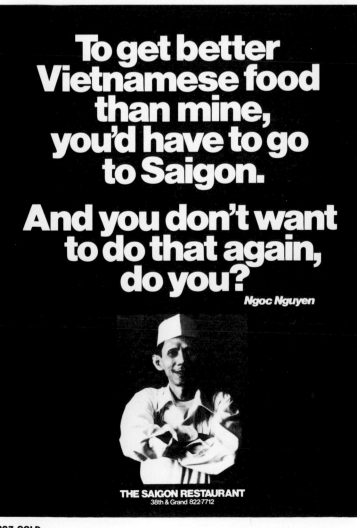

**To get better
Vietnamese food
than mine,
you'd have to go
to Saigon.**

**And you don't want
to do that again,
do you?**

Ngoc Nguyen

THE SAIGON RESTAURANT
38th & Grand 822-7712

388 SILVER
ART DIRECTOR
John Knight
WRITER
Lyndon Mallett
DESIGNER
Geoff Halpin
PHOTOGRAPHER
Billy Wrencher
CLIENT
Wolverhampton & Dudley
Breweries
AGENCY
TBWA/London

389
ART DIRECTOR
David Harrison
WRITER
Peter Little
DESIGNER
David Harrison
PHOTOGRAPHER
Derek Seagrim
CLIENT
Mainstop
AGENCY
Davidson Pearce/London

388 SILVER

390

He's got his father's eyes.
Cataracts and all.

For far too many children, the dark ages begin at an early age. With genetic disorders that cause cataracts and other serious eye problems.

The persistent work of the Eye Research Institute (the world's largest independent eye research center) gives physicians a greater ability to understand and treat these and many other blinding eye conditions.

In fact, the techniques and treatments we've developed help restore or preserve the vision of tens of thousands of people every year. With your support, we could help lots more.

Please send your tax deductible contribution to us at 20 Staniford Street, Dept. EB, Boston, MA 02114. Or write for further information.

If you see the light, chances are more visually impaired children will, too.

EYE RESEARCH INSTITUTE
Don't close your eyes to the problem of blindness.

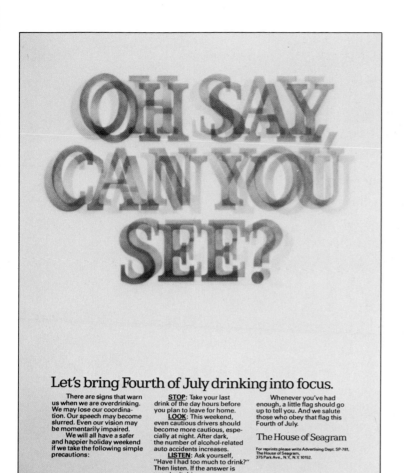

OH SAY, CAN YOU SEE?

Let's bring Fourth of July drinking into focus.

There are signs that warn us when we are overdrinking. We may lose our coordination. Our speech may become slurred. Even our vision may be momentarily impaired.

We will all have a safer and happier holiday weekend if we take the following simple precautions:

STOP: Take your last drink of the day hours before you plan to leave for home.
LOOK: This weekend, even cautious drivers should become more cautious, especially at night. After dark, the number of alcohol-related auto accidents increases.
LISTEN: Ask yourself, "Have I had too much to drink?" Then listen. If the answer is yes, don't drive.

Whenever you've had enough, a little flag should go up to tell you. And we salute those who obey that flag this Fourth of July.

The House of Seagram

For reprints please write Advertising Dept. SP-781,
The House of Seagram,
375 Park Ave., N.Y., N.Y. 10152.

391

It's New Year's Eve.

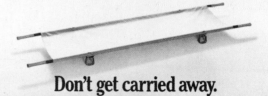

Don't get carried away.

There's no reason to beat around the bush when you're asking people not to kill themselves. If you're driving tonight, please drink responsibly.

If you've had too much to drink, don't get behind the wheel. Or you might find that you'll wind up in a more permanent resting place.

The way we see it, if one life is saved, this message is worth thousands of times the cost of publishing it. Have a happy and healthy New Year. **THE HOUSE OF SEAGRAM**

For reprints please write Advertising Dept. PE-1281,
The House of Seagram, 375 Park Ave., N.Y., N.Y. 10152

392 GOLD

The earthquake is over but the shock wave continues.

The quake in southern Italy happened back on November 23, 1980. Yet people are still homeless. Families still separated. Schools still shut. Hospitals still working overtime. Everywhere there are tens of thousands of people with only a past and very little future. They need your help. Please be generous and send a donation to the Red Cross.

That way the homeless will get shelter, the sick will get medicine, the hungry will get fed. Your donation could make a lot of people feel better. Including yourself.

The Italian Earthquake Relief Fund.

Yes, I would like to help the victims of the Italian earthquake. Here is my check for:

☐ $10 ☐ $20 ☐ Other _____

Name _____
Address _____
City _____
State _____ Zip _____

Make check to:
American Red Cross/Italian Earthquake Relief
Mail to: Jo Scott, 330 Madison Ave., 10th floor,
New York, N.Y. 10017

A public service announcement by the following U.S. advertising agencies:
N.W. Ayer ABH International • Ted Bates & Company, Inc. • BBDO International, Inc. • Benton & Bowles, Inc.
Compton Advertising Incorporated • Dancer Fitzgerald Sample, Inc. • Doyle Dane Bernbach Inc. • Foote, Cone & Belding
McCann-Erickson, Inc. • Ogilvy & Mather International Inc. • Young & Rubicam Inc.

393 SILVER

If these people have cancer, why are they so happy?

They're happy because they're winning the battle. Which is no longer a rare occurrence. In fact, of all the major diseases, cancer has one of the highest cure rates.

But we need your help to make sure the cure rate continues to improve. Please support the American Cancer Society by giving to the United Way.

 Give to the United Way. Because life is worth giving.

395 GOLD

That'll give you an idea of what it's like to be a victim of the Italian earthquake.

Over the next few weeks, the people at Y&R are being asked to make a contribution to help a few hundred thousand unfortunate people in Italy. Your money will go to the Red Cross. That way the homeless can get shelter, the sick can get medicine, the hungry can get fed. You could make a lot of people happy. Including yourself. Please be generous. Make your check payable to: American Red Cross/Italian Earthquake Relief. Mail to: Jo Scott, Y&R, 330 Madison Avenue, N.Y., N.Y. 10017

The Y&R Italian Earthquake Relief Fund.

The earthquake is over but the shock wave continues.

396

Sleep in the street tonight.

That'll give you an idea of what it's like to be a victim of the Italian earthquake.

Over the next few weeks, the people at Y&R are being asked to make a contribution to help a few hundred thousand unfortunate people in Italy. Your money will go to the Red Cross. That way the homeless can get shelter, the sick can get medicine, the hungry can get fed. You could make a lot of people happy. Including yourself. Please be generous. Make your check payable to: American Red Cross/Italian Earthquake Relief. Mail to: Jo Scott, Y&R, 330 Madison Avenue, N.Y., N.Y. 10017

The Y&R Italian Earthquake Relief Fund.
The earthquake is over but the shock wave continues.

397

Dogs can't read, but you can.

Obey the Pooper Scooper Law!

If you can read this, there's a chance you have glaucoma.

You can read an eye chart perfectly and still have glaucoma. Most forms of the disease progress painlessly, often with no symptoms. Which makes it difficult to detect. In fact, over one million Americans have glaucoma and don't know it.

The work of the Eye Research Institute (the world's largest independent eye research center) gives physicians a greater ability to understand and treat glaucoma and other blinding eye conditions.

Our discoveries help restore or preserve the vision of tens of thousands of people every year. There are many more we can't help. Not because finding a cure is difficult. But because finding the money is.

Please send your tax deductible contribution to us at 20 Staniford Street, Dept. EB, Boston, MA 02114. Or write for information.

Your gift could give someone the most precious gift of all. Vision.

EYE RESEARCH INSTITUTE
Don't close your eyes to the problem of blindness.

400
ART DIRECTOR
Rob Dalton
WRITER
Leslie Trinite Clark
DESIGNER
Rob Dalton
PHOTOGRAPHER
Rick Dublin
CLIENT
Courage Alpine Skiers
AGENCY
Brandt/Barringmann-Mpls.

401
ART DIRECTOR
John Triolo
WRITER
Ken Musto
DESIGNER
John Triolo
CLIENT
Italian Earthquake Relief
Fund
AGENCY
Young & Rubicam

402 SILVER
ART DIRECTOR
Ed Tajon
WRITER
Dave Newman
DESIGNER
Ed Tajon
ARTIST
Ken Orvidas
CLIENT
American Red Cross,
Portland Chapter
AGENCY
Borders, Perrin &
Norrander/Oregon

403
ART DIRECTOR
Arnold Wicht
WRITER
Tim Heintzman
PHOTOGRAPHER
Rudi von Tiedermann
CLIENT
Ontario Ministry of the
Attorney General
AGENCY
Camp Associates/Canada

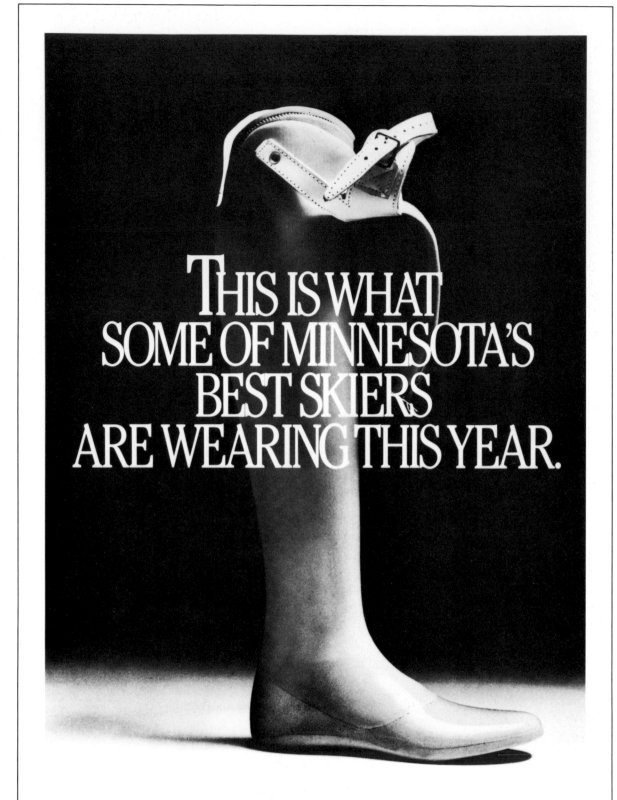

400

That'll give you an idea of what it's like to be a victim of the Italian earthquake.

Over the next few weeks, the people at Y&R are being asked to make a contribution to help a few hundred thousand unfortunate people in Italy. Your money will go to the Red Cross. That way the homeless can get shelter, the sick can get medicine, the hungry can get fed. You could make a lot of people happy. Including yourself. Please be generous. Make your check payable to: American Red Cross/Italian Earthquake Relief. Mail to: Jo Scott, Y&R, 330 Madison Avenue, N.Y., N.Y. 10017.

The Y&R Italian Earthquake Relief Fund.

The earthquake is over but the shock wave continues.

401

402 SILVER

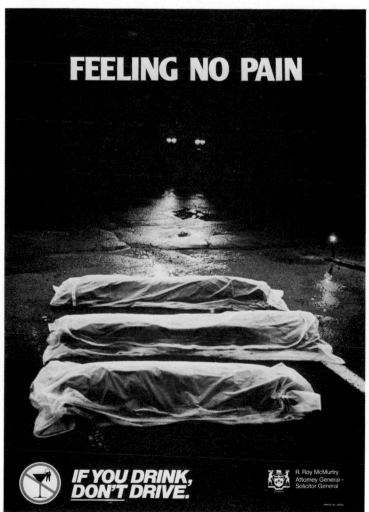

403

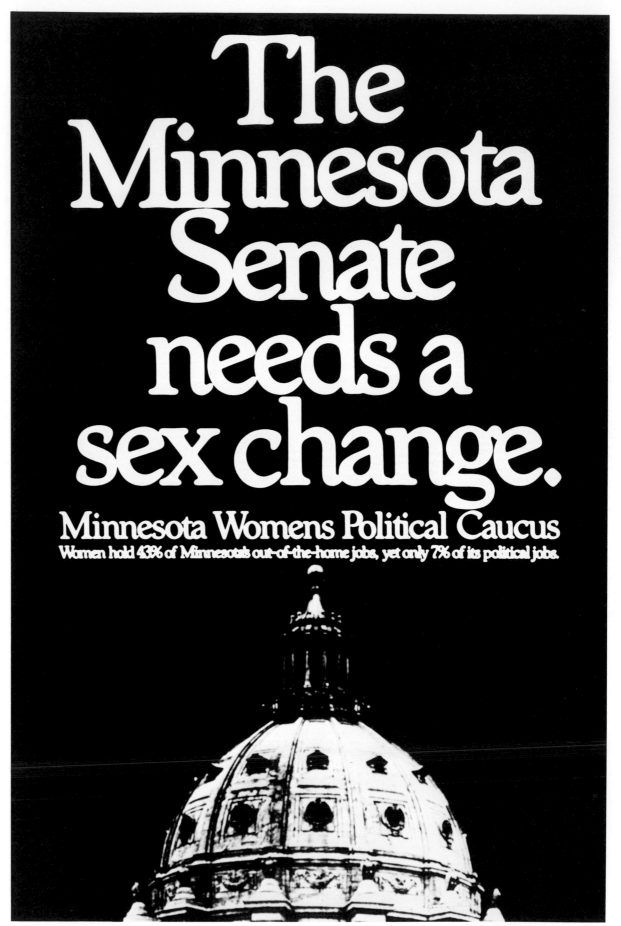

404

IN 1959, XEROX INVENTED THE XEROX.

TODAY THEY MAY WISH THEY INVENTED THE SAVIN.

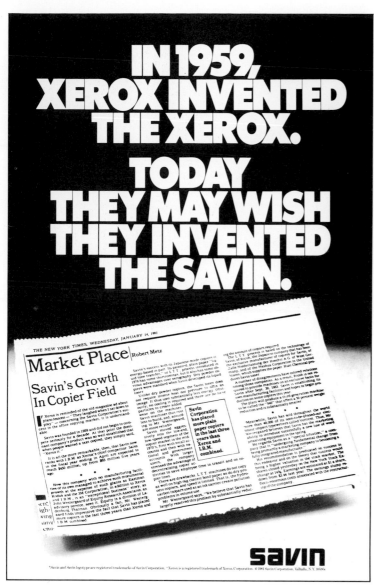

savin

405

WHEN YOU'RE 966 MILLION MILES IN SPACE, YOU CAN'T DROP YOUR PICTURES OFF AT THE CORNER DRUGSTORE.

The planet Saturn is so far away, it has taken Voyager 2, travelling several times the speed of sound, four years to get there. Even a radio message takes almost an hour and a half to make the trip. Imagine the challenge of sending back pictures.

And yet, the pictures get back. And with amazing clarity.

A Motorola communications system designed for the Jet Propulsion Laboratory and NASA transmits all the pictures from Voyager 2.

This Motorola system also provides the link for all other communications between Earth and the spacecraft, and relays the scientific information Voyager 2 gathers on this remarkable journey, just as one of our systems did for Voyager 1.

In fact, Motorola electronic systems have been part of U.S. space programs since Explorer I in 1958. Our equipment has been used on every manned and most unmanned space shots without a single failure affecting mission success. Not one.

Bringing pictures back from 966 million miles away is just another example of Motorola's advanced technology and reliability meeting challenges around the world. And beyond.

Ⓜ **MOTOROLA** *A World Leader In Electronics.*

Quality and productivity through employee participation in management.

406

Which bag would you prefer?

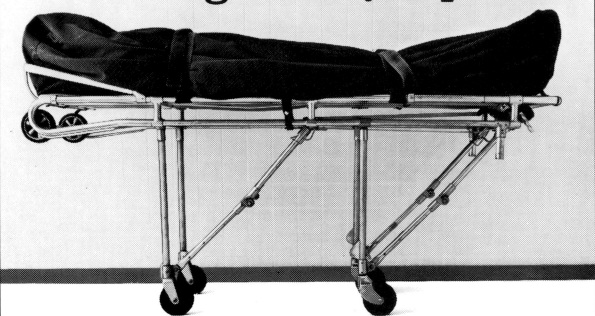

At this moment, President Reagan and his Cabinet are reviewing the future of U.S. Passive Restraint Legislation. (An act that would provide for factory installation of air bags in all cars.)

In Allstate's book, this is a perfectly reasonable and proper thing for the Executive Branch of the United States Government to be doing.

Except for one slightly disturbing note.

Whatever they decide will inevitably affect Canadians, because under the Canada-U.S. Auto Pact, most of our cars are designed in the U.S.

Why should Canadians worry about this?

After all, every car sold in Canada already has seat belts, and four provinces have even gone to the trouble of passing mandatory "buckle-up" laws.

And everybody knows that, even though nothing is perfect, seat belts provide reasonably good protection on the road.

In spite of these comforting thoughts, we think Canadians *should* worry.

Because seat belts by definition suffer from a potentially fatal flaw.

Human nature.

Unless the people in the car actually perform the voluntary act of doing up their seat belts, they end up with no protection at all.

And we all know about human nature when it comes to voluntary acts, even if they are life savers.

A typical example is drunk driving.

Why don't people perform the voluntary act of not driving when they're under the influence?

When you consider that impaired

driving is about as dangerous as Russian roulette, this particular voluntary act could be a real life saver.

It's the same with seat belts. By performing the voluntary act of buckling up, car occupants could help save their lives by the thousands.

(Not to mention the millions of dollars in hospital and highway emergency costs that are borne by us all.)

The sad truth is that even in provinces with strong "buckle up" laws, supported by advertising campaigns, seat belt use is *actually slipping.* (Example: in a recent B.C. survey, seat belt use was found to have slipped from 63% to 54% in just six months. Other provincial surveys could be worse.)

Without even counting in the people who are excluded from using seat belts such as Police, emergency vehicle drivers and individuals with certain medical

Allstate
A company with values

problems, this leaves a lot of Canadians dangerously unprotected. If only it weren't for human nature!

Do we have to stay on this merry-go-round?

No. Because there is an alternative.

Air bags.

Because they're in place, ready to operate 100% of the time, air bags don't depend on any voluntary act by the driver or passenger.

Because of this fundamental advantage over seat belts, and their protective capability proven by more than 750 million kilometres of actual highway driving experience, we estimate that if every car in Canada was equipped with air bags 900 lives and 6,500 injuries* could be saved in the next twelve months.

And because air bags could save some of the millions of dollars that insurance companies have to pay out now for death and injury claims, car insurance costs could better be brought under control.

Allstate understands the problems now being faced by the North American automobile industry.

We appreciate that losses of more than 4 billion dollars in 1980 can make car manufacturers somewhat reluctant to support air bag legislation that could add to the sticker price of their cars.

But Allstate also knows that because the technology exists, installing air bags on all cars at the factory would cost about the same as a vinyl roof or an AM/FM radio.

The choice is simple. A moderate investment in air bags to help save lives. Or another kind of bag.

Which would you prefer?

407 GOLD

DKG.
A NAME TO
FORGET.

It was a good name. And it stood for a lot of good things. Like award-winning creative. A blue-chip account list. And the kinds of marketing successes brand managers pray for. Which may be the reason DKG has received seven merger offers in the past twelve months.

After considering them carefully, we've decided. It's no dice.

We're not going to exchange our independence for someone else's stock. Or sacrifice our convictions to someone else's bottom line.

We're not going to merge.

Instead, we're going to emerge.

From now on, DKG will be known as Calet, Hirsch, Kurnit & Spector. After twenty years in the business, we're putting our names on the door. Our names. Not a combination of us and some merger-hungry monolith.

Because at Calet, Hirsch, Kurnit & Spector, the only ones we want to be responsible to are our clients.

AAMCO Transmissions
Alitalia Airlines
American Enka
Brown-Forman Distillers
Clairol Appliances
Corning Housewares
Corning Lenses
Dollar Savings Bank
Getty/Skelly
Martex/Lady Pepperell
Pocket Books
Ramada (Tropicana Hotel)
Remington Shavers
Ricoh Cameras
Simplicity Patterns
Talon Zippers
Thermos
Toshiba
True Temper
Uniroyal

Calet, Hirsch, Kurnit & Spector, Inc.

1271 AVENUE OF THE AMERICAS, NEW YORK, NY 10020/(212) 489-7300

AT SPERRY, LISTENING IS NOT A 9 TO 5 JOB.

A listener loose in a world of talkers has one unbeatable edge: the flow of new ideas through his ears to his mind never stops.

It's been said there's at least one thing to learn from everyone one meets. Provided one bothers to listen.

Unfortunately for most people, no one ever bothered to teach us how.

Which is why listening training is available to Sperry employees, worldwide.

Helping our people become better listeners helps make us a better corporation.

For one thing, it eliminates the enormous costs of simple listening errors.

But more than that, it's making our employees better thinkers. Better problem solvers. And ultimately, more open to the original and unexpected.

That's the most compelling reason of all for learning to listen.

You never know where the next great idea is coming from.

✦ SPERRY

We understand how important it is to listen.

Sperry is Sperry Univac computers, Sperry New Holland farm equipment, Sperry Vickers fluid power systems, and guidance and control equipment from Sperry division and Sperry Flight Systems.

To learn more about listening, write to Sperry, Dept. B3, 1290 Avenue of the Americas, New York, N.Y. 10104

Anyone who thinks there's a difference between a drunk driver and a stoned driver could be making a grave mistake.

Several months ago, Allstate ran an ad urging for more public understanding and discussion of the issues before decriminalization of marijuana was engraved in tablets of stone by Ottawa.

Response was excellent.

Individual Canadians and organizations expressed their views to us in the hundreds. Newspapers, radio stations and TV networks ran stories about the ad and the decriminalization issue nationally.

We even received some constructive letters from many prominent citizens and important political figures.

The only problem is, that in raising the decriminalization issue for public debate, we've also uncovered a minority belief that being stoned shouldn't necessarily prevent a person from driving a car.

A dangerous notion that driving performance is not impaired by cannabis and that the stoned driver is therefore a perfectly fit user of the highway.

In our opinion this idea is dead wrong. But just to show we're not alone in this belief, let's look at some conclusions that other people have reached.

MARIJUANA EFFECTS ON DRIVING: AMERICAN AUTOMOBILE ASSOCIATION FOUNDATION FOR TRAFFIC SAFETY, 1981.

"For young drivers who are in the early phase of the lengthy learning curve which characterizes the acquisition of driving skills, the risks and consequences of driving under the influence of marijuana are likely to be particularly severe."

THE ADDICTION RESEARCH FOUNDATION OF ONTARIO, 1980.

"It is now well recognized that even low doses of marijuana adversely affect driving performance, whether this is measured in a driving simulator, on a test track, or on city streets."

What are these reputable, recognized, authorities saying?

They have obviously concluded that marijuana can impair driving abilities.

Or in other words, that smoking grass and driving could turn out to be a potentially lethal error.

Disturbing news.

But what's even more disturbing is that the American Automobile Association 1981 study also found that "There are marijuana users who agree that it is unsafe to drive while high on marijuana but indicate that they do it anyway."

The attitude being expressed here is clearly "driving while high is O.K. for me."

What research doesn't conclusively prove (or conclusively disprove for that matter) is whether decriminalization or any liberalization of the laws will actually increase the frequency of marijuana-related accidents.

All we do know is that, even under our present severe laws, marijuana usage has been increasing for the past several years.

This trend is expected to continue.

And in our considered opinion, decriminalization alone, without consideration for controlling the fallout, can't but help worsen the trend.

How can we resolve this dilemma? Is it possible to have laws that treat cannabis use and possession in a humanitarian way but don't open the door to highway abuse?

Surely the place to start is with the monitoring and control of cannabis in and around driving situations.

We believe that with the introduction of the proposed decriminalization legislation, the Federal Government should negotiate with the Provincial and Territorial governments so that their highway acts will provide for additional, stronger penalties for possession of cannabis in any motor vehicle and authority for police to lay charges accordingly.

And as related activities, we suggest government support for consumer education about the issue and long-term monitoring of cannabis-related highway incidents.

At Allstate, we realize that it is not our business to be either for or against decriminalization of marijuana. That's up to the Government. But it is our business to be against needless death and injury on the highways of Canada. In Allstate's book, to be anything less would be a grave mistake.

Allstate A company with values

If you have an opinion on this issue, we'd appreciate hearing from you. Please write: Allstate, 255 Consumers Road, Willowdale, Ontario. M2J 1R4.

Which bag would you prefer?

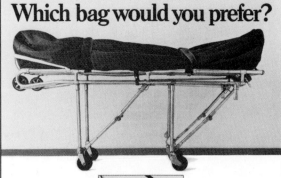

At this moment, President Reagan and his Cabinet are reviewing the future of U.S. Passive Restraint Legislation. (An act that would provide for factory installation of air bags in all cars.)

In Allstate's book, this is a perfectly reasonable and proper thing for the Executive Branch of the United States Government to be doing.

Except for one slightly disturbing note.

Whatever they decide will inevitably affect Canadians, because under the Canada-U.S. Auto Pact, most of our cars are designed in the U.S.

Why should Canadians worry about this?

After all, every car sold in Canada already has seat belts, and four provinces have even gone to the trouble of passing mandatory "buckle-up" laws.

And everybody knows that, even though nothing is perfect, seat belts provide reasonably good protection on the road.

In spite of these comforting thoughts, we think Canadians *should* worry.

Because seat belts by definition suffer from a potentially fatal flaw.

Human nature.

Unless the people in the car actually perform the voluntary act of doing up their seat belts, they end up with no protection at all.

And we all know about human nature when it comes to voluntary acts, even if they are life savers.

A typical example is drunk driving.

Why don't people perform the voluntary act of not driving when they're under the influence?

When you consider that impaired

driving is about as dangerous as Russian roulette, this particular voluntary act could be a real life saver.

It's the same with seat belts. By performing the voluntary act of buckling up, car occupants could help save their lives by the thousands.

(Not to mention the millions of dollars in hospital and highway emergency costs that are borne by us all.)

The sad truth is that even in provinces with strong "buckle up" laws, supported by advertising campaigns, seat belt use is *actually slipping*. (Example: in a recent B.C. survey, seat belt use was found to have slipped from 63% to 54% in just six months. Other provincial surveys could be worse.)

Without even counting in the people who are excluded from using seat belts such as Police, emergency vehicle drivers and individuals with certain medical problems, this leaves a lot of Canadians dangerously unprotected. If only it weren't for human nature!

Do we have to stay on this merry-go-round?

No. Because there is an alternative.

Air bags.

Because they're in place, ready to operate 100% of the time, air bags don't depend on any voluntary act by the driver or passenger.

Because of this fundamental advantage over seat belts, and their protective capability proven by more than 750 million kilometres of actual highway driving experience, we estimate that if every car in Canada was equipped with air bags 900 lives and 6,500 injuries* could be saved in the next twelve months.

And because air bags could save some of the millions of dollars that insurance companies have to pay out now for death and injury claims, car insurance costs could better be brought under control.

Allstate understands the problems now being faced by the North American automobile industry.

We appreciate that losses of more than 4 billion dollars in 1980 can make car manufacturers somewhat reluctant to support air bag legislation that could add to the sticker price of their cars.

But Allstate also knows that because the technology exists, installing air bags on all cars at the factory would cost about the same as a vinyl roof or an AM/FM radio.

The choice is simple. A moderate investment in air bags to help save lives.

Or another kind of bag.

Which would you prefer?

Allstate A company with values

If you have an opinion on this issue, or if you'd just like more air bag information, we'd like to hear from you. Please write: Consumer Information Group, Allstate Insurance Companies of Canada, 255 Consumers Road, Willowdale, Ontario. M2J 1R4.

*An estimate for Canada based on U.S. Department of Transport Studies.

Decriminalization of Marijuana. Let's understand all of the issues before it gets carved in tablets of stone.

Sometime in 1981, the House of Commons will debate a bill which will decriminalize the possession of marijuana.

If this legislation is subsequently passed into law, the act of possessing marijuana will be changed from a crime to a simple misdemeanor.

Which means something like a traffic ticket instead of a jail sentence if you're caught.

While the bill does not entirely legalize the act of smoking grass, the vast majority of people will interpret it as if it did.

After all, if you can practically carry it, you can smoke it.

And if you can smoke it, you can get stoned out of your mind on it.

Which brings us to the one discordant note in an otherwise humanitarian change in the law.

The Traffic Injury Research Foundation of Canada has irrefutable research findings obtained in a recent study of fatal highway accidents proving that one of every eight victims had been using cannabis.

In our book, this proves that the popular belief that grass doesn't interfere with psychomotor response is wrong.

Dead wrong. Grass can kill on the highway just as lethally as alcohol can.

Allstate's position on this life and death matter is simple.

It's not our business to be either for or against decriminalization of marijuana.

That's up to Parliament.

But it is our business to be against needless death and injury on the highways. From where we sit, we have a horrifyingly first-hand view of the increasing waste of life and money caused by road accidents and we know it has to be stopped.

So before Parliament passes a bill that may cause a road safety hazard as serious as that of alcohol, let's at least understand and discuss the issues.

Let's ask ourselves and our elected representatives if we have enough facts to justify such a far reaching move at this time.

If, in our enthusiasm for freeing young people from the stigma of a criminal record, we aren't at the same time condemning them to a self-inflicted death.

And equally to the point, if laws as they apply to cannabis should not be changed to mirror existing statutes that provide stiff penalties for carrying open bottles of liquor or beer in a motor vehicle.

Allstate urges you to consider these issues.

Before they get carved in tablets of stone.

Allstate A company with values

Like to know more about cannabis and its effect on driving? Write: Consumer Information Group, Allstate Insurance Companies of Canada, 255 Consumers Road, Willowdale, Ontario. M2J 1R4

WE USED TO BRING YOU THE SIX O'CLOCK NEWS. NOW WE ARE THE SIX O'CLOCK NEWS.

Back in the 1950s, when the 6 o'clock news first started finding its way into people's living rooms, Motorola was there.

Today, although we're no longer making television sets, we're still there when people all over the country sit down to the 6 o'clock news.

Except now, instead of making the sets they're watching, we're part of the history they're watching.

On November 12, 1980, a Motorola communications subsystem designed for the Jet Propulsion Laboratory and NASA sent photographs back to Earth from a billion miles away near the planet Saturn.

This equipment, the only link between Earth and the Voyager spacecraft, not only sent photos that thrilled a watching world, it also transmitted data that turned centuries of scientific thought upside down.

One month before, the world's largest auto maker was able to announce a giant step forward in improving gas mileage while at the same time decreasing emissions because of an engine management system that runs on a microprocessor Motorola designed.

And in the years ahead, technology we're pioneering may bring microelectronic devices into our lives that the world has only dreamed of before.

Like a portable telephone small enough to fit in your pocket.

Microprocessors that could allow industrial robots to function ten times faster than humans.

And microchips that make it possible to use computers to find oil miles beneath the earth's crust without drilling an inch.

All these advances and more are being pioneered by Motorola in our development centers around the world. And in many ways they're only the beginning of what we can do.

So the next time you see something on the 6 o'clock news that you never imagined possible, you'll know there's a chance someone at Motorola had a part in making it happen. And if that makes us sound like a company far different from the one that once made television sets for your living room, it's simply because we are.

Motorola and Ⓜ are registered trademarks of Motorola, Inc.

Making electronics history. Ⓜ **MOTOROLA**

WHEN YOU'RE 966 MILLION MILES IN SPACE, YOU CAN'T DROP YOUR PICTURES OFF AT THE CORNER DRUGSTORE.

The planet Saturn is so far away, it has taken Voyager 2, travelling several times the speed of sound, four years to get there. Even a radio message takes almost an hour and a half to make the trip. Imagine the challenge of sending back pictures.

And yet, the pictures get back. And with amazing clarity.

A Motorola communications system designed for the Jet Propulsion Laboratory and NASA transmits all the pictures from Voyager 2.

This Motorola system also provides the link for all other communications between Earth and the spacecraft, and relays the scientific information Voyager 2 gathers on this remarkable journey, just as one of our systems did for Voyager 1.

In fact, Motorola electronic systems have been part of U.S. space programs since Explorer I in 1958. Our equipment has been used on every manned and most unmanned space shots without a single failure affecting mission success. Not one.

Bringing pictures back from 966 million miles away is just another example of Motorola's advanced electronic and reliability meeting challenges around the world. And beyond.

Ⓜ **MOTOROLA** *A World Leader In Electronics.*

Quality and productivity through employee participation in management.

Motorola Inc. is one of the world's leading manufacturers of electronic equipment, systems and components, including: communications systems, semiconductors, equipment for military and aerospace use; industrial and automotive electronic equipment; and data communications products.

WE USED TO BRING YOU THE SIX O'CLOCK NEWS. NOW WE ARE THE SIX O'CLOCK NEWS.

Back in the 1950s, when the 6 o'clock news first started finding its way into people's living rooms, Motorola was there.

Today, although we're no longer making television sets, we're still there when people all over the world sit down to the 6 o'clock news.

Except now, instead of making the sets they're watching, we're part of the history they're watching.

On November 12, 1980, a Motorola communications subsystem designed for the Jet Propulsion Laboratory and NASA sent photographs back to Earth from a billion miles away near the planet Saturn.

This equipment, the only link between Earth and the Voyager spacecraft, not only sent photos that thrilled a watching world, it also transmitted data that turned centuries of scientific thought upside down.

One month before, the world's largest auto maker was able to announce a giant step forward in improving gas mileage while at the same time decreasing emissions because of an engine management system that runs on a microprocessor Motorola designed.

And in the years ahead, technology we're pioneering may bring microelectronic devices into our lives that the world has only dreamed of before.

Like a portable telephone small enough to fit in your pocket.

Microprocessors that could allow industrial robots to function ten times faster than humans.

And microchips that make it possible to use computers to find oil miles beneath the earth's crust without drilling an inch.

All these advances and more are being pioneered by Motorola in our development centers around the world.

And in many ways they're only the beginning of what we can do.

So the next time you see something on the 6 o'clock news that you never imagined possible, you'll know there's a chance someone at Motorola had a part in making it happen.

And if that makes us sound like a company far different from the one that once made television sets for your living room, it's simply because we are.

Making electronics history. Ⓜ **MOTOROLA**

LISTENING WELL DOESN'T MEAN SAYING YES.

It's human nature to suspect we aren't being listened to whenever we aren't agreed with.

To quote a pointed piece of office sarcasm: "If you don't agree with me, then I obviously haven't made myself clear."

But the fact is, no one's less likely to be a "yes man" than someone who listens well.

To us at Sperry, listening isn't just a selling tool. It's a corporate philosophy.

To our customers, it means we're committed to understanding their problems, without bias or preconception, and telling them the truth. Even if the truth isn't what they want to hear.

To our employees, it means we know management has no monopoly on good ideas. So we listen–even to things that _we_ don't want to hear.

Listening is making Sperry a better corporation, and a more exciting place to work.

As a company determined to be at the forefront of every industry we serve, no one better knows the need for unorthodox thinking, diverse ideas.

"Yes men" are a luxury we simply can't afford.

✦ SPERRY
We understand how important it is to listen.

Sperry is Sperry Univac computers, Sperry New Holland farm equipment, Sperry Vickers fluid power systems, and guidance and control equipment from Sperry division and Sperry Flight Systems.

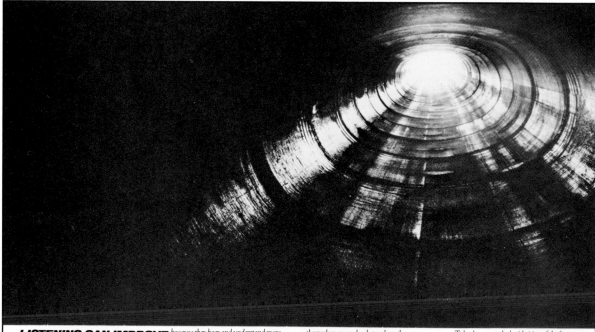

LISTENING CAN IMPROVE YOUR VISION.

Few, we've found, see as far or as clearly as those who listen well.

Good listeners think more broadly– because they hear and understand more facts and points of view.

They make better innovators. Because listeners look at problems with fresh eyes, combine what they learn in more unlikely ways, they're more apt to hit upon truly startling ideas.

Ultimately, good listeners attune themselves more closely to where the world is going–and the products, talents, and techniques it needs to get there.

That's the selfish reason Sperry's committed to listening.

To lead, you need a lucid vision of the future.

✦ SPERRY
We understand how important it is to listen.

Sperry is Sperry Univac computers, Sperry New Holland farm equipment, Sperry Vickers fluid power systems, and guidance and control equipment from Sperry division and Sperry Flight Systems.

To learn more about listening, write to Sperry, Dept. H4, 1290 Avenue of the Americas, New York, N.Y. 10104

412

IT PAYS TO LISTEN.

Columbus' ideas fell on deaf ears for years before Queen Isabella finally chose to listen.

It's a lesson that wasn't lost on Sperry. Listening keeps us alert to ever-expanding possibilities in computer science, aerospace, and defense.

What's more, it helps us expand them ourselves.

Real breakthroughs increasingly occur when seemingly unrelated advances get connected—and then, suddenly, explosively fuse.

This takes an attentive, imaginative kind of listener who combines the unlikely in unexpected ways.

It's why, at Sperry's Research Center, scientists from eighteen totally different disciplines regularly meet.

To listen to each other.

We at Sperry are convinced that listening well ignites new insights, guides us into uncharted areas of thought, and ultimately uncovers whole new worlds.

 SPERRY

We understand how important it is to listen.

Doesn't Cut
Corners

FOR HIGH QUALITY ILLUSTRATION AND DESIGN:

AB INDEWALD

Design developer

Caution! She is quick and precise with her work. Do not be surprised if she gets the job done before the deadline.

Refer to AB for all of your Design Jobs

To Achieve Professional Results, Choose
2 USE ABindewald
4.0 Yrs Ed.

Read This Notice: Anne McIntyre Bindewald is interested in illustrating and graphically designing for you. She is overflowing with an abundance of creative ideas and determination. Contact AB for all of your design needs.

Net Wt 145 Lbs 6 Oz (3.2 kg)

**Made in Durham, N.C. by
Mr. and Mrs. R.A. Bindewald
1309 Glendale Avenue, 27701**

ECU - BFA ILLUSTRATION

AMB 919-758-1460

413

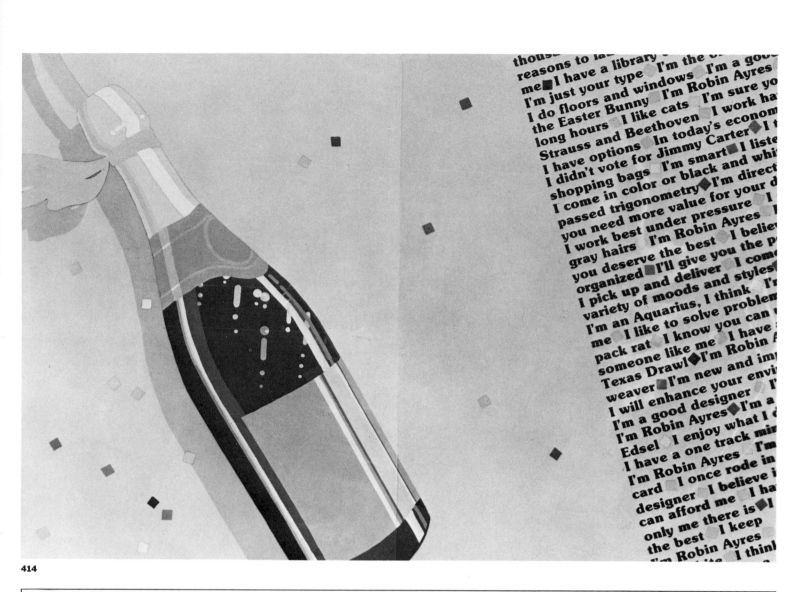

416 SILVER

417

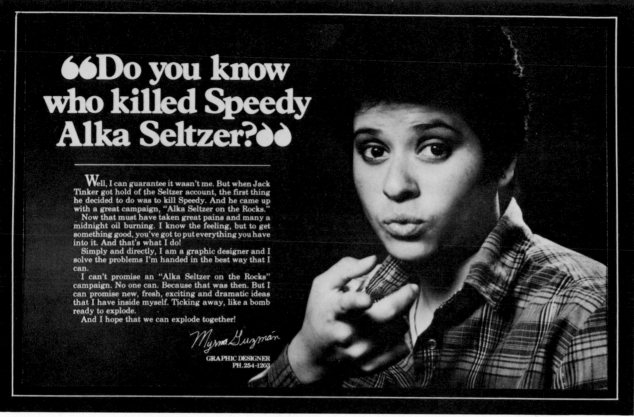

"Do you know who killed Speedy Alka Seltzer?"

Well, I can guarantee it wasn't me. But when Jack Tinker got hold of the Seltzer account, the first thing he decided to do was to kill Speedy. And he came up with a great campaign, "Alka Seltzer on the Rocks."

Now that must have taken great pains and many a midnight oil burning. I know the feeling, but to get something good, you've got to put everything you have into it. And that's what I do!

Simply and directly, I am a graphic designer and I solve the problems I'm handed in the best way that I can.

I can't promise an "Alka Seltzer on the Rocks" campaign. No one can. Because that was then. But I can promise new, fresh, exciting and dramatic ideas that I have inside myself. Ticking away, like a bomb ready to explode.

And I hope that we can explode together!

Myrna Guzman
GRAPHIC DESIGNER
PH. 254-1203

418

GOOD.

FOR NOTHING.

I'm good and I know what I want. I'm seeking an assistant Art Director position with an agency that has a wide range of challenging accounts. I want to work in print.

I'm a graduate of Art Center College of Design; advertising major. I have four years experience as a retail Art Director. I know how to coordinate ideas, photography, art, and production to keep deadlines and good office morale.

And now I'm ready to work for you for 30 days *for nothing*, if that's what it takes, to prove just how good I can be.

☐ Yes, I'd like to see a resume and samples of your work.

Agency
Address

Attn.
Mail to: Norm Johnson
2017 Berkshire Avenue
So. Pasadena, CA 91030
or call collect (213) 256-1270

419 GOLD

Radio Finalists

Consumer Radio Single

420
WRITERS
Deborah Polenberg
Mitch Epstein

CLIENT
Barney's

AGENCY PRODUCER
Neil Kraft

AGENCY
Epstein Raboy

421
WRITERS
Tom Thomas
David Tessler

CLIENT
BMW of North America

AGENCY PRODUCER
Colleen O'Connor

AGENCY
Ammirati & Puris

422
WRITER
Jim Weller

CLIENT
Indiana Telco

AGENCY PRODUCER
Lynne Kluger

AGENCY
Della Femina, Travisano &
Partners/California

423
WRITER
Jim Weller

CLIENT
BSR Systems

AGENCY PRODUCER
Jim Weller

AGENCY
Della Femina, Travisano &
Partners/California

424
WRITERS
Deborah Polenberg
Mitch Epstein

CLIENT
Barney's

AGENCY PRODUCER
Neil Kraft

AGENCY
Epstein Raboy

425
WRITERS
Tom Thomas
David Tessler

CLIENT
BMW of North America

AGENCY PRODUCER
Colleen O'Connor

AGENCY
Ammirati & Puris

426
WRITERS
Dick & Bert

CLIENT
Granada TV Rental

AGENCY PRODUCER
Shelley Muller

AGENCY
TBWA Advertising

420

ANNCR: Some of the finer stores keep the usual business hours. Unfortunately, they're usually the same business hours as yours. Still others stay open until 9 o'clock, two nights a week. The usual Mondays and Thursdays. But what if a Tuesday, or Saturday night is more convenient for you? Well, that leaves you with just one store. One store whose doors are open until 9:30 every night. Six nights a week. With a full complement of salespeople. A full complement of fitters. Free valet parking. And even a small elegant café. One store where a man can choose from the world's finest men's clothiers. Six nights a week. The name of that store? Barney's, New York. 7th Avenue and 17th Street. A place where a man—and a woman—can dress to the nines.

Till 9:30. Even on Saturdays.

421

ANNCR: It's ironic that while many prestigious luxury sedans succeed as status symbols, they disappoint as cars.

Apparently, it's easier to engineer a reputation than a true high-performance car.

Luxury car buyers, dissastisfied with this state of affairs, will find a perfect vehicle for dissent in the BMW 733i.

A car powered by an engine one critic termed "the most refined in-line six in the world."

With a suspension system so advanced it has been awarded an international patent.

It is, in short, a luxury car built on the radical belief that its owner might actually enjoy driving.

The BMW 733i.

The world's most elegant protest against mediocre engineering.

BMW. THE ULTIMATE DRIVING MACHINE.

422

TYPING SOUNDS AND FIRST MAN: OK now, Mr. Harnishshalger...

DR. HARNISHVAGER: No, that's Dr. Harnishvager...

FIRST MAN: OK, Dr. Harnishvager, let me get this straight...you're applying for a job at...

DR. HARNISHVAGER: Indiana Bell, Western Electric, Bell Labs or AT&T.

FIRST MAN: Right...and you're an experienced brain surgeon??

DR. HARNISHVAGER: Twelve year's surgery at Mt. Cranial General.

FIRST MAN: May I ask why?

DR. HARNISHVAGER: Well, I guess it started when I used to watch Ben Casey on TV...I was just a little...

FIRST MAN: No, no, no...why you're applying for a job at Indiana Bell.

DR. HARNISHVAGER: Oh...so I can open an Indiana Telco Credit Union share draft account.

FIRST MAN: Telco share draft...?

DR. HARNISVAGER: Yeah...you see a Telco share draft is like a regular checking account, only it pays you 6½% interest on your money.

FIRST MAN: Yes...it does.

DR. HARNISHVAGER: And there's no minimum balance or check-writing charge.

FIRST MAN: Mmmm...

DR. HARNISHVAGER: But you can't open a Telco share draft account unless you work at Indiana Bell...

FIRST MAN: ...Western Electric, Bell Labs or AT&T. Well, I'm afraid not, Dr. Harnishvager.

DR. HARNISHVAGER: Not????

FIRST MAN: I mean we just can't go around willy-nilly hiring every brain surgeon who wants to open a Telco account.

I mean next thing the podiatrists would be on our neck...

And then the chiropractors would start applying...pressure.

ANNNOUNCER: Indiana Telco Credit Union...We give you more for your money.

423

DECK THE HALLS MUSIC:
ANNCR: "Christmas is a great time of the year for Burglars. Because the more time you spend shopping, or visiting friends...the more time a burglar can spend robbing your home. I know, I'm Ray D. Johnson. And for 20 years, I made my living as a burglar. Today I make it telling people how to stop them. And the best way I know is with the BSR System X-10. The BSR system X-10 automatically controls the lights, television sets and appliances in your house. So it always looks and sounds like someone's home.

And no burglar wants to rob a house when someone's there. What's more, the X-10 requires no costly installation, you can help protect your home for under $150.

The BSR system X-10.

Because the man coming down the chimney may not be Santa Claus."

424

ANNCR: If you're looking for a suit in the neighborhood of, say, $175, you'd be hard-pressed to find a neighborhood with more to chose from than 7th Avenue and 17th Street.

There you'll find Barney's.

In Barney's Madison Room the traditionalist will see not just one interpretation of the natural-shoulder business suit, but subtle—and corporately correct—variations. In the neighborhood of $175.

If your milieu allows more self expression, Barney's New Yorker room helps you break with tradition in the same $175 neighborhood.

And for those who are willing to push tradition to its ultimate bounds, Barney's International House offers a broad spectrum of fashion in the European idiom. Also in the $175 area.

Of course, at Barney's alterations are free of charge.

Barney's. 7th Avenue and 17th Street. A place a man can call home in the neighborhood of $175. Free parking. Open 9 till 9:30.

425

ANNCR: Nobody purchases a stock with the expectation of watching its value plummet.

Why purchase a car where such losses are not only a possibility, but a virtual certainty?

Why, indeed, when it's possible to invest in the BMW 320i.

According to the NADA Used-Car Guide, if you had bought a new 320i at the beginning of 1980, and sold it at the end, your investment would have retained an astonishing 92.9% of its value. That's better than you'd have done with any of 318 stocks on the New York Exchange.

And the BMW 320i would have guaranteed you an important daily dividend:

The unfluctuating joy of driving one of the world's great performance sedans.

BMW. THE ULTIMATE DRIVING MACHINE.

426

BERT: (On phone filter) Hello?

MIR: Is this Bernie Blenstrum?

BERT: Yes...

MIR: The guy I met yesterday at the supermarket?

BERT: We grabbed the same rump roast.

MIR: And today, you sent me a brand new color television set?

BERT: Some guys send candy, or flowers, but *me*...

MIR: They're just delivering it, it's *gorgeous!*

BERT: Well, if anything happens to it, it'll be fixed for free!

MIR: What a man!

BERT: Yes I am!

MIR: Bernie, would you like to come over and...

BERT: Yes I would!

DICK: ...'scuse me, lady, could you sign this receipt from Granada TV Rental?

MIR: Rental? What rental?

BERT: Pay no attention to him, Gloria!

DICK: Granada TV Rental. It's the newest thing. You can rent new, brand name TVs for as little as $11.95 a month!

MIR: *$11.95???!*

DICK: So, you save hundreds of dollars renting, cuz there's no big cash outlay, and no repair bills!

MIR: Bernie, you spent a measly $11.95?

BERT: With the money I saved on renting from Granada, I was going to get you some flow...can... a...car! Yeah, a car!!

MIR: A car?? Oh, Bernie, you hurry right over!!!

SFX: (hang up)

BERT: Where's that number, rent a car, rent a car.

ANNCR: TV and VCR rental. A new concept in America from Granada. Fourteen locations in the New York metropolitan area. Look for us in the white pages.

Granada TV Rental. A whole new way of looking at TV.

427
WRITER
Steve Kasloff
CLIENT
Hebrew National Kosher Foods
AGENCY PRODUCER
David Perry
AGENCY
Scali, McCabe, Sloves

428
WRITER
Helayne Spivak
CLIENT
MCI
AGENCY PRODUCER
Jerry Haynes
AGENCY
Ally & Gargano

429
WRITERS
Deborah Polenberg
Mitch Epstein
CLIENT
Barney's
AGENCY PRODUCER
Neil Kraft
AGENCY
Epstein Raboy

430
WRITER
Jim Doherty
CLIENT
WABC—TV
AGENCY PRODUCER
Liz Triantafillou
AGENCY
Della Femina, Travisano
& Partners

431
WRITER
Steve Kasloff
CLIENT
Hebrew National Kosher Foods
AGENCY PRODUCER
David Perry
AGENCY
Scali, McCabe, Sloves

432
WRITERS
Deborah McDuffie
Allan Corwin
CLIENT
Kentucky Fried Chicken
AGENCY PRODUCERS
Caroline Jones
Deborah McDuffie
AGENCY
Mingo-Jones

433
WRITER
Kevin McKeon
CLIENT
Xerox
AGENCY PRODUCER
Sydelle Rangell
AGENCY
Needham, Harper & Steers

434
WRITER
Nancy Coyne
CLIENT
McCann Nugent
AGENCY PRODUCER
Nancy Coyne
AGENCY
Serino, Coyne and Nappi

427

MUSIC: *Tradition...tradition. Tradition!*

ANNCR: For 75 years, Hebrew National has made salami according to the most demanding tradition we know. Our own.

Our salami exceeds U.S. Government standards. We don't use cereals or sweeteners.

Our salami exceeds our competition's standards. We don't use meat by-products or fillers.

And because we don't use artificial flavor or color, our salami even exceeds *Kosher* standards.

So why buy just any salami when you can buy Hebrew National, the one made to the strictest tradition on earth...or off.

MUSIC: *Tradition...tradition. Tradition!*

ANNCR: Hebrew National. We make them like we used to.

MUSIC: *Tradition!*

428

(SOUND OF PHONE RINGING. FUMBLING WITH RECEIVER IS HEARD. A VERY SLEEPY VOICE SAYS...)

DENISE: Hullo?

HAROLD: Denise? It's me. Harold. Did I wake you?

DENISE: Not yet. But if you keep talking, you will.

HAROLD: Come on. This is a long distance call.

DENISE: What time is it?

HAROLD: 2 a.m. your time.

DENISE: Harold. I have to wake up all over again in four hours. Call me in the morning.

HAROLD: Denise. Wait. I can't. Look how much money I save by calling weekdays after 11 p.m.

DENISE: I can save you even more money, Harold.

HAROLD: How?

DENISE: (SOUND OF RECEIVER BEING HUNG UP.)

ANNCR: Bell suggests that to save the most money on your long distance calls, you should call after 11 p.m. We have a better suggestion: call MCI, the nation's long distance phone company, and save 30, 40 even 50% between the civilized weekday hours of 5 and 11 p.m. Not to mention the savings you can get all day long and weekends. So call MCI now. And stop talking in someone else's sleep.

429

ANNCR: To those men who view shopping as something less than the ultimate experience, imagine, if you will, this alternative.

A store with seven floors devoted to men's clothing. And four additional floors devoted to men's tailoring.

A store that offers a man free parking in a city that has seen the cost of parking almost double within recent memory.

A store where a man can actually make an appointment with his favorite salesman. And a salesman, who, in turn, is fully conversant with every corner of every floor. Furthermore, a store with a staff of fashion coordinators who, should you so desire, will help you accessorize your purchase.

And finally, a store that satisfies the inner man as well as the outer, by providing a café where he can enjoy a hearty bowl of soup, a glass of wine and a salad, or simply a cup of expresso.

Of course, New Yorkers don't have to imagine such a store. New York has Barney's. 7th Avenue and 17th Street. Free parking. Free alterations. Open 9 to 9:30.

430

ANNCR: New York is fast becoming the home of a new rat race—a breed of rat that's more powerful than the poisons used to exterminate it.

DIALOGUE: "They come in through the sewers...through garbage trucks...through deliveries. They will come into a food warehouse and ravage the warehouse."

ANNCR: Tonight at 6 and 11, in an Eyewitness News Special report, Kaity Tong shows how these creatures from the underworld could be taking over.

Watch "Super Rats in New York." Tonight at 6 and 11 on Channel 7. This is one rat race nobody's been able to beat.

431

MUSIC: *Tradition...tradition. Tradition!*

ANNCR: 75 years ago, a salami maker could make a salami out of most anything he wanted. There were no strict government standards. At Hebrew National, we set up our own. No meat by-products, no fillers, no sugar.

Today, the only thing that's really changed is the list of things Hebrew National say no to. It's longer now. No cereal, no soy protein, no artifical color or flavor. While the government does have some standards, what goes into a salami is left strictly up to the maker. Considering that you have to buy a salami on *faith*, doesn't it make sense to buy Hebrew National?

MUSIC: *Tradition...tradition. Tradition!*

ANNCR: Hebrew National. We make them like we used to.

MUSIC: *Tradition!*

432

SINGERS: *We do one thing*
Like no one else can do
We concentrate on making it great
We make it just for you

ANNOUNCER: Ladies and Gentlemen, Miss Gladys Knight.

GLADYS KNIGHT: When somebody says, "Gladys Knight" —what's the first thing that pops into your mind?

BROTHER BUBBA: The Pips!

GLADYS KNIGHT: Shut up Bubba! I would have said "singing". Okay. When somebody says Kentucky Fried Chicken you say...

BROTHER BUBBA: Original Recipe!

GLADYS KNIGHT: Right for a change. Chicken is what they do. Kentucky Fried Chicken Original Recipe with that secret blend of 11 herbs and spices. And that special pressure-cooking to seal it all in so it's finger-lickin' good. They do chicken right!

SINGERS: *Kentucky Fried Chicken*
We do it right
Kentucky Fried Chicken
We do chicken right.

433

ANNCR: You can get a Xerox desktop copier for only twenty-nine hundred and ninety-five dollars. Now, how do you get the $2995?

(SFX: DIALING.)

GERRY: Sidney, ole pal. Still in the finance business? (PAUSE) Great! How's your interest rates? You're kidding, right?

(SFX: CLICK! DIALING.)

GERRY: Steve, ole buddy. Gerry here. Listen, how'd you like to help out your best pal? (PAUSE) Gerry. Gerry Diebert.

(SFX: CLICK! DIALING.)

GERRY: Tony, you ole sawbuck! Hey, speaking of money...

(SFX: CLICK!)

ANNCR: At Xerox, we realize it isn't easy for small businesses to raise money. So we *make* it easy. First, we'll give you a generous trade-in on your old copier. Up to $1000.00 or more. Then, we'll help you finance your new copier, at low interest rates. Just call Xerox at 800-648-5000. 800-648-5000. Or in Nevada, 800-992-5710. We're easier to talk to than a lot of other people.

(SFX: DIALING)

GERRY: Hello, Ma?

(SFX: CLICK! THEN DIAL TONE.)

434

A.: I don't believe it.

B.: They say.

A.: I hear.

B.: They say.

A.: I don't believe it.

B.: The whole city is talking.

A.: You hear it all over.

B.: The cafes.

A.: The opera.

B.: The gutter.

A.: Incredible.

B.: I don't believe it.

A.: What a story.

B.: What a scandal.

A.: I don't believe it.

B.: Who can believe it?

A.: What horrors have you heard?

B.: Tell us.

A.: Tell us.

B.: Tell us at once.

A.: About Wolfgang.

B.: AMADEUS.

A.: Mozart.

B.: Mozart.

A.: Mozart.

B.: Mozart was dying.

A.: He claimed he'd been poisoned.

B.: Some said he accused a man.

A.: Some said that the man was Salieri.

B.: Salieri.

A.: Salieri.

B.: I don't believe it.

A.: All the same.

B.: Is it just possible?

A.: Did Salieri do it after all?

B.: Did he murder AMADEUS?

435
WRITER
Steve Kasloff
CLIENT
Hebrew National Kosher Foods
AGENCY PRODUCER
David Perry
AGENCY
Scali, McCabe, Sloves

436
WRITERS
Charley Gowl
Hal Goluboff
CLIENT
Great Waters of France/Perrier
AGENCY PRODUCER
Barbara Gans Russo
AGENCY
Mathieu, Gerfen & Bresner

437
WRITER
Helayne Spivak
CLIENT
MCI
AGENCY PRODUCER
Jerry Haynes
AGENCY
Ally & Gargano

438
WRITER
Kerry Feuerman
CLIENT
Hot Springs Auto Wash
AGENCY PRODUCER
Kerry Feuerman
AGENCY
Siddall, Matus & Coughter/
Virginia

439
WRITER:
Renee Rockoff Vetter
CLIENT:
Hinckley & Schmitt
AGENCY PRODUCER:
Jerry Inglehart
AGENCY:
Inglehart & Partners/Chicago

440
WRITER
Nancy Coyne
CLIENT
Cameron Macintosh
AGENCY PRODUCER
Nancy Coyne
AGENCY
Serino, Coyne and Nappi

441
WRITER
Larry Plapler
CLIENT
People Express Airlines
AGENCY PRODUCER
Rachel Novak
AGENCY
Levine, Huntley, Schmidt,
Plapler & Beaver

442
WRITER
Al Ragin
CLIENT
Joseph Schlitz Brewing
AGENCY PRODUCER
Sandy Wilbur
AGENCY
Benton & Bowles

435

MUSIC: *Tradition…tradition. Tradition!*

ANNCR: 75 years ago, when Hebrew National started making hot dogs, all hot dogs were naturally smoked. Over real hickory chips in a real smoke-house. For a real old-fashioned, beefy flavor.

Over the years, hot dog makers began switching to something newer. And cheaper. Liquid smoke. It smells like smoke. Even tastes like smoke. It just isn't smoke. It's artificial.

So how can you tell if your hot dog is naturally smoked or phoney baloney smoked? Just look for the words Hebrew National. Because buying anything less than a naturally smoked hot dog is simply burning money.

MUSIC: *Tradition…tradition. Tradition!*

ANNCR: Hebrew National. We make them like we used to.

MUSIC: *Tradition!*

436

WELLES: He rode across the burning sands of the Great African Desert; a tall, pale figure in robes of white. (MUSIC:) They called him a Mystic, a Madman. But he was a shy Englishman, named T.E. Lawrence: The Legendary Lawrence of Arabia…who once traveled 300 miles across the blazing Benghazi. 300 scorching, searing miles across the cruelest desert on earth…until, finally, delirious and crazed with thirst, he found a small, unmarked oasis. He dropped to his knees, and drank. Then he spoke:

LAWRENCE: It is good. But it is not Perrier.

(SFX: MUSIC, UP!)

WELLES: As usual, the Legendary Lawrence was right. There is but one Perrier. It's Only Natural. Cold, crackling, deeply thirst-quenching Perrier. The most refreshing drink under the sun. Perrier. It's Only Natural.

437

(SOUND OF INTERCOM-LIKE BUZZ)

PICKING: Sara. Is the WATS line free?

SARA: No, Mr. Picking, it isn't.

PICKING: Call me when it is.

SARA: Sure will. (BUZZ) Yes?

LORD: Sara. I'd like the WATS line?

SARA: Sorry, Mr. Lord. Mr. Picking's next in line.

LORD: Forget Picking. Put me next.

SARA: Sure will. (BUZZ) Yes?

PICKING: Picking here. Is the WATS free yet?

SARA: Listen, Mr. Picking. Mr. Lord says his call should be next.

PICKING: We'll see about that. (BUZZ)

SARA: Yes?

KELLY: It's Mr. Kelly. Give me the WATS line.

SARA: Mr. Picking and Mr. Lord are waiting too, Mr. Kelly.

KELLY: Whose name is on your check every week, Sara?

SARA: Why, I believe the line is free now.

ANNCR: If you spend more in time than you save in money with Bell's WATS line, call MCI. The nation's long distance phone company. MCI offers your company many economical alternatives to Bell's services. Including one that will save you 30% more than their famous WATS line. So call MCI. Because your company hasn't been calling too much. You've just been paying too much.

438

ANNCR: For the next sixty seconds, you are going to experience something quite remarkable: a technological breakthrough.

(SFX: HIGH TECH MUSIC AND SOUND EFFECTS UNDER)

ANNCR: Inside a tunnel is a large object.

A computer calculates its exact shape and size and feeds the information into a control center.

The process is now set into motion.

Photo-electric sensors feel their way along the object's exterior. Never touching it. Instead, they guide jets of hot water. The water removes any corrosive particles while heating the surface to 140 degrees Farenheit.

With the surface at the ideal temperature, a transparent liquid is applied. Within seconds, it dries into an incredibly hard, protective shell.

Once again, the object is heated. This time with two blasts of hot air.

And the computer indicates that it is now ready for inspection.

(SFX: SFX AND MUSIC OUT)

What have we done? We've just washed your car.

Hot Springs Autowash. Midlothian Turnpike. Exterior wash, two dollars and ninety cents.

439

(MUSIC: THE PURE WATER RAG)

ANNCR: The Hinckley & Schmitt Water Lillies

WATER LILLIES: Ah one. Ah two. Ah three.
I drink pure water,
Clear as can be.

(CLINK, CLINK OF ICE CUBES)

There ain't no water,
So healthy for me.

(POURING OF WATER INTO GLASS)

No salt, no chlorine,
Drink up and keep fit.

(TAPPING NOTES ON CRYSTAL)

There's nothing hiding,
In Hinckley & Schmitt.

(SWISH THROUGH THE WATER)

Get some pure water,
Pick up the phone,

(FOUR NOTES IN SEQUENCE ON TOUCH TONE)

You'll love pure water,
Delivered at home.

(BUBBLING UP OF SPRING)

Once you have tried it,
You won't want to quit.
Oh so delicious,
Hinckley & Schmitt!

ANNCR: If you don't love your water, try Hinckley & Schmitt. Discover how delicious water tastes when it's free of salt, chlorine, chemicals and additives. A water so good, you'll want to sing its praises too.

WATER LILLIES: Get some pure water,
From Hinckley & Schmitt (SPLASH) Ahhhh!

ANNCR: Dial 229-1800.

440

ANNCR: You are about to spend less money for more entertainment than you ever thought possible.

You are about to get more laughs per song than you ever imagined.

You are about to experience TOM FOOLERY.

The songs and sagacity of Tom Lehrer dumped into a musical extravaganza at the Top of the Village Gate.

None of the Royal Shakespeare Company.

Five costumes.

One wig.

Eleven pounds of scenery plus twenty-seven swell songs.

All the Tom Lehrer lyrics you love.

All the Tom Lehrer lyrics you hate.

Every uncivilised family should call for tickets now.
982-9292

For TOM FOOLERY. The theatrical event of the week.

Tickets at the Top of the Gate box office, Bleecker and Thompson Streets.

For Tom Foolery.
Everything you've ever wanted in a musical but have had the good taste not to ask for.

441

ANNCR: Do a lot of airline commercials sound like this to you?

FIRST VO: We're the sixth largest carrier in the north western free world. The sky is ours. The world is ours. You are ours.

SECOND VO: I'm the president of an important airline—every day. I want you to fly with us—every day. So I'm going to keep reminding you—every day.

DOUBLETALK: Anyone can take advantage of our low, low airline prices.

As long as you're a child over 80 years old or an adult under 2 years old or fly with a koala bear.

Of course this offer is limited to 2:00 a.m. departures in leap years.

And to selected destinations—selected by us, not you.

ANNCR: Well, there is an airline that believes in straight talk...People Express. Because we have what you really want: Prices that are often less than one third of what you're accustomed to paying—without any gimmicks or restrictions. And frequent flights around the clock each business day—with choice seats available at the last minute. What's more, People Express is the first airline where attitude is as important as altitude.

People Express

Fly Smart

442

(MUSIC: ORIGINAL MUSIC UNDER THROUGHOUT)

MILLIE: You know, when my man gets home the first thing he wants is a brew that's cold, bold, and with a lot of taste. I say to him, how about some malt liquor? The man says, Bull! I got really up-tight. Then he laid it down for me and said—

(SINGS)

When you say malt liquor say Schlitz Malt Liquor.
When you say malt liquor say Bull!
When you say malt liquor say Schlitz Malt Liquor.
When you say malt liquor say Bull!
Want a bold malt liquor, say Schlitz Malt Liquor.
Want a smooth malt liquor say Bull!
'Cause no one does it like Schlitz Malt Liquor.
No one does it like the Bull!
When you say malt liquor say Schlitz Malt Liquor.
When you say malt liquor say Bull!
'Cause no one does it like Schlitz Malt Liquor.
No one does it like the Bull!
No one does it like the Bull!

ANNCR: Joseph Schlitz Brewing Company, Milwaukee.

443

ANNCR: Music is a very private experience. It can ignite every sense. It can touch you so deeply that it hurts. It can wash over you like a summer rain. Or it can fill you with a beauty and passion almost frightening in its intensity. And that's why Sony invented the Walkman. With the Walkman, you can ski, or stroll, or lie on a beach, and the music will make the experience that much more wonderful. The sound of the Walkman will be unlike any sound you have ever heard. And instantly, you'll know why the Sony Walkman will be unlike any sound you have ever heard. And instantly, you'll know why the Sony Walkman stereo cassette player, with its tiny featherweight headphones, has been perhaps the most revolutionary invention in the history of sound. And now there's even an FM Walkman. But it all comes down to three things: The music...the Walkman...and you. The Walkman. From Sony. The One and Only.

TAG: Hear the fabulous cassette Walkman and the new FM Walkman at your local Sony dealer.

444 GOLD

(A PHONE RINGS. THEN A VERY TIRED WOMAN'S VOICE.)

MOM: Hullo?

DAVE: Hi, Mom. Surprise. It's Dave.

MOM: Hullo?

DAVE: Mom. Wake up. It's your son, Dave. I'm calling long distance.

MOM: (STILL ASLEEP BUT KNOWS HIS NAME.) Dave?

DAVE: I'm sorry I'm calling so late, but the rates are cheapest weekdays after 11 pm.

MOM: (SOUND OF FEMALE SNORING.)

DAVE: Mom? Mom! Come on. Give the phone to Dad.

MOM: Here, Frank. It's for you.

DAD: (LOUD MASCULINE SNORING)

DAVE: Dad. It's me. Dave. Dad? Come on, Dad. Mom. Are you still there? (SOUND OF TWO PEOPLE SNORING.) Wake Dad! Wake Dad! Don't do this to me. Mom...Dad...

ANNCR: Reach out. Reach out and wake someone. That's one suggestion on how to get Bells' lowest rates on long distance calls. Want a better suggestion? Try MCI, the nation's long distance phone company, and save 30, 40, even 50% weekdays by calling after the very decent hour of 5:00 p.m. So call MCI. And find out how to save money when you want to. Not when Bell tells you to.

445

(MUSIC: MUSIC UP AND UNDER)

ANNCR: For nearly half a century, scientists have been baffled by the homing instincts of the Monarch Butterfly. Each fall they migrate south and land on the exact spot where previous generations had landed. Same trees. Same telephone wires. Scientists have gone so far as to disguise the trees, and still the butterflies find them. We believe, for the past three decades thousands of these baffling creatures have spent one night of their migration on the sign at Highams Cadillac/Rolls-Royce. But now that Highams Cadillac/Rolls-Royce has changed its name to McGinnis Cadillac/Rolls-Royce and moved to a new location, we will be curiously watching to detect any change in the migratory habits of the colorful lepidoptora. If you're a scientist, you're welcome to wait at McGinnis Cadillac/Rolls-Royce, and perhaps take advantage of the exceptional values on 1981 Cadillacs during our Grand Opening. And if you're a Monarch Butterfly, please note the change of address. McGinnis Cadillac/Rolls-Royce, quietly doing things very well, on the Katy Freeway at Dairy-Ashford.

(MUSIC: MUSIC RESOLVES.)

446

MAN: Hi!

WOMAN: Uh, hi.

MAN: This is a beautiful spot. Do you mind if I make camp here?

WOMAN: Yeh, it is. Hey, I really wanted to be alone, if you don't mind.

MAN: Oh well, no. Okay. Well, that's fine. That's fine with me.

WOMAN: Is that all your stuff?

MAN: Sorry. Yeh. This is my camping stuff.

WOMAN: A cooler? That's all you brought?!

MAN: Yeh, it's full of Molson Golden Ale. It's imported from Canada.

WOMAN: Funny. I was just thinking how great it would be to have a Molson Golden.

MAN: Really?! Ah...it's a wonderful brew. Clean taste. Crisp, clear, fresh, pure.

WOMAN: I've got an extra hamburger. Are you hungry? You don't want an extra hamburger?

MAN: No. I'd love a hamburger. Sure. Yeh. That would be great.

WOMAN: What are you going to do if it rains?

MAN: Ah. I don't really know. Make...

WOMAN: Hey. I've got a drop cloth here. You could borrow it. I mean...we can,...you can...make a tent and...

MAN: That's a good idea. Yeh, I like it.

WOMAN: That's all you brought? A cooler of Molson Golden?

MAN: That's all I ever bring.

(LAUGHING...)

ANNCR: If you're thirsting for the best of Canada, make sure it's Molson Golden, with the fresh, clean, taste of Canada. Molson Golden. Imported by Martlet Importing Company, Great Neck, New York.

MAN: So!...Is?...Ah, well...would you like a Molson?

WOMAN: Sure, I would!! I thought you'd never ask.

MAN: You have a bottle opener? Right?

WOMAN: Yeh. (LAUGHING...)

447

WELLES (MUSIC UNDER): He was the tall stranger dressed in black, who rode with a vengeance across the High Plains of the Great American West. Gunfighter. Bounty Hunter. Devil. He answered no call. He loved no woman. And on that fateful day, he walked through the doors of that Laredo saloon and spun a dusty double eagle across the bar. Slowly, he raised a bottle to his dry, parched lips to drink. Instantly he lowered it, turned, and spoke, with red hatred in his eyes:

GUNFIGHTER: It's good. But it ain't Perrier.

(SFX: MUSIC, UP!)

WELLES: Six good men paid the price for a bartender's honest mistake. It's Only Natural. There is but one Perrier. Sparkling with Nature's own carbonation. Pure, with nothing artificial and not one single calorie. Perrier. It's Only Natural.

448

MUSIC: *Tradition...tradition. Tradition!*

ANNCR: For 75 years Hebrew National has resisted temptation. Unlike others, we haven't made changes in our salami simply for the sake of the almighty dollar.

In the 20's we resisted the temptation of using meat-by-products and sugars. Even though the competition swore by them.

In the 40's, we resisted the temptation of using artificial colors and flavors.

In the 50's, we resisted the temptation of meat trimming machines, and kept right on trimming by hand.

Where has all this resisting temptation gotten us? It's made Hebrew National the salami more and more people just can't resist.

MUSIC: *Tradition...tradition. Tradition!*

ANNCR: Hebrew National. We make them like we used to.

MUSIC: *Tradition!*

449

ANNCR: Ever since he was a small child, Basil played the piano.

MUSIC: (MUSIC UP: CHOPSTICKS—ONE FINGER)

ANNCR: He practiced for hours a day while the other children played sporting games beside his parlour window.

MUSIC: (MUSIC CONT: CHOPSTICKS)

ANNCR: His parents' service on the board of endowments at Juilliard allowed him to enroll on scholarship at age nine. There...he refined his skill.

MUSIC: (MUSIC CONT: CHOPSTICKS—TWO FINGERS)

ANNCR: He spent a year abroad studying under a savant once employed by the Vienna Boys Choir, where he accelerated his learning.

MUSIC: (MUSIC CONT: CHOPSTICKS—DOUBLE TIME)

ANNCR: Upon his return he opened a small studio near Highams Cadillac, where he tutored promising students night and day.

MUSIC: (MUSIC UP: MANY PIANOS, OUT OF TUNE)

ANNCR: Highams Cadillac, quietly doing things very well, offered the pompous virtuoso an unspecified sum to kindly relocate.

MUSIC: (MUSIC UP AND UNDER—MC GINNIS THEME)

ANNCR: Failing that, Highams Cadillac changed its name to McGinnis Cadillac/Rollys-Royce and moved to a new location. On the Katy Freeway at Dairy-Ashford. McGinnis Cadillac/Rollys-Royce. Again. Quietly doing things very well...

450 SILVER

BERT: You're sure this is the newest video cassette recorder? Huh?

DICK: The KX-2 records, plays back, freeze-frames, and has a laser-powered digital chronographical instrumentation panel.

BERT: Ooh, what's that?

DICK: A clock

BERT: Oh Boy. Here's my check!

DICK: And here's your KX-2.

GUY: Hey Mack, I got those video KX-3's here.

BERT: KX-3's?

DICK: Yeah, this one selects the best show on the air, edits out the commercials and chills beer.

BERT: What about my KX-2's?

DICK: It's now officially obsolete.

BERT: Obsolete?

ANNCR: Video cassette recorders are changing fast. So, why buy one for hundreds of dollars when you can rent a new brand name VCR from Granada TV Rental for as low as $29.95 a month? And, when you want a newer model, no problem. And no cost for delivery, installation or repairs. Granada believes that when it comes to TV's and VCR's, the only thing that's obsolete is the idea of "buying" one.

BERT: So the KX-3 is the state of the art, huh.

DICK: For at least a week.

BERT: A week!

DICK: Maybe 2 days

BERT: 2 days?

DICK: What time is it? Maybe an hour.

ANNCR: TV and VCR rental. A new concept in America from Granada. Fourteen locations in the New York metropolitan area. Look for us in the white pages. Granada TV rental. A whole new way of looking at TV.

451

(MUSIC UP AND UNDER)

FEMALE: There was this guy.

MALE: I met this girl.

FEMALE: It was just before breakfast.

MALE: I saw her classified ad in The Houston Post.

FEMALE: He gave me a call.

MALE: She was selling her Xylophone.

FEMALE: We decided to meet.

MALE: I went to her home.

FEMALE: He asked if he could play it.

MALE: It was in perfect condition.

FEMALE: He offered me a check.

MALE: But she wanted cash.

FEMALE: He said he'd be back.

MALE: She said she'd wait.

FEMALE: But he hasn't returned.

MALE: I tried to phone her but her line was busy.

FEMALE: I've so many calls from that one little Post ad.

MALE: I'll bet she's already sold it.

FEMALE: I promised him I'd hold it.

ANNCR: If you want to sell something fast, remember... morning home delivery can get same day results only in The Houston Post.

(SFX: TELEPHONE RINGS)

FEMALE: Hello, what took you so long, I was saving the Xylophone for you...(FADE OUT...)

ANNCR: For same day classified results dial 666-1000 and Houston Post your ad.

452

(MUSIC IN, UNDER)

ANNCR: Your friends at FPL have a tip or two. To tell you 'bout somethin' comin' up that we don't want anymore than you...

CHORUS: *Big Bill.*

ANNCR: Never fails round these parts, summer comes, heat starts. Air conditioners hum, go on the bum, it's time again for Big Bill.

CHORUS: *Big Bill.*

ANNCR: There *is* somethin' a dude can do; weatherstrip, caulk, and insulate too. Set the thermostat at seventy eight, now that's a savin' thing to do.

CHORUS: *Big Bill.*

ANNCR: Oil's costin' us a bundle, fuel adjustment's gonna suffer. Those high oil costs 'll make your bill do another upper. FPL's doin' all it can, just scramblin' 'n generatin'. Sending folders to help folks who aren't insulatin'. To tell 'em *now* to start savin'... and start holdin' down...

CHORUS: *Big Bill! Big Bill!*

ANNCR: Florida Power & Light.

453

(SFX: TRIBAL CHANTS AND EXOTIC DRUMS)

ANNCR: There is a tribe of people who live in a dense jungle on an island in the Indian Ocean. They have nearly everything we have. But they only have one of each. They have an electric typewriter. A set of golf clubs and a can of frozen orange juice. They also have a museum. The typewriter, the golf clubs and the orange juice are in the museum. They have nearly everything. But they don't have a cadillac. So they built a 60 foot schooner. And set sail for Houston.

(SFX: CITY TRAFFIC)

ANNCR: Upon arriving they were directed to McGinnis Cadillac/Rolls-Royce.

(MUSIC UP AND UNDER—MC GINNIS THEME)

ANNCR: The tribe, having done their research carefully, chose McGinnis Cadillac because of the large selection of new cadillacs ready for immediate delivery. Then, they returned to their homeland and added the McGinnis cadillac to their museum. If you'd like to see this extraordinary motor car, their museum is open one day a year. Or you can visit the new showrooms of McGinnis Cadillac/Rolls-Royce, formerly Highams. Now quietly doing things very well on the Katy Freeway at Dairy-Ashford.

(MUSIC: MUSIC RESOLVES)

454

ANNCR: This commercial message is about drinking water...and cancer. The Council on Environmental Quality recently reported on studies linking chlorinated water with cancer of the bladder and digestive tract. Alarming, because chlorine treatment is used to treat tap water in almost all municipal supply systems—including our own Lake Michigan water. The water we've trusted all our lives. This is not a public service announcement... this is a commercial message from Hinckley & Schmitt, a company which has been serving Chicago with pure, non-chlorinated drinking water since 1893. For the complete report on Cancer and Drinking Water write the National Technical Information Service. U.S. Department of Commerce, Springfield Virginia 22161. For information on Hinckley & Schmitt drinking water call 229-1800.

455

(SFX: BATTLEGROUND SKIRMISHES, MISSILES AND MACHINE GUNS FIRING, ETC.)

ANNCR (VO): This year alone, the U.S. will lose more lives to the war against cancer than it did in World War II, the Korean War, and Vietnam.

In fact, after billions of dollars in research, your chances of surviving most kinds of cancer are about the same as they were in 1956.

Tonight, in an Eyewitness News Special Report, Tracy Egan reveals the truth about the fight against cancer.

Watch "Cancer Research: Is it more hype than hope?" Tonight at 11 on Channel 7.

If fighting cancer is a losing battle, it could be we've made it that way.

456
WRITER
Steve Kasloff
CLIENT
Hebrew National Kosher Foods
AGENCY PRODUCER
David Perry
AGENCY
Scali, McCabe, Sloves

457 GOLD
WRITER
Helayne Spivak
CLIENT
MCI
AGENCY PRODUCER
Jerry Haynes
AGENCY
Ally & Gargano

458
WRITER
Jim Doherty
CLIENT
WABC-TV
AGENCY PRODUCER
Liz Triantafillou
AGENCY
Della Femina, Travisano
& Partners

459
WRITER
Jack Supple
CLIENT
Oak Grove Dairy
AGENCY
Carmichael-Lynch/Mpls.

460 SILVER
WRITERS
Dick & Bert
CLIENT
Granada TV Rental
AGENCY PRODUCER
Shelley Muller
AGENCY
TBWA Advertising

461
WRITERS
Mark Schneider
John Gruen
CLIENT
General Foods
AGENCY PRODUCER
Creina Gahan
AGENCY
Ogilvy & Mather

456

MUSIC: *Tradition...tradition. Tradition!*

ANNCR: When Hebrew National first started making salami, we were just a six story walk-up on New York's lower east side, out to please the toughest customers in the world. Butchers.

They would tell us, "Make it leaner. Don't make it leaner. Add more spice. Add less spice." And the price. They *always* complained about the price. But deep down they knew it took better ingredients to make a better salami. Today, Hebrew National runs a huge 125,000 square foot plant. But we still make salami the same way. And still have to please the toughest customer in the world. Our president. The grandson of a butcher.

MUSIC: *Tradition...tradition. Tradition!*

ANNCR: Hebrew National. We make them like we used to.

MUSIC: *Tradition!*

457 GOLD

(SOUND OF INTERCOM-LIKE BUZZ)

PICKING: Sara. Is the WATS line free?

SARA: No, Mr. Picking, it isn't.

PICKING: Call me when it is.

SARA: Sure will. (BUZZ) Yes?

LORD: Sara. I'd like the WATS line?

SARA: Sorry, Mr. Lord. Mr. Picking's next in line.

LORD: Forget Picking. Put me next.

SARA: Sure will. (BUZZ) Yes?

PICKING: Picking here. Is the WATS free yet?

SARA: Listen, Mr. Picking. Mr. Lord says his call should be next.

PICKING: We'll see about that. (BUZZ)

SARA: Yes?

KELLY: It's Mr. Kelly. Give me the WATS line.

SARA: Mr. Picking and Mr. Lord are waiting too, Mr. Kelly.

KELLY: Whose name is on your check every week, Sara?

SARA: Why, I believe the line is free now.

ANNCR: If you spend more in time than you save in money with Bell's WATS line, call MCI. The nation's long distance phone company. MCI offers your company many economical alternatives to Bell's services. Including one that will save you 30% more than their famous WATS line. So call MCI. Because your company hasn't been calling too much. You've just been paying too much.

458

ANNCR: Philippe Petit did something most of us wouldn't think of doing in our wildest dreams. He crossed a high wire that spanned the Twin Towers.

Philippe was living out a dream. A dream in which he walked gracefully among the clouds. Like Philippe, all of us walk that fine line between dreams and reality.

Tonight, in an Eyewitness Special Report, Tracy Egan explores dream analysis.

Watch "The Reality of Dreams." Tonight at 11 on Channel 7. The difference between night and day is smaller than you think.

459

FRAN: In the little town of Norwood, Minnesota, Ort Paulson regularly takes folks through the Oak Grove Dairy. Now that can lead to a lot of questions, especially from the children...

(SFX: COWS MOO IN BACKGROUND)

ORT: A lot of kids ask me about cows. They hear me on the radio and figure, well, Ort knows his cows and so they ask me things, y'know. I know this one time a boy asked me, "Hey Ort, do all cows say moo?" (LAUGH) Everybody laughed y'know. But I knew what he was gettin' at. And I told him "Not all do say moo with an 'M.' Some of 'em go 'nnnnnnnooooo' with an 'N' as in Norwood. Or 'oooooo' with an 'O' as in Oak Grove. But it's very difficult for them to pronounce 'Moo' just like that.

FRAN: Next time you're asked what a cow says, tell 'em what Ort Paulson says. Oak Grove Dairy. They really know their cows.

(SFX: MOO)

ORT: Oak Grove cows are pretty good at it. You've got to watch their lips.

(SFX: MOOOOOOOOO)

BERT: (On phone filter) Hello?

MIR: Is this Bernie Blenstrum?

BERT: Yes...

MIR: The guy I met yesterday at the supermarket?

BERT: We grabbed the same rump roast.

MIR: And today, you sent me a brand new color television set?

BERT: Some guys send candy, or flowers, but *me*...

MIR: They're just delivering it, it's *gorgeous!*

BERT: Well, if anything happens to it, it'll be fixed for free!

MIR: What a man!

BERT: Yes I am!

MIR: Bernie, would you like to come over and...

BERT: Yes I would!

DICK: ...'scuse me, lady, could you sign this receipt from Granada TV Rental?

MIR: Rental? What rental?

BERT: Pay no attention to him, Gloria!

DICK: Granada TV Rental. It's the newest thing. You can rent new, brand name TVs for as little as $11.95 a month!

MIR: *$11.95???!*

DICK: So you save hundreds of dollars renting, cuz there's no big cash outlay, and no repair bills!

MIR: Bernie, you spent a measly $11.95?

BERT: With the money I saved on renting from Granada, I was going to get you some flow... can...a...car! Yeah, a car!!

MIR: A car?? Oh, Bernie, you hurry right over!!!

(SFX: HANG UP)

BERT: Where's that number, rent a car, rent a car...

ANNCR: TV and VCR rental. A new concept in America from Granada. Fourteen locations in the New York metropolitan area. Look for us in the white pages.

Granada TV Rental. A whole new way of looking at TV.

VERSE: *Dinner's done, the day has ended,*
Peace and quiet have descended,
Now it's just the two of you,
And your Maxwell House.

Pour a cup, enjoy that flavor,
Talk about what's new,
Spend some precious time together,
Maxwell House and you—

CHORUS: *Get that "Good To The Last Drop" feeling*
With Maxwell House, only Maxwell House
Gives you the "Good To The Last Drop" feeling
Maxwell House

ANNCR: Maxwell House has a taste, a feeling that no other coffee can give you. 'Cause Maxwell House is always good to the last drop.

CHORUS: *Get that "Good To The Last Drop" feeling*
Maxwell House

462
WRITER
Grant Swain

CLIENT
Gold Circle Stores

AGENCY PRODUCERS
Grant Swain
Tom Plapper

AGENCY
Howard Swink/Ohio

463
WRITER
Ilon Specht

CLIENT
Norcliff-Thayer

AGENCY PRODUCER
Peter Cohen

AGENCY
Specht, Gilbert & Partners

464
WRITER
Deborah McDuffie

CLIENT
Miller Brewing

AGENCY PRODUCER
Caroline Jones

AGENCY
Mingo-Jones

465
WRITER
Larry Plapler

CLIENT
People Express Airlines

AGENCY PRODUCER
Rachel Novak

AGENCY
Levine, Huntley, Schmidt,
Plapler & Beaver

466
WRITER
Mike Hughes

CLIENT
Mobil Chemical

AGENCY PRODUCER
Craig Bowlus

AGENCY
The Martin Agency/Virginia

467
WRITER
David Smyrl

CLIENT
Bambu Sales

AGENCY PRODUCER
Barry Z. Levine

AGENCY
Levy, Sussman & Levine

462

JACK: Oops, there's my car pool. Leonard's horn must be broken.

CASEY: Jack, will you be home at your usual time tonight?

JACK: Well, if my boss Mister Meany remembers to unlock my leg irons.

CASEY: (laughs) Seriously.

JACK: Yeah, I'll be home, he'll do it.

CASEY: You don't have any big plans?

JACK: No... Well, *Gilligan's Island* is on!

CASEY: See, I'm gonna go to Gold Circle and I thought you might like to come along.

JACK: Gold Circle?

CASEY: Yes, Gold Circle.

JACK: I suppose I could miss Gilligan for that.

CASEY: I suppose so. Now—

JACK: Of course, this could be the week they get rescued!

CASEY: (laughs) Jack! I just want to get a few things we need.

JACK: Oh yeah, how few?

CASEY: Oh, maybe a top and some diapers.

JACK: A top and some *what?*

CASEY: Some diapers. You know, like Pampers or Luvs.

JACK: Why do we need diapers?

CASEY: That's what I like about Gold Circle—they always have a good selection of brand name stuff.

JACK: Why do we need diapers?

CASEY: Did you know that Gold Circle keeps more merchandise in stock now than ever before and nine out of ten times they'll have exactly what you want and always at a great discount price?

JACK: Why do we need diapers?

CASEY: Why do you think?

JACK: You mean I'm gonna be a fa—

CASEY: Yes, Jack.

JACK: A fa—

CASEY: An uncle (laughs)

JACK: Aw!

SINGERS: *You're glad you've got Gold Circle.*

CASEY: Had you going there, didn't I?

463

ANNCR: This commercial is dedicated to losers.

To those who, at this very moment, are losing out on the benefits of benzoyl peroxide.

To those totally unresponsible for making Oxy 5, Oxy 10 and Oxy Wash the #1 benzoyl peroxide pimple medication in this country.

To those who scorn us, reject us and, worst of all, have managed not to get the message for lo! these past 4 years...

that most dermatologists prefer benzoyl peroxide, the active ingredient in Oxy 5 and Oxy 10.

that people prefer benzoyl peroxide. That the only ones who don't prefer benzoyl peroxide are pimples!!!

In plain talk...it will help make your pimples go away faster and better than anything else you can buy without a prescription.
Let me ask you...

are you hard of hearing?

are you stubborn?

are *you* crazy!!!

Then *try* Oxy 5 or extra strength Oxy 10.

464

ANNCR: It's Miller Time with Larry Graham

LARRY GRAHAM AND SINGERS: *Strumming my guitar
In my favorite neighborhood bar
I love to play my music
(Play his music)
For people I meet*

*Folks from near and far
Come to hear me play my guitar
There's love in my music
(In his music)
I play it so sweet*

*Oh, while the music man plays
Pass another Miller Beer
(When it's time to relax)
Bring another Miller here
(We've got the beer)*

(REPEAT TO FADE)

ANNCR: Miller Brewing Company, Milwaukee

465

(SFX: MUSIC THROUGHOUT)

(VO): You can take a bus to Jacksonville for $103.00.

WOMAN: Harry, are we there yet?

(VO): You can take a train to Jacksonville for $111.00.

WOMAN: Harry are we there yet?

(VO): The Federal government estimates it costs you $188.00 to drive to Jacksonville.

WOMAN: Harry are we there yet?

(VO): People Express will fly you to Jacksonville for $49 all day Saturday and Sunday and evenings, and for $79 weekdays, every seat—every flight.

(VO): People Express Airlines
Fly Smart

WOMAN: Harry, we're there!

466

DON: What do you do?

CRAVEN: Oh, I'm a cotton farmer.

DON: Do you use defoliants?

CRAVEN: Yes sir, we use a Folex.

CRAVEN: Around here, uh, most people appreciate 'em givin' that buck to the Cotton...

DON: (UNDER) Cotton Research?

CRAVEN: Right.

DON: Would you say that there's no better cotton defoliant than Folex?

CRAVEN: Well, I haven't found one, I'll say it that way.

DON: So that buck that Folex gives automatically to Cotton Foundation Research for every can you buy, is important to you.

CRAVEN: Sure it is, sure.

DON: Well, Folex is a 100% cotton and in your mind you're 100% cotton.

CRAVEN: Yes sir, 100% cotton.

DON: Does that say cotton on your belt buckle?

CRAVEN: Yes sir! That's cotton boy, cotton britches...

DON: Those are made of cotton...

CRAVEN: Shirt's 100%.

DON: Anything that's not cotton?

CRAVEN: Just my shoes, I've even got some brand-new Sears Roebuck all cotton shorts on this morning.

DON: (LAUGHS) Does it say 100% cotton on 'em?

CRAVEN: 100%, Yes sir! They say 100% in the back on the label.

DON: They don't say I'm a 100% cotton.

CRAVEN: Oh, no, no, they don't say that.

DON: You say that.

CRAVEN: I say that.

DON: You could be Folex Man of the Year.

CRAVEN: Yeah. (LAUGHS)

467

MAN NO. 1: You roll your own cigarettes?

MAN NO. 2: Yes and I enjoy them more because I roll them, not some greasy machine I don't even know.

MAN NO. 1: Yours has a little hump right there.

MAN NO. 2: If I didn't want a hump, I wouldn't have rolled one, besides aren't you tired of smoking cigarettes that all look alike?

MAN NO. 1: Hhhmmmmmm, that's a good question.

468
WRITER
Barry J. Magarick

CLIENT
Anti-Defamation League
of B'nai B'rith

AGENCY PRODUCER
Barry J. Magarick

AGENCY
Barry Magarick Advertising/
Philadelphia

469
WRITERS
Leland Rosemond
Tony Lamont
Richard Middendorf

CLIENT
New Jersey Water Crisis Project

AGENCY PRODUCER
Rick Paynter

AGENCY
Bozell & Jacobs/New Jersey

**Corporate Radio
Single**

470
WRITER
Jerry Inglehart

CLIENT
Hinckley & Schmitt

AGENCY PRODUCER
Jerry Inglehart

AGENCY
Inglehart & Partners/Chicago

471
WRITER
Neil Calet

CLIENT
Calet, Hirsch, Kurnit & Spector

AGENCY PRODUCER
Ron Weber

AGENCY
Calet, Hirsch, Kurnit & Spector

ANNCR: You know, some folks think the good Lord would have done a lot better if he'd left out Jews all together.

'Course, we'd have to give up a few things here and there...

Like the music of Leonard Bernstein, Isaac Stern, Bob Dylan.

There'd never have been a George Gershwin or a Richard Rodgers or Irving Berlin's "God Bless America."

We wouldn't have the laughter of Fanny Brice, Danny Kaye, Jolson or the Marx Brothers. And you could forget you ever heard the name Houdini.

Kids might be dying of polio again, because Jonas Salk and Albert Sabin wouldn't have lived.

And of course, we'd have to write off the likes of Albert Einstein, Sigmund Freud, Louis Brandeis, even Sandy Koufax's fast balls.

Oh yes, one more name would have to go. Humble fellow, worked with his hands...believe he was a carpenter from Galilee...

This message was brought to you by the Anti-Defamation League of B'nai B'rith and this station in hopes of promoting understanding among all peoples.

ALAN ALDA: This is Alan Alda for New Jersey's Water Crisis Project. If you don't know what it feels like to run out of water, lock yourself out of the bathroom for 24 hours. Please, let's save water.

MAN: We're talking to a pet clam who has just moved out on his owners because of the water he was getting...

CLAM: You bet, Man! The old lady stuck me in a tank of *tap* water! Chlorine, salts, chemicals, grossed me out. Who wants to gulp chlorine all day?

MAN: Do other pet clams have this problem?

CLAM: To each his own, Baby. Some hard hat wanna live in tap water from Lake Michigan, that's his business. I'd had it. I split, Man. Didn't even wanna *bathe* in that stuff.

MAN: Do clams really bathe?

CLAM: This one does. (PAUSE) Hey, I'm not pumping you on *your* personal habits.

MAN: Sorry. Look, here's an aquarium full of Hinckley & Schmitt Pure Drinking Water. (SPLASH, SPLASH). Care to try it?

CLAM: Hinckley & *who?*

MAN: Hinckley & Schmitt water with no impurities. Perhaps you'll like it.

CLAM: Shade your eyes a sec while I slip outa my cuttoffs. (SPLASH, PAUSE, EMERGING, SWIMMING SOUNDS) Hey, that's clean an' *beautiful*, Man, like a mountain spring! Where does this Hinckley & Schmitt live?

MAN: They deliver pure water to any home or office in town. You can call them at 229-1800.

CLAM: Gotta jot that down. 229-1800. You gotta ball point? This felt tip smears underwater.

ANNCR: In June, 1976, over fettucine primavera and a chilled soave, DKG Advertising received its first proposal of merger.

In February, '78, over a lobster huge enough to cover the cost of a thirty seconds network spot, an equally huge *agency* made us our second offer.

And in 1980 alone, seven giant agencies proposed a merger with DKG.

Well, we've decided.

It's no dice.

We're not going to exchange our independence for someone else's stock. Or our convictions for someone else's bottom line.

DKG is not going to merge. We're going to *e*merge.

From now on, we'll be known as Calet, Hirsch, Kurnit & Spector. After twenty years in business, we're putting our names on the door. *Our* names... and not a combination of us and some merger-hungry monolith.

Because at Calet, Hirsch, Kurnit & Spector, the only ones we want to be responsible to are our clients!

1982 Television Finalists

Television Finalists

472

SINGERS: *We bring new friends to play.*

LITTLE GIRL: Hi!

SINGERS: *Show how much you care.*

MAN: I wrote this just for you.

SINGERS: *We make you smile.*
G.E.
We bring good things to living.
We bring good things to living.
We bring good things to life.
We let you live it again.
Bring a song to your night.
We help you to create.
We keep you looking right.
We bring you closer, closer and closer...
to the ones you love.
G.E.
We bring good things to living.
We bring good things.
Bring good things.

LITTLE GIRL: Good bye!

SINGERS: *We bring good things to life.*

473

PA: Attention please, will the owner of... the blue Mercedes, license number (static) please come... to the parking lot. Your car has been in a minor accident.

VO: If you're looking for a well-built European luxury sedan... that offers the amenities a person of means expects... but you don't... want to follow... the crowd, consider a Volvo. It's not outrageously priced. And it's not for people who are running around... looking for status.

WOMAN: Your drink Mr. Baily?

VO: Volvo's a car for people who already have it.

474

ANNCR: Atari brings the computer age home.

DAD: Ready, we don't have much time. Go ahead, say it.

COMPUTER: Bonjour.

SON: Bonjeer.

DAD: Not quite, try it one more time.

ANNCR: With an Atari 400 Home Computer you can learn a new language, link up to a world of information by phone.

HUSBAND: Da-dum! Chinese Meat Loaf!

WIFE: Recipes from the computer?!...Great idea, George! Now...does it clean up?

ANNCR: Or take your best shot playing Missile Command. In fact, for a price that isn't out of this world...the Atari 400 Home Computer can open a world of possibilities.

SON/DAD: Le Pere, La Mere, Merci. It's so simple, a child can use it alone...yet so advanced, it could even change your life.

SON: Bonjour Grandmere, Grandpere. Comment allez-vous.

ANNCR: The Atari 400 Home Computer...We've brought the computer age home.

475

(MUSIC)

BOY: Hey Patty, what do you have to do to be a Pepper?

PATTY: It's easy.

PATTY (SINGING): *To be a Pepper, original like a Pepper all you gotta do is taste.*

SINGERS: *Be a Pepper to know the pleasure of a flavor you will treasure. All you gotta do is taste. Be a Pepper. The flavor's got a feeling, original and appealing, and all you gotta do is taste. To be a Pepper, open up a Dr Pepper, and all you gotta do is taste. Be a Pepper, drink Dr Pepper. Be a Pepper, yeah. The more you pour it, the more you will adore it. All you gotta do is taste. To be a Pepper. Open up a Dr Pepper. And all you gotta do is taste. Be a Pepper, drink Dr Pepper, yeah.*

476
ART DIRECTOR
Bob Czernysz

WRITER
Sue Read

CLIENT
Jamaica Tourist Board

DIRECTOR
Jeff Lovinger

PRODUCTION CO.
Lovinger, Tardio, Melsky

AGENCY PRODUCER
Scott Kulok

AGENCY
Young & Rubicam

477
ART DIRECTOR
Tom Peck

WRITER
Geraldine Newman

CLIENT
Eastman Kodak

DIRECTOR
Dick Miller

PRODUCTION CO.
Dick Miller Associates

AGENCY PRODUCER
Scott Kulok

AGENCY
Young & Rubicam

478 GOLD
ART DIRECTOR
Michael Tesch

WRITER
Patrick Kelly

CLIENT
Federal Express

DIRECTOR
Joe Sedelmaier

PRODUCTION CO.
Sedelmaier Films/Chicago

AGENCY PRODUCER
Maureen Kearns

AGENCY
Ally & Gargano

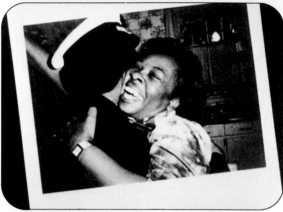

476

(MUSIC UNDER)

WOMAN SINGS: *Come back to Jamaica.*

MAN: Come back to gentility.

WOMAN SINGS: *What's old is what's new.*

WOMAN: Come back to our beauty.

WOMAN SINGS: *We want you to join us.*

MAN: Come back to our people.

WOMAN SINGS: *We made it for you.*

WOMAN: Come back to hospitality.

WOMAN SINGS: *So make it Jamaica.*

WOMAN: Come back to our bounty.

WOMAN SINGS: *Make it your own.*

WOMAN: Come back to tranquility.

WOMAN SINGS: *Make it Jamaica.*

WOMAN: Come back to romance.

WOMAN SINGS: *Your new island home.*

MAN: Come back to the way things used to be. Make it Jamaica again and make it your own.

CHORUS SINGS: *Make it Jamaica,*

(MUSIC) *your new island home.*

477

(MUSIC UNDER)

WOMAN SINGS: *I'll be seeing you in all the old familiar places, that this heart of mine embraces all year through.*

ANNCR: (VO) Christmas. When everyone comes home.

WOMAN SINGS: *I'll be seeing you, your smiling face this holiday.*

ANNCR: (VO) Share every glorious instant, in glorious instant pictures by Kodak

WOMAN SINGS: *Share love and joy the special way.*

ANNCR: (VO) This Christmas bring home the gift of a smile, the gift of love and the gift that lets you share them.

The Kodak Colorburst Instant Camera.

WOMAN SINGS: *When we share these special times, I'll be seeing you.*

ANNCR: (VO) Give the gift of instant joy.

478 GOLD

MR. SPLEEN(OC): OkayEunice,travelplans.Ineedtobe
inNewYorkonWednesday,LAonThursday,NewYorkon
Friday.Gotit?

EUNICE (VO): Got it.

MR. SPLEEN (OC): Soyouwanttoworkhere,wellwhatmakes
youthinkyoudeserveajobhere?

GUY: Wellsir,Ithinkonmyfeet,I'mgoodwithfiguresandI
haveasharpmind.

SPLEEN: Excellent.CanyoustartMonday? Guy: Yessir.
Absolutelywithouthesitation.

SPLEEN: Congratulation,welcomeaboard.

(SFX) (OC): Wonderful,wonderful,wonderful.Andin
conclusionJim,Bill,Bob,Paul,Don,Frank,andTed,

businessisbusinessandasweallknow,inordertoget
somethingdoneyou'vegottodosomething.Inordertodo
somethingyou'vegottogettoworksolet'sallgettowork.

Thankyouforattendingthismeeting. (SFX)

(OC): Peteryoudidabang-upjobI'mputtingyouin
chargeofPittsburgh.

PETER: (oc) Pittsburgh,perfect.

SPLEEN: Iknowit'sperfectPeterthat'swhyIpicked
Pittsburgh. Pittsburgh'sperfectPeter.
MayIcallyouPete?

PETER: CallmePete. SPLEEN: Pete.

SECRETARY (OC): there'saMr.Snitlerheretoseeyou.

SPLEEN (OC): Tellhimtowait15seconds.

SECRETARY: Canyouwait15seconds.

MAN: I'll wait 15 seconds.

SPLEEN (OC): CongratulationsonyourdealinDenverDavid.
I'mputtingyoudowntodealinDallas.Donisitadeal?Do
wehaveadeal?It'sadeal.Ihaveacallcomingin...

ANNCR (VO): In this fast moving high pressure,
get-it-done-yesterday world.

(VO): Aren't you glad that there's one company that can
keep up with it all?

SPLEEN (OC): Dickwhat'sthedealwiththedeal.Arewe
dealing?We'redealing.Daveit'sadealwithDon,Dork
andDick.Dorkit'sadealwithDon,DaveandDick.

Dickit'saDorkwithDonDealandDave.Dave,gotago,
disconnecting.Dorkgotago,disconnecting.Dick
gottago,disconnecting...

ANNCR (VO): Federal Express. (SFX) When it absolutely,
positively has to be there overnight.

479
ART DIRECTOR
Bob Gage

WRITER
Jack Dillon

CLIENT
Polaroid

DIRECTOR
Bob Gage

PRODUCTION CO.
Directors' Studio

AGENCY PRODUCERS
Joseph Scibetta
Jane Liepshutz

AGENCY
Doyle Dane Bernbach

480
ART DIRECTOR
Hy Varon

WRITERS
Martin Kaufman
David Curtis

CLIENT
IBM General Systems

DIRECTOR
R.O. Blechman

PRODUCTION CO.
The Ink Tank

AGENCY PRODUCER
Lois Goldberg

AGENCY
Leber Katz

479

JIM: Now you don't worry where the sun is when you take a picture.

MARI: As long as it's on what you're shooting.

JIM: No more. Now the sun can be behind you, in front of you or not even out.

MARI: The sun's gotta be somewhere.

JIM: Got it right in here. There's a piece of the sun in Polaroid's new Sun Camera.

MARI: Not the real sun?

JIM: Don't quibble. It's a new system with the fastest color print film made. 600 speed. Now you can turn bad light into good pictures. Here, I'll shoot you with the sun behind you.

MARI: You'll get a silhouette.

JIM: (WHOOSH!) Not any more.
(OVER PIC) You see? You're glowing. You've never been so sure of an instant picture.

MARI: Wonderful. But what if you shoot me in good light?

JIM: Then it uses just enough of its own light (WHOOSH) to touch up the small shadows.

(OVER PIC) See, mixing in our light can make any picture better. You use it on every shot.

MARI: Until you run out of money.

JIM: You could save money. Why waste film in bad light? Besides, you never buy flash or extra batteries.

MARI: Swell. But if they put a piece of the sun in every camera, there won't be any sun left.

JIM: That's a Production problem. I'm in Sales.

A little IBM can mean a lot of freedom.

480

ANNCR (VO): Do you sometimes feel like you're carrying your whole business on your back?

SECRETARY: Harvey's Hardware, please hold. Harvey, these accounts payable are piling up.

HARVEY: I'm working on it.

ANNCR (VO): Are you a businessman or a beast of burden?

WORKER: What about the inventory?

HARVEY: I'm working on it!

ANNCR (VO): Are you running your business, or is your business running you?

WORKERS: Harvey, how about the payroll?

ANNCR (VO): Wouldn't you like to get it all off your back?

HARVEY: With what, a forklift?

ANNCR (VO): No, with a small business computer from IBM.

HARVEY: IBM makes small computers?

ANNCR (VO): As only IBM can. This one, for instance—a low cost, desktop computer with the power to help free you from all that drudgery.

HARVEY: Ahh.

ANNCR (VO): And because it's easy to use and backed by IBM, it can even help free you from a lot of your worries about computerizing. So you're free to think. To plan. To be a titan of industry.

SECRETARY: Harvey's International.

ANNCR (VO): A little IBM can mean a lot of freedom.

SUPER: IBM LOGO. General Systems Division. 800-241-2003

481
ART DIRECTOR
Alan Sprules

WRITER
Roger Proulx

CLIENT
Peugeot

DIRECTOR
Gerard Hameline

PRODUCTION CO.
1/33 Productions

AGENCY PRODUCER
Bernard C. Wesson

AGENCY
Ogilvy & Mather

482
ART DIRECTOR
Len McCarron

WRITER
Dennis Berger

CLIENT
General Electric

DIRECTOR
Steve Horn

PRODUCTION CO.
Steve Horn Productions

AGENCY PRODUCER
Barbara Mullins

AGENCY
BBDO

483
ART DIRECTOR
Ed Maslow

WRITERS
Elin Jacobson
Phil Dusenberry

CLIENT
Pepsi-Cola

DIRECTOR
Rick Levine

PRODUCTION CO.
Levine Pytka

AGENCY PRODUCER
Mickey Paradise

AGENCY
BBDO

484
ART DIRECTOR
Joe Sedelmaier

WRITER
Tom McElligott

CLIENT
Mr. Coffee

DIRECTOR
Joe Sedelmaier

PRODUCTION CO.
Sedelmaier Films/Chicago

AGENCY PRODUCER
Howard Teitler

AGENCY
Fallon McElligot Rice/Mpls.

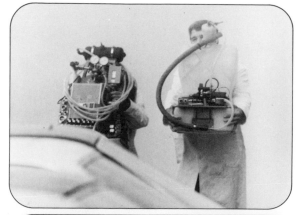

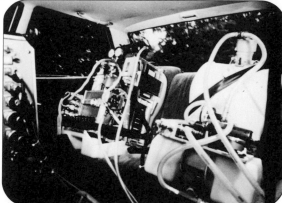

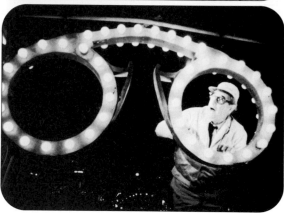

481

ANNCR: The car is a Peugeot 505S. The road, so brutal that Peugeot will not subject human test drivers to the ordeal. In their place, robots like Robert and Mathilde. An electromagnetic cable buried under the road will guide the Peugeot 505S around the test track...and around...and around...day in...day out.

Testing the strength of the Peugeot body, welded in three thousand, nine hundred and thirty-two places. Testing the Peugeot shock absorbers, designed to last up to one hundred thousand kilometers. Testing...testing...more testing. Peugeot has little tolerance for poorly made cars.

482

SINGERS: *We light your way back home. Make a wish come true.*

BOY: Wow!

RADIO (AVO): Due to the snow, all schools are closed.

SINGERS: *We keep you company. We celebrate with you.*

COP: Oh guys, you shouldn't have.

SINGERS: *We show how pretty you are.*
We make you smile.
G.E.
We bring good things to living.
We bring good things to life.
We bring you closer, closer...to the ones you love.
G.E.
We bring good things to living.
We bring good things to life.

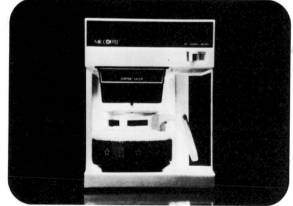

483

484

SINGERS: *You've got a Pepsi generation way of tasting life.*
I can see it in your style, your look, your laugh,
your smile.
You're tasting life and you're comin' back for more.
And each day's a little bit better than it was the day
before.
You're the Pepsi generation sharing one great taste
for life.
Pepsi's got your taste for life.
Come on and taste all that life can be—that Pepsi
spirit lives in you and me.
C'mon, C'mon, C'mon, C'mon.
You're the Pepsi generation sharing one great taste
for life.
Pepsi's got your taste for life.

ANNCR (VO): All across America people are getting fed
up with bad coffee.

Fortunately, they have an alternative. Mr. Coffee.
Only Mr. Coffee precisely controls coffee brewing
time and temperature for perfect coffee everytime.

Mr. Coffee…America's perfect coffee maker. With
a patent to prove it.

485
ART DIRECTOR
Bob Steigelman

WRITER
Charlie Breen

CLIENT
Miller Brewing

DIRECTOR
Ed Barnett

PRODUCTION CO.
Johnston Films

AGENCY PRODUCER
Sandy Udoff

AGENCY
Backer & Spielvogel

486
ART DIRECTOR
Terry Holben

WRITER
Peter Sugden

CLIENT
Ford

DIRECTOR
Richard Loncraine

PRODUCTION CO.
James Garret & Partners

AGENCY PRODUCER
Peter Harrison

AGENCY
Ogilvy & Mather/London

487 SILVER
ART DIRECTOR AND WRITER
Ray Black

CLIENT
Tip Top Bakery

DIRECTOR
Ray Lawrence

PRODUCTION CO.
Window Productions/Australia

AGENCY PRODUCER
Robert Bateson

AGENCY
Pope & Kiernan & Black/
Australia

488
ART DIRECTOR
Jim Nawrocki

WRITER
Josephine Cummings

CLIENT
McDonald's

DIRECTOR
Rob Lieberman

PRODUCTION CO.
Harmony Pictures/Chicago

AGENCY PRODUCER
Sheila Hayden

AGENCY
Needham, Harper & Steers/
Chicago

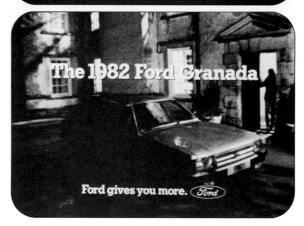

485

HERO: (BLOWS WHISTLE) Beach is closed! It's Miller Time.

SECOND HERO: Man, what a day. Let's go for a beer.

HERO: Yeah, we've earned it.

(SONG BEGINS):
*I've got the direction,
Now everybody get in the car.
Bring your money and your affections,
We're going down to the Shipwreck Bar.
Boiled shrimp are in season,
The crowd is in full swing.
Miller time so pleasin'
Makes everybody sing.
Sing about a happy hour, happy times, happy
nights,
Yours and mine.
Happy hour, happy year, happy times, Miller Beer.
When its time to relax,
One beer stands clear.
Yeah, for a happy hour, happy time,
Miller's got the beer.*

486

(MUSIC THROUGHOUT)

(SFX: CAR NOISES)

MVO: I'd never driven the new Grenada, so Bob and I
swopped cars for the weekend.

After a day like I'd just had it was nice to get some
peace.

His car was a Ghia. A 1981 model with the 2.8 fuel
injected engine.

And he'd chosen all the latest equipment.

I had 200 miles to go and I was beginning to look
forward to it.

Why does it always rain on Fridays?

The corners don't feel quite as sharp as usual—
makes all the difference—the new suspension.

Huh! That was easy.

I wonder if Bob likes my car as much as I like his
Grenada Ghia.

MVO: You'll never believe how good the new Grenada is
until you drive it.

487 SILVER

(SINGERS): *No other multigrain is quite like*
    Bornhoffen...
    There's flaxseed, malted grain, buckwheat and
    bran...
    so the aroma and taste of Bornhoffen is something
    to look forward to...
    Bornhoffen Wholefood bread.
    Man does not live on bread alone...
    However, with Bornhoffen he comes close.

488

MALE SOLO: *Where did all the day go*

GIRL SOLO: *I'm so sleepy, goodnight*

MALE SOLO: *Miss her more than she knows*
    Sometimes you can't seem to find...

GIRL SOLO: *Do you have to go Dad?*

MALE SOLO: *...A minute of time,*
    There's so much to be said.

GIRL SOLO: *I've got homework to do...*

MALE SOLO: *How can it be so tough...*

GIRL SOLO: *Have to go to my class.*

DAD SOLO: *A little time's all you need,*
    You never see her enough

GROUP: *Get together, get away*

GIRL: Yes, I'll have a cheeseburger and fries...

DAD: And a sundae?

GIRL: Yeah!

GROUP: *You deserve a break today*

GIRL SOLO: *At McDonald's.*

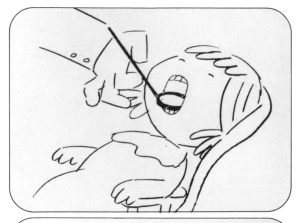

489

MALE (VO): Ten years ago...this was the picture...
...of decay in the typical eight year old.
Not very pleasant.
Today, partly due to fluoride toothpastes...

...the picture isn't...

...quite so painful. But what we and every mum
would like is...

...no fillings at all.

Today, after ten years of research, we can announce
an important step forward—an advanced fluoride
formula.

For three whole years we've been testing...

...one of the best fluoride toothpastes available—
Crest—against this new formula.

After continuous checking by independent dentists,
the evidence shows...

...you get demonstrably greater protection against
decay with this advanced fluoride formula.

CHILDREN: Hurray!

MALE (VO): And its name? It's Crest +.
It's such a real plus...

...we think every mum in the land...

will want to use it.

Crest + ...a real step forward in the fight...

...to make tooth decay a thing of the past.

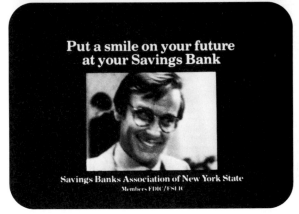

**Put a smile on your future
at your Savings Bank**

Savings Banks Association of New York State
Members FDIC/FSLIC

490

YOUNG MAN: Hi...(SLOW DOUBLE TAKE)...You look *very*
familiar...

My future?
(TO SELF)
My future? Ah...How *am* I...er...how *are* you?

Er...Excuse me, did you say "Savings Bank?"

Gee thanks. After all, that's what a Savings Bank is
for...the...ah...future.

YOUNG MAN: I will. Ah, here's our floor.
Okay, I'll be seeing ya...and keep smilin'. (DOORS
CLOSE) Nice guy.

ANNCR (VO): You can put a smile on *your* future...at
your Savings Bank. There's never been a better
time.

SUPER: PUT A SMILE ON YOUR FUTURE AT
YOUR SAVINGS BANK.

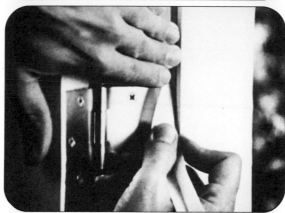

491

ANNCR (VO): In the wee small hours, the world is asleep. And a sleeping world doesn't use much electricity. The generators making it don't even have to breathe hard. So it's cheaper to provide. When the world wakes up, though, the demand goes way up. Way up.

And all our people, all our generators, have to go all out. We even have to add generators that guzzle expensive oil. So electricity costs a lot more to make. And that means everybody has to pay more for it.

Now, if we could all use a little less during the day, wait till nine or ten p.m. to run our dishwashers or our clothes dryers, easy things like that... it can keep the cost of electricity from... getting away from us. And help us get some control over tomorrow.

492

ANNCR (VO): In just 3 seconds, about this much cold air... leaks in through the unweatherstripped cracks around this window. About this much around the door. This is 3M's flexible V-Seal Weather Strip. How much difference would it make? With this house... in just one day, it could amount to enough air... to fill these three balloons! Enough to cut the heating bill more than 20%. You just pull it out... fold it... expose this adhesive... and stick it in place. 3M V-Seal blocks drafts around windows and doors better than brass, felt or foam. It's been lab tested to withstand 2½ million door openings and closings. You'll find it here, along with other energy saving products at the 3M Energy-Saving center. You could cut your heating bill more than 20%. 3M V-Seal Weather Strip... a great way to fight rising energy costs.

493
ART DIRECTOR
Bob Kuperman

WRITER
Robert Saxon

CLIENT
Fisher

DIRECTOR
Melvin Sokolsky

PRODUCTION CO.
Sunlight Pictures/Los Angeles

AGENCY PRODUCER
Jim Baier

AGENCY
BBDO/West

494
ART DIRECTORS
John Koelle
Dennis McVey

WRITERS
Hal Riney
Jeff Goodby

CLIENT
California First Bank

DIRECTOR
Denny Harris

PRODUCTION CO.
Denny Harris Productions

AGENCY PRODUCER
Debbie King

AGENCY
Ogilvy & Mather/San Francisco

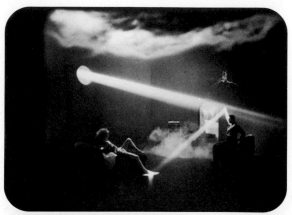

493

(MUSIC: Rod Stewart Song, "Do You Think I'm Sexy?"):

> *She sits alone, waiting for suggestions.*
> *He's so nervous, avoiding all the questions.*
> *His lips are dry; her heart is gently pounding.*
> *Don't you just know exactly what they're thinking?*

ANNCR (VO): Recording by Rod Stewart. Authentic reproduction by the Fisher 8500. A perfectly matched component system with Fisher's programmable direct-drive turntable, quartz digital tuner, direct drive cassette deck, graphic equalizer, Fisher 900 series speakers, plus 100 watts of power per channel.

The Fisher System 8500.

(MUSIC—UP)
> *Relax, baby, now we're all alone.*

ANNCR (VO): Why listen to the first names in music on anything less than one of the first names in high fidelity?

494

ED: They shoulda called by now...

ANNCR: Ed Bonestroo and John Haagsma once dreamed of starting a hay business.

JOHN: They'll call.

ANNCR: They had the hay...

ED: You told 'em about the hay?

JOHN: Uh huh.

ANNCR: They had something to haul it with...

ED: You told 'em about the truck?

JOHN: Uh huh.

ANNCR: But they didn't have a bank.

ED: Banks!

ANNCR: Oh, they'd gone to a number of banks, but none of them seemed interested.

ED: you shoulda worn a suit...

ANNCR: Until they came to California First...

ED: They're not gonna call.

ANNCR: At California First, we thought if their dream was that important to them...

JOHN: They'll call.

ANNCR: It was important to us, too.

SFX (PHONE RINGS)

ANNCR: After sixteen years, we're still Ed and John's bank.

ED: You tell 'em about the hay?

JOHN: Uh huh.

ANNCR: And we're still helping them dream.

ED: 'N about the trucks?

ANNCR: After all...

JOHN: Uh huh.

ANNCR: What's life without dreams?

ED: They aren't gonna call.

SFX (PHONE RINGS)

MUSIC: Come and meet the people at California First.

Consumer Television
60 Seconds Single

495
ART DIRECTOR
Susan Emerson

WRITER
Jim Glover

CLIENT
McDonald's

DIRECTOR
Lear Levin

PRODUCTION CO.
Lear Levin Productions

AGENCY PRODUCER
Susan Emerson

AGENCY
Needham Harper & Steers
/Chicago

496
WRITER
Tom Mabley

CLIENT
Savings Banks Association of
New York State

DIRECTOR
Stu Hagmann

PRODUCTION CO.
Hagmann, Impastato,
Stephens, Kerns

AGENCY PRODUCER
Robert L. Dein

AGENCY
Lord, Geller, Federico, Einstein

495

SINGER: *Nobody*
Rises up in the city
Quite the way we do.
Up with the dawn
Hot coffee's on
Another day is headed toward you.
Early showers
Those bloomin' flowers
Say it's morning
Won't you stroll on in
With our Egg McMuffin
We do it
Nobody can do it
Like only . . .
McDonald's can.

BRIDE: Hello, thank you for coming.

BRIDE'S FUTURE: Hi, you don't know us, but we're your futures.

BRIDE: George, darling... Mr. and Mrs. Future.

GROOM'S FUTURE: No, we're *your* futures. Take a good look at us, Mary.

BRIDE: Oh, you're *our* future... Oh my goodness.

GROOM'S FUTURE: We came here so we could thank you two.

GROOM: Thank us? For what?

BRIDE'S FUTURE: For what you're doing for us at the Savings Bank.

GROOM: The Savings Bank...

GROOM'S FUTURE: Like that All Savers Certificate... Up to $2,000 in tax free interest. Smart move George.

BRIDE'S FUTURE: It was her idea.

BRIDE'S FUTURE: You're making wise investments at the Savings Bank. Believe us, this is *no* time to be taking a lot of risks.

BRIDE: You look so happy.

GROOM'S FUTURE: Hey, we're smilin' because of you.

BRIDE'S FUTURE: Come on, dear; the babysitter...

GROOM: Babysitter...

GROOM'S FUTURE: So long, young man.

GROOM: But aren't you going to kiss the bride?

GROOM'S FUTURE: You do it for me.

ANNCR (VO): You can put a smile on *your* future... at your Savings Bank. There's never been a better time.

Consumer Television 60 Seconds Campaign

497

ART DIRECTOR
Lee Gleason

WRITERS
David Lamb
David Klehr

CLIENT
Anheuser-Busch

DIRECTOR
Joe Pytka

PRODUCTION CO.
Levine Pytka

AGENCY PRODUCER
David Lamb

AGENCY
Needham, Harper & Steers/
Chicago

498

ART DIRECTOR
Ed Maslow

WRITER
Phil Dusenberry

CLIENT
Pepsi Cola

DIRECTOR
Rick Levine

PRODUCTION CO.
Levine Pytka

AGENCY PRODUCER
Mickey Paradise

AGENCY
BBDO

499 GOLD

ART DIRECTORS
Jim Nawrocki
Lynn Crosswaite
Rich Seidelman

WRITERS
Josephine Cummings
Bob Scarpelli
Christie McMahon

CLIENT
McDonald's

DIRECTORS
Rob Lieberman
Dan Nichols
Denny Harris

PRODUCTION COS.
Harmony Pictures
Michael/Daniel Productions
Denny Harris

AGENCY PRODUCERS
Sheila Hayden
Helmut Dorger
Patricia Caruso

AGENCY
Needham, Harper & Steers/
Chicago

497

(MUSIC)

ATHLETE: I wasn't drafted til the seventh round.
   They don't even know my name.

SINGERS: *Bring out your best.*

ANNCR: The best never comes easy. That's why there's
   nothing else like it. Budweiser Light.

SINGERS: *Bring out your best*
   Budweiser Light
   Bring out your best
   Budweiser Light
   Bring out your best

ANNCR: The best.

(SFX): WHISTLE

ATHLETE: Kroeter, huh.

ANNCR: You've found it in yourself and now you've found
   it in the beer you drink.

SINGERS: *Budweiser Light.*

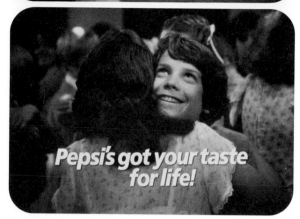

498

(SINGERS): *You've got a Pepsi generation way of tasting life.*
I can see it in your style, your look, your laugh, your smile.
You're tasting life and you're comin' back for more.
And each day's a little bit better than it was the day before.
You're the Pepsi generation sharing one great taste for life.
Pepsi's got your taste for life.
Come on and taste all that life can be—that Pepsi spirit lives in you and me.
C'mon, C'mon, C'mon, C'mon.
You're the Pepsi generation sharing one great taste for life.
Pepsi's got your taste for life.

499 GOLD

DENISE (VO): Chrissie's my very best friend in the whole world. We're exactly alike. We both have trouble with math.

CHRISSIE (OC): What's the square root of 164?

DENISE (VO): We both love horses. And we both hate our hair.

GIRLS (OC): Yuck!!

DENISE (VO): We even liked the same guy. Then we found out he likes Marcia Wilk.

GIRLS (OC): Marcia Wilk?!

SINGERS: *No two are closer than you*
She shares in all that you do
A best friend's someone to care
Someone who'll always be there
Everything is more fun
When it's done with someone
We've got a place to get away
When you deserve a break today
At McDonald's.

DENISE (VO): The best thing about Chrissie is...she's my best friend.

SINGERS: *Here's to the two of you.*

500 SILVER
ART DIRECTORS
Nicholas Gisonde
Eric Steinhauser
Doreen Fox
Mark Nussbaum

WRITERS
Barry Udoff
Charlie Breen
Charlie Ryant

CLIENT
Miller Brewing

DIRECTORS
Steve Horn
Bob Giraldi
Jeff Lovinger

PRODUCTION COS.
Steve Horn Productions
Bob Giraldi Productions
Lovinger, Tardio, Melsky

AGENCY PRODUCERS
Eric Steinhauser
Marc Mayhew

AGENCY
Backer & Spielvogel

501
ART DIRECTORS
Susan Emerson
Bernard Nosbaum

WRITERS
Jim Glover
Jennifer Fields

CLIENT
McDonald's

DIRECTORS
Lear Levin
Andy Jenkins

PRODUCTION COS.
Lear Levin Productions
Jenkins-Covington

AGENCY PRODUCERS
Sue Emerson
Ed Larson

AGENCY
Needham, Harper & Steers/
Chicago

502
ART DIRECTORS
Dennis McVey
John Koelle

WRITERS
Jeff Goodby
Hal Riney

CLIENT
California First Bank

DIRECTORS
Denny Harris
Haskell Wexler

PRODUCTION COS.
Denny Harris
Haskell Wexler

AGENCY PRODUCER
Debbie King

AGENCY
Ogilvy & Mather/San Francisco

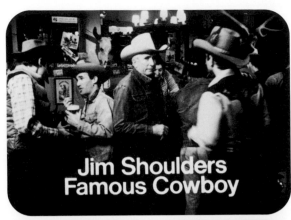

500 SILVER

SHOULDERS: I can tell a real cowboy from the drugstore kind clean across Texas. The way he wears his hat'll tell you. And the beer that they drink is a sure-fire give-away too. A lot of us drink Lite beer from Miller. We love the taste, but we surely appreciate that it's got a third less calories than their regular kind. You see, you don't wanna be filled up when you're out there punching doggies...right, cowboy?

MARTIN: I didn't punch that doggie!

ANNCR (VO): Lite Beer from Miller. Everything you always wanted in a beer. And less.

501

SINGER: *Nobody*
Rises up in the city
Quite the way we do
Up with the dawn
Hot coffee's on
Another day is headed toward
You
Early showers
Those bloomin' flowers
Say it's morning
Won't you stroll on in
With our Egg McMuffin
We do it
Nobody can do it
Like only...
McDonald's can.

502

WILL: You may be wondering why I've called you all together...

ANNCR: Will Chadwick had a dream.

WILL: Well, I've got some news...

ANNCR: After years of collecting toys in his garage, he had decided to go into business.

WILL: We're gonna open a toy store.

ANNCR: But it takes more than toys to open a toy store...

WILL: So...

ANNCR: It takes money.

WILL: We're going to the bank. Any volunteers? We'll talk about cash flow...

ANNCR: And so, Will went to the bank.

WILL: I'll bring up return on investment.

ANNCR: A bank that had been helping California people for years and years...

WILL: Tell them what we have to offer in capital depreciation...

ANNCR: A bank called California First.

WILL: We want to open a toy store.

ANNCR: Today, in Escondido, California, Will Chadwick has his store. A store full of dreams for other people. We were glad to help.

SING: *Come and meet the people...*

ANNCR: After all, what's life without dreams?

SING: *...at California First.*

503

ART DIRECTORS
Ralph Palamidessi
Frank Murakami

WRITERS
Carl Casselman
Drake Sparkman

CLIENT
Van Munching

DIRECTOR
Phil Marco

PRODUCTION CO.
Phil Marco Productions

AGENCY PRODUCER
Eric Brenner

AGENCY
SSC&B

504

ART DIRECTORS
Anthony Angotti
Ralph Ammirati

WRITER
Elizabeth Cutler

CLIENT
Club Med

DIRECTOR
Rick Levine

PRODUCTION CO.
Levine Pytka

AGENCY PRODUCER
Colleen O'Connor

AGENCY
Ammirati & Puris

505

ART DIRECTOR
Ralph Woods

WRITER
Leo Hartz

CLIENT
Stokely-Van Camp

DIRECTOR
Sid Avery

PRODUCTION CO.
Avery Film Group

AGENCY PRODUCER
Gordon Byrd

AGENCY
Clinton E. Frank/Chicago

506

ART DIRECTOR
Stanley Block

WRITER
Frank DiGiacomo

CLIENT
Dow Chemical

DIRECTOR
Geoffrey Mayo

PRODUCTION CO.
Bob Giraldi Productions

AGENCY PRODUCER
Peter Yahr

AGENCY
Della Femina, Travisano
& Partners

503

MEL BOUDROT (VO): Someday soon you could very well
have the best of everything. But you will have to
begin somewhere. And the best place to begin is
with the very best beer in the world. The best
tasting beer wherever you go. When you think
about it, why would you ever have anything else.
Come to think of it, I'll have a Heineken.

504

(VO): The trouble with most vacations in this so-called
civilized world...

...is an uncivilized devotion to separating you from
your money.

MAN: Seventeen dollars for pancakes?

(VO): At Club Med, we have a different attitude.

Here, everything is included.

The sports...

The food...

The wine.

Everything.

At Club Med, you play, play, play instead of pay,
pay, pay.

SONG: *The Club Med vacation. The antidote for
civilization.*

505

(vo): An egg . . . one of the richest sources of nutrition surprisingly has no more iron than four ounces of Van Camp's Pork and Beans. In fact, a 16 ounce can of beans is an economical source of many nutrients. It provides as much iron as 11 ounces of beef . . . 20 percent of the U.S. RDA for calcium . . . and as much protein as 14 ounces of milk.

Good tasting Van Camp's.

Good nutrition for the price of beans.

506

(vo): Since 1974, Chicken is up 24%.

WOMAN: That's for the birds.

(vo): Fish 84%.

MAN: That's a lot of clams!

(vo): Hamburger 64%.

WOMAN: OOOH, Whee!

(vo): In today's economy you need the strength of Ziploc Freezer Bags. With their unique seal, Ziploc Freezer Bags are a zip to lock, and they stay locked . . . for the best protection against freezer burn.

(vo): Pork Chops are up 36%.

PORKY PIG: Puh, puh, puh, Pork Chops?

(vo): Ziploc Freezer Bags. There's no better way to protect your investment.

507
ART DIRECTOR
Roy Tuck

WRITER
Bill Appelman

CLIENT
Merrill Lynch

DIRECTOR
Dick Miller

PRODUCTION CO.
Dick Miller Associates

AGENCY PRODUCER
Scott Kulok

AGENCY
Young & Rubicam

508
ART DIRECTOR
George Euringer

WRITER
Tom Messner

CLIENT
MCI

DIRECTOR
Joe Sedelmaier

PRODUCTION CO.
Sedelmaier Films/Chicago

AGENCY PRODUCER
Maureen Kearns

AGENCY
Ally & Gargano

509
ART DIRECTORS
Tom Shortlidge
Frank Parke

WRITER
Jim Carey

CLIENT
West Bend

DIRECTOR
Phil Marco

PRODUCTION CO.
Phil Marco Productions

AGENCY PRODUCER
Lee Lunardi

AGENCY
Young & Rubicam/Chicago

510
ART DIRECTOR
Greta Carlstrom

WRITER
L. Kovel

CLIENT
General Foods

DIRECTOR
Norm Griner

PRODUCTION CO.
Myers & Griner/Cuesta

AGENCY PRODUCER
Jerry Rice

AGENCY
Young & Rubicam

507

ANNCR (VO): Looking for the right fields to invest in, and the right investments in these fields, can be frustrating. That's why Merrill Lynch does the groundwork with research. To seek out the best investments, Merrill Lynch brought together the best researchers. And it is turning up the unseen or over-looked...that makes us what we are.
MERRILL LYNCH, A BREED APART.

508

(MUSIC UNDER, LAUGHTER)

ANNCR (VO): Bell Telephone's done a wonderful job helping people stay close.

You've seen those "reach out and touch someone" commercials.

We, at MCI, thought you'd like to see something they never show you:

What goes on when the bill arrives.

(SFX)

If your long distance bills are $25.00 or more, call MCI and start saving 30, 40, even 50% on long distance.

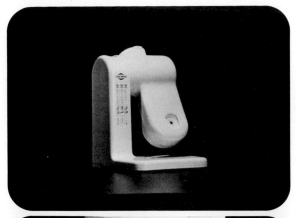

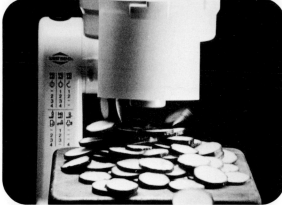

509

ANNCR (VO): Watch closely. For this new machine from West Bend is one of many disguises.

Just move its revolutionary swing arm and it changes...

from a mixer

to a meat grinder...

to a slicer/shredder

and a blender.

The new Food Preparation System from West Bend.

Never has an appliance done so much...in so little counter space.

510

BILL COSBY: I remember when I was a little baby and I had my very first bit of Jell-O Pudding, you know. Tasted so rich and creamy. Very first words out of my mouth that I ever spoke were "More Jell-O Pudding, please."

CHILD: You said that?

COSBY: Um hm.

ANNCR (VO): Kids love Jell-O Brand Pudding. And because you make it with fresh milk, you know it's wholesome.

COSBY: Did she just say something? More Jell-O Pudding, please.

CHILD: You said that.

COSBY: Listen

BABY: (BABY TALK)

COSBY: See?

511
ART DIRECTORS
Anthony Angotti
Ralph Ammirati

WRITER
Elizabeth Cutler

CLIENT
Club Med

DIRECTOR
Rick Levine

PRODUCTION CO.
Levine Pytka

AGENCY PRODUCER
Colleen O'Connor

AGENCY
Ammirati & Puris

512
ART DIRECTOR
Frank La Commare

WRITERS
Richard Mercer
Robert Summers

CLIENT
Carnation

DIRECTOR
Elbert Budin

PRODUCTION CO.
Ampersand

AGENCY PRODUCER
Nicholas Pellegrino

AGENCY
SSC&B

513
ART DIRECTOR
Barry Vetere

WRITER
Ron Berger

CLIENT
Dunkin' Donuts

DIRECTORS
Tim Newman
Jack Zanders

PRODUCTION COS.
Jenkins-Covington-Newman
Zanders Animation Parlour

AGENCY PRODUCER
Maureen Kearns

AGENCY
Ally & Gargano

514
ART DIRECTOR
Ted Shaine

WRITER
Jay Taub

CLIENT
Chemical Bank

DIRECTOR
Bob Giraldi

PRODUCTION CO.
Bob Giraldi Productions

AGENCY PRODUCER
Dominique Bigar

AGENCY
Della Femina, Travisano
& Partners

511

(VO): The trouble with most vacations in this so-called civilized world...

...is an uncivilized devotion to separating you from your money.

At Club Med, we have a different attitude.

Here, everything is included.

The sports...

The food...

The wine.

Everything.

At Club Med, you play, play, play instead of pay, pay, pay.

SONG: *The Club Med vacation. The antidote for civilization.*

512

MARTY INGELS (VO): Is your cat trying to tell you something? Could be! For years cats have been trying to say: "Fish!...The taste of fish is what I want!" 'Cause real fish flavor is what cats love. That's why they love Fish Ahoy, the only dry cat food with the real taste of salmon, cod and tuna. And it's nutritionally complete. So listen to your cat when he's talking fish flavor and feed him Fish Ahoy fish flavored cat dinner. It's what your cat's been trying to tell you!

513

(MUSIC AND SFX THROUGHOUT)

GUY 1: Hey, how ya doin'?

GUY 2: Here comes the jelly! (Little men giggle)

FATHER (OC): Hmmm...

GUY 1: Here you go. Put that in the coconut.

GUY 2: Whoops!

GUY 3: Whoa!

GUY 1: Shhh! Quiet!!!

FATHER (OC): Hmmm...?!?

GUY 1: That was close. Watch out!!!

GUY 3: Get it!!!

GUY 4: There it goes!!!

ANNCR (VO): Munchkin donut hole treats from Dunkin'
   Donuts. They're made just for kids.

514

(SINGING): *If I was a rich man, ya, ba, ba, ba, ba, ba...*
   Ya, ba, ba, ba, ba, ba, ba, ba, bum,
   All day long I'd...

   Bitty, bitty, bum, If I were a wealthy man...

   I wouldn't have to work hard

(UNDER): deedle, deedle, deeedle, bum, bumm, bum.

(FULL) ANNCR: This message is brought to you from
   Chemical Bank, whose Savings Programs can make
   you a little richer.

(UNDER): *All day long I'd bitty, bitty, bum...*

   If I were a wealthy man.

ANNCR: The Chemistry's just right for savers at
   CHEMICAL.

Consumer Television
30 Seconds Single

515
ART DIRECTOR
Harvey Hoffenberg

WRITER
Susan Procter

CLIENT
Diet Pepsi

DIRECTOR
Tony Scott

PRODUCTION CO.
Sunlight Pictures

AGENCY PRODUCER
Ed Pollack

AGENCY
BBDO

516
ART DIRECTOR
Lester Feldman

WRITER
Mike Mangano

CLIENT
GTE

DIRECTOR
Joe DeVoto

PRODUCTION CO.
Joel Productions

AGENCY PRODUCER
Phil Bodwell

AGENCY
Doyle Dane Bernbach

517
ART DIRECTOR
Stanley Block

WRITER
Frank DiGiacomo

CLIENT
Dow Chemical

DIRECTOR
Geoffrey Mayo

PRODUCTION CO.
Bob Giraldi Productions

AGENCY PRODUCER
Peter Yahr

AGENCY
Della Femina, Travisano
& Partners

518
ART DIRECTOR
Bob Gage

WRITER
Jack Dillon

CLIENT
Polaroid

DIRECTOR
Bob Gage

PRODUCTION CO.
Directors' Studio

AGENCY PRODUCERS
Joseph Scibetta
Jane Liepshutz

AGENCY
Doyle Dane Bernbach

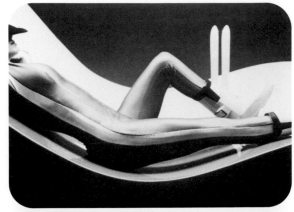

515

(SINGERS): *Now you see it*
Now you don't.
Here you have it
Here you won't.
Diet Pepsi one small calorie
Now you see it
Now you don't.
That great Pepsi taste
Diet Pepsi
Won't go to your waist.
Now you see it
Now you don't.
Diet Pepsi one small calorie
Now you see it
Now you don't.

516

(VO): If you can restrain your family from calling long distance till after 5PM, you can save yourself a lot of money.

517

(VO): Since 1975, lettuce is up 61%.

MAN: That's a lot of cabbage.

(VO): Mushrooms 46%.

WOMAN: Indeed!

(VO): Grapes? 82%!

MAN: It's fruitless.

(VO): In today's economy, you need Ziploc Storage Bags. With their unique seal, Ziploc Bags are a zip to lock, and they stay locked...so foods stay fresher, longer.

BUGS BUNNY: What's up Doc?

(VO): Carrots! 138%

BUGS: Oh, no!

(VO): Ziploc Storage Bags. There's no better way to protect your investment.

518

JIM: There's a piece of the sun in Polaroid's new Sun Camera. So you don't have to drag people out in the sun to take pictures.

MARI: I don't have to stand out there and squint?

JIM: Nope. It's a new system.

MARI: Why waste a shot in this light?

JIM: (WHOOSH!) We turn bad light into good pictures.
Didn't waste that shot.
You've never been so sure of an instant picture.

MARI: Perfect. But isn't it expensive?

JIM: No, but wasting film in bad light is. Besides, you never buy flash or extra batteries.

MARI: How'd they get that sun in there?

JIM: They did it at night.

519
ART DIRECTOR
Michael Tesch

WRITER
Patrick Kelly

CLIENT
Saab-Scania

DIRECTOR
Mike Cuesta

PRODUCTION CO.
Myers & Griner/Cuesta

AGENCY PRODUCER
Janine Marjollet

AGENCY
Ally & Gargano

520
ART DIRECTOR
F. Paul Pracilio

WRITER
Robert Neuman

CLIENT
American Express

DIRECTOR
Dominic Rossetti

PRODUCTION CO.
Rossetti Films

AGENCY PRODUCER
Nancy Perez

AGENCY
Ogilvy & Mather

521
ART DIRECTOR
George Euringer

WRITER
Tom Messner

CLIENT
MCI

DIRECTOR
Dick Loew

PRODUCTION CO.
Gomes Loew

AGENCY PRODUCER
Jerry Haynes

AGENCY
Ally & Gargano

522
ART DIRECTOR
Paul Basile

WRITERS
Jay Taub
Jerry Della Femina

CLIENT
WNBC Radio

DIRECTOR
Ralph DeVito

PRODUCTION CO.
Ralph DeVito Productions

AGENCY PRODUCERS
Linda Tesa
Peter Yahr

AGENCY
Della Femina, Travisano
& Partners

519

(SFX AND MUSIC THROUGHOUT)

ANNCR (VO): Some people think Saabs are not the most
beautiful cars in the world.

(SFX: ENGINE ROAR)

But what do you call a car that can go like this?
Stop like this?
Corner like this?
Climb like this?
Save gas like this?
And survive something like this?
Some say Saabs aren't beautiful but if this isn't
beautiful, what is?

(SILENT)

520

MILLS BROS: (Singing refrain of "Glow Worm")

HARRY: Do you know us?

DON: You know our songs.

GROUP SINGING: *Shine little glow worm, glimmer,
glimmer...*

HERB: But our faces hardly get a glimmer of recognition.

DON: So we carry the American Express Card.

Without it we'd be (SINGING) *up a lazy river without
a you know what.*

ANNCR: To apply for the Card, look for this display
wherever the Card is welcomed.

DON: The American Express Card.

ALL: Don't leave home without it.

521

(SFX: TABULATOR UNDER)

ANNCR (VO): Here are two businessmen making credit
card calls to the same place at the same time.

Look at the difference with MCI, the nation's long
distance phone company.

Then multiply those savings by the thousands of
calls your company makes every year.

And consider that you get those savings without
installing anything, without any investment in new
equipment.

(SFX: OUT) Call MCI for more information.

Over 100,000 companies now use MCI. Why pay any
more for long distance than they do?

522

IMUS: We need 47,000 people

ANNCR (OVER): ...and I want people from all over this
great stadium to come up here...
To hit the 3 million mark, WNBC needs 47,000 more
listeners in the worst way, and that's exactly how
we're getting them.

IMUS: Hey brother, I wonder if I can get you to listen to
WNBC?

IMUS: Hi, Uh, do you listen to WNBC?

MAN: I don't understand. (In Chinese)

ANNCR: For more listeners, WNBC offers all the most
popular songs, more prizes and more IMUS.

IMUS: Do you listen to WNBC?

MAN: Do you play Tchaikovsky?

IMUS: We need 47,000 more listeners and you're gonna
be one of them.

MAN: Hey Wait... You guy...

523
ART DIRECTOR
Angelo DeSantis

WRITER
Peter Bregman

CLIENT
Stroh's Beer

DIRECTOR
Ron Finley

PRODUCTION CO.
Iris Films

AGENCY PRODUCER
Jim Callan

AGENCY
Doyle Dane Bernbach

524
ART DIRECTOR
Mike Withers

WRITER
Hy Abady

CLIENT
AAMCO Transmissions

DIRECTOR
Joe Sedelmaier

PRODUCTION CO.
Sedelmaier Films/Chicago

AGENCY PRODUCER
Frank DiSalvo

AGENCY
Calet, Hirsch, Kurnit
& Spector

525
ART DIRECTOR
Jack Piccolo

WRITER
Marvin Honig

CLIENT
Citicorp

DIRECTOR
Norm Griner

PRODUCTION CO.
Myers & Griner/Cuesta

AGENCY PRODUCER
Justin Crasto

AGENCY
Doyle Dane Bernbach

526
ART DIRECTOR
Barry Vetere

WRITER
Richard Goodman

CLIENT
Pentax

DIRECTOR
Steve Horn

PRODUCTION CO.
Steve Horn Productions

AGENCY PRODUCER
Beth Forman

AGENCY
Ally & Gargano

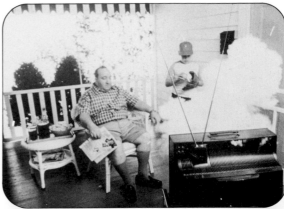

523

COACH: Barishnikiki, tell me. One tour in United States and you defected??!!

BARISHNIKIKI: That's right, comrade.

COACH: In people's Republic you were big star. Here you are "thrrrpppp!!!!"

BARISHNIKIKI: Da! I know.

COACH: They give you country home in Babutchki. television set, washing machine...

BARISHNIKIKI: Da. Even blue jeans.

COACH: So why, Barishnikiki? Why???

BARISHNIKIKI: Because, comrade...they could not give me Stroh's!

COACH: Da! Stroh's!!

BOTH: Nastrovya!!!!

524

ANNCR (VO): Ever notice how things break down right after the warranty expires? Most warranties only last a short time.

But if you ever have a transmission problem, you can get a warranty that lasts as long as you own your car.

It's AAMCO's car-ownership warranty. You get free annual checkups, and you never have to pay for transmission repair again.

Wouldn't it be nice if every warranty was this way?

AAMCO. (BEEP-BEEP) Why go anywhere else?

525

(MUSIC UNDER THROUGHOUT)

STRANGER: They got everything—even my travellers checks.

OLD MAN: No travel office here.

STRANGER: I'll use Citicorp—you got a Western Union?

OLD MAN: Over there—next to our Civic Center.

(VO): Citicorp Travelers Checks. In the U.S., even if you end up no place, we can get you emergency funds through Western Union. Every day of the year.

STRANGER: Any good French restaurants in town?

OLD MAN: Nope.

(VO): Travel with Citicorp. America's leading financial institution, worldwide.

526

(MUSIC UNDER)

ANNCR (VO): In Japan, people demand a lot from a 35mm camera.

That's why thousands of Japanese have gone beyond ordinary automatic 35's (SFX OF CAMERA) to the Pentax ME Super.

(SFX) The ME Super is really two cameras. On manual, you use it like a professional camera.

(SFX)

But on automatic, It's as easy to use as any 35. The Pentax ME Super.

One reason we've sold more 35 SLR cameras (SFX) than any other company in Japan...or, in the world.

527
ART DIRECTOR
Paul Rubinstein

WRITER
Larry Kopald

CLIENT
TWA

DIRECTOR
Linda Mevorach

PRODUCTION CO.
Eye Video

AGENCY PRODUCERS
Linda Mevorach
Kathleen Reagan

AGENCY
Ogilvy & Mather

528
ART DIRECTOR
Bob Gage

WRITER
Jack Dillon

CLIENT
Polaroid

DIRECTOR
Bob Gage

PRODUCTION CO.
Directors' Studio

AGENCY PRODUCERS
Joseph Scibetta
Jane Liepshutz

AGENCY
Doyle Dane Bernbach

529
ART DIRECTOR
Robert Anderson

WRITER
John Williams

CLIENT
Warner-Lambert Canada

DIRECTOR
Ray Kellgren

PRODUCTION CO.
Owl Productions

AGENCY PRODUCER
Cathy McLewin

AGENCY
Ted Bates/Canada

530
ART DIRECTOR
Barbara Siebel

WRITER
John Greenberger

CLIENT
Black & Decker

DIRECTOR
Andreas Zoller

PRODUCTION CO.
Jim Johnston Films

AGENCY PRODUCER
Luis Cruz

AGENCY
BBDO

527

(MUSIC UNDER)

ANNCR (VO): Right before your eyes, TWA is creating a brand new way for business flyers to fly coast-to-coast. It's a separate business class with bigger, wider seats than in coach. But less seats, so you're less crowded. It's TWA's new Ambassador Class to California. With enough room... for anybody.

CHAMBERLAIN: Even if you're seven foot one.

JABBAR: Or taller.

CHAMBERLAIN: Taller?

JABBAR: A little.

SINGERS: *You're going to like us... TWA...*

528

JIM: Guess what I've got in here?

MARI: What?

JIM: A piece of the sun.

MARI: No wonder I can't get a tan.

JIM: It's Polaroid's new Sun Camera. A new system that can turn bad light into good pictures. Go on, take my picture.

MARI: (WHOOSH!) You know you'll be dark.

JIM: Nope. You've never been so sure of an instant picture.

MARI: Great. But doesn't this cost a lot?

JIM: No, but wasting film in bad light does. Besides, you never buy flash or extra batteries.

MARI: That sun looks the same. Where'd they take the piece from?

JIM: The other side.

529

530

(SFX): MUSIC STARTS AND CONTINUES THROUGHOUT.

MALE (VO): Skin Deep works without grease, works without waiting.

ANNCR (VO): Introducing the Cutter.

Black & Decker's most powerful string trimmer yet.

The Cutter

powers through grass,

powers through weeds.

And with the Cutter's Command Feed, just the touch of a button keeps the string at its most powerful cutting length.

The Cutter, with Command Feed, from Black & Decker.

It can cut the time of trimming your yard.

531

SPOKESMAN (OC): Last year, MCI started its long distance discounts in the home.

The response has been...gratifying...to say the least.

GLASS (OC): My bills have been running over $100. MCI cut them in half.

COLE (OC): This is the greatest thing since pizza and beer.

NOLEN (OC): Since sliced bread.

GEIGER (OC): Since the wheel.

BEALE (OC): Your service is the greatest thing since the ball point pen.

SPOKESMAN (VO): If your long distance bills are $25 or more, call MCI and join the rest of the country in cutting them down to size.

532

(MUSIC UP AND UNDER)

ANNCR (VO): The taste of chocolate. There's nothing in the world like it.

Maybe that's why there are so many ways to enjoy it. But one of the best ways is when it comes fortified with seven essential vitamins and minerals. And that's when it comes this way.

Ovaltine.
Add Ovaltine flavoring to milk and you turn an...

...ordinary glass of milk...

...into an extraordinary treat.

So, if you're looking for a chocolate taste that's nutritious and delicious...

...look no further.

533

(MUSIC UP AND UNDER)

ANNCR (VO): Isn't it time you saw America from a different point of view?

MUSIC: *"Something about a train that's magic . . .*

". . . There's something about a train that's magic.

". . . Something about a train that's magic . . ."

ANNCR (VO): If you want to see how beautiful America really is . . .

ANNCR (VO): See it at see level.

MUSIC: *"America's getting into training . . .*

". . . Training the Amtrak way!"

534

PILOT: Blue GCA, this is Army two one two, seven miles northwest, low fuel, heavy weather.

GCA: Army two one two, radar contact. Turn right, heading one five zero.

PILOT: Roger.

GCA: Begin descent, on glide path two miles from touchdown.

PILOT: Roger.

GCA: Below glide path, coming up slowly.

PILOT: Roger.

GCA: Over landing threshold . . .

PILOT: Runway in sight. Thanks for your help.

GCA: Roger.

ANNCR: With a dozen lives and six million dollars worth of helicopters hanging on your every word it doesn't matter if you're a man or a woman . . . only that you're good.

(SFX): Helicopter rotors.

PILOT: (FILTERED OVER RADIO) Roger, tower visibility very poor.

CONTROLLER: We've got you on radar. We'll bring you in one at a time.

SINGERS: *Be all that you can be*

SERGEANT: Good work, Johnson

SINGERS: *'Cause we need you in the Army.*

535
ART DIRECTOR
Joe Sedelmaier

WRITER
Tom McElligott

CLIENT
Mr. Coffee

DIRECTOR
Joe Sedelmaier

PRODUCTION CO.
Sedelmaier Films/Chicago

AGENCY PRODUCER
Howard Teitler

AGENCY
Fallon McElligott Rice/Mpls.

536
ART DIRECTOR
Dennis D'Amico

WRITER
Ron Berger

CLIENT
Timberland

DIRECTOR
Henry Sandbank

PRODUCTION CO.
Sandbank Films

AGENCY PRODUCER
Beth Forman

AGENCY
Ally & Gargano

537
ART DIRECTOR
Bob Gage

WRITER
Jack Dillon

CLIENT
Polaroid

DIRECTOR
Bob Gage

PRODUCTION CO.
Directors' Studio

AGENCY PRODUCERS
Joseph Scibetta
Jane Liepshutz

AGENCY
Doyle Dane Bernbach

538
ART DIRECTOR
Harvey Hoffenberg

WRITER
Susan Procter

CLIENT
Pepsi Cola (Diet Pepsi)

DIRECTOR
Tony Scott

PRODUCTION CO.
Sunlight Pictures

AGENCY PRODUCER
Ed Pollack

AGENCY
BBDO

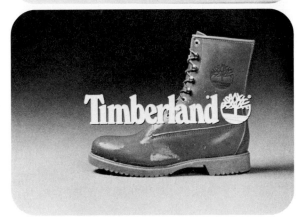

535

(NATURAL SFX THROUGHOUT)

ANNCR (VO): 1951, Lorenzo Lini tried to convince the U.S. Patent Office he could make better coffee by stamping on the beans. He failed.

1963, The Yuent Brothers tried to patent the Yuent Combustion Process. They failed.

1972, Vincent Marotta tried to patent a way to make coffee perfectly by controlling brewing time and temperature. He succeeded.

Mr. Coffee. America's perfect coffee maker. With a patent to prove it.

536

ANNCR (VO): Here's what you could be getting into when you buy a pair of work boots. This is a $45 boot after 3 hours in water.

(SFX)

This, a $60 boot.

This, an $80 boot.

While this is a Timberland work boot. Timberland, waterproof, insulated boots start at about $60. So if you're spending $45 or more and not getting work boots as good as Timberlands, your feet aren't the only thing getting soaked.

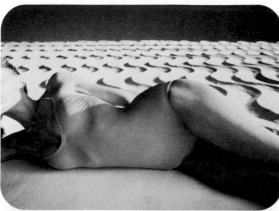

537

MARI: O.K. I'm beautiful.

JIM: I want proof of this!

MARI: No, you don't, we're late already.

JIM: Don't worry, this is the world's fastest developing color. You see it in seconds now, not minutes.

MARI: Well there's your proof. But go on. Get it *all* out of your system.

JIM: The Time-Zero OneStep and Time-Zero Supercolor film are made for each other. That's why they both come together in Polaroid's new Made-For-Each-Other-Pack.

MARI: Feel better now?

JIM: O.K. Let's go.

MARI: You're not taking *that* to the party.

JIM: Why not? I'm taking you!

538

SINGERS: *Now you see it*
Now you don't.
Here you have it
Here you won't.
Diet Pepsi one small calorie
Now you see it
Now you don't.
That great Pepsi taste
Diet Pepsi
Won't go to your waist.
Now you see it
Now you don't.
Diet Pepsi one small calorie
Now you see it
Now you don't.

539
ART DIRECTOR
Curtis B. Loftis

WRITERS
Gabe Massimi
Sarah Cotton

CLIENT
Atlanta High Museum of Art

DIRECTORS
Jamie Cook
Curtis B. Loftis

PRODUCTION CO.
Cook & Clemens Productions

AGENCY PRODUCER
Curtis B. Loftis

AGENCY
Burton-Campbell/Atlanta

540
ART DIRECTOR
Dave Lowenbein

WRITER
Carey Fox

CLIENT
Getty Refining & Marketing

DIRECTOR
Dick Clark

PRODUCTION CO.
Stone/Clark Productions

AGENCY PRODUCER
Ron Weber

AGENCY
Calet, Hirsch, Kurnit
& Spector

541
ART DIRECTOR
Michael Tesch

WRITER
Patrick Kelly

CLIENT
Federal Express

DIRECTOR
Joe Sedelmaier

PRODUCTION CO.
Sedelmaier Films/Chicago

AGENCY PRODUCER
Maureen Kearns

AGENCY
Ally & Gargano

542
ART DIRECTOR
Rich Martel

WRITER
Al Merrin

CLIENT
General Electric

DIRECTOR
Henry Sandbank

PRODUCTION CO.
Sandbank Films

AGENCY PRODUCER
Jeff Fischgrund

AGENCY
BBDO

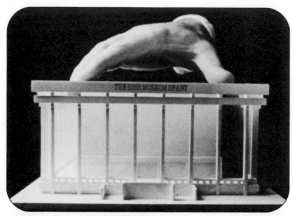

539

ANNCR (VO): Most people think Atlanta's High Museum of Art is that big building on Peachtree Street.

But take away...

the Atlanta College of Art.

Symphony Hall,

The Alliance Theater,

auditorium, lounges,

and offices...

What's left is the High Museum... so small, only one out of every five works of art can be displayed.

Help build a museum big enough for Atlanta... to replace that little building on Peachtree Street.

540

(SFX: POORLY RUNNING CAR)

Does your car sound like it needs a tune-up? Listen... what you hear may be nothing more than cold starts, knocks and run-ons.

Before you get a costly tune-up, try a Getty fill-up. With Getty Premium Unleaded. It can help absorb the knocks and pings and keep your car running soundly between tune-ups.

(SFX: HEALTHY ENGINE RUNNING)

Try Getty Premium Unleaded.

It can help you get the most out of your car.

541

(MUSIC: THEME)

ANNCR (VO): These days the American business person is under a great deal of pressure. (SFX: THUD)

(SFX: KNOCKING) What with the economy the way it is, the pressure is really on to perform...

To do the job flawlessly, to not mess up, not even one tiny, little bit, or it's all over...finished...kaput.

So isn't it nice to know that when you are under this much pressure,

(SFX: KNOCKING) There's someone you can count on to take some of the pressure away?

Federal Express. When it absolutely, positively has to be there overnight.

542

(MUSIC THROUGHOUT)

(VO): Presenting the incredible Grill/Griddle range from General Electric.

(MUSIC UP)

The GE Grill/Griddle range.
It makes cooking almost as much fun as eating.

SINGERS: *GE. We bring good things to life.*

543
ART DIRECTOR
Bob Gage

WRITER
Jack Dillon

CLIENT
Polaroid

DIRECTOR
Bob Gage

PRODUCTION CO.
Directors' Studio

AGENCY PRODUCERS
Joseph Scibetta
Jane Liepshutz

AGENCY
Doyle Dane Bernbach

544
ART DIRECTOR
Mike Withers

WRITER
Hy Abady

CLIENT
AAMCO Transmissions

DIRECTOR
Joe Sedelmaier

PRODUCTION CO.
Sedelmaier Films/Chicago

AGENCY PRODUCER
Frank DiSalvo

AGENCY
Calet, Hirsch, Kurnit
& Spector

545
ART DIRECTOR
Ron Becker

WRITER
Rick Meyer

CLIENT
Luden's

DIRECTOR
Joe DeVoto

PRODUCTION CO.
Joel Productions

AGENCY PRODUCER
Jean Muchmore

AGENCY
Geers Gross Advertising

546
ART DIRECTOR
Richard Dearing

WRITER
Rick Sear

CLIENT
Ranks Hovis McDougall

DIRECTOR
Des Serjeant & Harris

PRODUCTION CO.
Serjeant Productions

AGENCY PRODUCER
Alan Saunders

AGENCY
Young & Rubicam/London

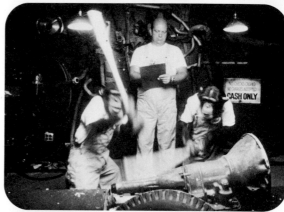

543

JIM: This is Polaroid's new Sun Camera—a new system
with the fastest color print film made—600 speed.
But it needs one more thing to turn bad light into
good pictures.

MARI: What's that?

JIM: A piece of the sun.

MARI: Daddy longlegs.

JIM: There...a piece of the sun does it.

MARI: Turns bad light into a good picture.

JIM: (WHOOSH!) Sure, you use this on every shot.

See, you've never been so sure of an instant picture.

MARI: Lovely, now you just reach up.

JIM: Well, don't waste it.

544

ANNCR (VO): If your transmission ever breaks down...
you'll probably imagine all sorts of horrors.

SVCE MGR (ECHOED): Fix your transmission? Fine. We
have a 15-year waiting list.

BACKGROUND VO (ECHOED): Don't worry. *Our* mechanics
are experts.

MGR (ECHOED): That'll be 22,000 dollars.

MECHANIC (ECHOED): Twenty-two...two...two.

ANNCR (VO): Don't let your fears run wild. Call the
transmission specialist that's...fast, reliable, with
over 900 locations coast to coast.

MAN: AAMCO?

ANNCR (VO): AAMCO. (BEEP-BEEP)

Why go anywhere else?

545

FIRST MAN: I just broke into the mint.

SECOND MAN: Was it hard?

FIRST MAN: No, it was soft.

SECOND MAN: You mean it was a piece of cake?

FIRST MAN: No, it was a piece of candy.

ANNCR (VO): When you've got a Mellomint you've got it soft.

WOMAN: My ex-husband said he was going to leave me a mint and I'd have it soft for the rest of my life.

ANNCR (VO): Soft, refreshing peppermint surrounded by rich, dark chocolate.

FATHER: Son, getting a mint today isn't hard. It's soft. The hard part is keeping it.

Look, you just lost your first mint.

ANNCR (VO): Mellomint. The soft mint.

546

(BRASS BAND MUSIC UNDER THROUGHOUT)

(SFX: CRUNCH!)

(SFX: CRUNCH!)

(SFX: CRUNCH!)

(SFX: CRUNCH!)

MALE VO: Cracottes. They're all crunch and no crumble.

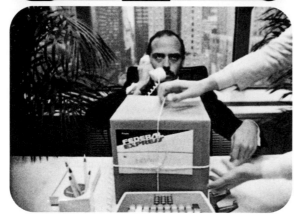

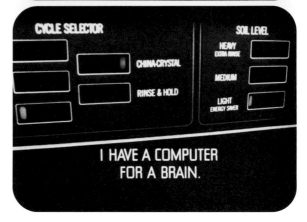

547 SILVER

MR. SPLEEN (OC): OkayEunice,travelplans. Ineedtobe
inNewYorkonMonday,LAonTuesday,NewYorkon
Wednesday,LAonThursday,

andNewYorkonFriday. Gotit? Soyouwanttowork
here,wellwhatmakesyouthinkyoudeserveajobhere?

GUY: Wellsir,Ithinkonmyfeet,I'mgoodwithfiguresandI
haveasharpmind.

SPLEEN: Excellent.CanyoustartMonday?

(OC): AndinconclusionJim,Bill,Bob,andTed,
Businessisbusinesssolet'sgettowork. Thankyoufor
takingthismeeting.

(OC): Peteryoudidabang-upjobI'mputtingyouinchargeof
Pittsburgh.

PETER (OC): Pittsburgh'sperfect.

SPLEEN: Iknowit'sperfect,Peter,that'swhyIpicked
Pittsburgh. Pittsburgh'sperfect,Peter,MayIcall
youPete?

SPLEEN (OC): CongratulationsonyourdealinDenverDavid.
I'mputtingyoudowntodealinDallas.

ANNCR (VO): In this fast moving, high pressure, get-it-
done-yesterday world, aren't you glad there's one
company that can keep up with it all?

ANNCR (VO): Federal Express. (SFX) When it absolutely,
positively has to be there overnight.

548

(SFX: BEEP, BEEP, BEEP THROUGHOUT)

(SUPER): HELLO.

ALLOW ME TO INTRODUCE MY REMARK-
ABLE SELF.

I AM THE NEW GE 2500 DISHWASHER.

I HAVE A COMPUTER FOR A BRAIN.

I CAN PUT 25 CLEANING CYCLES AT YOUR
FINGERTIPS.

I CAN CLEAN YOUR POTS

...PAMPER YOUR CHINA

...HELP YOU SAVE ENERGY

...AND TELL YOU WHEN YOUR DISHES
WILL BE CLEAN.

ANNCR(VO): The GE 2500. It can do almost everything... but
talk.

SINGERS: *GE ... We bring good things to life.*

SFX: (BEEP, BEEP.)

549

ANNCR (VO): We at American Tourister know that waiting for every suitcase is the unexpected.

That's why we reinforce our beautiful American Tourister lightweights with a steel frame, rugged rubber wheels, and tough protective corners.

To us at American Tourister...

It's not just how good it looks...

It's how long it looks good.

550

(SFX: NATURAL PRESENCE.)

(VO): When you have your hands full, even simple things can become difficult.

Like pouring a cup of coffee.

So Thermos invented the Flip 'N' Pour Stopper.

It's easy to open, easy to pour...and easy to close.

The new Flip 'N' Pour. What could be easier than that?

The Flip 'N' Pour.

Only from Thermos.

Consumer Television
30 Seconds Single

551
ART DIRECTOR
George Euringer

WRITER
Helayne Spivak

CLIENT
Kayser-Roth

DIRECTOR
Joe Sedelmaier

PRODUCTION CO.
Sedelmaier Films/Chicago

AGENCY PRODUCER
Jerry Haynes

AGENCY
Ally & Gargano

552
ART DIRECTOR
Barbara Siebel

WRITER
John Greenberger

CLIENT
Black & Decker

DIRECTOR
Matthew Brady

PRODUCTION CO.
Matthew Brady Productions

AGENCY PRODUCER
Neal Bergman

AGENCY
BBDO

553
ART DIRECTOR
Dianne Fiumara

WRITER
Ron Burkhardt

CLIENT
Minolta

DIRECTOR
Joe Sedelmaier

PRODUCTION CO.
Sedelmaier Films/Chicago

AGENCY PRODUCER
Bonnie Singer

AGENCY
Bozell & Jacobs

554
ART DIRECTOR
John Eding

WRITER
Jane Talcott

CLIENT
Volkswagen

DIRECTOR
Henry Sandbank

PRODUCTION CO.
Sandbank Films

AGENCY PRODUCER
Mark Sitley

AGENCY
Doyle Dane Bernbach

551

(MUSIC THROUGHOUT)

ANNCR (VO): Just a reminder from Interwoven that the only times that you should ever have to think about your socks are when you put them on, when you take them off, and when you buy them. So next time, think of the No. 1 sock in department and other fine stores.

552

(MUSIC UNDER: OH MINE PAPA)

To the families of America, Black & Decker would like to say, this Father's Day your participating Black & Decker dealer is offering many exciting specials on some of our most popular tools.

To the fathers of America, Black & Decker would like to say, Happy Father's Day.

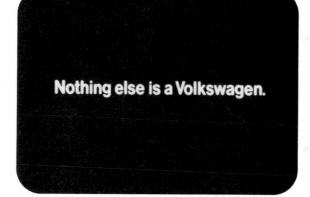

Nothing else is a Volkswagen.

553

MAN: "Is it workin'?"

(vo): When you overwork a small copier...

WOMAN: "Is it workin'?"

(vo): and make it do the job of a big copier...

ANOTHER MAN: "Is it workin'?"

(vo): it can break down.

(SFX): Machine grinds and sputters.

OLD WOMAN: "It's *not* workin!"

(vo): That's why your next copier should be the Minolta EP 520. It makes crisp, clear copies on any kind of paper, and works harder than an ordinary small copier. Because it was designed to do a bigger job. The Minolta EP 520.

OLD WOMAN: "It's workin!!"

554

(vo): At Volkswagen, we pull Rabbits off our American assembly line, at random, and give them this little test...

...We test every weld to make absolutely sure the metal breaks before the weld does. There's no law in any book that says we have to do this, but we let some Rabbits die so that yours will live longer.

Consumer Television
30 Seconds Single

555
ART DIRECTOR
Harvey Hoffenberg

WRITER
Susan Procter

CLIENT
Pepsi Cola (Diet Pepsi)

DIRECTOR
Tony Scott

PRODUCTION CO.
Sunlight Pictures

AGENCY PRODUCER
Ed Pollack

AGENCY
BBDO

556
ART DIRECTOR
Mike Withers

WRITER
Hy Abady

CLIENT
AAMCO Transmissions

DIRECTOR
Joe Sedelmaier

PRODUCTION CO.
Sedelmaier Films/Chicago

AGENCY PRODUCER
Frank DiSalvo

AGENCY
Calet, Hirsch, Kurnit
& Spector

557
ART DIRECTOR
Ron Taylor

WRITERS
Bob Mallin
Valerie Burns

CLIENT
R.J. Reynolds

DIRECTOR
Barry Lategan

PRODUCTION CO.
Fred Levinson Productions

AGENCY PRODUCER
Arnie Blum

AGENCY
BBDO / International

558
ART DIRECTOR
Tom McConnaughy

WRITER
Ron Hawkins

CLIENT
Marriott's Great America

DIRECTORS
Sid Myers
Andy Jenkins

PRODUCTION COS.
Myers & Griner/Cuesta
Jenkins-Covington

AGENCY PRODUCER
Gary Conway

AGENCY
Ogilvy & Mather/Chicago

555

SINGERS: *Now you see it*
Now you don't.
Here you have it
Here you won't.
Diet Pepsi one small calorie
Now you see it
Now you don't.
That great Pepsi taste
Diet Pepsi
Won't go to your waist.
Now you see it
Now you don't.
Diet Pepsi one small calorie
Now you see it
Now you don't.

556

WOMAN: A little demitasse?

ANNCR (VO): When you buy a foreign car, everything is wonderful.

DEALER: But of course, I'll take care of your slightest problem *immediately*.

ANNCR (VO): But when you go back to the dealer with a transmission problem, that's a different story.

DEALER: Y'gotta wait, fella. I got a hundred cars back there with all kinds of problems...Bon jour?

ANNCR (VO): Take your foreign car to the place that fixes more foreign-car transmissions than anyone.

AAMCO. We'll have your car back to you fast.

AAMCO. (BEEP-BEEP) Why go anywhere else?

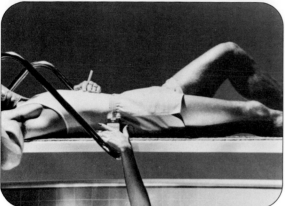

557

SINGERS: *Give me flavor.*
   Give me Winston.
   Give me pleasure.
   Give me Winston.
   Give me Winston.
   That smooth rich flavor is there.
   Give me Winston.
   Give me Winston.
   That great Winston taste.
   Yeah, it's your kind, it's my kind of taste.
   Give me pleasure.
   Give me Winston.
   Give me Winston.
   That smooth rich flavor is there.
   Give me Winston.
   Give me Winston.

558

MUSIC: THREATENING, EERIE

ANNCR (VO): This is the Demon.

   The nine-story drop.

   The loops.

   The tunnel.

   The corkscrew.

   The Demon. It's everything you were afraid it would be.

Consumer Television
30 Seconds Single

559
ART DIRECTOR
Ervin Jue

WRITER
Nicole Cranberg

CLIENT
GTE

DIRECTOR
Mark Story

PRODUCTION CO.
Pfeifer Story

AGENCY PRODUCER
Jim Callan

AGENCY
Doyle Dane Bernbach

560
ART DIRECTOR
Chris Blum

WRITER
Mike Koelker

CLIENT
Levi Strauss

DIRECTOR
Robert Abel

PRODUCTION CO.
Robert Abel & Associates

AGENCY PRODUCER
Steve Neely

AGENCY
Foote, Cone & Belding/
Honig-San Francisco

561
ART DIRECTOR
Gene Taylor

WRITERS
Gene Taylor
Sharon Kirk
Keith Condon

CLIENT
Kings Island

DIRECTOR
Gene Taylor

PRODUCTION CO.
Richard Williams Productions

AGENCY PRODUCER
Anne Chambers

AGENCY
Lawler Ballard/Ohio

562
ART DIRECTOR
Dennis McVey

WRITERS
Andy Berlin
Jeff Goodby

CLIENT
National Subscription
Television

AGENCY PRODUCER
Barbro Eddy

AGENCY
Ogilvy & Mather/San
Francisco

559

MAN: Guess what? You're all grandparents!

ANNCR (VO): With a GTE conference call, you can talk to all four grandparents at once. Even if one set lives in...Cleveland...

GRANDPA 1: He has my nose and your eyes...

ANNCR (VO): ...and the other set lives in Chicago.

GRANDMA 2: He has your hair. (GRANDPA LAUGHS)

ANNCR (VO): Say you're calling this evening from Tampa. You can all talk for ten minutes for under $16.00 So next time you have something important to say...
(BABY CRIES)...say it to everyone at once.

560

SFX: (throughout the commercial) INDUSTRIAL

ANNCR: He's the working man,
  Forging dreams with fire,
  Building,

(MUSIC UP)

ANNCR: Moving mountains,
  Always reaching higher.
  He's the wheels that move a nation,

  The stitching in the seams,
  He holds it all together,
  He wears Levi's jeans.

  'Cause he knows...we still build the Levi's jeans,

(MUSIC OUT)

ANNCR: that helped build America.

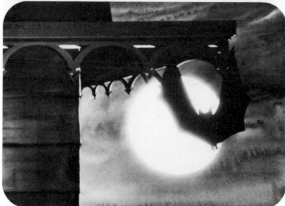

561

ANNCR: Hidden in the shadows of falling darkness,
wings of the night creature await their
silent signal from the moon.
Darting madly through a starless sky...
the frenzied flight of The Bat takes you
by surprise and leaves you breathless.
Hanging in mid-air... captured alive by
The Bat.
Fly The Bat at Kings Island.
It's a non-stop fright.

562

RAY: I don't usually discuss my strategy before a
fight...

TOMMY: I'm gonna hit him...

RAY: But there are a lot of things I can do to him...

TOMMY: ...and hit him...

RAY: I can go inside and work his body, real hard...

TOMMY: ...and hit him...

RAY: ...or I can just lay back and dance, and move on
him...

TOMMY: ...and hit him...

RAY: ...and look for an opening...

TOMMY: ...and hit him...

RAY: ...and hit him...

TOMMY: ...and knock him out.

(SFX FIGHT BELL AND MUSIC. CROWD UP.)

ANNCR: The showdown. Live, September 16th...
...from ON. Just $15, *if* you're a subscriber. If not,
call now and get installed in time for the fight.

563
ART DIRECTOR
Mas Yamashita

WRITER
John Annarino

CLIENT
Comprehensive Care

DIRECTOR
Ron Phillips

PRODUCTION CO.
Leawood Productions

AGENCY PRODUCER
Randy Zook

AGENCY
Doyle Dane Bernbach/West

564 GOLD
ART DIRECTOR
Dean Hanson

WRITER
Tom McElligott

CLIENT
Donaldsons

DIRECTOR
Jim Lund

PRODUCTION CO.
EmCom

AGENCY PRODUCERS
Dean Hanson
Tom McElligott

AGENCY
Fallon McElligott Rice/Mpls.

565
ART DIRECTOR
Dave Bradley

WRITERS
Jim Longstaff
Jim Stein

CLIENT
Ray-O-Vac

DIRECTOR
Howard Morris

PRODUCTION CO.
Coast Productions/Los Angeles

AGENCY PRODUCERS
Dave Bradley
Jim Longstaff

AGENCY
Campbell-Mithun/Mpls.

566
ART DIRECTOR
Bernard Aronson

WRITER
Jon Goward

CLIENT
Colonnade

DIRECTOR
Marc Yale

PRODUCTION CO.
Cinemagraphics

AGENCY PRODUCERS
Bernard Aronson
Jon Goward

AGENCY
ClarkeGowardCarr & Fitts/
Boston

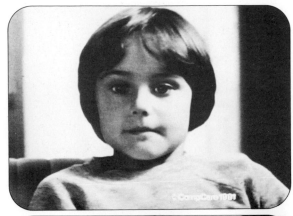

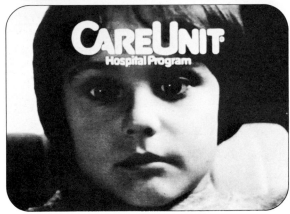

563

FATHER: What do you do? Drink all day?

MOTHER: (SLURRED) Oh I had a couple a drinks.

FATHER: Here let me do that.

MOTHER: (ANGRILY) I can do it!

FATHER: Someday you're gonna' burn the house down.

ANNCR: If you're living with an alcoholic, call CareUnit—the largest private provider of alcoholism treatment in the country.

FATHER: Where's Bobby?

MOTHER: He's aroun' someplace.

(SUPER APPEARS)

ANNCR: Call CareUnit now.

ANNCR: Some day not only your kids will thank you for it. So will the alcoholic.

564 GOLD

ANNCR (VO): Christmas may be for *children*...but *after* Christmas is for *adults*.

MAN: I want a new color TV!

ANNCR (VO): Donaldsons presents the *After* Christmas Sale and Clearance.

WOMAN: And a coffee pot and a sweater and a toaster...

ANNCR (VO): ...with *20 to 50 percent savings* on housewares, clothing and more.

MAN: I want a new ski jacket and gloves...

ANNCR (VO): Donaldsons After Christmas Sale and Clearance...

WOMAN: And if I don't get it, I'm going to hold my breath!

565

VOA: George Burns.

GEORGE: That's my name, too.

VOA: George, what's the secret of long life?

GEORGE: Ray-O-Vac Alkaline batteries.

VOA: Ray-O-Vac Alkaline batteries?

GEORGE: They'll play the Minute Waltz 4000 times...or...

TAPE: (GEORGE SINGS) *You're the flower of my heart, Sweet Alkaline.*

GEORGE: (TO GIRL) Pretty...you too...too tall.

VOA: But the secret of long life can't be a battery!

GEORGE: (OPENING COAT TO REVEAL BATTERIES). Are you kidding? (POINTS TO ONE BATTERY) This one's for dancing.

VOA: Ray-O-Vac Alkalines really are the secret of long life.

SECOND VOA: Ray-O-Vac Alkaline.

GEORGE: Power for the long run.

566

ANNCR: In Europe, one may spend upwards of 20 years learning to prepare gourmet cuisine before being acknowledged as a master chef. So why is it that in the Colonnade Hotel in Boston, a master European chef will spend hours creating something that no one will ever eat? Because there are people in this world who will appreciate such attention to detail.

SUPER: THE COLONNADE
BOSTON'S EUROPEAN
GRAND HOTEL

567
ART DIRECTOR
Donald Gill

WRITER
Peter Burkhard

CLIENT
H. J. Wilson

DIRECTOR
Mark Story

PRODUCTION CO.
Pfeifer Story

AGENCY PRODUCER
Susan Hayes

AGENCY
Green & Burkhard/Atlanta

568
ART DIRECTORS
Gene Trentacoste
Betty Freedman

WRITERS
Jack Aaker
Betty Freedman

CLIENT
General Foods

PRODUCTION CO.
Dove Films

AGENCY PRODUCER
Maura Dausey

AGENCY
Grey Advertising

569
ART DIRECTORS
Gene Taylor
Cliff Schwandner

WRITER
Keith Condon

CLIENT
Kings Island

DIRECTOR
Thom Ferrell

PRODUCTION CO.
Thom 2

AGENCY PRODUCER
Anne Chambers

AGENCY
Lawler Ballard/Ohio

570
ART DIRECTOR
Rick McQuiston

WRITER
Bill Borders

CLIENT
Burgerville, U.S.A.

DIRECTOR
Gary Noreen

PRODUCTION CO.
Kaye-Smith Productions

AGENCY PRODUCER
Bill Borders

AGENCY
Borders, Perrin & Norrander/
Oregon

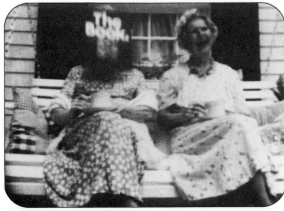

567

(vo): This week, Wilson's Jeweler's Catalog Showroom is throwing the book...

(vo): ...at over 20 million Americans

(SFX): plop

LADY: laughs

(SFX): snore

MAN: Ooooh...

(vo): It can save you hundreds of dollars on housewares, sporting goods,...

(vo): ...cameras, gifts, electronics,

(SFX): plop!

(vo): ...and toys, watches and fine jewelry.

(SFX): Whomp!

EXECUTIVE: Hrruumph!

(vo): So, if you want to save money on things, you want to go by the book at Wilson's.

568

MUSIC (BEETHOVEN'S FIFTH PIANO CONCERTO)

ANNCR (VO): Presenting world champion catcher—Ashley Whippet, age 10. He's a Cycle dog. He follows the Cycle Feeding Program.

(MUSIC)

ANNCR (VO): Cycle Dog Foods can help your dog...be in peak condition for life.

569

ANNCR: There's only one place on earth where people come in search of beasts, bats and demons.

It's a place where savage beasts grip you with fear.

Where screaming demons send shivers down your spine.

Where haunting bats make your hair stand on end.

Year after year, the best thrills the world has to offer are at Kings Island.

570

GEORGE: If you were president of Burgerville, where would you put the company's money: Into games that a few people win...

Or into more costly beef that everyone can enjoy?

That's what I thought, too. (with mouth full) And *I am* President of Burgerville.

(VO): Premium, fresh, local beef...instead of fun and games. At Burgerville, fast food doesn't mean taking short cuts.

GEORGE: We put our money where your mouth is.

571
ART DIRECTOR
Matt Basile

WRITERS
Ken Musto
Klaus Gensheimer

CLIENT
Gulf Motor Oil

DIRECTOR
D. Devries

PRODUCTION CO.
Nadel Film Consortium

AGENCY PRODUCERS
Manny Perez
Ian Shand

AGENCY
Young & Rubicam

572
ART DIRECTORS
Rich Silverstein
Jeff Goodby

WRITERS
John Crawford
Jeff Goodby

CLIENT
The Oakland A's

DIRECTOR
Bob Eggers

PRODUCTION CO.
Eggers Films

AGENCY PRODUCER
Deborah Wagner

AGENCY
Ogilvy & Mather/San
Francisco

573
ART DIRECTOR
Nicholas Gisonde

WRITER
Charlie Ryant

CLIENT
Miller Brewing

DIRECTOR
Steve Horn

PRODUCTION CO.
Steve Horn Productions

AGENCY PRODUCER
Eric Steinhauser

AGENCY
Backer & Spielvogel

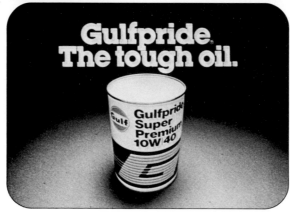

571

(MUSIC UNDER)

WOMAN: Didn't have to happen, Harold.

HAROLD: I know.

WOMAN: Should've taken better care.

HAROLD: I know.

ANNCR (VO): Thousands of cars meet their fate before
their time. That's why there's Gulfpride Motor Oil,
an oil so tough, it was tested over a million miles
without a single engine failure.

HAROLD: Next time I'll take better care.

MAN: Protect your engine with Gulfpride, the tough oil.
It could save you a lot of grief.

(MUSIC OUT)

572

TIMID SOUL: Reserved seat, pl—...oh...

MARTIN: Right. And I s'ppose you came out here just to
sit on your hands.

TS: uh...no...

MARTIN: Okay, Armas is up. Three and one. Let's hear
it.

TS: (HESITANTLY) Uh...hey go, Tony.

MARTIN: C'mon, talk it up!

TS: (STILL EMBARRASSED) Atta way, Tony.

MARTIN: Let's hear some chatter!

TS: (BUILDING) Atta way to watch him, Tony.

MARTIN: C'mon! C'mon!

TS: This guy's got nothin, Tony! Make him pitch to you.
That's not an arm, that's a noodle.

MARTIN: (CUTTING HIM OFF) Okay. We'll give you a tryout.

ANNCR: Billyball. It's a different brand of baseball.

573

BUTKUS: Over the years, us guys and Lite Beer from Miller have had a lot of laughs, but this time we'd like to share some personal sentiments. Boog...

POWELL: Have a very Merry Christmas.

SMITH: Yeah, and a Happy New Year, too.

HONOCHICK: Yeah.

GRESHAM: This holiday, may there be bass under all your lily pads.

MIZERAK: May all your pockets be full.

PALOMINO: Feliz Navidad.

MARTIN: Peace.

MADDEN: We wish you everything you always wanted in a Christmas.

HEINSOHN: And more.

THRONEBERRY: You know, I'm glad they asked me to do this commercial. Merry Christmas.

GROUP: Merry Christmas.

574
ART DIRECTORS
Michael Ridel
Don Gillies

WRITERS
Cliff Einstein
Lee Lefton

CLIENT
American Honda

DIRECTOR
Dick Rucker

PRODUCTION CO.
Bluebird Productions

AGENCY PRODUCER
Steve Banks

AGENCY
Dailey & Associates/
Los Angeles

575
ART DIRECTOR
Mas Yamashita

WRITER
John Annarino

CLIENT
Comprehensive Care

DIRECTOR
Ron Phillips

PRODUCTION CO.
Leawood Productions

AGENCY PRODUCER
Randy Zook

AGENCY
Doyle Dane Bernbach/West

576
ART DIRECTOR
Peter Cherry

WRITER
Paul Jones

CLIENT
McWilliam's Wines

DIRECTOR
Peter Cherry

PRODUCTION CO.
The French Film Company

AGENCY PRODUCER
Amanda Berry

AGENCY
The Weston Company/
Australia

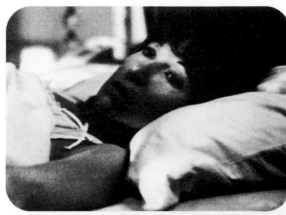

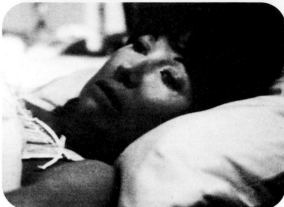

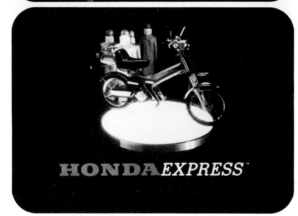

574

GUIDE (OC): And by the 1980's, a new mode of transportation had emerged.

The Honda Urban Express. It started electrically.

It was quite stylish.

EARTHLING NO. 1: Stylish?

EARTHLING NO. 2: Did superior design cause its popularity?

GUIDE: No. It was fun.

EARTHLING NO. 1: Fun?

EARTHLING NO. 2: Fun?

EARTHLING NO. 3: Fun?

GUIDE: And it got up to 100 miles to the gallon.

EARTHLING NO. 2: Gallons of what?

GUIDE: We don't know.

ANNCR (VO): The Honda Express. It's fun.

EARTHLINGS: Fun?...Fun?...

575

(VO): "How many nights have you lain awake waiting? Afraid that he might not make it home but dreading the moment he does."

(VO): "If you're living with an alcoholic..."

(VO): ...find out what to do about it. Call CareUnit—the largest private provider of alcoholism treatment in the country.

(VO): "Call CareUnit now."

HUSBAND'S VOICE: "Ah, the little woman."

(VO): "Isn't it time you put an end to the nightmare?"

576

(vo): Drink the wine the wine tasters drink.
  McWilliam's Chablis.

577
ART DIRECTOR
Ron Anderson

WRITER
Tom McElligott

CLIENT
Poppin Fresh Pie Restaurants

DIRECTOR
Joe Sedelmaier

PRODUCTION CO.
Sedelmaier Films/Chicago

AGENCY PRODUCER
Ron Anderson

AGENCY
Bozell & Jacobs/Mpls.

578
ART DIRECTORS
Greta Carlstrom
Marilyn Susser

WRITERS
L. Kovel
Walter Forys

CLIENT
General Foods

DIRECTORS
Norm Griner
Ed Bianchi

PRODUCTION COS.
Meyers & Griner/Cuesta
Stage I

AGENCY PRODUCERS
Jerry Rice
Sandy Breakstone

AGENCY
Young & Rubicam

579 GOLD
ART DIRECTOR
Michael Tesch

WRITER
Patrick Kelly

CLIENT
Federal Express

DIRECTOR
Joe Sedelmaier

PRODUCTION CO.
Sedelmaier Films/Chicago

AGENCY PRODUCER
Maureen Kearns

AGENCY
Ally & Gargano

580
ART DIRECTOR
Bob Gage

WRITER
Jack Dillon

CLIENT
Polaroid

DIRECTOR
Bob Gage

PRODUCTION CO.
Directors' Studio

AGENCY PRODUCER
Joseph Scibetta

AGENCY
Doyle Dane Bernbach

577

(MUSIC UP AND UNDER...)

FAT MAN: Hey, I'll bet you didn't know Poppin Fresh put out a taco salad like this...huh? huh?

Look...look at the fresh crisp lettuce and tomatoes and cheese and beef and tortilla chips.

You know you oughta taste this. It's perfect for the diet.

Go ahead amigo, try it...go ahead...

Mean time I'll just get started on this French silk pie.

578

BILL COSBY: You know, you remind me of my brother Russell. He loves smooth and creamy Jell-O Pudding so much, my mother said Russell, you're gonna turn into a bowl of Jell-O Pudding. I'm not kidding. And one day, poof! I'm telling you, I looked down and I had a bowl of Jell-O Pudding for a brother.

ANNCR (VO): Kids love Jell-O Brand Pudding. And because you make it with fresh milk, you know it's wholesome.

COSBY: I don't believe it. He turned into a bowl of Jell-O Pudding just like my brother Rus...Oh! There he...(LAUGHS)

(CHILD LAUGHS)

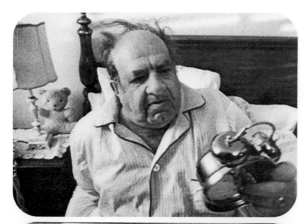

579 GOLD

(MUSIC THROUGHOUT) (SFX: BIRDS CHIRPING)

(SFX: RATTLE OF ALARM CLOCK)

(SFX: ENGINE)

(SFX: FLAT TIRE)

(SFX: DOG BARKING)

ANNCR (VO): You can't count on anything these days...

(SFX: FOOTSTEPS)

(SFX: TYPING)

MAN (OC): Did you type the letter I told you to type?

SECRETARY (OC): No.

ANNCR (VO): With possibly one exception: Federal Express.

When it absolutely, positively has to be there overnight.

580

KERMIT: (RUSHING IN) Quick, where's my OneStep?

PIGGY: Why? What's happening?

KERMIT: Nothing. This party's dead.

PIGGY: I hear laughing.

KERMIT: They're laughing at the hors d'œuvres.

PIGGY: Oh...

KERMIT: I got it.

PIGGY: (SADLY) And I worked so hard.

KERMIT: Smile, everybody!

STATLER: Why, is the party over?

KERMIT: (WHOOSH!) No, it just started.

FOZZIE: Hey, everybody looks happy.

WALDORF: I thought cameras didn't lie.

KERMIT: A Polaroid OneStep brings a dead party to life in seconds.

PIGGY: More hors d'œuvres everybody.

WALDORF: They're funnier than the pictures.

PIGGY: Out! Everybody out!

GANG: (SINGING TO US) *Polaroid means fun.*

KERMIT: With the OneStep.

581
ART DIRECTOR
Harvey Hoffenberg

WRITER
Susan Procter

CLIENT
Pepsi Cola (Diet Pepsi)

DIRECTOR
Tony Scott

PRODUCTION CO.
Sunlight Pictures

AGENCY PRODUCER
Ed Pollack

AGENCY
BBDO

582
ART DIRECTOR
Joe Sedelmaier

WRITER
Tom McElligott

CLIENT
Mr. Coffee

DIRECTOR
Joe Sedelmaier

PRODUCTION CO.
Sedelmaier Films/Chicago

AGENCY PRODUCER
Howard Teitler

AGENCY
Fallon McElligott Rice/Mlps.

583
ART DIRECTOR
Mike Withers

WRITER
Hy Abady

CLIENT
AAMCO Transmissions

DIRECTOR
Joe Sedelmaier

PRODUCTION CO.
Sedelmaier Films/Chicago

AGENCY PRODUCER
Frank DiSalvo

AGENCY
Calet, Hirsch, Kurnit
& Spector

584
ART DIRECTOR
George Euringer

WRITER
Tom Messner

CLIENT
MCI

DIRECTORS
Joe Sedelmaier
Dick Loew

PRODUCTION COS.
Sedelmaier Films/Chicago
Gomes Loew

AGENCY PRODUCERS
Maureen Kearns
Jerry Haynes

AGENCY
Ally & Gargano

581

SINGERS: *Now you see it*
Now you don't.
Here you have it
Here you won't.
Diet Pepsi one small calorie
Now you see it
Now you don't.
That great Pepsi taste
Diet Pepsi
Won't go to your waist.
Now you see it
Now you don't.
Diet Pepsi one small calorie
Now you see it
Now you don't.

582

(NATURAL SFX THROUGHOUT)

ANNCR (VO): Remember your first cup of coffee?

Did it ever get any better...

...or did you just get used to it?

Mr. Coffee thinks it's about time you tasted coffee the way it was meant to be...

Mr. Coffee. America's perfect coffee maker. With a patent to prove it.

583

ANNCR (VO): Ever notice how things break down right
after the warranty expires?

Most warranties only last a short time.

But if you ever have a transmission problem, you
can get a warranty that lasts as long as you own
your car.

It's AAMCO's car-ownership warranty. You get free
annual checkups, and you never have to pay for
transmission repair again.

Wouldn't it be nice if every warranty was this way?

AAMCO. (BEEP-BEEP) Why go anywhere else?

584

(MUSIC UNDER LAUGHTER)

ANNCR (VO): Bell Telephone's done a wonderful job
helping people stay close.

You've seen those "reach out and touch someone"
commercials.

We, at MCI, thought you'd like to see something
they never show you:

What goes on when the bill arrives.

(SFX)

If your long distance bills are $25.00 or more, call
MCI and start saving 30, 40, even 50% on long
distance.

585
ART DIRECTOR
Jean Govoni

WRITER
Cliff Freeman

CLIENT
General Mills (Yoplait Yogurt)

PRODUCTION COS.
Lovinger, Tardio, Melsky
The Ink Tank
Johnston Films

AGENCY PRODUCER
Janet Pangborn

AGENCY
Dancer, Fitzgerald, Sample

586
ART DIRECTOR
Joe Shyllit

WRITER
Jerry Kuleba

CLIENT
Henry's & Company

DIRECTOR
Graham Hunt

PRODUCTION COS.
Boardwalk
Rosnick Productions

AGENCY
Kuleba & Shyllit/Canada

587
ART DIRECTOR
David Mitchell

WRITER
Mike Pettle

CLIENT
Sony/U.K.

DIRECTOR
Robert Young

PRODUCTION CO.
A.B. & C.

AGENCY PRODUCER
Stephen Spencer

AGENCY
Benton & Bowles/London

588
ART DIRECTOR AND WRITER
Lou Musachio

CLIENT
Procter & Gamble–Zest

DIRECTOR
Michael Ulick

PRODUCTION CO.
Michael Ulick Productions

AGENCY PRODUCER
Rick Wysocki

AGENCY
Benton & Bowles

585

ANNCR (VO): The yogurt of France is called Yoplait. To some Americans just saying it's the yogurt of France means nothing till they first taste Yoplait. Then they'll believe it's creamy, smooth, all natural yogurt with real fruit. It's just amazing what happens when a real American gets his first taste of French culture.

JUDD HIRSCH: Yoplait est délicieux. Et les fruits sont naturels. C'est si crémeux, si doux. Yoplait est incroyable! Naturellement les Americans aiment Yoplait.

ANNCR: Yoplait Yogurt. Get a little taste of French culture.

586

ANNCR (VO): Why is it when you go into some camera stores, the salesperson talks your ear off? They work on commission. The more they sell, the more they make. Why is it when you go into some camera stores, you don't get answers to your questions? How can you get experienced part-time help?

At Henry's our salespeople are experienced and full-time. None work on commission. So when they shoot their mouth off, you won't hear a sales pitch. Just good advice. Like for example on Nikon equipment. (MUSIC THEME SIGN OFF.)

Where Photography is more than selling cameras.

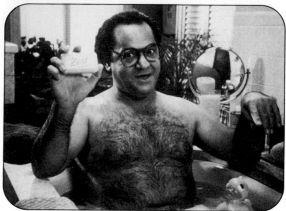

587

(SFX: DEMONSTRATOR TALKING UNDER.)

JOHN: Those awfully nice Sony people want me to tell you what makes my Sony Trinitron so unique. But I'm not going to. All that jargon about one electron lens instead of three—very boring. This is what you're interested in.

(SFX: RAPS)

JOHN: A brighter, sharper picture that'll look good even longer than she will. And those cakes: good enough to eat aren't they—in fact, I think I will eat one.

Mmmm.

I wonder if there's anything to eat on BBC 1.

(SFX: FOOTBALL MATCH)

JOHN: Yah—football!

(SFX: SNOOKER MATCH.)

JOHN: Ah snooker. That's much better.

MVO: Sony Trinitron. A more lifelike picture. A longer lasting set.

JOHN: Always like the strawberry ones.

REF: Oi—give me my ball back.

588

MAN: Ya wanna know why some people hate taking baths?

Schmutz! That sticky film from soap. On my skin...on the tub...

...even on my duck.

Schmutz is in the shower too. Believe me.

Here I am again...the only thing different...

Zest.

A deodorant bar with great lather.

But the main thing...no Schmutz!

So I feel cleaner, the tub feels cleaner, even my duck feels cleaner.

MAN (VO): Zest. Feel cleaner...

MAN: Without the Schmutz! Quack, quack, quack.

589
ART DIRECTOR
Bernard Aronson

WRITER
Jon Goward

CLIENT
Colonnade

DIRECTOR
Marc Yale

PRODUCTION CO.
Cinemagraphics

AGENCY PRODUCERS
Bernard Aronson
Jon Goward

AGENCY
Clarke Goward Carr &
Fitts/Boston

590
ART DIRECTOR
Wayne Graydon

WRITER
Tom Zager

CLIENT
Ford

DIRECTOR
Ron Jacobs

PRODUCTION CO.
Jaguar Productions

AGENCY PRODUCERS
Jerry Cammisa
Peggy Devinne

AGENCY
Young & Rubicam/Detroit

591 SILVER
ART DIRECTORS
Rich Silverstein
Jeff Goodby

WRITERS
John Crawford
Jeff Goodby

CLIENT
The Oakland A's

DIRECTOR
Bob Eggers

PRODUCTION CO.
Eggers Films

AGENCY PRODUCER
Deborah Wagner

AGENCY
Ogilvy & Mather/San
Francisco

592
ART DIRECTOR
John Porter

WRITERS
Bower Yousse
John Porter

CLIENT
King Soopers

DIRECTOR
Steve Griak

PRODUCTION CO.
Wilson–Griak

AGENCY PRODUCERS
John Porter
Bower Yousse

AGENCY
Frye–Sills/Colorado

589

ANNCR: In Europe, one may spend upwards of 20 years learning to prepare gourmet cuisine before being acknowledged as a master chef. So why is it that in the Colonnade Hotel in Boston, a master European chef will spend hours creating something that no one will ever eat? Because there are people in this world who will appreciate such attention to detail.

SUPER: THE COLONNADE
BOSTON'S EUROPEAN
GRAND HOTEL

590

(MUSIC: UP AND UNDER)

ANNCR: You're looking at the enemy of your engine.

Abrasive dirt in the oil.

It can wear out your engine before its time.

(SFX: MUSIC EFFECT)

ANNCR: Motorcraft Oil Filters fight the enemy.

Motorcraft FL-1A Oil Filters trap more dirt... last longer... than any other leading filter. Motorcraft Oil Filters.

For the future of your car.

For sure.

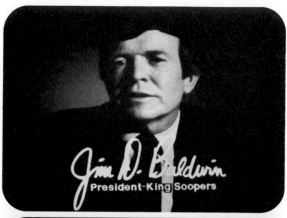

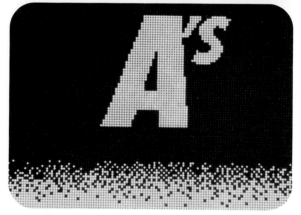

591 SILVER

UMPIRE: He's *out*, Billy!

MARTIN: (MILDLY) Gosh, Ron, from the dugout it sure looked like he held up on that pitch.

UMPIRE: He swung, Billy!

MARTIN: Of course, you have a much better vantage point than I.

UMPIRE: (BELLIGERENTLY) You wanna appeal, go ahead!

MARTIN: That won't be necessary, Ron. Your word is good enough for me. If you say he went around, I'm sure he went around. (WALKING OFF) My mistake... my mistake.

UMPIRE: (REACTS)

ANNCR: It's a different brand of baseball: It's Billyball.

592

GUARANTEE: BONNIE SIMMONS, CUSTOMER

BALDWIN: You know what's irritating? Getting home from the grocery store and finding your bakery items under a ten pound watermelon. Well, not even the people who sack groceries at King Soopers are perfect every time. Bonnie Simmons, I got your letter. I'm truly sorry about this incident. We've sent you a gift certificate to help make up for the damage and your inconvenience. Thank you for bringing this to our attention, it will help all of us do a better job in the future.

593 SILVER
ART DIRECTOR
Michael Tesch

WRITER
Patrick Kelly

CLIENT
Federal Express

DIRECTOR
Joe Sedelmaier

PRODUCTION CO.
Sedelmaier Films/Chicago

AGENCY PRODUCER
Maureen Kearns

AGENCY
Ally & Gargano

594
ART DIRECTOR
George Euringer

WRITER
Helayne Spivak

CLIENT
Kayser-Roth

DIRECTOR
Joe Sedelmaier

PRODUCTION CO.
Sedelmaier Films/Chicago

AGENCY PRODUCER
Jerry Haynes

AGENCY
Ally & Gargano

595
ART DIRECTOR
Earl Cavanah

WRITER
Larry Cadman

CLIENT
Playboy Enterprises

DIRECTOR
Tim Newman

PRODUCTION CO.
Jenkins–Covington–Newman

AGENCY PRODUCER
Karen Spector

AGENCY
Scali, McCabe, Sloves

596 GOLD
ART DIRECTOR
Michael Tesch

WRITER
Patrick Kelly

CLIENT
Federal Express

DIRECTOR
Joe Sedelmaier

PRODUCTION CO.
Sedelmaier Films/Chicago

AGENCY PRODUCER
Maureen Kearns

AGENCY
Ally & Gargano

593 SILVER

SPLEEN (OC): Congratulationsonyourdealin Denver, David. I'mputtingyoudowntodealwithDon.

Donisitadeal? Dowehaveadeal? Ihaveacallcoming through.

ANNCR (VO): In this fast paced world aren't you glad there's one company that can keep up with it all?

SPLEEN: Dick, what'sthedealwiththedeal? Arewedealing?

SUPER: Federal Express.

594

(MUSIC THROUGHOUT)

Don't you think it's time to change your socks? To INTERWOVEN.

595

MAN: I read the Wall Street Journal every business day.
It's succinct.
It's precise.
It's all business.
That's why I also read Playboy.
SUPER: 17 MILLION MEN ROUND OUT THEIR
LIVES WITH PLAYBOY.

596 GOLD

ANNCR (VO): Federal Express is so easy to use, all you
have to do is pick up the phone.

(SFX: RRRRRRRIIIIIIIPPPPPPPPPPPPPPPP!!)
(SFX: WATER)

597
ART DIRECTOR
Ted Shaine

WRITER
Jay Taub

CLIENT
Chemical Bank

DIRECTOR
Steve Horn

PRODUCTION CO.
Steve Horn Productions

AGENCY PRODUCER
Linda Tesa

AGENCY
Della Femina, Travisano
& Partners

598
ART DIRECTOR
George Euringer

WRITER
Helayne Spivak

CLIENT
Kayser–Roth

DIRECTOR
Joe Sedelmaier

PRODUCTION CO.
Sedelmaier Films/Chicago

AGENCY PRODUCER
Jerry Haynes

AGENCY
Ally & Gargano

599
ART DIRECTOR
Michael Tesch

WRITER
Patrick Kelly

CLIENT
Federal Express

DIRECTOR
Joe Sedelmaier

PRODUCTION CO.
Sedelmaier Films/Chicago

AGENCY PRODUCER
Maureen Kearns

AGENCY
Ally & Gargano

600
ART DIRECTOR
Paul Basile

WRITERS
Jay Taub
Jerry Della Femina

CLIENT
WNBC Radio

DIRECTOR
Ralph DeVito

PRODUCTION CO.
Ralph DeVito Productions

AGENCY PRODUCERS
Linda Tesa
Peter Yahr

AGENCY
Della Femina, Travisano
& Partners

597

MAN: I recently invested a chunk of money on a sure
thing. Know what happened?

ANNCR: Right now, Chemical Bank guarantees
a _____% interest rate on $10,000.

SUPER: $10,000 Six Month Certificate

Chemical Bank
The Chemistry's just right for savers at Chemical.

*Substantial interest penalty required for early
withdrawal. Federal regulations prohibit com-
pounding of interest. Additional information available at any branch. Member FDIC.

598

(MUSIC THROUGHOUT)

Don't you think it's time to change your socks? To
INTERWOVEN.

599

(SFX UNDER)

ANNCR (VO): The Post Office handles over 300 million pieces of mail a day.

And you're going to put your important business letter in that pile. (SFX OUT)

Federal Express has an alternative.

600

IMUS: We need 47,000 more listeners and you're going to be one of them.

ATTENDANT: Yells...

ANNCR: At WNBC, we won't give up until we hit the 3,000,000 (three million) mark.

Consumer Television
10 Seconds Single

601
ART DIRECTOR
George Euringer

WRITER
Tom Messner

CLIENT
MCI

DIRECTOR
Joe Sedelmaier

PRODUCTION CO.
Sedelmaier Films/Chicago

AGENCY PRODUCER
Maureen Kearns

AGENCY
Ally & Gargano

602
ART DIRECTOR
George Euringer

WRITER
Helayne Spivak

CLIENT
Kayser–Roth

DIRECTOR
Joe Sedelmaier

PRODUCTION CO.
Sedelmaier Films/Chicago

AGENCY PRODUCER
Jerry Haynes

AGENCY
Ally & Gargano

603
ART DIRECTOR
Michael Tesch

WRITER
Patrick Kelly

CLIENT
Federal Express

DIRECTOR
Joe Sedelmaier

PRODUCTION CO.
Sedelmaier Films/Chicago

AGENCY PRODUCER
Maureen Kearns

AGENCY
Ally & Gargano

604
ART DIRECTOR
Rick McQuiston

WRITER
Bill Borders

CLIENT
Burgerville U.S.A.

DIRECTOR
Gary Noreen

PRODUCTION CO.
Kaye–Smith Productions

AGENCY PRODUCER
Bill Borders

AGENCY
Borders, Perrin &
Norrander/Oregon

601

ANNCR (VO): Are your long distance bills more than $25.00 a month?

(MUSIC UNDER) Call MCI. You aren't talking too much. Just paying too much.

602

(MUSIC THROUGHOUT)

Don't you think it's time to change your socks? To INTERWOVEN.

603

ANNCR (VO): The nice thing about Federal Express is
(SFX: HORN) we'll come to your office and pick up the
package. You don't have to take it anywhere.
(SFX: HORN)

604

GEORGE: Some places put their money into fancy games.
Burgerville puts it into better beef.
And you can sure taste the difference.

605
ART DIRECTOR
Earl Cavanah

WRITER
Larry Cadman

CLIENT
Playboy Enterprises

DIRECTOR
Tim Newman

PRODUCTION CO.
Jenkins–Covington–Newman

AGENCY PRODUCER
Karen Spector

AGENCY
Scali, McCabe, Sloves

606 SILVER
ART DIRECTOR
Lindy Junor

WRITER
Keith Davidson

CLIENT
Australian Apple & Pear
Corporation

DIRECTORS
John Street
Pablo Albers

PRODUCTION CO.
Zoetrope Film Productions

AGENCY PRODUCERS
Keith Dunn
Heather Moors

AGENCY
Ogilvy & Mather/Australia

607
ART DIRECTOR
George Euringer

WRITER
Helayne Spivak

CLIENT
Kayser–Roth

DIRECTOR
Joe Sedelmaier

PRODUCTION CO.
Sedelmaier Films/Chicago

AGENCY PRODUCER
Jerry Haynes

AGENCY
Ally & Gargano

608 GOLD
ART DIRECTOR
Michael Tesch

WRITER
Patrick Kelly

CLIENT
Federal Express

DIRECTOR
Joe Sedelmaier

PRODUCTION CO.
Sedelmaier Films/Chicago

AGENCY PRODUCER
Maureen Kearns

AGENCY
Ally & Gargano

605

MAN: I'm a reader of U.S. News and World Report.

There's no trivia; no jokes...no fun.

That's why I also read Playboy.

SUPER: 17 MILLION MEN ROUND OUT THEIR
LIVES WITH PLAYBOY.

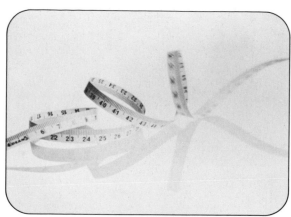

606 SILVER

(VO): Most snacks are cruel to diets.

(SFX: WHIPLASH)

But not apples. For a diet snack, grab an apple.

(SFX: CRUNCH)

607

(MUSIC THROUGHOUT)

Don't you think it's time to change your socks?
To INTERWOVEN.

608 GOLD

(VO): Federal Express is so easy to use. All you have to
do is pick up the phone.

(SFX: RRRRRRRIIIIIIIIPPPPPPPPPPPPPPPPPP!!!!)

(SFX: WATER)

609

ANNCR: It's 7:40 AM. Do you know where your
President is right now?

TOWNSEND: . . .the President journeys to Capitol Hill. . .

ANNCR: KTRH Radio, 740 AM. The difference is fact.

610

MAN: You know (SFX: COFFEE CUP SET DOWN) I keep seeing
these product recall notices. Look, I don't have time
for that sort of thing. (SFX: PUSH DOWN TOASTER, FRIDGE
DOOR OPENING) One notice says my toaster has a bad
(SFX: FRIDGE DOOR CLOSING) connection. (SFX: TOAST
POPPING OUT) And another one says my hot water
heater might be faulty. Later, Carl. And there are
all kinds of recall notices on my kid's toys, (SFX: FRIDGE
DOOR OPEN) my lawnmower, all telling me these
products could (SFX: SHOCK SHOCK) be hazardous to
my health. Later, Carl. Look if I had to worry. . .

ANNCR: Every year a lot of people pay no attention to
recall notices and get injured or killed.

So take recall notices seriously. And write the
Consumer Product Safety Commission for free
important information on recalls. (SFX: OVEN DOOR
FALLING OPEN)

MAN: Recall Notices? Nothing ever happens to me. (SFX:
ROOM FALLING APART SOUND)

ANNCR: Write Recalls, Washington, DC 20207. Or call
toll free. Product Safety. It's no accident.

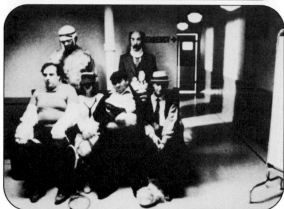

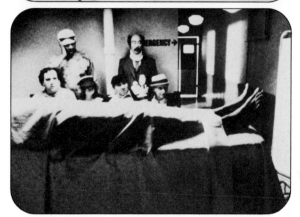

611 SILVER

ANNCR: It's often assumed that people with mental or physical disabilities cannot participate in today's complex society. We've produced this commercial to set the record straight. Of the 68 people involved in this production, 42 are mentally or physically disabled; among them, the director, the cameraman, the set designer and the builders, the sound engineer, many of the musicians, and Beethoven who was deaf when he wrote this music.

Even me. I'm blind.

We put it all together to make this point: consider what we *can* do—LABEL US ABLE.

612

ANNCR (VO): Every year thousands of people aren't careful with the products they use and hurt or kill themselves. So choose your products carefully. Use and maintain them properly.

And write the Consumer Product Safety Commission (SFX: DOLLY WHEELS SQUEAKING) for free and vital information on product safety. Write Safety, Washington, D.C. 20207.

Public Service
Television Single

613
ART DIRECTOR AND WRITER
Peter Mitchell

CLIENT
State Pollution Control Commission of New South Wales

DIRECTORS
Ross Nichols
Peter Mitchell

PRODUCTION CO.
Ross Nichols Productions

AGENCY PRODUCER
Peter Mitchell

AGENCY
Fortune/Australia

Public Service
Television Campaign

614
ART DIRECTOR
Asa Duff

WRITERS
Irene Block
John Wagner

CLIENT
Illinois Department of Children
and Family Services

DIRECTOR
John Wagner

PRODUCTION CO.
Haboush Co./Chicago

AGENCY PRODUCER
Susan Thurston

AGENCY
McCann–Erickson/Chicago

Corporate
Television Single

615 GOLD
ART DIRECTORS
Phil Dusenberry
Ted Sann

WRITERS
Phil Dusenberry
Ted Sann

CLIENT
General Electric

DIRECTOR
Bob Giraldi

PRODUCTION CO.
Bob Giraldi Productions

AGENCY·PRODUCER
Jeff Fischgrund

AGENCY
BBDO

616
ART DIRECTOR
F. Paul Pracilio

WRITER
Robert Neuman

CLIENT
Smith Barney Harris Upham

DIRECTOR
Norm Griner

PRODUCTION CO.
Griner/Cuesta

AGENCY PRODUCER
Nancy Perez

AGENCY
Ogilvy & Mather

613

(SINGERS): *When you're there*
Without a care
Don't forget that little thing
Do the Right Thing

Do your part
And do it smart
Oh, with everything you bring
Do the Right Thing
Do the Right Thing

For everything
Just use the bin
C'mon everybody sing
Do the Right Thing

We all know
That litter shows
C'mon everybody sing
Do the Right Thing
Do the Right Thing
Do the Right Thing

614

ROOSEVELT: I want to be a governor 'cause a governor lives in a mansion.

CHRIS: I want to be a lawyer to help people.

ADRIENNE: I'd like to be a model.

ROOSEVELT: Probably I want to be a Senator 'cause a Senator meets a lot of people.

ANNCR (VO) (OVER ROOSEVELT'S DIALOGUE): *You* can make a homeless child's dream come true. By being *his* parent.

ROOSEVELT: I want to be a President.

DANA: I want to be an artist when I grow up because I enjoy painting...

JAMES: I want to be a doctor.

ANNCR (VO) (OVER JAMES' DIALOGUE): Even if you're single, even if you don't make a lot of money, you can be that parent by calling the Adoption Information Center of Illinois.

CIGDEM: I wanna be a ve-vet-veterarian because...

ANNCR (VO) (OVER CIGDEM DIALOGUE): Call the Adoption Information Center of Illinois. And give a child what he *wants most.*

CHRIS: Most of all I want to be a son.

DANA: I wanna be a daughter

JAMES: I wanna be a son.

615 GOLD

(MUSIC)

(AVO): On a summer's evening in 1924, in Lynn, Massachusetts, perhaps the most significant game in the long history of baseball was played.

It wasn't the pitching that was so extraordinary, nor the hitting. And the fielding, well, it was less than exemplary.

No, what made this game truly historic was the time of day. (SFX)

Nightfall!

For it was on this night that this small group of GE engineers ushered in the era of night baseball. Baseball under the lights.

And while the names of "Yugo" Fee and Tommy Perkins and Hank Innes will never be recorded in the Hall of Fame...

It was this earnest band of GE pioneers that made possible for us all the many brilliant nights to come. (SFX)

SINGERS: *GE. We bring good things to life.*

616

ANNCR (VO): John Houseman for the investment firm of Smith Barney.

JOHN HOUSEMAN: Being born with a silver spoon in one's mouth is not enough.

How quickly it can tarnish in today's topsy turvy economy.

When it comes to growth and the preservation of capital,

many prudent investors look to Smith Barney.

Smith Barney.

(SFX: BABY): They make money the old-fashioned way, they earn it.

Corporate
Television Single

617
ART DIRECTOR
Tony Romeo
WRITER
Joe Nunziata
CLIENT
IBM
DIRECTOR
Neil Tardio
PRODUCTION CO.
Lovinger, Tardio, Melsky
AGENCY PRODUCER
Tony Perrotto
AGENCY
Doyle Dane Bernbach

618 SILVER
ART DIRECTORS
Ted Sann
Phil Dusenberry
Mike Moir
WRITERS
Ted Sann
Phil Dusenberry
CLIENT
General Electric
DIRECTOR
Bob Giraldi
PRODUCTION CO.
Bob Giraldi Productions
AGENCY PRODUCER
Jeff Fischgrund
AGENCY
BBDO

619
ART DIRECTOR
Herb Strauss
WRITER
Michael Solow
CLIENT
Viacom Radio
DIRECTOR
Herb Strauss
PRODUCTION CO.
Herb Strauss Productions
AGENCY PRODUCER
Dianne DeArmond
AGENCY
Viacom Radio

Corporate
Television Campaign

620 GOLD
ART DIRECTORS AND WRITERS
Phil Dusenberry
Ted Sann
CLIENT
General Electric
DIRECTOR
Bob Giraldi
PRODUCTION CO.
Bob Giraldi Productions
AGENCY PRODUCER
Jeff Fischgrund
AGENCY
BBDO

617

ANNCR (VO): Deaf people can't hear...but they can work.

Blind people can't see... but they can work.

There are over 15 million disabled Americans... with the ability to work. For the past 40 years, we've learned that being disabled hardly stops

anyone

from doing quality work.

MAN: Here's my report.

ANNCR (VO): 15 million disabled Americans who can help *your* business like they're

helping ours.

618 SILVER

(MUSIC)

(AVO): To all you students of innovation, to you, inspired to try what's never been tried before,

To all those consumed with an insatiable curiosity,

a penchant for ingenuity,

To you who seek and search

And blaze new trails,

Who try and fail and try again;

To all you children of imagination,

You sons and daughters and mothers of invention,

Dreamers and doers, thinkers and

Tinkerers all, we at General Electric salute you.

For, as advanced as our technology has become, we've never forgotten that from small beginnings big ideas grow.

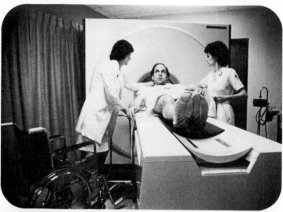

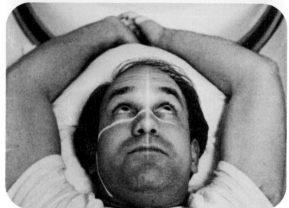

619

(MUSIC-"LOOKIN' FOR LOVE")

BUSINESSMAN: Don't mess with my radio station.

(VOICE OVER) Washington's Radio Station WMZQ-98 FM.

(MUSIC OUT)

620 GOLD

(MUSIC)

ANNCR (VO): You're about to see surgery performed without anesthesia, without sutures, even without a scalpel. This is the CT Scanner by GE.

It's a remarkable machine that lets doctors see and explore the human body without a single incision.

It actually takes tens of thousands of images and assembles them into a clear precise picture. This allows doctors to see clearly the most intricate details of the human anatomy, which until now could only be seen through conventional surgery.

The CT Scanner by GE.

NURSE: That's it.

PATIENT: That's it?

DOCTOR: That's it.

(VO): Bringing new vision to exploratory medicine.

PATIENT: I'm okay.

WIFE: Oh, great!

PATIENT: Let's go home.

(VO): GE. We bring good things to life.

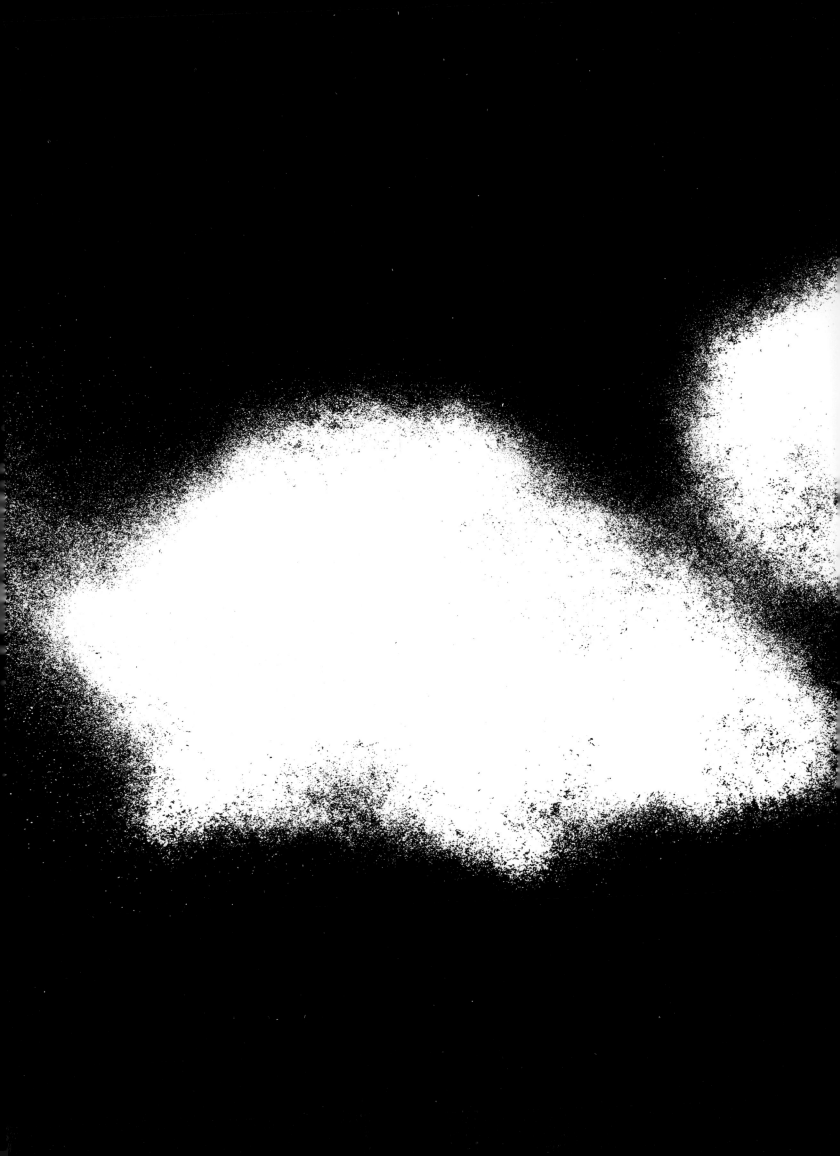

Index

Production Companies

Agencies

THE RETOUCHER'S

TRADE
COLOR PAGE OR SPREAD

GOLD
Art Director: Dean Stefanides
Writer: Earl Carter
Designer: Dean Stefanides
Photographer: Hashi
Client: Nikon
Agency: Scali, McCabe, Sloves
Retoucher: Spano/Roccanova

One of the few things on the Space Shuttle that didn't have a backup system.

Backup systems are essential to any manned space flight.

But space inside the shuttle is precious. How did the crew of the NASA Space Shuttle Columbia get a 35mm camera they could depend on, without having to take along a lot of 35mm cameras?

They took off with a Nikon.*

With good reason.

No Nikon has ever failed on a NASA space mission. In every manned mission into space since 1971, no Nikon has had structural damage from blast off. Or jammed.

Or had a mechanical problem. Or any problem that affected its performance.

A Nikon, as you may have gathered, is incredibly reliable.

So reliable it's the choice of more professional photographers than all other 35mm cameras combined.

There are four Nikon models designed for your special professional needs. The F3, the finest Nikon ever built for the professional photographer. The FE, a compact full-featured automatic. The FM which offers full manual control. And the

Nikonos IV-A—the world's only fully automatic 35mm underwater camera.

Whatever your needs as a professional, one thing is certain. Whether up in space, down on earth, or underwater, there's a Nikon to help take pictures that are out of this world.

Nikon
We take the world's greatest pictures.

*Camera used was a modified Nikon F. Future flights will use a modified F3 that has been customized with special wiring, lubrication and finish for use in space. © Nikon Inc., 1981. Garden City, New York 11530

SPANO/ROCCANOVA. THE QUALITY OF OUR WORK IS

SPANO/ROCCANOVA RETOUCHING, INC. 16 WEST

ONE SHOW AWARDS.

RETOUCHING OTHER STUDIOS OUT OF THE PICTURE.

46 STREET   NEW YORK, N.Y. 10036   212 840-7450